Chevrolet
Venture
Oldsmobile
Silhouette
Pontiac
Trans Sport
and Montana
Automotive
Repair
Manual

by Bob Henderson
and John H Haynes
Member of the Guild of Motoring Writers

Models covered:
Chevrolet Venture and Oldsmobile Silhouette - 1997 through 2001, Pontiac Trans Sport models - 1997 and 1998, Pontiac Montana models - 1999 through 2001

(10E1 - 38036)

ABCDE
FGHIJ
KLMNO

Haynes Publishing Group
Sparkford Nr Yeovil
Somerset BA22 7JJ England

Haynes North America, Inc
861 Lawrence Drive
Newbury Park
California 91320 USA

Acknowledgements

Wiring diagrams provided exclusively for Haynes North America, Inc. by Valley Forge Technical Information Services. Technical consultants who contributed to this project include Jeff Kibler and Eric Godfrey.

© **Haynes North America, Inc. 2001**

With permission from J.H. Haynes & Co. Ltd.

A book in the Haynes Automotive Repair Manual Series

Printed in the U.S.A.

ISBN 1 56392 422 6

Library of Congress Control Number 2001088741

While every attempt is made to ensure that the information in this manual is correct, no liability can be accepted by the authors or publishers for loss, damage or injury caused by any errors in, or omissions from, the information given.

Contents

Haynes photographer, mechanic and author with 1997 Oldsmobile Silhouette

About this manual

Its purpose

The purpose of this manual is to help you get the best value from your vehicle. It can do so in several ways. It can help you decide what work must be done, even if you choose to have it done by a dealer service department or a repair shop; it provides information and procedures for routine maintenance and servicing; and it offers diagnostic and repair procedures to follow when trouble occurs.

We hope you use the manual to tackle the work yourself. For many simpler jobs, doing it yourself may be quicker than arranging an appointment to get the vehicle into a shop and making the trips to leave it and pick it up. More importantly, a lot of money can be saved by avoiding the expense the shop must pass on to you to cover its labor and overhead costs. An added benefit is the sense of satisfaction and accomplishment that you feel after doing the job yourself.

Using the manual

The manual is divided into Chapters. Each Chapter is divided into numbered Sections, which are headed in bold type between horizontal lines. Each Section consists of consecutively numbered paragraphs.

At the beginning of each numbered Section you will be referred to any illustrations which apply to the procedures in that Section. The reference numbers used in illustration captions pinpoint the pertinent Section and the Step within that Section. That is, illustration 3.2 means the illustration refers to Section 3 and Step (or paragraph) 2 within that Section.

Procedures, once described in the text, are not normally repeated. When it's necessary to refer to another Chapter, the reference will be given as Chapter and Section number. Cross references given without use of the word "Chapter" apply to Sections and/or paragraphs in the same Chapter. For example, "see Section 8" means in the same Chapter.

References to the left or right side of the vehicle assume you are sitting in the driver's seat, facing forward.

Even though we have prepared this manual with extreme care, neither the publisher nor the author can accept responsibility for any errors in, or omissions from, the information given.

NOTE

A **Note** provides information necessary to properly complete a procedure or information which will make the procedure easier to understand.

CAUTION

A **Caution** provides a special procedure or special steps which must be taken while completing the procedure where the Caution is found. Not heeding a Caution can result in damage to the assembly being worked on.

WARNING

A **Warning** provides a special procedure or special steps which must be taken while completing the procedure where the Warning is found. Not heeding a Warning can result in personal injury.

Introduction to the Chevrolet Venture, Oldsmobile Silhouette, and Pontiac Trans Sport and Montana

The models covered by this manual are available in five-door minivan body styles only.

The engine used in all models is the 3.4L OHV V6. All models are equipped with Sequential Multi-port Fuel Injection (SMPFI).

The transversely mounted engine transmits power to the front wheels through an electronically controlled four-speed automatic transaxle via independent driveaxles.

The independent front suspension features MacPherson struts and control arms to locate the steering knuckle assembly at each wheel. The rear suspension is a beam axle with integral trailing arms, suspended by coil springs and shock absorbers and located laterally by a track bar. Some vehicles are equipped with an optional Electronic Level Control (ELC) system.

The rack-and-pinion steering unit is mounted behind the engine with power-assist as standard equipment.

The brakes are disc at the front and drums at the rear, with power assist and an Anti-lock Braking System (ABS) as standard equipment.

Vehicle identification numbers

Modifications are a continuing and unpublicized part of vehicle manufacturing. Since spare parts manuals and lists are compiled on a numerical basis, the individual vehicle numbers are essential to correctly identify the component required.

Vehicle Identification Number (VIN)

This very important identification number is etched on a plate attached to the left side of the dashboard and is visible through the driver's side of the windshield **(see illustration)**. The VIN also appears on the Vehicle Certificate of Title and Registration. It contains valuable information such as where and when the vehicle was manufactured, the model year and the body style.

VIN engine and model year codes

Two particularly important pieces of information found in the VIN are the engine code and the model year code. Counting from the left, the engine code letter designation is the 8th digit and the model year code letter designation is the 10th digit.

On the models covered by this manual the engine code is:

E 3.4L V6

On the models covered by this manual the model year codes are:

V.. 1997
W... 1998
X.. 1999
Y.. 2000
1.. 2001

Vehicle Certification/Tire label

The Vehicle Certification/Tire label is attached to the rear edge of the driver's door **(see illustration)**. The label contains the name of the manufacturer, the month and year of production, the Gross Vehicle Weight Rating (GVWR), the Gross Axle Weight Rating (GAWR) and the certification statement.

This label also contains information on tire sizes, tire pressures, and tire speed rating,

Service Parts Identification label

Located on the inside of the left-side access panel in the cargo area, this label contains information about the options on your vehicle and the paint and trim codes **(see illustration)**. This information is important when ordering parts or when bodywork and repainting is done.

Engine identification numbers

The engine identification numbers are located on a machined pad on the front (left) side of the engine block by the transaxle bellhousing **(see illustration)**.

Automatic transaxle identification number

The transaxle identification information is found on a bar code tag located on the

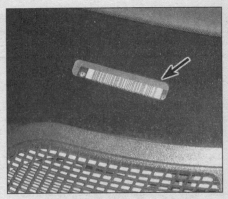

The Vehicle Identification Number (VIN) is visible through the driver's side of the windshield

right rear of the transaxle, visible from underneath the vehicle **(see illustration)**.

Vehicle Emissions Control Information label

This label is found on the underside of the hood. See Chapter 6 for more information on this label.

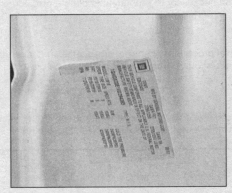

The Vehicle Certification/Tire label is affixed to the end of the driver's door

The Service Parts Identification label contains information on options and trim/paint codes

Engine Identification Number locations

A Engine ID number *B VIN number*

Location of the transaxle bar code tag (arrow)

Buying parts

Replacement parts are available from many sources, which generally fall into one of two categories - authorized dealer parts departments and independent retail auto parts stores. Our advice concerning these parts is as follows:

Retail auto parts stores: Good auto parts stores will stock frequently needed components which wear out relatively fast, such as clutch components, exhaust systems, brake parts, tune-up parts, etc. These stores often supply new or reconditioned parts on an exchange basis, which can save a considerable amount of money. Discount auto parts stores are often very good places to buy materials and parts needed for general vehicle maintenance such as oil, grease, filters, spark plugs, belts, touch-up paint, bulbs, etc. They also usually sell tools and general accessories, have convenient hours, charge lower prices and can often be found not far from home.

Authorized dealer parts department: This is the best source for parts which are unique to the vehicle and not generally available elsewhere (such as major engine parts, transmission parts, trim pieces, etc.).

Warranty information: If the vehicle is still covered under warranty, be sure that any replacement parts purchased - regardless of the source - do not invalidate the warranty!

To be sure of obtaining the correct parts, have engine and chassis numbers available and, if possible, take the old parts along for positive identification.

Maintenance techniques, tools and working facilities

Maintenance techniques

There are a number of techniques involved in maintenance and repair that will be referred to throughout this manual. Application of these techniques will enable the home mechanic to be more efficient, better organized and capable of performing the various tasks properly, which will ensure that the repair job is thorough and complete.

Fasteners

Fasteners are nuts, bolts, studs and screws used to hold two or more parts together. There are a few things to keep in mind when working with fasteners. Almost all of them use a locking device of some type, either a lockwasher, locknut, locking tab or thread adhesive. All threaded fasteners should be clean and straight, with undamaged threads and undamaged corners on the hex head where the wrench fits. Develop the habit of replacing all damaged nuts and bolts with new ones. Special locknuts with nylon or fiber inserts can only be used once. If they are removed, they lose their locking ability and must be replaced with new ones.

Rusted nuts and bolts should be treated with a penetrating fluid to ease removal and prevent breakage. Some mechanics use turpentine in a spout-type oil can, which works quite well. After applying the rust penetrant, let it work for a few minutes before trying to loosen the nut or bolt. Badly rusted fasteners may have to be chiseled or sawed off or removed with a special nut breaker, available at tool stores.

If a bolt or stud breaks off in an assembly, it can be drilled and removed with a special tool commonly available for this purpose. Most automotive machine shops can perform this task, as well as other repair procedures, such as the repair of threaded holes that have been stripped out.

Flat washers and lockwashers, when removed from an assembly, should always be replaced exactly as removed. Replace any damaged washers with new ones. Never use a lockwasher on any soft metal surface (such as aluminum), thin sheet metal or plastic.

Fastener sizes

For a number of reasons, automobile manufacturers are making wider and wider use of metric fasteners. Therefore, it is important to be able to tell the difference between standard (sometimes called U.S. or SAE) and metric hardware, since they cannot be interchanged.

All bolts, whether standard or metric, are sized according to diameter, thread pitch and length. For example, a standard 1/2 - 13 x 1 bolt is 1/2 inch in diameter, has 13 threads per inch and is 1 inch long. An M12 - 1.75 x 25 metric bolt is 12 mm in diameter, has a thread pitch of 1.75 mm (the distance between threads) and is 25 mm long. The two bolts are nearly identical, and easily confused, but they are not interchangeable.

In addition to the differences in diameter, thread pitch and length, metric and standard bolts can also be distinguished by examining the bolt heads. To begin with, the distance across the flats on a standard bolt head is measured in inches, while the same dimension on a metric bolt is sized in millimeters (the same is true for nuts). As a result, a standard wrench should not be used on a metric bolt and a metric wrench should not be used on a standard bolt. Also, most stan-

dard bolts have slashes radiating out from the center of the head to denote the grade or strength of the bolt, which is an indication of the amount of torque that can be applied to it. The greater the number of slashes, the greater the strength of the bolt. Grades 0 through 5 are commonly used on automobiles. Metric bolts have a property class (grade) number, rather than a slash, molded into their heads to indicate bolt strength. In this case, the higher the number, the stronger the bolt. Property class numbers 8.8, 9.8 and 10.9 are commonly used on automobiles.

Strength markings can also be used to distinguish standard hex nuts from metric hex nuts. Many standard nuts have dots, stamped into one side, while metric nuts are marked with a number. The greater the number of dots, or the higher the number, the

greater the strength of the nut.

Metric studs are also marked on their ends according to property class (grade). Larger studs are numbered (the same as metric bolts), while smaller studs carry a geometric code to denote grade.

It should be noted that many fasteners, especially Grades 0 through 2, have no distinguishing marks on them. When such is the case, the only way to determine whether it is standard or metric is to measure the thread pitch or compare it to a known fastener of the same size.

Standard fasteners are often referred to as SAE, as opposed to metric. However, it should be noted that SAE technically refers to a non-metric fine thread fastener only. Coarse thread non-metric fasteners are referred to as USS sizes.

Grade 1 or 2   Grade 5   Grade 8

Bolt strength marking (standard/SAE/USS; bottom - metric)

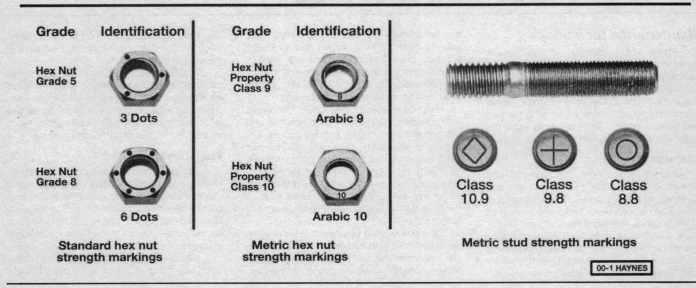

Grade	Identification
Hex Nut Grade 5	3 Dots
Hex Nut Grade 8	6 Dots

Standard hex nut strength markings

Grade	Identification
Hex Nut Property Class 9	Arabic 9
Hex Nut Property Class 10	Arabic 10

Metric hex nut strength markings

Class 10.9   Class 9.8   Class 8.8

Metric stud strength markings

Since fasteners of the same size (both standard and metric) may have different strength ratings, be sure to reinstall any bolts, studs or nuts removed from your vehicle in their original locations. Also, when replacing a fastener with a new one, make sure that the new one has a strength rating equal to or greater than the original.

Tightening sequences and procedures

Most threaded fasteners should be tightened to a specific torque value (torque is the twisting force applied to a threaded component such as a nut or bolt). Overtightening the fastener can weaken it and cause it to break, while undertightening can cause it to eventually come loose. Bolts, screws and studs, depending on the material they are made of and their thread diameters, have specific torque values, many of which are noted in the Specifications at the beginning of each Chapter. Be sure to follow the torque recommendations closely. For fasteners not assigned a specific torque, a general torque value chart is presented here as a guide. These torque values are for dry (unlubricated) fasteners threaded into steel or cast iron (not aluminum). As was previously mentioned, the size and grade of a fastener determine the amount of torque that can safely be applied to it. The figures listed here are approximate for Grade 2 and Grade 3 fasteners. Higher grades can tolerate higher torque values.

Fasteners laid out in a pattern, such as cylinder head bolts, oil pan bolts, differential cover bolts, etc., must be loosened or tightened in sequence to avoid warping the component. This sequence will normally be shown in the appropriate Chapter. If a specific pattern is not given, the following procedures can be used to prevent warping.

Metric thread sizes	Ft-lbs	Nm
M-6	6 to 9	9 to 12
M-8	14 to 21	19 to 28
M-10	28 to 40	38 to 54
M-12	50 to 71	68 to 96
M-14	80 to 140	109 to 154
Pipe thread sizes		
1/8	5 to 8	7 to 10
1/4	12 to 18	17 to 24
3/8	22 to 33	30 to 44
1/2	25 to 35	34 to 47
U.S. thread sizes		
1/4 - 20	6 to 9	9 to 12
5/16 - 18	12 to 18	17 to 24
5/16 - 24	14 to 20	19 to 27
3/8 - 16	22 to 32	30 to 43
3/8 - 24	27 to 38	37 to 51
7/16 - 14	40 to 55	55 to 74
7/16 - 20	40 to 60	55 to 81
1/2 - 13	55 to 80	75 to 108

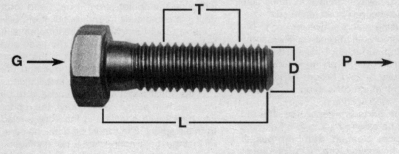

00-2 HAYNES

Standard (SAE and USS) bolt dimensions/grade marks

G   Grade marks (bolt strength)
L   Length (in inches)
T   Thread pitch (number of threads per inch)
D   Nominal diameter (in inches)

Metric bolt dimensions/grade marks

P   Property class (bolt strength)
L   Length (in millimeters)
T   Thread pitch (distance between threads in millimeters)
D   Diameter

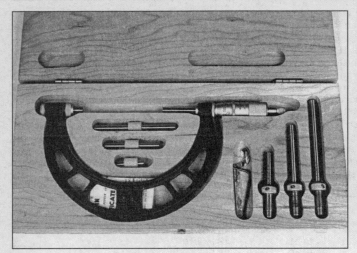

Micrometer set

Dial indicator set

Initially, the bolts or nuts should be assembled finger-tight only. Next, they should be tightened one full turn each, in a criss-cross or diagonal pattern. After each one has been tightened one full turn, return to the first one and tighten them all one-half turn, following the same pattern. Finally, tighten each of them one-quarter turn at a time until each fastener has been tightened to the proper torque. To loosen and remove the fasteners, the procedure would be reversed.

Component disassembly

Component disassembly should be done with care and purpose to help ensure that the parts go back together properly. Always keep track of the sequence in which parts are removed. Make note of special characteristics or marks on parts that can be installed more than one way, such as a grooved thrust washer on a shaft. It is a good idea to lay the disassembled parts out on a clean surface in the order that they were removed. It may also be helpful to make sketches or take instant photos of components before removal.

When removing fasteners from a component, keep track of their locations. Sometimes threading a bolt back in a part, or putting the washers and nut back on a stud, can prevent mix-ups later. If nuts and bolts cannot be returned to their original locations, they should be kept in a compartmented box or a series of small boxes. A cupcake or muffin tin is ideal for this purpose, since each cavity can hold the bolts and nuts from a particular area (i.e. oil pan bolts, valve cover bolts, engine mount bolts, etc.). A pan of this type is especially helpful when working on assemblies with very small parts, such as the carburetor, alternator, valve train or interior dash and trim pieces. The cavities can be marked with paint or tape to identify the contents.

Whenever wiring looms, harnesses or connectors are separated, it is a good idea to identify the two halves with numbered pieces of masking tape so they can be easily reconnected.

Gasket sealing surfaces

Throughout any vehicle, gaskets are used to seal the mating surfaces between two parts and keep lubricants, fluids, vacuum or pressure contained in an assembly.

Many times these gaskets are coated with a liquid or paste-type gasket sealing compound before assembly. Age, heat and pressure can sometimes cause the two parts to stick together so tightly that they are very difficult to separate. Often, the assembly can be loosened by striking it with a soft-face hammer near the mating surfaces. A regular hammer can be used if a block of wood is placed between the hammer and the part. Do not hammer on cast parts or parts that could be easily damaged. With any particularly stubborn part, always recheck to make sure that every fastener has been removed.

Avoid using a screwdriver or bar to pry apart an assembly, as they can easily mar the gasket sealing surfaces of the parts, which must remain smooth. If prying is absolutely necessary, use an old broom handle, but keep in mind that extra clean up will be necessary if the wood splinters.

After the parts are separated, the old gasket must be carefully scraped off and the gasket surfaces cleaned. Stubborn gasket material can be soaked with rust penetrant or treated with a special chemical to soften it so it can be easily scraped off. A scraper can be fashioned from a piece of copper tubing by flattening and sharpening one end. Copper is recommended because it is usually softer than the surfaces to be scraped, which reduces the chance of gouging the part. Some gaskets can be removed with a wire brush, but regardless of the method used, the mating surfaces must be left clean and smooth. If for some reason the gasket surface is gouged, then a gasket sealer thick enough to fill scratches will have to be used during reassembly of the components. For most applications, a non-drying (or semi-drying) gasket sealer should be used.

Hose removal tips

Warning: *If the vehicle is equipped with air conditioning, do not disconnect any of the A/C hoses without first having the system depressurized by a dealer service department or a service station.*

Hose removal precautions closely parallel gasket removal precautions. Avoid scratching or gouging the surface that the hose mates against or the connection may leak. This is especially true for radiator hoses. Because of various chemical reactions, the rubber in hoses can bond itself to the metal spigot that the hose fits over. To remove a hose, first loosen the hose clamps that secure it to the spigot. Then, with slip-joint pliers, grab the hose at the clamp and rotate it around the spigot. Work it back and forth until it is completely free, then pull it off. Silicone or other lubricants will ease removal if they can be applied between the hose and the outside of the spigot. Apply the same lubricant to the inside of the hose and the outside of the spigot to simplify installation.

As a last resort (and if the hose is to be replaced with a new one anyway), the rubber can be slit with a knife and the hose peeled from the spigot. If this must be done, be careful that the metal connection is not damaged.

If a hose clamp is broken or damaged, do not reuse it. Wire-type clamps usually weaken with age, so it is a good idea to replace them with screw-type clamps whenever a hose is removed.

Tools

A selection of good tools is a basic requirement for anyone who plans to maintain and repair his or her own vehicle. For the owner who has few tools, the initial investment might seem high, but when compared to the spiraling costs of professional auto maintenance and repair, it is a wise one.

To help the owner decide which tools are needed to perform the tasks detailed in this manual, the following tool lists are offered: *Maintenance and minor repair,*

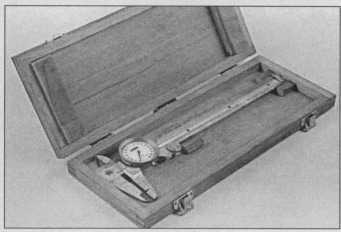

Dial caliper

Hand-operated vacuum pump

Timing light

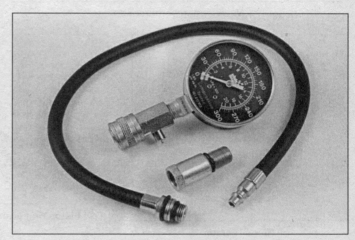

Compression gauge with spark plug hole adapter

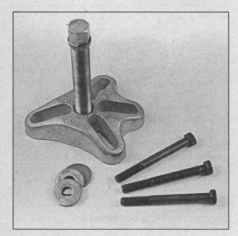

Damper/steering wheel puller

General purpose puller

Hydraulic lifter removal tool

Repair/overhaul and *Special*.

The newcomer to practical mechanics should start off with the *maintenance and minor repair* tool kit, which is adequate for the simpler jobs performed on a vehicle. Then, as confidence and experience grow, the owner can tackle more difficult tasks, buying additional tools as they are needed.

Eventually the basic kit will be expanded into the *repair and overhaul* tool set. Over a period of time, the experienced do-it-yourselfer will assemble a tool set complete enough for most repair and overhaul procedures and will add tools from the special category when it is felt that the expense is justified by the frequency of use.

Maintenance and minor repair tool kit

The tools in this list should be considered the minimum required for performance of routine maintenance, servicing and minor repair work. We recommend the purchase of combination wrenches (box-end and open-

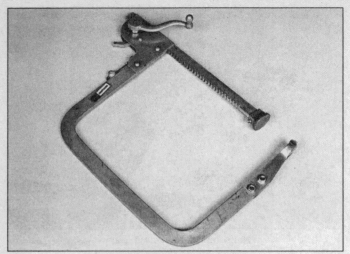

Valve spring compressor

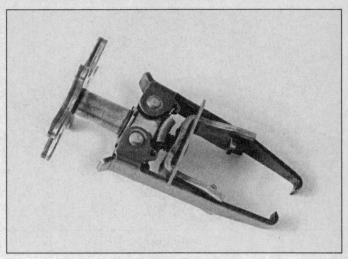

Valve spring compressor

Ridge reamer

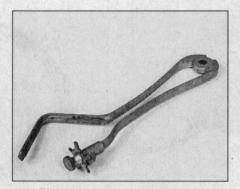

Piston ring groove cleaning tool

Ring removal/installation tool

Ring compressor

end combined in one wrench). While more expensive than open end wrenches, they offer the advantages of both types of wrench.

> Combination wrench set (1/4-inch to
>   1 inch or 6 mm to 19 mm)
> Adjustable wrench, 8 inch
> Spark plug wrench with rubber insert
> Spark plug gap adjusting tool
> Feeler gauge set
> Brake bleeder wrench
> Standard screwdriver (5/16-inch x
>   6 inch)
> Phillips screwdriver (No. 2 x 6 inch)
> Combination pliers - 6 inch
> Hacksaw and assortment of blades
> Tire pressure gauge
> Grease gun
> Oil can
> Fine emery cloth
> Wire brush
> Battery post and cable cleaning tool
> Oil filter wrench
> Funnel (medium size)
> Safety goggles
> Jackstands (2)
> Drain pan

Note: *If basic tune-ups are going to be part of routine maintenance, it will be necessary to purchase a good quality stroboscopic timing*

light and combination tachometer/dwell meter. Although they are included in the list of special tools, it is mentioned here because they are absolutely necessary for tuning most vehicles properly.

Repair and overhaul tool set

These tools are essential for anyone who plans to perform major repairs and are in addition to those in the maintenance and minor repair tool kit. Included is a comprehensive set of sockets which, though expensive, are invaluable because of their versatility, especially when various extensions and drives are available. We recommend the 1/2-inch drive over the 3/8-inch drive. Although the larger drive is bulky and more expensive, it has the capacity of accepting a very wide range of large sockets. Ideally, however, the mechanic should have a 3/8-inch drive set and a 1/2-inch drive set.

> Socket set(s)
> Reversible ratchet
> Extension - 10 inch
> Universal joint
> Torque wrench (same size drive as
>   sockets)
> Ball peen hammer - 8 ounce
> Soft-face hammer (plastic/rubber)

> Standard screwdriver (1/4-inch x 6 inch)
> Standard screwdriver (stubby -
>   5/16-inch)
> Phillips screwdriver (No. 3 x 8 inch)
> Phillips screwdriver (stubby - No. 2)
> Pliers - vise grip
> Pliers - lineman's
> Pliers - needle nose
> Pliers - snap-ring (internal and external)
> Cold chisel - 1/2-inch

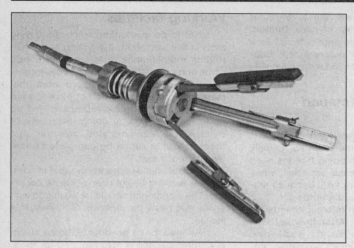

Cylinder hone

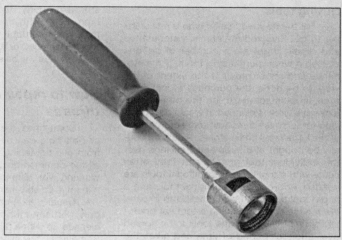

Brake hold-down spring tool

Scribe
Scraper (made from flattened copper
    tubing)
Centerpunch
Pin punches (1/16, 1/8, 3/16-inch)
Steel rule/straightedge - 12 inch
Allen wrench set (1/8 to 3/8-inch or
    4 mm to 10 mm)
A selection of files

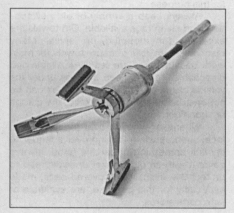

Brake cylinder hone

Wire brush (large)
Jackstands (second set)
Jack (scissor or hydraulic type)

Note: *Another tool which is often useful is an electric drill with a chuck capacity of 3/8-inch and a set of good quality drill bits.*

Special tools

The tools in this list include those which are not used regularly, are expensive to buy, or which need to be used in accordance with their manufacturer's instructions. Unless these tools will be used frequently, it is not very economical to purchase many of them. A consideration would be to split the cost and use between yourself and a friend or friends. In addition, most of these tools can be obtained from a tool rental shop on a temporary basis.

This list primarily contains only those tools and instruments widely available to the public, and not those special tools produced by the vehicle manufacturer for distribution to dealer service departments. Occasionally, references to the manufacturer's special tools are included in the text of this manual. Generally, an alternative method of doing the job without the special tool is offered. How-

ever, sometimes there is no alternative to their use. Where this is the case, and the tool cannot be purchased or borrowed, the work should be turned over to the dealer service department or an automotive repair shop.

Valve spring compressor
Piston ring groove cleaning tool
Piston ring compressor
Piston ring installation tool
Cylinder compression gauge
Cylinder ridge reamer
Cylinder surfacing hone
Cylinder bore gauge
Micrometers and/or dial calipers
Hydraulic lifter removal tool
Balljoint separator
Universal-type puller
Impact screwdriver
Dial indicator set
Stroboscopic timing light (inductive
    pick-up)
Hand operated vacuum/pressure pump
Tachometer/dwell meter
Universal electrical multimeter
Cable hoist
Brake spring removal and installation
    tools
Floor jack

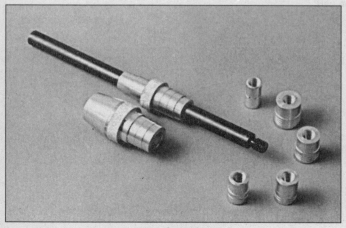

Clutch plate alignment tool

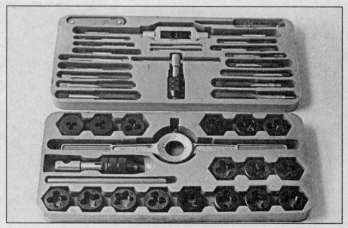

Tap and die set

Buying tools

For the do-it-yourselfer who is just starting to get involved in vehicle maintenance and repair, there are a number of options available when purchasing tools. If maintenance and minor repair is the extent of the work to be done, the purchase of individual tools is satisfactory. If, on the other hand, extensive work is planned, it would be a good idea to purchase a modest tool set from one of the large retail chain stores. A set can usually be bought at a substantial savings over the individual tool prices, and they often come with a tool box. As additional tools are needed, add-on sets, individual tools and a larger tool box can be purchased to expand the tool selection. Building a tool set gradually allows the cost of the tools to be spread over a longer period of time and gives the mechanic the freedom to choose only those tools that will actually be used.

Tool stores will often be the only source of some of the special tools that are needed, but regardless of where tools are bought, try to avoid cheap ones, especially when buying screwdrivers and sockets, because they won't last very long. The expense involved in replacing cheap tools will eventually be greater than the initial cost of quality tools.

Care and maintenance of tools

Good tools are expensive, so it makes sense to treat them with respect. Keep them clean and in usable condition and store them properly when not in use. Always wipe off any dirt, grease or metal chips before putting them away. Never leave tools lying around in the work area. Upon completion of a job, always check closely under the hood for tools that may have been left there so they won't get lost during a test drive.

Some tools, such as screwdrivers, pliers, wrenches and sockets, can be hung on a panel mounted on the garage or workshop wall, while others should be kept in a tool box or tray. Measuring instruments, gauges, meters, etc. must be carefully stored where they cannot be damaged by weather or impact from other tools.

When tools are used with care and stored properly, they will last a very long time. Even with the best of care, though, tools will wear out if used frequently. When a tool is damaged or worn out, replace it. Subsequent jobs will be safer and more enjoyable if you do.

How to repair damaged threads

Sometimes, the internal threads of a nut or bolt hole can become stripped, usually from overtightening. Stripping threads is an all-too-common occurrence, especially when working with aluminum parts, because aluminum is so soft that it easily strips out.

Usually, external or internal threads are only partially stripped. After they've been cleaned up with a tap or die, they'll still work. Sometimes, however, threads are badly damaged. When this happens, you've got three choices:

1) *Drill and tap the hole to the next suitable oversize and install a larger diameter bolt, screw or stud.*

2) *Drill and tap the hole to accept a threaded plug, then drill and tap the plug to the original screw size. You can also buy a plug already threaded to the original size. Then you simply drill a hole to the specified size, then run the threaded plug into the hole with a bolt and jam nut. Once the plug is fully seated, remove the jam nut and bolt.*

3) *The third method uses a patented thread repair kit like Heli-Coil or Slimsert. These easy-to-use kits are designed to repair damaged threads in straight-through holes and blind holes. Both are available as kits which can handle a variety of sizes and thread patterns. Drill the hole, then tap it with the special included tap. Install the Heli-Coil and the hole is back to its original diameter and thread pitch.*

Regardless of which method you use, be sure to proceed calmly and carefully. A little impatience or carelessness during one of these relatively simple procedures can ruin your whole day's work and cost you a bundle if you wreck an expensive part.

Working facilities

Not to be overlooked when discussing tools is the workshop. If anything more than routine maintenance is to be carried out, some sort of suitable work area is essential.

It is understood, and appreciated, that many home mechanics do not have a good workshop or garage available, and end up removing an engine or doing major repairs outside. It is recommended, however, that the overhaul or repair be completed under the cover of a roof.

A clean, flat workbench or table of comfortable working height is an absolute necessity. The workbench should be equipped with a vise that has a jaw opening of at least four inches.

As mentioned previously, some clean, dry storage space is also required for tools, as well as the lubricants, fluids, cleaning solvents, etc. which soon become necessary.

Sometimes waste oil and fluids, drained from the engine or cooling system during normal maintenance or repairs, present a disposal problem. To avoid pouring them on the ground or into a sewage system, pour the used fluids into large containers, seal them with caps and take them to an authorized disposal site or recycling center. Plastic jugs, such as old antifreeze containers, are ideal for this purpose.

Always keep a supply of old newspapers and clean rags available. Old towels are excellent for mopping up spills. Many mechanics use rolls of paper towels for most work because they are readily available and disposable. To help keep the area under the vehicle clean, a large cardboard box can be cut open and flattened to protect the garage or shop floor.

Whenever working over a painted surface, such as when leaning over a fender to service something under the hood, always cover it with an old blanket or bedspread to protect the finish. Vinyl covered pads, made especially for this purpose, are available at auto parts stores.

Booster battery (jump) starting

Observe the following precautions when using a booster battery to start a vehicle:

a) *Before connecting the booster battery, make sure the ignition switch is in the Off position.*

b) *Turn off the lights, heater and other electrical loads.*

c) *Your eyes should be shielded. Safety goggles are a good idea.*

d) *Make sure the booster battery is the same voltage as the dead one in the vehicle.*

e) *The two vehicles MUST NOT TOUCH each other.*

f) *Make sure the transmission is in Neutral (manual transaxle) or Park (automatic transaxle).*

g) *If the booster battery is not a maintenance-free type, remove the vent caps and lay a cloth over the vent holes.*

Connect the red jumper cable to the positive (+) terminals of each battery **(see illustration)**. **Note:** *The battery on the vehicles covered by this manual is mounted in such a way that it would be very difficult to connect jumper cables directly to the battery terminals, so a remote positive terminal, located at the front of the underhood fuse/relay center is provided for this purpose* **(see illustration)**.

Connect one end of the black cable to the negative (-) terminal of the booster battery. The other end of this cable should be connected to a good ground on the engine block. Make sure the cable will not come into contact with the fan, drivebelts or other moving parts of the engine.

Start the engine using the booster battery, then, with the engine running at idle speed, disconnect the jumper cables in the reverse order of connection.

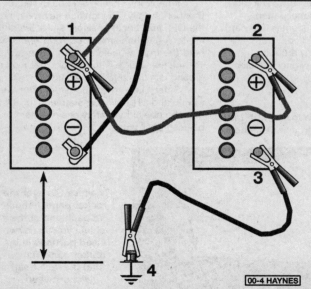

Make the booster battery cable connections in the numerical order shown (note that the negative cable from the booster battery is NOT attached to the negative terminal of the dead battery)

These vehicles have a remote positive battery terminal at the right front of the engine compartment

Anti-theft audio system

1997 through 1999 models

General information

1   Some of these models are equipped with THEFTLOCK audio systems, which include an anti-theft feature that will render the stereo inoperative if stolen. If the power source to the stereo is cut with the anti-theft feature activated, the stereo will be inoperative. Even if the power source is immediately re-connected, the stereo will not function.

2   If your vehicle is equipped with this anti-theft system, do not disconnect the battery, remove the stereo or disconnect related components unless you have either turned off the feature or have the individual ID (code) number for the stereo.

Disabling the anti-theft feature

3   Press the stereo's 1 and 4 buttons at the same time for five seconds with the ignition on and the radio power off. The display will show SEC, indicating the unit is in the secure mode (anti-theft feature enabled).

4   Press the MN button. The display will show "000".

5   Press the MN button until the last two numbers are the same as your secret code.

6   Press HR until the first one or two numbers displayed match your code. The numbers will be displayed as entered.

7   Press the AM/FM button. If the display shows "_ _ _" you have successfully disabled the anti-theft feature. If SEC is displayed, the code you entered was incorrect and the anti-theft feature is still enabled.

Unlocking the stereo after a power loss

8   When the power is restored to the stereo, the stereo won't turn on and LOC will appear on the display. Enter your ID code as follows; pause no more than 15 seconds between Steps.

9   Turn the ignition switch to ON, but leave the stereo off.

10   Press the MN button. "000" should display.

11   Press the MN button again to make the last two numbers match your code, then release the button.

12   Press the HR button until the first one or two numbers match your code.

13   Once you correct code has been displayed, press AM/FM. SEC should appear indicating the stereo is unlocked. If LOC appears, the numbers you entered were not correct and the stereo is still inoperative.

14   If you forget your code, contact a dealer service department.

2000 and later models

15   Anti-theft radios in these models automatically "learn" part of the vehicle's identification number and will only work with that particular vehicle. If the radio is installed in another vehicle, it won't work. No precautions have to be taken when removing the radio or disconnecting the battery on these models, aside from writing down the radio station presets (these will be lost when the battery is disconnected and must be reset).

Jacking and towing

Jacking

Warning: *The jack supplied with the vehicle should only be used for changing a tire or placing jackstands under the frame. Never work under the vehicle or start the engine while this jack is being used as the only means of support.*

The vehicle should be on level ground. Place the shift lever in Park. Block the wheel diagonally opposite the wheel being changed. Set the parking brake.

Remove the spare tire and jack from stowage. Remove the wheel cover (on steel wheels) with the tapered end of the lug nut wrench by inserting and twisting the handle and then prying against the back of the wheel cover. On aluminum wheels, use a small screwdriver to pry out the center hub cap. Loosen the wheel lug nuts about 1/4-to-1/2 turn each.

Place the scissors-type jack under the side of the vehicle and adjust the jack height until it fits between the raise portions of the vertical rocker panel flange nearest the wheel to be changed. There is a front and rear jacking point on each side of the vehicle **(see illustration)**.

Turn the jack handle clockwise until the tire clears the ground. Remove the lug nuts and pull the wheel off. Replace it with the spare.

Install the lug nuts with the beveled edges facing in. Tighten them snugly. Don't attempt to tighten them completely until the vehicle is lowered or it could slip off the jack. Turn the jack handle counterclockwise to lower the vehicle. Remove the jack and tighten the lug nuts in a diagonal pattern.

Install the wheel cover (center hub cap on aluminum wheels) and be sure it's snapped into place all the way around.

Stow the tire, jack and wrench. Unblock the wheels.

Towing

These vehicles *must* be towed with the front (drive) wheels off the ground. A flatbed car carrier is the preferred method, but a tow truck with wheel lift equipment can be used. Tow trucks with a sling-type lift *cannot* be used.

If the front wheels can't be raised, place them on a dolly. The ignition key must be in the OFF (*not* Lock) position, since the steering lock mechanism isn't strong enough to hold the front wheels straight while towing. Towing the vehicle with all four wheels on the ground can damage the drivetrain.

Safety is a major consideration when towing and all applicable state and local laws must be obeyed. A safety chain system must be used at all times.

The jack fits over the rocker panel flange; at each end of the vehicle you'll see two raised portions in the rocker panel flange that the jack head fits between

Automotive chemicals and lubricants

A number of automotive chemicals and lubricants are available for use during vehicle maintenance and repair. They include a wide variety of products ranging from cleaning solvents and degreasers to lubricants and protective sprays for rubber, plastic and vinyl.

Cleaners

Carburetor cleaner and choke cleaner is a strong solvent for gum, varnish and carbon. Most carburetor cleaners leave a dry-type lubricant film which will not harden or gum up. Because of this film it is not recommended for use on electrical components.

Brake system cleaner is used to remove grease and brake fluid from the brake system, where clean surfaces are absolutely necessary. It leaves no residue and often eliminates brake squeal caused by contaminants.

Electrical cleaner removes oxidation, corrosion and carbon deposits from electrical contacts, restoring full current flow. It can also be used to clean spark plugs, carburetor jets, voltage regulators and other parts where an oil-free surface is desired.

Demoisturants remove water and moisture from electrical components such as alternators, voltage regulators, electrical connectors and fuse blocks. They are non-conductive, non-corrosive and non-flammable.

Degreasers are heavy-duty solvents used to remove grease from the outside of the engine and from chassis components. They can be sprayed or brushed on and, depending on the type, are rinsed off either with water or solvent.

Lubricants

Motor oil is the lubricant formulated for use in engines. It normally contains a wide variety of additives to prevent corrosion and reduce foaming and wear. Motor oil comes in various weights (viscosity ratings) from 0 to 50. The recommended weight of the oil depends on the season, temperature and the demands on the engine. Light oil is used in cold climates and under light load conditions. Heavy oil is used in hot climates and where high loads are encountered. Multi-viscosity oils are designed to have characteristics of both light and heavy oils and are available in a number of weights from 5W-20 to 20W-50.

Gear oil is designed to be used in differentials, manual transmissions and other areas where high-temperature lubrication is required.

Chassis and wheel bearing grease is a heavy grease used where increased loads and friction are encountered, such as for wheel bearings, balljoints, tie-rod ends and universal joints.

High-temperature wheel bearing grease is designed to withstand the extreme temperatures encountered by wheel bearings in disc brake equipped vehicles. It usually contains molybdenum disulfide (moly), which is a dry-type lubricant.

White grease is a heavy grease for metal-to-metal applications where water is a problem. White grease stays soft under both low and high temperatures (usually from -100 to +190-degrees F), and will not wash off or dilute in the presence of water.

Assembly lube is a special extreme pressure lubricant, usually containing moly, used to lubricate high-load parts (such as main and rod bearings and cam lobes) for initial start-up of a new engine. The assembly lube lubricates the parts without being squeezed out or washed away until the engine oiling system begins to function.

Silicone lubricants are used to protect rubber, plastic, vinyl and nylon parts.

Graphite lubricants are used where oils cannot be used due to contamination problems, such as in locks. The dry graphite will lubricate metal parts while remaining uncontaminated by dirt, water, oil or acids. It is electrically conductive and will not foul electrical contacts in locks such as the ignition switch.

Moly penetrants loosen and lubricate frozen, rusted and corroded fasteners and prevent future rusting or freezing.

Heat-sink grease is a special electrically non-conductive grease that is used for mounting electronic ignition modules where it is essential that heat is transferred away from the module.

Sealants

RTV sealant is one of the most widely used gasket compounds. Made from silicone, RTV is air curing, it seals, bonds, waterproofs, fills surface irregularities, remains flexible, doesn't shrink, is relatively easy to remove, and is used as a supplementary sealer with almost all low and medium temperature gaskets.

Anaerobic sealant is much like RTV in that it can be used either to seal gaskets or to form gaskets by itself. It remains flexible, is solvent resistant and fills surface imperfections. The difference between an anaerobic sealant and an RTV-type sealant is in the curing. RTV cures when exposed to air, while an anaerobic sealant cures only in the absence of air. This means that an anaerobic sealant cures only after the assembly of parts, sealing them together.

Thread and pipe sealant is used for sealing hydraulic and pneumatic fittings and vacuum lines. It is usually made from a Teflon compound, and comes in a spray, a paint-on liquid and as a wrap-around tape.

Chemicals

Anti-seize compound prevents seizing, galling, cold welding, rust and corrosion in fasteners. High-temperature anti-seize, usually made with copper and graphite lubricants, is used for exhaust system and exhaust manifold bolts.

Anaerobic locking compounds are used to keep fasteners from vibrating or working loose and cure only after installation, in the absence of air. Medium strength locking compound is used for small nuts, bolts and screws that may be removed later. High-strength locking compound is for large nuts, bolts and studs which aren't removed on a regular basis.

Oil additives range from viscosity index improvers to chemical treatments that claim to reduce internal engine friction. It should be noted that most oil manufacturers caution against using additives with their oils.

Gas additives perform several functions, depending on their chemical makeup. They usually contain solvents that help dissolve gum and varnish that build up on carburetor, fuel injection and intake parts. They also serve to break down carbon deposits that form on the inside surfaces of the combustion chambers. Some additives contain upper cylinder lubricants for valves and piston rings, and others contain chemicals to remove condensation from the gas tank.

Miscellaneous

Brake fluid is specially formulated hydraulic fluid that can withstand the heat and pressure encountered in brake systems. Care must be taken so this fluid does not come in contact with painted surfaces or plastics. An opened container should always be resealed to prevent contamination by water or dirt.

Weatherstrip adhesive is used to bond weatherstripping around doors, windows and trunk lids. It is sometimes used to attach trim pieces.

Undercoating is a petroleum-based, tar-like substance that is designed to protect metal surfaces on the underside of the vehicle from corrosion. It also acts as a sound-deadening agent by insulating the bottom of the vehicle.

Waxes and polishes are used to help protect painted and plated surfaces from the weather. Different types of paint may require the use of different types of wax and polish. Some polishes utilize a chemical or abrasive cleaner to help remove the top layer of oxidized (dull) paint on older vehicles. In recent years many non-wax polishes that contain a wide variety of chemicals such as polymers and silicones have been introduced. These non-wax polishes are usually easier to apply and last longer than conventional waxes and polishes.

Conversion factors

Length (distance)

Inches (in)	X	25.4	= Millimetres (mm)	X 0.0394	= Inches (in)
Feet (ft)	X	0.305	= Metres (m)	X 3.281	= Feet (ft)
Miles	X	1.609	= Kilometres (km)	X 0.621	= Miles

Volume (capacity)

Cubic inches (cu in; in^3)	X	16.387	= Cubic centimetres (cc; cm^3)	X 0.061	= Cubic inches (cu in; in^3)
Imperial pints (Imp pt)	X	0.568	= Litres (l)	X 1.76	= Imperial pints (Imp pt)
Imperial quarts (Imp qt)	X	1.137	= Litres (l)	X 0.88	= Imperial quarts (Imp qt)
Imperial quarts (Imp qt)	X	1.201	= US quarts (US qt)	X 0.833	= Imperial quarts (Imp qt)
US quarts (US qt)	X	0.946	= Litres (l)	X 1.057	= US quarts (US qt)
Imperial gallons (Imp gal)	X	4.546	= Litres (l)	X 0.22	= Imperial gallons (Imp gal)
Imperial gallons (Imp gal)	X	1.201	= US gallons (US gal)	X 0.833	= Imperial gallons (Imp gal)
US gallons (US gal)	X	3.785	= Litres (l)	X 0.264	= US gallons (US gal)

Mass (weight)

Ounces (oz)	X	28.35	= Grams (g)	X 0.035	= Ounces (oz)
Pounds (lb)	X	0.454	= Kilograms (kg)	X 2.205	= Pounds (lb)

Force

Ounces-force (ozf; oz)	X	0.278	= Newtons (N)	X 3.6	= Ounces-force (ozf; oz)
Pounds-force (lbf; lb)	X	4.448	= Newtons (N)	X 0.225	= Pounds-force (lbf; lb)
Newtons (N)	X	0.1	= Kilograms-force (kgf; kg)	X 9.81	= Newtons (N)

Pressure

Pounds-force per square inch (psi; lbf/in^2; lb/in^2)	X	0.070	= Kilograms-force per square centimetre (kgf/cm^2; kg/cm^2)	X 14.223	= Pounds-force per square inch (psi; lbf/in^2; lb/in^2)
Pounds-force per square inch (psi; lbf/in^2; lb/in^2)	X	0.068	= Atmospheres (atm)	X 14.696	= Pounds-force per square inch (psi; lbf/in^2; lb/in^2)
Pounds-force per square inch (psi; lbf/in^2; lb/in^2)	X	0.069	= Bars	X 14.5	= Pounds-force per square inch (psi; lbf/in^2; lb/in^2)
Pounds-force per square inch (psi; lbf/in^2; lb/in^2)	X	6.895	= Kilopascals (kPa)	X 0.145	= Pounds-force per square inch (psi; lbf/in^2; lb/in^2)
Kilopascals (kPa)	X	0.01	= Kilograms-force per square centimetre (kgf/cm^2; kg/cm^2)	X 98.1	= Kilopascals (kPa)

Torque (moment of force)

Pounds-force inches (lbf in; lb in)	X	1.152	= Kilograms-force centimetre (kgf cm; kg cm)	X 0.868	= Pounds-force inches (lbf in; lb in)
Pounds-force inches (lbf in; lb in)	X	0.113	= Newton metres (Nm)	X 8.85	= Pounds-force inches (lbf in; lb in)
Pounds-force inches (lbf in; lb in)	X	0.083	= Pounds-force feet (lbf ft; lb ft)	X 12	= Pounds-force inches (lbf in; lb in)
Pounds-force feet (lbf ft; lb ft)	X	0.138	= Kilograms-force metres (kgf m; kg m)	X 7.233	= Pounds-force feet (lbf ft; lb ft)
Pounds-force feet (lbf ft; lb ft)	X	1.356	= Newton metres (Nm)	X 0.738	= Pounds-force feet (lbf ft; lb ft)
Newton metres (Nm)	X	0.102	= Kilograms-force metres (kgf m; kg m)	X 9.804	= Newton metres (Nm)

Vacuum

Inches mercury (in. Hg)	X	3.377	= Kilopascals (kPa)	X 0.2961	= Inches mercury
Inches mercury (in. Hg)	X	25.4	= Millimeters mercury (mm Hg)	X 0.0394	= Inches mercury

Power

Horsepower (hp)	X	745.7	= Watts (W)	X 0.0013	= Horsepower (hp)

Velocity (speed)

Miles per hour (miles/hr; mph)	X	1.609	= Kilometres per hour (km/hr; kph)	X 0.621	= Miles per hour (miles/hr; mph)

Fuel consumption*

Miles per gallon, Imperial (mpg)	X	0.354	= Kilometres per litre (km/l)	X 2.825	= Miles per gallon, Imperial (mpg)
Miles per gallon, US (mpg)	X	0.425	= Kilometres per litre (km/l)	X 2.352	= Miles per gallon, US (mpg)

Temperature

Degrees Fahrenheit = (°C x 1.8) + 32

Degrees Celsius (Degrees Centigrade; °C) = (°F - 32) x 0.56

*It is common practice to convert from miles per gallon (mpg) to litres/100 kilometres (l/100km), where mpg (Imperial) x l/100 km = 282 and mpg (US) x l/100 km = 235

Fraction/Decimal/Millimeter Equivalents

DECIMALS TO MILLIMETERS

Decimal	mm	Decimal	mm
0.001	0.0254	0.500	12.7000
0.002	0.0508	0.510	12.9540
0.003	0.0762	0.520	13.2080
0.004	0.1016	0.530	13.4620
0.005	0.1270	0.540	13.7160
0.006	0.1524	0.550	13.9700
0.007	0.1778	0.560	14.2240
0.008	0.2032	0.570	14.4780
0.009	0.2286	0.580	14.7320
0.010	0.2540	0.590	14.9860
0.020	0.5080		
0.030	0.7620		
0.040	1.0160	0.600	15.2400
0.050	1.2700	0.610	15.4940
0.060	1.5240	0.620	15.7480
0.070	1.7780	0.630	16.0020
0.080	2.0320	0.640	16.2560
0.090	2.2860	0.650	16.5100
		0.660	16.7640
0.100	2.5400	0.670	17.0180
0.110	2.7940	0.680	17.2720
0.120	3.0480	0.690	17.5260
0.130	3.3020		
0.140	3.5560		
0.150	3.8100		
0.160	4.0640	0.700	17.7800
0.170	4.3180	0.710	18.0340
0.180	4.5720	0.720	18.2880
0.190	4.8260	0.730	18.5420
		0.740	18.7960
0.200	5.0800	0.750	19.0500
0.210	5.3340	0.760	19.3040
0.220	5.5880	0.770	19.5580
0.230	5.8420	0.780	19.8120
0.240	6.0960	0.790	20.0660
0.250	6.3500		
0.260	6.6040	0.800	20.3200
0.270	6.8580	0.810	20.5740
0.280	7.1120	0.820	21.8280
0.290	7.3660	0.830	21.0820
0.300	7.6200	0.840	21.3360
0.310	7.8740	0.850	21.5900
0.320	8.1280	0.860	21.8440
0.330	8.3820	0.870	22.0980
0.340	8.6360	0.880	22.3520
0.350	8.8900	0.890	22.6060
0.360	9.1440		
0.370	9.3980		
0.380	9.6520		
0.390	9.9060	0.900	22.8600
0.400	10.1600	0.910	23.1140
0.410	10.4140	0.920	23.3680
0.420	10.6680	0.930	23.6220
0.430	10.9220	0.940	23.8760
0.440	11.1760	0.950	24.1300
0.450	11.4300	0.960	24.3840
0.460	11.6840	0.970	24.6380
0.470	11.9380	0.980	24.8920
0.480	12.1920	0.990	25.1460
0.490	12.4460	1.000	25.4000

FRACTIONS TO DECIMALS TO MILLIMETERS

Fraction	Decimal	mm	Fraction	Decimal	mm
1/64	0.0156	0.3969	33/64	0.5156	13.0969
1/32	0.0312	0.7938	17/32	0.5312	13.4938
3/64	0.0469	1.1906	35/64	0.5469	13.8906
1/16	0.0625	1.5875	9/16	0.5625	14.2875
5/64	0.0781	1.9844	37/64	0.5781	14.6844
3/32	0.0938	2.3812	19/32	0.5938	15.0812
7/64	0.1094	2.7781	39/64	0.6094	15.4781
1/8	0.1250	3.1750	5/8	0.6250	15.8750
9/64	0.1406	3.5719	41/64	0.6406	16.2719
5/32	0.1562	3.9688	21/32	0.6562	16.6688
11/64	0.1719	4.3656	43/64	0.6719	17.0656
3/16	0.1875	4.7625	11/16	0.6875	17.4625
13/64	0.2031	5.1594	45/64	0.7031	17.8594
7/32	0.2188	5.5562	23/32	0.7188	18.2562
15/64	0.2344	5.9531	47/64	0.7344	18.6531
1/4	0.2500	6.3500	3/4	0.7500	19.0500
17/64	0.2656	6.7469	49/64	0.7656	19.4469
9/32	0.2812	7.1438	25/32	0.7812	19.8438
19/64	0.2969	7.5406	51/64	0.7969	20.2406
5/16	0.3125	7.9375	13/16	0.8125	20.6375
21/64	0.3281	8.3344	53/64	0.8281	21.0344
11/32	0.3438	8.7312	27/32	0.8438	21.4312
23/64	0.3594	9.1281	55/64	0.8594	21.8281
3/8	0.3750	9.5250	7/8	0.8750	22.2250
25/64	0.3906	9.9219	57/64	0.8906	22.6219
13/32	0.4062	10.3188	29/32	0.9062	23.0188
27/64	0.4219	10.7156	59/64	0.9219	23.4156
7/16	0.4375	11.1125	15/16	0.9375	23.8125
29/64	0.4531	11.5094	61/64	0.9531	24.2094
15/32	0.4688	11.9062	31/32	0.9688	24.6062
31/64	0.4844	12.3031	63/64	0.9844	25.0031
1/2	0.5000	12.7000	1	1.0000	25.4000

Safety first!

Regardless of how enthusiastic you may be about getting on with the job at hand, take the time to ensure that your safety is not jeopardized. A moment's lack of attention can result in an accident, as can failure to observe certain simple safety precautions. The possibility of an accident will always exist, and the following points should not be considered a comprehensive list of all dangers. Rather, they are intended to make you aware of the risks and to encourage a safety conscious approach to all work you carry out on your vehicle.

Essential DOs and DON'Ts

DON'T rely on a jack when working under the vehicle. Always use approved jackstands to support the weight of the vehicle and place them under the recommended lift or support points.

DON'T attempt to loosen extremely tight fasteners (i.e. wheel lug nuts) while the vehicle is on a jack - it may fall.

DON'T start the engine without first making sure that the transmission is in Neutral (or Park where applicable) and the parking brake is set.

DON'T remove the radiator cap from a hot cooling system - let it cool or cover it with a cloth and release the pressure gradually.

DON'T attempt to drain the engine oil until you are sure it has cooled to the point that it will not burn you.

DON'T touch any part of the engine or exhaust system until it has cooled sufficiently to avoid burns.

DON'T siphon toxic liquids such as gasoline, antifreeze and brake fluid by mouth, or allow them to remain on your skin.

DON'T inhale brake lining dust - it is potentially hazardous (see *Asbestos* below).

DON'T allow spilled oil or grease to remain on the floor - wipe it up before someone slips on it.

DON'T use loose fitting wrenches or other tools which may slip and cause injury.

DON'T push on wrenches when loosening or tightening nuts or bolts. Always try to pull the wrench toward you. If the situation calls for pushing the wrench away, push with an open hand to avoid scraped knuckles if the wrench should slip.

DON'T attempt to lift a heavy component alone - get someone to help you.

DON'T rush or take unsafe shortcuts to finish a job.

DON'T allow children or animals in or around the vehicle while you are working on it.

DO wear eye protection when using power tools such as a drill, sander, bench grinder, etc. and when working under a vehicle.

DO keep loose clothing and long hair well out of the way of moving parts.

DO make sure that any hoist used has a safe working load rating adequate for the job.

DO get someone to check on you periodically when working alone on a vehicle.

DO carry out work in a logical sequence and make sure that everything is correctly assembled and tightened.

DO keep chemicals and fluids tightly capped and out of the reach of children and pets.

DO remember that your vehicle's safety affects that of yourself and others. If in doubt on any point, get professional advice.

Asbestos

Certain friction, insulating, sealing, and other products - such as brake linings, brake bands, clutch linings, torque converters, gaskets, etc. - may contain asbestos. Extreme care must be taken to avoid inhalation of dust from such products, since it is hazardous to health. If in doubt, assume that they do contain asbestos.

Fire

Remember at all times that gasoline is highly flammable. Never smoke or have any kind of open flame around when working on a vehicle. But the risk does not end there. A spark caused by an electrical short circuit, by two metal surfaces contacting each other, or even by static electricity built up in your body under certain conditions, can ignite gasoline vapors, which in a confined space are highly explosive. Do not, under any circumstances, use gasoline for cleaning parts. Use an approved safety solvent.

Always disconnect the battery ground (-) cable at the battery before working on any part of the fuel system or electrical system. Never risk spilling fuel on a hot engine or exhaust component. It is strongly recommended that a fire extinguisher suitable for use on fuel and electrical fires be kept handy in the garage or workshop at all times. Never try to extinguish a fuel or electrical fire with water.

Fumes

Certain fumes are highly toxic and can quickly cause unconsciousness and even death if inhaled to any extent. Gasoline vapor falls into this category, as do the vapors from some cleaning solvents. Any draining or pouring of such volatile fluids should be done in a well ventilated area.

When using cleaning fluids and solvents, read the instructions on the container carefully. Never use materials from unmarked containers.

Never run the engine in an enclosed space, such as a garage. Exhaust fumes contain carbon monoxide, which is extremely poisonous. If you need to run the engine, always do so in the open air, or at least have the rear of the vehicle outside the work area.

If you are fortunate enough to have the use of an inspection pit, never drain or pour gasoline and never run the engine while the vehicle is over the pit. The fumes, being heavier than air, will concentrate in the pit with possibly lethal results.

The battery

Never create a spark or allow a bare light bulb near a battery. They normally give off a certain amount of hydrogen gas, which is highly explosive.

Always disconnect the battery ground (-) cable at the battery before working on the fuel or electrical systems.

If possible, loosen the filler caps or cover when charging the battery from an external source (this does not apply to sealed or maintenance-free batteries). Do not charge at an excessive rate or the battery may burst.

Take care when adding water to a non maintenance-free battery and when carrying a battery. The electrolyte, even when diluted, is very corrosive and should not be allowed to contact clothing or skin.

Always wear eye protection when cleaning the battery to prevent the caustic deposits from entering your eyes.

Household current

When using an electric power tool, inspection light, etc., which operates on household current, always make sure that the tool is correctly connected to its plug and that, where necessary, it is properly grounded. Do not use such items in damp conditions and, again, do not create a spark or apply excessive heat in the vicinity of fuel or fuel vapor.

Secondary ignition system voltage

A severe electric shock can result from touching certain parts of the ignition system (such as the spark plug wires) when the engine is running or being cranked, particularly if components are damp or the insulation is defective. In the case of an electronic ignition system, the secondary system voltage is much higher and could prove fatal.

Troubleshooting

Contents

Engine and performance

1 Engine will not rotate when attempting to start

1   Battery terminal connections loose or corroded. Check the cable terminals at the battery; tighten cable clamp and/or clean off corrosion as necessary (see Chapter 1).
2   Battery discharged or faulty. If the cable ends are clean and tight on the battery connections, turn the key to the On position and switch on the headlights or windshield wipers. If they don't work, the battery is discharged.
3   Automatic transaxle not engaged in park (P) or Neutral (N).
4   Broken, loose or disconnected wires in the starting circuit. Inspect all wires and connectors at the battery, starter solenoid and ignition switch (on steering column).
5   Starter motor pinion jammed in driveplate ring gear. Remove starter (Chapter 5) and inspect pinion and driveplate (Chapter 2) at earliest convenience.
6   Starter solenoid faulty (Chapter 5).
7   Starter motor faulty (Chapter 5).
8   Ignition switch faulty (Chapter 12).
9   Engine seized. Try to turn the crankshaft with a large socket and breaker bar on the pulley bolt (see Chapter 2).

2 Engine rotates but will not start

1   Fuel tank empty.
2   Battery discharged (engine rotates slowly). Check the operation of electrical components as described in previous Section.
3   Battery terminal connections loose or corroded. See previous Section.
4   Fuel not reaching fuel injectors. Check for clogged fuel filter or lines and defective fuel pump. Also make sure the tank vent lines aren't clogged (Chapter 4).
5   Faulty ignition coil (Chapter 5).
6   Low cylinder compression. Check as described in Chapter 2.
7   Water in fuel. Drain tank and fill with new fuel.
8   Dirty or clogged fuel injectors.
9   Faulty emissions or engine control systems (Chapter 6).
10   Wet or damaged ignition components (Chapters 1 and 5).
11   Worn, faulty or incorrectly gapped spark plugs (Chapter 1).
12   Broken, loose or disconnected wires in the ignition circuit.
13   Broken, loose or disconnected wires at the ignition coils or faulty coils (Chapter 5).
14   Timing chain failure or wear affecting valve timing (Chapter 2).

3 Starter motor operates without turning engine

1   Starter pinion sticking. Remove the starter (Chapter 5) and inspect.
2   Starter pinion or driveplate teeth worn or broken. Remove the inspection cover on the left side of the engine and inspect.

4 Engine hard to start when cold

1   Battery low or discharged. Check as described in Chapter 1.
2   Fuel not reaching the fuel injectors. Check the fuel filter and lines (Chapters 1 and 4).
3   Defective spark plugs (Chapter 1).
4   Intake manifold vacuum leaks. Make sure all mounting bolts/nuts are tight and all vacuum hoses connected to the manifold are attached properly and in good condition.
5   Faulty emissions or engine control systems (Chapter 6).

5 Engine hard to start when hot

1   Air filter dirty (Chapter 1).
2   Bad engine ground connection.
3   Fuel not reaching the injectors (Chapter 4).
4   Loose connection in the ignition system (Chapter 5).
5   Faulty emissions or engine control systems (Chapter 6).

6 Starter motor noisy or engages roughly

1   Pinion or flywheel/driveplate teeth worn or broken. Remove the inspection cover and inspect.
2   Starter motor mounting bolts loose or missing.

7 Engine starts but stops immediately

1   Loose or damaged wiring in the ignition system.
2   Intake manifold vacuum leaks. Make sure all mounting bolts/nuts are tight and all vacuum hoses connected to the manifold are attached properly and in good condition.
3   Faulty emissions or engine control systems (Chapter 6).

8 Engine 'lopes' while idling or idles erratically

1   Vacuum leaks. Check mounting bolts at the intake manifold or plenum for tightness.

Make sure that all vacuum hoses are connected and in good condition. Use a stethoscope or a length of fuel hose held against your ear to listen for vacuum leaks while the engine is running. A hissing sound will be heard. A soapy water solution will also detect leaks. Check the intake manifold or plenum gasket surfaces.
2   Leaking EGR valve or plugged PCV valve (Chapter 6).
3   Clogged air filter (Chapter 1).
4   Leaking head gasket. Perform a cylinder compression check (Chapter 2).
5   Worn timing chain (Chapter 2).
6   Worn camshaft lobes (Chapter 2).
7   Valves burned or otherwise leaking (Chapter 2).
8   Ignition system not operating properly (Chapter 5).
9   Clogged or dirty injectors (Chapter 4).
10   Faulty emissions or engine control systems (Chapter 6).

9 Engine misses at idle speed

1   Spark plugs faulty or not gapped properly (Chapter 1).
2   Faulty spark plug wires (Chapter 1).
3   Ignition components damaged or wet (Chapter 1).
4   Short circuits in spark plug wires, ignition or coils (Chapter 5).
5   Emissions or engine control systems faulty (Chapter 6).
6   Clogged fuel filter and/or foreign matter in fuel. Replace the fuel filter (Chapter 1).
7   Vacuum leaks at intake manifold or plenum or hose connections. Check as described in Section 8.
8   Cylinder compression low or uneven. Check as described in Chapter 2.
9   Fuel injectors clogged or dirty (Chapter 4).
10   Leaky EGR valve (Chapter 6).
11   Emissions or engine control systems faulty (Chapter 6).

10 Excessively high idle speed

1   Sticking throttle linkage (Chapter 4).
2   Idle Air Control system problem (Chapter 6).
3   Faulty emissions or engine control systems (Chapter 6).

11 Battery will not hold a charge

1   Drivebelt defective or not adjusted properly (Chapter 1).
2   Battery cables loose or corroded (Chapter 1).
3   Alternator not charging properly (Chapter 5).
4   Loose, broken or faulty wires in the charging circuit (Chapter 5).
5   Continuous drain on the battery caused

by a short circuit (Chapter 12).
6 Battery defective internally.
7 Faulty regulator (Chapter 5).

12 Alternator light stays on

1 Alternator or charging circuit fault (Chapter 5).
2 Drivebelt defective or not properly adjusted (Chapter 1).

13 Alternator light fails to come on when key is turned on

1 Faulty bulb (Chapter 12).
2 Defective alternator (Chapter 5).
3 Fault in the printed circuit, dash wiring or bulb holder (Chapter 12).

14 Engine misses throughout driving speed range

1 Fuel filter clogged and/or impurities in the fuel system. Check fuel filter (Chapter 1) or clean system (Chapter 4).
2 Faulty or incorrectly gapped spark plugs (Chapter 1).
3 Ignition system wires disconnected or damaged ignition system components (Chapter 1).
4 Defective spark plug wires (Chapter 1).
5 Emissions or engine control system components faulty (Chapter 6).
6 Low or uneven cylinder compression pressures. Check as described in Chapter 2.
7 Ignition coils faulty or weak (Chapter 5).
8 Ignition system faulty or weak (Chapter 5).
9 Vacuum leaks at intake manifold or plenum or vacuum hoses (see Section 8).
10 Fuel injector dirty or clogged (Chapter 4).

15 Hesitation or stumble during acceleration

1 Ignition system not operating properly (Chapter 5).
2 Clogged or dirty fuel injectors (Chapter 4).
3 Fuel pressure low. Check for proper operation of the fuel pump and for restrictions in the fuel filter and lines (Chapter 4).
4 Emissions or engine control system components faulty (Chapter 6).

16 Engine stalls

1 Idle Air Control valve faulty (Chapter 6).
2 Fuel filter clogged and/or water and impurities in the fuel system (Chapter 1).
3 Wet or damaged ignition system wires

or components.
4 Idle Air Control system faulty (Chapter 6).
5 Emissions or engine control system components faulty (Chapter 6).
6 Faulty or incorrectly gapped spark plugs (Chapter 1). Also check the spark plug wires (Chapter 1).
7 Vacuum leak at the intake manifold or plenum or vacuum hoses. Check as described in Section 8.

17 Engine lacks power

1 Check for faulty ignition wires, etc. (Chapter 1).
2 Faulty or incorrectly gapped spark plugs (Chapter 1).
3 Dirty air filter (Chapter 1).
4 Ignition coils faulty (Chapter 5).
5 Brakes binding (Chapters 1 and 9).
6 Automatic transaxle fluid level incorrect, causing slippage (Chapter 1).
7 Fuel filter clogged and/or impurities in the fuel system (Chapters 1 and 4).
8 EGR system not functioning properly (Chapter 6).
9 Use of sub-standard octane fuel. Fill tank with proper octane fuel.
10 Low or uneven cylinder compression pressures. Check as described in Chapter 2B.
11 Air (vacuum) leak at intake manifold or plenum (check as described in Section 8).

18 Engine backfires

1 EGR system not functioning properly (Chapter 6).
2 Vacuum leak (refer to Section 8).
3 Damaged valve springs or sticking valves (Chapter 2).
4 Intake air (vacuum) leak (see Section 8).

19 Engine surges while holding accelerator steady

1 Intake air (vacuum) leak (see Section 8).
2 Fuel pump not working properly.
3 Idle Air Control system faulty (Chapter 6).
4 Emissions or engine control system components faulty (Chapter 6).

20 Pinging or knocking engine sounds when engine is under load

1 Use of incorrect octane fuel. Fill tank with fuel of the proper octane rating.
2 Problem in the ignition system (Chapter 5).
3 Carbon build-up in combustion chambers. Remove cylinder head(s) and clean

combustion chambers (Chapter 2).
4 Incorrect spark plugs (Chapter 1).
5 Knock sensor system not functioning properly (Chapter 6).

21 Engine diesels (continues to run) after being turned off

1 Idle speed too high (Chapter 4).
2 Incorrect spark plug heat range (Chapter 1).
3 Intake air (vacuum) leak (see Section 8).
4 Carbon build-up in combustion chambers. Remove the cylinder head and clean the combustion chambers (Chapter 2).
5 Valves sticking (Chapter 2).
6 EGR system not operating properly (Chapter 6).
7 Leaking fuel injector(s) (Chapter 4).
8 Overheating. Check for causes (Section 27).

22 Low oil pressure

1 Improper oil grade.
2 Oil pump regulator valve not operating properly (Chapter 2).
3 Oil pump worn or damaged (Chapter 2).
4 Engine overheating (refer to Section 27).
5 Clogged oil filter (Chapter 1).
6 Clogged oil strainer (Chapter 2).
7 Oil pressure gauge not working properly (Chapter 2).

23 Excessive oil consumption

1 Oil pan drain plug loose.
2 Oil pan gasket or bolts loose or damaged (Chapter 2).
3 Front cover gasket or bolts loose or damaged (Chapter 2).
4 Crankshaft front or rear oil seal(s) leaking (Chapter 2).
5 Valve cover gasket bolts loose or damaged (Chapter 2).
6 Oil filter loose (Chapter 1).
7 Loose or damaged oil pressure switch (Chapter 2).
8 Pistons and cylinders worn excessively (Chapter 2).
9 Piston rings not installed correctly on pistons (Chapter 2).
10 Worn or damaged piston rings (Chapter 2).
11 Intake and/or exhaust valve oil seals worn or damaged (Chapter 2).
12 Worn valve stems.
13 Valves and or guides worn or damaged (Chapter 2).

24 Excessive fuel consumption

1 Dirty or clogged air filter element (Chapter 1).

2   Low tire pressure or incorrect tire size (Chapter 10).
3   Fuel leakage. Check all connections, lines and components in the fuel system (Chapter 4).
4   Fuel injectors clogged or dirty (Chapter 4).
5   Problem in the fuel injection system (Chapter 4).

25   Fuel odor

1   Fuel leaking out. Check all connections, lines and components in the fuel system (Chapter 4).
2   Fuel tank overfilled. Fill only to automatic shut-off.
3   Charcoal canister filter in Evaporative Emissions Control system clogged (Chapter 6).
4   Vapor leaks from Evaporative Emissions Control system lines (Chapter 6).

26   Miscellaneous engine noises

1   A strong dull noise that becomes more rapid as the engine accelerates indicates worn or damaged crankshaft bearings or an unevenly worn crankshaft. To pinpoint the trouble spot, remove the spark plug wire from one plug at a time and crank the engine over. If the noise stops, the cylinder with the removed plug wire indicates the problem area. Replace the bearing and/or service or replace the crankshaft (Chapter 2).
2   A similar (yet slightly higher pitched) noise to the crankshaft knocking described in the previous paragraph, that becomes more rapid as the engine accelerates, indicates worn or damaged connecting rod bearings (Chapter 2). The procedure for locating the problem cylinder is the same as described in Paragraph 1.
3   An overlapping metallic noise that increases in intensity as the engine speed increases, yet diminishes as the engine warms up indicates abnormal piston and cylinder wear (Chapter 2). To locate the problem cylinder, use the procedure described in Paragraph 1.
4   A rapid clicking noise that becomes faster as the engine accelerates is an indication of a worn piston pin or piston pin hole. Each time the piston hits the highest and lowest points in the stroke this sound will happen (Chapter 2). The procedure for locating the problem piston is described in Paragraph 1.
5   A metallic clicking noise coming from the water pump indicates worn or damaged water pump bearings or pump. Replace the water pump with a new one (Chapter 3).
6   A rapid tapping sound or clicking sound that becomes faster as the engine speed increases indicates "valve tapping" or stuck valve lifters. Holding one end of a section of hose to your ear and placing the other end at different spots along the rocker arm cover will help you identify this sound. The point where the sound is loudest indicates the problem valve or lifter (Chapter 2A).
7   A steady metallic rattling or rapping sound coming from the area of the timing chain cover indicates a worn, damaged or out-of-adjustment timing chain. Service or replace the chain and related components (Chapter 2).

Cooling system

27   Overheating

1   The system coolant level is low (Chapter 1).
2   Drivebelt defective or out of adjustment (Chapter 1).
3   Radiator core blocked or grille restricted (Chapter 3).
4   Thermostat faulty (Chapter 3).
5   The fan blades broken or cracked (Chapter 3).
6   Cap on the coolant reservoir is not maintaining proper pressure (Chapter 3).

28   Overcooling

The thermostat is faulty (Chapter 3).

29   External coolant leakage

1   Deteriorated/damaged hoses or loose clamps (Chapters 1 and 3).
2   Water pump seal defective (Chapters 1 and 3).
3   Leakage from radiator core or header tank (Chapter 3).
4   Engine drain or water jacket core plugs leaking (Chapter 2).
5   Leak at engine oil cooler (Chapter 3).

30   Internal coolant leakage

1   Leaking cylinder head gasket (Chapter 2).
2   The cylinder bore or cylinder head is cracked (Chapter 2).

31   Coolant loss

1   Too much coolant in system (Chapter 1).
2   Coolant boiling away because of overheating (Chapter 3).
3   The coolant reservoir cap is faulty (Chapter 3).

32   Poor coolant circulation

1   Water pump is faulty (Chapter 3).

2   Restriction in cooling system (Chapters 1 and 3).
3   Drivebelt defective or out of adjustment (Chapter 1).
4   Sticking thermostat (Chapter 3).

Automatic transaxle

Note: *Due to the complexity of the automatic transaxle, it's difficult for the home mechanic to properly diagnose and service this component. For problems other than the following, the vehicle should be taken to a dealer service department or a transmission shop.*

33   Fluid leakage

1   Automatic transmission fluid is a deep red color. Fluid leaks should not be confused with engine oil, which can easily be blown by the flow of air to the transaxle.
2   Pinpoint a leak by first removing all built-up dirt and grime from the transaxle housing with degreasing agents and/or steam cleaning. Drive the vehicle at low speeds so the flow of air will not blow the leak far from its source. Raise the vehicle and determine where the leak is coming from. Common areas of leakage are:

   a) *Pan (Chapters 1 and 7)*
   b) *Filler pipe (Chapter 7)*
   c) *Transaxle oil lines (Chapter 7)*
   d) *Vehicle Speed Sensor (Chapter 6)*

34   Transaxle fluid brown or has a burned smell

The transaxle has been overheated. Change the fluid (Chapter 1).

35   General shift mechanism problems

1   Chapter 7 deals with checking and adjusting the shift linkage on automatic transaxles. Common problems that may be attributed to poorly adjusted linkage are:

   a) *Engine starting in gears other than Park or Neutral.*
   b) *Indicator on shifter pointing to a gear other than the one actually being used.*
   c) *Vehicle moves when in Park.*
2   Refer to Chapter 7 for the shift linkage adjustment procedure.

36   Transaxle will not downshift with accelerator pedal pressed to the floor

Pressure control valve solenoid faulty. On electronically controlled transaxles, this type of problem - which is caused by a malfunction in the control unit, a sensor or solenoid, or the circuit itself - is beyond the scope of this book. Take the vehicle to a dealer service department or a competent automatic transmission shop.

37 Engine will start in gears other than Park or Neutral

Defective or misadjusted Park/Neutral Position (PNP) switch (Chapter 7).

38 Transaxle slips, shifts roughly, is noisy or has no drive in forward or reverse gears

There are many probable causes for the above problems, but the home mechanic should be concerned with only one possibility - fluid level. Before taking the vehicle to a repair shop, check the level and condition of the fluid as described in Chapter 1.

Correct the fluid level as necessary or change the fluid and filter if needed. If the problem persists, have a professional diagnose the probable cause.

Driveaxles

39 Clicking noise in turns

Worn or damaged outer CV joint. Check for cut or damaged boots (Chapter 1). Repair as necessary (Chapter 8).

40 Knock or clunk when accelerating after coasting

Worn or damaged CV joint. Check for cut or damaged boots (Chapter 1). Repair as necessary (Chapter 8).

41 Shudder or vibration during acceleration

1   Worn or damaged CV joints. Repair or replace as necessary (Chapter 8).
2   Inboard joint assembly is sticking. Correct or replace as necessary (Chapter 8).

Brakes

Note: *Before assuming that a brake problem exists, make sure . . .*
a) *The tires are in good condition and properly inflated (Chapter 1).*
b) *The front-end alignment is correct (Chapter 10).*
c) *The vehicle isn't loaded with weight in an unequal manner.*

42 Vehicle pulls to one side during braking

1   Tire pressures incorrect (Chapter 1).
2   Front end out of line (have the front end aligned).
3   Unmatched tires on same axle.
4   Brake lines or hoses are restricted (Chapter 9).
5   Malfunctioning caliper or wheel cylinder (Chapter 9).
6   Suspension parts are loose (Chapter 10).
7   Brake calipers are loose (Chapter 9).
8   Brake linings contaminated (Chapters 1 and 9).

43 Noise (high-pitched squeal when the brakes are applied)

Front disc brake pads worn out. The noise comes from the wear sensor rubbing against the disc. Replace pads with new ones immediately (Chapter 9).

44 Brake roughness or chatter (pedal pulsates)

Note: *Brake pedal pulsation during operation of the Anti-Lock Brake System (ABS) is normal.*
1   Excessive front brake disc lateral runout (Chapter 9).
2   Parallelism not within specifications (Chapter 9).
3   Defective brake disc (Chapter 9).

45 Excessive pedal effort required to stop vehicle

1   Malfunctioning power brake booster (Chapter 9).
2   Partial system failure (Chapter 9).
3   Excessively worn pads (Chapter 9).
4   One or more caliper pistons or wheel cylinders seized or sticking (Chapter 9).
5   Brake pads contaminated with oil or grease (Chapter 9).
6   New pads installed and not yet seated. It will take a while for the new material to seat.

46 Excessive brake pedal travel

1   Partial brake system failure (Chapter 9).
2   Fluid level in master cylinder low (Chapters 1 and 9).
3   Air trapped in system (Chapters 1 and 9).
4   Rear shoes excessively worn (Chapter 9).

47 Dragging brakes

1   Master cylinder pistons not returning correctly (Chapter 9).
2   Restricted brakes lines or hoses (Chapters 1 and 9).
3   Parking brake adjustment incorrect (Chapter 9).
4   Pistons sticking in the calipers (Chapter 9).

48 Grabbing or uneven braking action

1   Malfunction of proportioning valves (Chapter 9).
2   Malfunction of power brake booster unit (Chapter 9).
3   Binding brake pedal mechanism (Chapter 9).
4   Pistons sticking in the calipers (Chapter 9).

49 Brake pedal feels spongy when depressed

1   Air in the hydraulic lines (Chapter 9).
2   Master cylinder mounting bolts loose (Chapter 9).
3   The master cylinder is defective (Chapter 9).

50 Brake pedal travels to the floor with little resistance

Little or no fluid in the master cylinder reservoir caused by leaking caliper or wheel cylinder pistons, loose, damaged or disconnected brake lines (Chapter 9).

51 Parking brake does not hold

Check the parking brake (Chapter 9).

Suspension and steering systems
Note: *Before attempting to diagnose the suspension and steering systems, perform the following preliminary checks:*
a) *Check the tire pressures and look for uneven wear.*
b) *Check the steering universal joints or coupling from the column to the steering gear for loose fasteners and wear.*
c) *Check the front and rear suspension and the steering gear assembly for loose and damaged parts.*
d) *Look for out-of-round or out-of-balance tires, bent rims and loose and/or rough wheel bearings.*

52   Vehicle pulls to one side

1   The tires are uneven or mismatched (Chapter 10).
2   Broken or sagging springs (Chapter 10).
3   Front wheel alignment incorrect (Chapter 10).
4   Front brakes dragging (Chapter 9).

53   Abnormal or excessive tire wear

1   Wheel alignment incorrect (Chapter 10).
2   Sagging or broken springs (Chapter 10).
3   Tire out-of-balance (Chapter 10).
4   Worn shock absorber (Chapter 10).
5   Overloaded vehicle.
6   Tires not rotated regularly.

54   Wheel makes a "thumping" noise

1   Tire blister or bump (Chapter 1).
2   Improper shock absorber action (Chapter 10).

55   Shimmy, shake or vibration

1   Tire or wheel out-of-balance or out-of-round (Chapter 10).
2   Worn or loose wheel bearings (Chapter 10).
3   Worn tie-rod ends (Chapter 10).
4   Worn balljoints (Chapter 10).
5   Wheel runout is excessive (Chapter 10).
6   Tire blister or bump (Chapter 1).

56   Hard steering

1   Worn balljoints, tie-rod ends and steering gear assembly (Chapter 10).
2   Front wheel alignment incorrect (Chapter 10).
3   Tire pressure low (Chapter 1).

57   Steering wheel does not return to center position correctly

1   Worn balljoints or tie-rod ends (Chapter 10).
2   Binding in steering column (Chapter 10).
3   Defective rack-and-pinion assembly (Chapter 10).
4   Front wheel alignment problem (Chapter 10).

58   Abnormal noise at the front end

1   Worn balljoints and tie-rod ends (Chapter 1).
2   Upper strut mount loose (Chapter 10).
3   Worn tie-rod ends (Chapter 10).
4   Stabilizer bar loose (Chapter 10).
5   Wheel lug nuts loose (Chapter 1).
6   Suspension bolts loose (Chapter 10).

59   Wander or poor steering stability

1   Tires mismatched or uneven (Chapter 10).
2   Worn balljoints or tie-rod ends (Chapters 1 and 10).
3   Shock absorbers worn or faulty (Chapter 10).
4   Stabilizer bar loose (Chapter 10).
5   Broken or sagging springs (Chapter 10).
6   Wheel alignment incorrect (Chapter 10).
7   Worn steering gear clamp bushings (Chapter 10).

60   Erratic steering when braking

1   Worn wheel bearings (Chapters 8 and 10).
2   Broken or sagging springs (Chapter 10).
3   Leaking wheel cylinder or caliper (Chapter 9).
4   Brake discs warped (Chapter 9).
5   Worn steering gear clamp bushings (Chapter 10).

61   Excessive pitching and/or rolling around corners or during braking

1   Stabilizer bar loose (Chapter 10).
2   Shock absorbers or mounts worn or damaged (Chapter 10).
3   Broken or sagging springs (Chapter 10).
4   Overloaded vehicle.

62   Suspension bottoms

1   Vehicle overloaded.
2   Shock absorbers worn or faulty (Chapter 10).
3   Incorrect, broken or sagging springs (Chapter 10).

63   Cupped tires

1   Wheel alignment incorrect (Chapter 10).
2   Shock absorbers worn or faulty (Chapter 10).
3   Worn wheel bearings (Chapters 8 and 10).
4   Tire or wheel runout excessive (Chapter 10).
5   Balljoints worn (Chapter 10).

64   Excessive tire wear on outside edge

1   Tire inflation pressures incorrect (Chapter 1).
2   Excessive speed in turns.
3   Wheel alignment incorrect (excessive toe-in or positive camber). Have professionally aligned.
4   Suspension arm bent or twisted (Chapter 10).

65   Excessive tire wear on inside edge

1   Tire pressure inflation incorrect (Chapter 1).
2   Wheel alignment incorrect (toe-out or excessive negative camber). Have professionally aligned.
3   Steering components damaged or loose (Chapter 10).

66   Tire tread worn in one place

1   Tires out-of-balance.
2   Wheel damaged or buckled. Inspect and replace if necessary.
3   Tire defective (Chapter 1).

67   Excessive play or looseness in steering system

1   Worn wheel bearings (Chapter 10).
2   Tie-rod end loose or worn (Chapter 10).
3   Steering gear loose (Chapter 10).

68   Rattling or clicking noise in rack-and-pinion

Steering gear mounting clamps loose (Chapter 10).

Chapter 1
Tune-up and routine maintenance

Contents

1

Specifications

Recommended lubricants and fluids

Note: *Listed here are manufacturer recommendations at the time this manual was written. Manufacturers occasionally upgrade their fluid and lubricant specifications, so check with your local auto parts store for current recommendations.*

Engine oil .... API grade "certified for gasoline engines"
Viscosity.. See accompanying chart

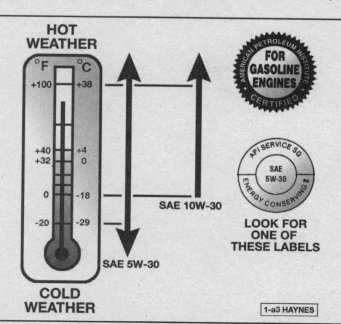

HOT WEATHER

SAE 10W-30

SAE 5W-30

COLD WEATHER

FOR GASOLINE ENGINES — AMERICAN PETROLEUM INSTITUTE — CERTIFIED

API SERVICE SG — SAE 5W-30 — ENERGY CONSERVING II

LOOK FOR ONE OF THESE LABELS

Engine oil viscosity chart - For best fuel economy and cold starting, select the lowest SAE viscosity grade for the expected temperature range

1-a3 HAYNES

Recommended lubricants and fluids (continued)

Fuel	Unleaded gasoline, 87 octane minimum
Automatic transaxle fluid	DEXRON III automatic transaxle fluid
Power steering fluid	GM power steering fluid
Brake fluid	DOT 3 brake fluid
Engine coolant	50/50 mixture of DEX-COOL coolant and de-mineralized water
Hood, door and trunk hinge lubricant	Lubriplate, aerosol spray lubricant
Door hinge and check spring grease	NLGI no. 2 multi-purpose grease
Door latch lubricant	NLGI no. 2 multi-purpose grease or equivalent
Hood latch assembly lubricant	Lubriplate, aerosol spray lubricant
Key lock cylinder lubricant	Graphite spray

Capacities*

Engine oil (including filter) .... 4.5 qts

Automatic transaxle
  1997
    Fluid and filter change .... 6.0 qts
    From dry, including torque converter .... 8.0 qts
  1998, 1999
    Fluid and filter change .... 8.0 qts
    From dry, including torque converter .... 13.4 qts
  2000
    Fluid and filter change .... 7.4 qts
    From dry, including torque converter .... 13.4 qts

Cooling system
  1997 through 1999
    Without heavy-duty cooling system
      With front air conditioning only .... 9.5 qts
      With front and rear air conditioning .... 12.1 qts
    With heavy-duty cooling system
      With front air conditioning only .... 10.5 qts
      With front and rear air conditioning .... 13.2 qts
  2000
    With front air conditioning only .... 9.6 qts
    With rear climate control .... 11.9 qts

*All capacities approximate. Add as necessary to bring to appropriate level.

24048-1-B HAYNES

Engine cylinder identification and coil terminal locations

Brakes

Disc brake pad wear limit .... 1/8 inch
Drum brake shoe wear limit .... 1/16 inch

Ignition system

Spark plug type and gap .... AC type 41-940 platinum, or equivalent @ 0.060 inch
Firing order 1-2-3-4-5-6

Torque specifications

Ft-lbs (unless otherwise indicated)

Spark plugs 20
Drivebelt tensioner bolt 37
Wheel lug nuts 100
Automatic transaxle fluid pan bolts .... 120 in-lbs

1 Chevrolet Venture, Oldsmobile Silhouette, Pontiac Montana and Trans Sport maintenance schedule

The following maintenance intervals are based on the assumption that the vehicle owner will be doing the maintenance or service work, as opposed to having a dealer service department do the work. Although the time/mileage intervals are loosely based on factory recommendations, most have been shortened to ensure, for example, that such items as lubricants and fluids are checked/changed at intervals that promote maximum engine/driveline service life. Also, subject to the preference of the individual owner interested in keeping his or her vehicle in peak condition at all times, and with the vehicle's ultimate resale in mind, many of the maintenance procedures may be performed more often than recommended in the following schedule. We encourage such owner initiative.

When your vehicle is new, follow the maintenance schedule to the letter, record the maintenance performed in your owners manual and keep all receipts to protect the new vehicle warranty. In many cases, the initial maintenance check is done at no cost to the owner.

Every 250 miles or weekly, whichever comes first

Check the engine oil level (Section 4)
Check the engine coolant level (Section 4)
Check the windshield washer fluid level (Section 4)
Check the brake fluid level (Section 4)
Check the tires and tire pressures (Section 5)
Check the operation of all lights
Check the horn operation

Every 3000 miles or 3 months, whichever comes first

All items listed above plus:
Check the power steering fluid level (Section 6)
Check the automatic transmission fluid level (Section 7)
Change the engine oil and filter (Section 8)

Every 6000 miles or 6 months, whichever comes first

All items listed above plus:
Check the battery (Section 9)
Check the cooling system (Section 10)
Inspect the underhood hoses (Section 11)
Check the engine drivebelt (Section 12)
Rotate the tires (Section 13)
Inspect the seat belts (Section 14)

Every 15,000 miles or 12 months, whichever comes first

Check the suspension, steering and driveaxle boots (Section 15)
Check the brakes (Section 16)*
Inspect the exhaust system (Section 17)
Inspect and replace, if necessary, the windshield wiper blades (Section 18)
Replace the interior ventilation filter (Section 19)

Every 30,000 miles or 24 months, whichever comes first

All items listed above plus:
Replace the air filter (Section 20)
Inspect the PCV valve (Section 21)
Inspect the spark plug wires (Section 22)
Replace the spark plugs (conventional [non-platinum] spark plugs) (Section 23)
Replace the fuel filter (Section 24)
Inspect the fuel system (Section 25)
Change the brake fluid (Section 26)

Every 60,000 miles or 48 months, whichever comes first

Replace the spark plugs (platinum-tipped spark plugs) (Section 23)
Change the automatic transaxle fluid and filter (Section 27)**
Service the cooling system (drain, flush and refill) (Section 28)

* If the vehicle frequently tows a trailer, is operated primarily in stop-and-go conditions or its brakes receive severe usage for any other reason, check the brakes every 3000 miles or three months.
** If operated under one or more of the following conditions, change the automatic transmission fluid every 30,000 miles:
In heavy city traffic where the outside temperature regularly reaches 90-degrees F (32-degrees C) or higher.
In hilly or mountainous terrain.
Frequent trailer pulling.

Typical engine compartment layout

1	Windshield washer fluid reservoir	
2	Drivebelt	
3	Engine oil filler cap	
4	Automatic transmission fluid dipstick	
5	Brake fluid reservoir	
6	Air filter housing	
7	Coolant reservoir	
8	Radiator hose	
9	Positive Crankcase Ventilation (PCV) valve	
10	Engine oil dipstick	
11	Radiator cap	
12	Battery	
13	Fuse and relay center	

Typical engine compartment underside components

1	Radiator drain valve	
2	Brake caliper	
3	Outer CV joint boot	
4	Inner CV joint boot	
5	Exhaust system	
6	Automatic transaxle fluid pan	
7	Engine oil drain plug	
8	Engine oil filter	
9	Strut/coil spring assembly	

Typical rear underside components

1	Resonator	4	Muffler	7	Coil spring		
2	Parking brake cable	5	Fuel tank	8	Shock absorber		
3	Brake drum	6	Rear axle beam				

2   Introduction

This Chapter is designed to help the home mechanic maintain the Chevrolet Malibu, Oldsmobile Cutlass and Alero, and Pontiac Grand Am models with the goals of maximum performance, economy, safety and reliability in mind.

Included is a master maintenance schedule, followed by procedures dealing specifically with each item on the schedule. Visual checks, adjustments, component replacement and other helpful items are included. Refer to the accompanying illustrations of the engine compartment and the underside of the vehicle for the locations of various components.

Adhering to the mileage/time maintenance schedule and following the step-by-step procedures, which is simply a preventive maintenance program, will result in maximum reliability and vehicle service life. Keep in mind that it's a comprehensive program - maintaining some items but not others at the specified intervals will not produce the same results.

As you service the vehicle, you'll discover that many of the procedures can - and

should - be grouped together because of the nature of the particular procedure you're performing or because of the close proximity of two otherwise unrelated components to one another.

For example, if the vehicle is raised, you should inspect the exhaust, suspension, steering and fuel systems while you're under the vehicle. When you're rotating the tires, it makes good sense to check the brakes, since the wheels are already removed. Finally, let's suppose you have to borrow or rent a torque wrench. Even if you only need it to tighten the spark plugs, you might as well check the torque of as many critical fasteners as time allows.

The first step in this maintenance program is to prepare before the actual work begins. Read through all the procedures you're planning to do, then gather up all the parts and tools needed. If it looks like you might run into problems during a particular job, seek advice from a mechanic or an experienced do-it-yourselfer.

Caution: *On models equipped with the Theft-lock audio system, be sure you have the correct activation code before performing any procedure which requires disconnecting the battery (see the front of this manual).*

3   Tune-up general information

The term tune-up is used in this manual to represent a combination of individual operations rather than one specific procedure.

If, from the time the vehicle is new, the routine maintenance schedule is followed closely and frequent checks are made of fluid levels and high wear items, as suggested throughout this manual, the engine will be kept in relatively good running condition and the need for additional work due to lack of regular maintenance will be minimized. This is even more likely if a used vehicle, which has not received regular and frequent maintenance checks, is purchased. In such cases, an engine tune-up will be needed outside of the regular routine maintenance intervals.

The first step in any tune-up or diagnostic procedure to help correct a poor running engine is a cylinder compression check. A compression check (see Chapter 2, Part B) will help determine the condition of internal engine components and should be used as a guide for tune-up and repair procedures. If, for instance, a compression check indicates serious internal engine wear, a conventional tune-up won't improve the performance of

4.2 The engine oil dipstick is located at the front side of the engine

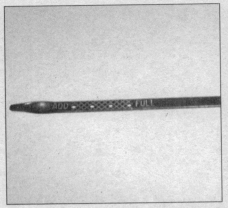

4.4 The oil level should be at or near the upper hole or in the cross-hatched area on the dipstick - if it's below the ADD line, add enough oil to bring the level into the upper hole or top of the cross-hatched area

4.6 The engine oil filler cap (arrow) is clearly marked and threads into the tube on the front valve cover - turn it counterclockwise to remove it

the engine and would be a waste of time and money. Because of its importance, the compression check should be done by someone with the right equipment and the knowledge to use it properly.

The following procedures are those most often needed to bring a generally poor running engine back into a proper state of tune.

Minor tune-up

Check all engine related fluids (Section 4)
Clean, inspect and test the battery (Section 9)
Check the cooling system (Section 10)
Check all underhood hoses (Section 11)
Check and adjust the drivebelt (Section 12)
Check the air filter (Section 19)
Check the PCV valve (Section 20)
Inspect the spark plug wires (Section 22)
Replace the spark plugs (Section 23)

Major tune-up

All items listed under Minor tune-up plus . . .

Replace the air filter (Section 20)
Replace the spark plug wires (Section 22)
Replace the fuel filter (Section 24)
Check the fuel system (Section 25)
Check the ignition timing (Chapter 5)
Check the charging system (Chapter 5)
Check the EGR system (Chapter 6)

---

4   Fluid level checks (every 250 miles or weekly)

Note: *The following are fluid level checks to be done on a 250 mile or weekly basis. Additional fluid level checks can be found in specific maintenance procedures that follow. Regardless of intervals, be alert to fluid leaks under the vehicle, which would indicate a problem to be corrected immediately.*

1   Fluids are an essential part of the lubrication, cooling, brake and windshield washer systems. Because the fluids gradually become depleted and/or contaminated during normal operation of the vehicle, they must be periodically replenished. See *Recommended lubricants and fluids* at the beginning of this Chapter before adding fluid to any of the following components. **Note:** *The vehicle must be on level ground when fluid levels are checked.*

Engine oil

Refer to illustrations 4.2, 4.4 and 4.6

2   The engine oil level is checked with a dipstick **(see illustration)**. The dipstick extends through a metal tube down into the oil pan.

3   The oil level should be checked before the vehicle has been driven, or about 5 minutes after the engine has been shut off. If the oil is checked immediately after driving the vehicle, some of the oil will remain in the upper part of the engine, resulting in an inaccurate reading on the dipstick.

4   Pull the dipstick from the tube and wipe all the oil from the end with a clean rag or paper towel. Insert the clean dipstick all the way back into the tube and pull it out again. Note the oil at the end of the dipstick. Add oil as necessary to keep the level above the ADD mark in the cross hatched area of the dipstick **(see illustration)**.

5   Do not overfill the engine by adding too much oil since this may result in oil fouled spark plugs, oil leaks or oil seal failures.

6   Oil is added to the engine after removing a twist-off cap located on the valve cover **(see illustrations)**. A funnel may help to reduce spills.

7   Checking the oil level is an important preventive maintenance step. A consistently low oil level indicates oil leakage through damaged seals, defective gaskets or past worn rings or valve guides. If the oil looks milky in color or has water droplets in it, the cylinder head gasket may be blown or the head or block may be cracked. The engine should be checked immediately. The condition of the oil should also be checked. Whenever you check the oil level, slide your thumb

and index finger up the dipstick before wiping off the oil. If you see small dirt or metal particles clinging to the dipstick, the oil should be changed (see Section 8).

Engine coolant

Refer to illustration 4.8

Warning: *Do not allow antifreeze to come in contact with your skin or painted surfaces of the vehicle. Rinse off spills immediately with plenty of water. Antifreeze is highly toxic if ingested. Never leave antifreeze lying around in an open container or in puddles on the floor; children and pets are attracted by its sweet smell and may drink it. Check with local authorities on disposing of used anti-freeze. Many communities have collection centers that will see that antifreeze is disposed of safely.*

Note: *Non-toxic antifreeze is now manufactured and available at local auto parts stores, but even this type should be disposed of properly.*

Caution: *Never mix green-colored ethylene glycol anti-freeze and orange-colored "DEX-COOL" silicate-free coolant because doing so will destroy the efficiency of the "DEX-COOL" coolant.*

8   All vehicles covered by this manual are equipped with a pressurized coolant recovery system. A white plastic coolant reservoir located in the engine compartment is connected by a hose to the radiator filler neck **(see illustration)**.

9   The coolant level in the reservoir should be checked regularly. **Warning:** *Do not remove the pressure cap to check the coolant level when the engine is warm.* The level of coolant in the reservoir varies with the temperature of the engine. When the engine is cold, the coolant level should be at or slightly above the MIN mark on the reservoir. Once the engine has warmed up, the level should be at or near the MAX mark. If it isn't, add coolant to the reservoir. To add coolant simply twist open the cap and add a 50/50 mixture of ethylene glycol based antifreeze and water.

4.8 The coolant reservoir is located in the left rear corner of the engine compartment - the coolant level can be checked by observing it through the translucent tank

4.14 Location of the windshield washer fluid reservoir

10   Drive the vehicle and recheck the coolant level. If only a small amount of coolant is required to bring the system up to the proper level, water can be used. However, repeated additions of water will dilute the antifreeze and water solution. In order to maintain the proper ratio of antifreeze and water, always top up the coolant level with the correct mixture. An empty plastic milk jug or bleach bottle makes an excellent container for mixing coolant. Do not use rust inhibitors or additives.

11   If the coolant level drops consistently, there may be a leak in the system. Inspect the radiator, hoses, filler cap, drain plugs and water pump (see Section 10). If no leaks are noted, have the radiator cap tested by a service station.

12   If you have to remove the radiator cap, wait until the engine has cooled completely, then wrap a thick cloth around the cap and turn it to the first stop. If coolant or steam escapes, let the engine cool down longer, then remove the cap.

13   Check the condition of the coolant as well. It should be relatively clear. If it is brown or rust colored, the system should be drained, flushed and refilled. Even if the coolant appears to be normal, the corrosion inhibitors wear out, so it must be replaced at the specified intervals. If the system is filled with standard green coolant/water, it must be flushed and replaced more frequently than if the original "DEX-COOL" coolant is retained.

Windshield washer fluid

Refer to illustration 4.14

14   Fluid for the windshield washer system is located in a plastic reservoir on the right rear corner of the engine compartment **(see illustration)**. In milder climates, plain water can be used in the reservoir, but it should be kept no more than two-thirds full to allow for expansion if the water freezes. In colder climates, use windshield washer system

antifreeze, available at any auto parts store, to lower the freezing point of the fluid. Mix the antifreeze with water in accordance with the manufacturer's directions on the container. **Caution:** *Do not use cooling system antifreeze - it will damage the vehicle's paint.*

15   To help prevent icing in cold weather, warm the windshield with the defroster before using the washer.

Battery electrolyte

16   All vehicles covered by this manual are equipped with a battery that is permanently sealed (except for vent holes) and has no filler caps. Water does not have to be added to these batteries at any time.

Brake fluid

Refer to illustration 4.18

17   The brake fluid level is checked by looking through the plastic reservoir mounted on the master cylinder. The master cylinder is mounted on the front of the power booster unit in the left (driver's side) rear corner of the engine compartment.

18   The fluid level should be at or near the base of the reservoir filler neck **(see illustration)**. If the fluid level is low, wipe the top of the reservoir and the lid with a clean rag to prevent contamination of the system as the lid is pried off.

19   When adding fluid, pour it carefully into the reservoir to avoid spilling it on surrounding painted surfaces. Be sure the specified fluid is used, since mixing different types of brake fluid can cause damage to the system. See *Recommended lubricants and fluids* at the front of this Chapter or your owner's manual. **Warning:** *Brake fluid can harm your eyes and damage painted surfaces, so use extreme caution when handling or pouring it. Do not use brake fluid that has been standing open or is more than one year old. Brake fluid absorbs moisture from the air. Excess moisture can cause a dangerous loss of braking*

effectiveness.

20   At this time the fluid and master cylinder can be inspected for contamination. The system should be drained and refilled if deposits, dirt particles or water droplets are seen in the fluid.

21   After filling the reservoir to the proper level, make sure the cap is tightened securely to prevent fluid leakage.

22   The brake fluid level in the master cylinder will drop slightly as the front brake pads wear down during normal operation. If the master cylinder requires repeated replenishing to keep it at the proper level, this is an indication of leakage in the brake system, which should be corrected immediately. Check all brake lines and connections (see Section 16 for more information).

23   If, when checking the master cylinder fluid level, you discover one or both reservoirs empty or nearly empty, the brake system should be bled and inspected for leaks (see Chapter 9).

4.18 The fluid level inside the brake fluid reservoir can easily be checked by observing the level through the translucent sides of the reservoir - if it is necessary to add fluid, a long funnel will be required- DO NOT OVERFILL

1

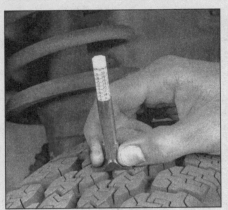

5.2　Use a tire tread depth gauge to monitor tire wear - they are available at auto parts stores and service stations and cost very little

5　Tire and tire pressure checks (every 250 miles or weekly)

Refer to illustrations 5.2, 5.3, 5.4a, 5.4b and 5.8

1　Periodic inspection of the tires may spare you the inconvenience of being stranded with a flat tire. It can also provide you with vital information regarding possible problems in the steering and suspension systems before major damage occurs.

2　The original tires on this vehicle are equipped with 1/2-inch wide bands that appear when tread depth reaches 1/16-inch, indicating the tires are worn out. Tread wear can be monitored with a simple, inexpensive device known as a tread depth indicator **(see illustration)**.

3　Note any abnormal tread wear **(see illustration)**. Tread pattern irregularities such as cupping, flat spots and more wear on one side than the other are indications of front end alignment and/or balance problems. If any of these conditions are noted, take the vehicle to a tire shop or service station to correct the problem.

4　Look closely for cuts, punctures and embedded nails or tacks. Sometimes a tire will hold air pressure for short time or leak down very slowly after a nail has embedded itself in the tread. If a slow leak persists, check the valve stem core to make sure it's tight **(see illustration)**. Examine the tread for an object that may have embedded itself in the tire or for a "plug" that may have begun to leak (radial tire punctures are repaired with a plug that's installed in a puncture). If a puncture is suspected, it can be easily verified by spraying a solution of soapy water onto the suspected area **(see illustration)**. The soapy solution will bubble if there's a leak. Unless the puncture is unusually large, a tire shop or service station can usually repair the tire.

5　Carefully inspect the inner sidewall of each tire for evidence of brake fluid. If you see any, inspect the brakes immediately.

6　Correct air pressure adds miles to the lifespan of the tires, improves mileage and enhances overall ride quality. Tire pressure cannot be accurately estimated by looking at a tire, especially if it's a radial. A tire pressure gauge is essential. Keep an accurate gauge in the vehicle. The pressure gauges attached to the nozzles of air hoses at gas stations are often inaccurate.

7　Always check tire pressure when the tires are cold. Cold, in this case, means the vehicle has not been driven over a mile in the three hours preceding a tire pressure check. A pressure rise of four to eight pounds is not uncommon once the tires are warm.

8　Unscrew the valve cap protruding from the wheel or hubcap and push the gauge firmly onto the valve stem **(see illustration)**. Note the reading on the gauge and compare the figure to the recommended tire pressure shown on the label attached to the inside of the glove compartment door. Be sure to reinstall the valve cap to keep dirt and moisture out of the valve stem mechanism. Check all four tires and, if necessary, add enough air to bring them up to the recommended pressure.

9　Don't forget to keep the spare tire inflated to the specified pressure (refer to your owner's manual or the tire sidewall).

6　Power steering fluid level check (every 3000 miles or 3 months)

Refer to illustrations 6.2 and 6.6

1　The power steering system relies on fluid that may, over a period of time, require replenishing.

UNDERINFLATION

INCORRECT TOE-IN OR EXTREME CAMBER

CUPPING

Cupping may be caused by:
- Underinflation and/or mechanical irregularities such as out-of-balance condition of wheel and/or tire, and bent or damaged wheel.
- Loose or worn steering tie-rod or steering idler arm.
- Loose, damaged or worn front suspension parts.

OVERINFLATION

FEATHERING DUE TO MISALIGNMENT

5.3　This chart will help you determine the condition of the tires, the probable cause(s) of abnormal wear and the corrective action necessary

5.4a If a tire loses air on a steady basis, check the valve core first to make sure it's snug (special inexpensive wrenches are commonly available at auto parts stores)

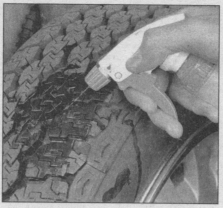

5.4b If the valve core is tight, raise the corner of the vehicle with the low tire and spray a soapy water solution onto the tread as the tire is turned slowly - leaks will cause small bubbles to appear

5.8 To extend the life of the tires, check the air pressure at least once a week with an accurate gauge (don't forget the spare)

2   The fluid reservoir for the power steering pump is mounted on the right side of the engine by the engine drivebelt **(see illustration)**.
3   For the check, the front wheels should be pointed straight ahead and the engine should be off.
4   Use a clean rag to wipe off the reservoir cap and the area around the cap. This will help prevent any foreign matter from entering the reservoir during the check.
5   Twist off the cap and check the temperature of the fluid at the end of the dipstick with your finger.
6   Wipe off the fluid with a clean rag, reinsert the cap, then withdraw it and read the fluid level. The level should be at the HOT mark if the fluid was hot to the touch **(see illustration)**. It should be at the COLD mark if the fluid was cool to the touch.
7   If additional fluid is required, pour the specified type directly into the reservoir, using a funnel to prevent spills.
8   If the reservoir requires frequent fluid additions, all power steering hoses, hose connections, the power steering pump and the rack and pinion assembly should be carefully checked for leaks.

7   Automatic transaxle fluid level check (every 3000 miles or 3 months)

Refer to illustrations 7.3 and 7.6

1   The automatic transaxle fluid level should be carefully maintained. Low fluid level can lead to slipping or loss of drive, while overfilling can cause foaming and loss of fluid.
2   With the parking brake set, start the engine, then move the shift lever through all the gear ranges, ending in Park. The fluid level must be checked with the vehicle level and the engine running at idle. **Note:** *Incorrect fluid level readings will result if the vehicle has just been driven at high speeds for an extended period, in hot weather in city traffic, or if it has been pulling a trailer. If any of these conditions apply, wait until the fluid has cooled (about 30 minutes).*
3   With the transaxle at normal operating temperature, remove the dipstick from the filler tube. The dipstick is located at the rear of the engine compartment on the driver's side **(see illustration)**.

6.2 The power steering fluid reservoir is located on the right (passenger's) end of the engine

4   Wipe the fluid from the dipstick with a clean rag and push it back into the filler tube until the cap seats.
5   Pull the dipstick out again and note the fluid level.
6   The level should be in the crosshatched area, near the MAX line **(see illustration)**. If additional fluid is required, add it directly into the tube using a funnel. It takes about one

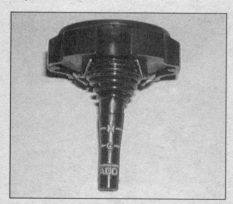

6.6 The marks on the dipstick indicate the safe fluid range

7.3 The automatic transmission fluid dipstick is located at the rear of the engine compartment, near the brake fluid reservoir

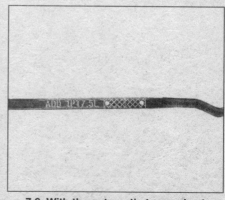

7.6 With the automatic transaxle at normal operating temperature, the fluid level must be maintained within the crosshatched area on the dipstick

1

pint to raise the level from the bottom of the crosshatched area to the MAX line with a hot transmission, so add the fluid a little at a time and keep checking the level until it's correct.

7   The condition of the fluid should also be checked along with the level. If the fluid at the end of the dipstick is a dark reddish-brown color, or if it smells burned, it should be changed. If you are in doubt about the condition of the fluid, purchase some new fluid and compare the two for color and smell.

8   Engine oil and filter change (every 3000 miles or 3 months)

Refer to illustrations 8.2, 8.7, 8.12 and 8.14

1   Frequent oil changes are the best preventive maintenance the home mechanic can give the engine, because aging oil becomes diluted and contaminated, which leads to premature engine wear. **Note:** *Some later models have an Oil Change Indicator light on the instrument panel. We recommend that you change your oil according to the Maintenance Schedule at the beginning of this Chapter, even if the Oil Change light has not come on.*

2   Make sure you have all the necessary tools before you begin this procedure **(see illustration)**. You should also have plenty of rags or newspapers handy for mopping up any spills.

3   Access to the underside of the vehicle is greatly improved if the vehicle can be lifted on a hoist, driven onto ramps or supported by jackstands. **Warning:** *Do not work under a vehicle that is supported only by a hydraulic or scissors-type jack.*

4   If this is your first oil change, get under the vehicle and familiarize yourself with the locations of the oil drain plug and the oil filter. The engine and exhaust components will be warm during the actual work, so try to anticipate any potential problems before the engine and accessories are hot.

5   Park the vehicle on a level spot. Start the engine and allow it to reach its normal operating temperature. Warm oil and sludge will flow out more easily. Turn off the engine when it's warmed up. Remove the filler cap from the valve cover.

6   Raise the vehicle and support it securely on jackstands. **Warning:** *Never get beneath the vehicle when it is supported only by a jack. The jack provided with your vehicle is designed solely for raising the vehicle to remove and replace the wheels. Always use jackstands to support the vehicle when it becomes necessary to place your body underneath the vehicle.*

7   Being careful not to touch the hot exhaust components, place the drain pan under the drain plug in the bottom of the pan and remove the plug **(see illustration)**. You may want to wear gloves while unscrewing the plug the final few turns if the engine is hot.

8   Allow the old oil to drain into the pan. It may be necessary to move the pan farther under the engine as the oil flow slows to a trickle. Inspect the old oil for the presence of metal shavings and chips.

9   After all the oil has drained, wipe off the drain plug with a clean rag. Even minute metal particles clinging to the plug would immediately contaminate the new oil.

10   Clean the area around the drain plug opening, reinstall the plug and tighten it to the torque listed in this Chapter's Specifications.

11   Move the drain pan into position under the oil filter.

12   Loosen the oil filter **(see illustration)** by turning it counterclockwise with the filter wrench. Use a quality filter wrench of the correct size and be careful not to collapse the canister as you apply pressure. Once the filter is loose, use your hands to unscrew it from the block. Just as the filter is detached from the block, immediately tilt the open end up to prevent the oil inside the filter from spilling out.

13   With a clean rag, wipe off the mounting surface on the block. If a residue of old oil is allowed to remain, it will smoke when the

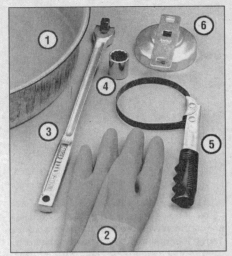

8.2 These tools are required when changing the engine oil and filter

1   *Drain pan - It should be fairly shallow in depth, but wide to prevent spills*

2   *Rubber gloves - When removing the drain plug and filter, you will get oil on your hands (the gloves will prevent burns)*

3   *Breaker bar - Sometimes the oil drain plug is tight, and a long breaker bar is needed to loosen it*

4   *Socket - To be used with the breaker bar or a ratchet (must be the correct size to fit the drain plug)*

5   *Filter wrench - This is a metal band-type wrench, which requires clearance around the filter to be effective*

6   *Filter wrench - This type fits on the bottom of the filter and can be turned with a ratchet or breaker bar (different-size wrenches are available for different types of filters)*

block is heated up. Also make sure that none of the old gasket remains stuck to the mounting surface. It can be removed with a scraper if necessary.

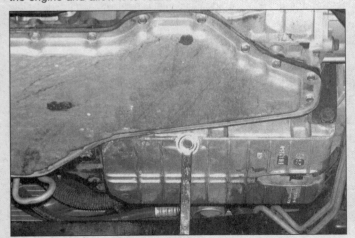

8.7 The engine oil drain plug is located at the rear of the oil pan - it is usually very tight, so use a socket or box-end wrench to avoid rounding off the hex

8.12 The oil filter is usually on very tight as well and will require a special wrench for removal - DO NOT use the wrench to tighten the new filter!

8.14 Lubricate the oil filter gasket with clean engine oil before installing the filter on the engine

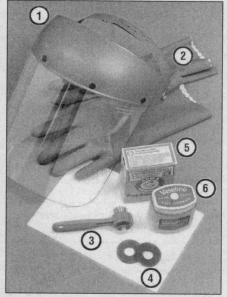

9.1 Tools and materials required for battery maintenance

1 *Face shield/safety goggles* - When removing corrosion with a brush, the acidic particles can easily fly up into your eyes
2 *Rubber gloves* - Another safety item to consider when servicing the battery - remember that's acid inside the battery!
3 *Battery terminal/cable cleaner* - This wire brush cleaning tool will remove all traces of corrosion from the battery and cable
4 *Treated felt washers* - Placing one of these on each terminal, directly under the cable end, will help prevent corrosion (be sure to get the correct type for side-terminal batteries)
5 *Baking soda* - A solution of baking soda and water can be used to neutralize corrosion
6 *Petroleum jelly* - A layer of this on the battery terminal bolts will help prevent corrosion

14 Compare the old filter with the new one to make sure they are the same type. Smear some clean engine oil on the rubber gasket of the new filter and screw it into place **(see illustration)**. Because overtightening the filter will damage the gasket, do not use a filter wrench to tighten the filter. Tighten it by hand until the gasket contacts the seating surface. Then seat the filter by giving it an additional 3/4-turn.
15 Remove all tools, rags, etc. from under the vehicle, being careful not to spill the oil in the drain pan, then lower the vehicle.
16 Add new oil to the engine through the oil filler cap. Use a funnel, if necessary, to prevent oil from spilling onto the top of the engine. Pour three quarts of fresh oil into the engine. Wait a few minutes to allow the oil to drain into the pan, then check the level on the oil dipstick (see Section 4 if necessary). If the oil level is at or near the upper hole on the dipstick, install the filler cap hand tight, start the engine and allow the new oil to circulate.
17 Allow the engine to run for about a minute. While the engine is running, look under the vehicle and check for leaks at the oil pan drain plug and around the oil filter. If either is leaking, stop the engine and tighten the plug or filter.
18 Wait a few minutes to allow the oil to

Terminal end corrosion or damage.

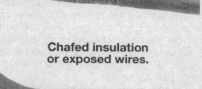

Insulation cracks.

Chafed insulation or exposed wires.

Burned or melted insulation.

9.4 Typical battery cable problems

trickle down into the pan, then recheck the level on the dipstick and, if necessary, add enough oil to bring the level to the upper hole.
19 During the first few trips after an oil change, make it a point to check frequently for leaks and proper oil level. **Note:** *If your vehicle is equipped with the Change Oil light, you must reset the light. With the Key in the RUN position and the engine off, depress the accelerator pedal to the floor three times slowly, but within five seconds. Turn the ignition key off, then on again, to make sure the light monitor has reset.*
20 The old oil drained from the engine cannot be re-used in its present state and should be recycled. Check with your local auto parts store, disposal facility or environmental agency to see if they will accept the oil for recycling. Don't pour used oil into drains or onto the ground. After the oil has cooled, it can be drained into a suitable container (capped plastic jugs, topped bottles, milk cartons, etc.) for transport to one of these recycling sites.

9 Battery check, maintenance and charging (every 6000 miles or 6 months)

Refer to illustrations 9.1, 9.4, 9.5a, 9.5b and 9.5c
Warning: *Hydrogen gas is produced by the battery, so keep open flames and lighted tobacco away from it at all times. Always wear eye protection when working around the battery. Rinse off spilled electrolyte immediately with large amounts of water. When removing the battery cables, always detach the negative cable first and hook it up last!*
Caution: *On models equipped with the Theft-lock audio system, be sure you have the correct activation code before performing any procedure which requires disconnecting the battery (see the front of this manual).*
1 Battery maintenance is an important procedure that will help ensure you aren't stranded because of a dead battery. Several tools are required for this procedure **(see illustration)**.
2 A sealed battery is standard equipment on all vehicles covered by this manual. Although this type of battery has many advantages over the older, capped cell type, and never requires the addition of water, it should still be routinely maintained according to the procedures that follow.

Check

3 The battery is located in the right front corner of the engine compartment, underneath the fuse/relay center. The battery removal procedure is described in Chapter 5.
4 Check the tightness of the battery cable terminals and connections to ensure good electrical connections and check the entire length of each cable for cracks and frayed conductors **(see illustration)**.

9.5a   A tool like this one (available at auto parts stores) is used to clean the side terminal type battery contact area

9.5b   Use the brush to finish the cleaning job

9.5c   The result should be a clean, shiny terminal area

5   If corrosion (visible as white, fluffy deposits) is evident, remove the cables from the terminals, clean them with a battery brush and reinstall the cables **(see illustrations)**. Corrosion can be kept to a minimum by using special treated fiber washers available at auto parts stores or by applying a layer of petroleum jelly to the terminals and cables after they are assembled.

6   Make sure that the battery tray is in good condition and the hold-down clamp bolt is tight. If the battery is removed from the tray, make sure no parts remain in the bottom of the tray when the battery is reinstalled. When reinstalling the hold-down clamp bolt, do not overtighten it. **Note:** *Always reinstall the battery's protective insulating sleeve when putting the battery back in the vehicle.*

7   Information on removing and installing the battery can be found in Chapter 5. Information on jump-starting can be found at the front of this manual. For more detailed battery checking procedures, refer to the *Haynes Automotive Electrical Manual.*

Cleaning

8   Corrosion on the hold-down components, battery case and surrounding areas can be removed with a solution of water and baking soda. Thoroughly rinse all cleaned areas with plain water.

9   Any metal parts of the vehicle damaged by corrosion should be covered with a zinc-based primer, then painted.

Charging

Warning: *When batteries are being charged, hydrogen gas, which is very explosive and flammable, is produced. Do not smoke or allow open flames near a charging or a recently charged battery. Wear eye protection when near the battery during charging. Also, make sure the charger is unplugged before connecting or disconnecting the battery from the charger.*

10   Slow-rate charging is the best way to restore a battery that's discharged to the point where it will not start the engine. It's also a good way to maintain the battery

charge in a vehicle that's only driven a few miles between starts. Maintaining the battery charge is particularly important in the winter when the battery must work harder to start the engine and electrical accessories that drain the battery are in greater use.

11   It's best to use a one or two-amp battery charger (sometimes called a "trickle" charger). They are the safest and put the least strain on the battery. They are also the least expensive. For a faster charge, you can use a higher amperage charger, but don't use one rated more than 1/10th the amp/hour rating of the battery. Rapid boost charges that claim to restore the power of the battery in one to two hours are hardest on the battery and can damage batteries that aren't in good condition. This type of charging should only be used in emergency situations.

12   The average time necessary to charge a battery should be listed in the instructions that come with the charger. As a general rule, a trickle charger will charge a battery in 12 to 16 hours.

13   Remove all of the cell caps (if equipped) and cover the holes with a clean cloth to prevent spattering electrolyte. Disconnect the negative battery cable and hook the battery charger leads to the battery posts (positive to positive, negative to negative), then plug in the charger. Make sure it is set at 12-volts if it has a selector switch.

14   If you're using a charger with a rate higher than two amps, check the battery regularly during charging to make sure it doesn't overheat. If you're using a trickle charger, you can safely let the battery charge overnight after you've checked it regularly for the first couple of hours.

15   If the battery has removable cell caps, measure the specific gravity with a hydrometer every hour during the last few hours of the charging cycle. Hydrometers are available inexpensively from auto parts stores - follow the instructions that come with the hydrometer. Consider the battery charged when there's no change in the specific gravity reading for two hours and the electrolyte in the cells is gassing (bubbling) freely. The specific gravity reading from each cell should be very

close to the others. If not, the battery probably has a bad cell(s).

16   Your original sealed factory battery has a built-in hydrometer on the top that indicate the state of charge by the color displayed in the hydrometer window. Normally, a bright-colored hydrometer indicates a full charge and a dark hydrometer indicates the battery still needs charging. Check the battery manufacturer's instructions to be sure you know what the colors mean.

17   If the battery has a sealed top and no built-in hydrometer, you can hook up a digital voltmeter across the battery terminals to check the charge. A fully charged battery should read 12.5-volts or higher.

10   Cooling system check (every 6000 miles or 6 months)

Refer to illustration 10.4
Caution: *Never mix green-colored ethylene glycol anti-freeze and orange-colored "DEX-COOL" silicate-free coolant because doing so will destroy the efficiency of the "DEX-COOL" coolant.*

1   Many major engine failures can be attributed to a faulty cooling system. If the vehicle is equipped with an automatic transmission, the cooling system also cools the transmission fluid and plays an important role in prolonging transmission life.

2   The cooling system should be checked with the engine cold. Do this before the vehicle is driven for the day or after the engine has been shut off for at least three hours.

3   Remove the radiator cap by turning it slowly counterclockwise to the first stop. If you hear any hissing sounds (indicating there is still pressure in the system), wait until it stops. Now depress the cap and continue turning to the left until the cap can be removed. Thoroughly clean the cap, inside and out, with clean water. Also clean the filler neck on the radiator. All traces of corrosion should be removed. The coolant inside the radiator should be relatively transparent. If it is rust colored, the system should be drained and refilled (see Section 28). If the coolant

Check for a chafed area that could fail prematurely.

Check for a soft area indicating the hose has deteriorated inside.

Overtightening the clamp on a hardened hose will damage the hose and cause a leak.

Check each hose for swelling and oil-soaked ends. Cracks and breaks can be located by squeezing the hose.

10.4 Hoses, like drivebelts, have a habit of failing at the worst possible time - to prevent the inconvenience of a blown radiator or heater hose, inspect them carefully as shown here

level is not up to the bottom of the filler neck, add additional antifreeze/coolant mixture to the radiator, and also to the coolant reservoir, if necessary (see Section 4).

4   Carefully check the large upper and lower radiator hoses along with any smaller diameter heater hoses that run from the engine to the firewall. Inspect each hose along its entire length, replacing any hose that is cracked, swollen or shows signs of deterioration. Cracks may become more apparent if the hose is squeezed **(see illustration)**.

5   Make sure all hose connections are tight. A leak in the cooling system will usually show up as white or rust-colored deposits on the areas adjoining the leak. If wire-type clamps are used at the ends of the hoses, it may be wise to replace them with more secure, screw-type clamps.

6   Use compressed air or a soft brush to remove bugs, leaves, etc. from the front of the radiator or air conditioning condenser. Be careful not to damage the delicate cooling fins or cut yourself on them.

7   Every other inspection, or at the first indication of cooling system problems, have the cap and system pressure tested. If you don't have a pressure tester, most gas stations and repair shops will do this for a minimal charge.

11   Underhood hose check and replacement (every 6000 miles or 6 months)

General

1   **Warning:** *Replacement of air conditioning hoses must be left to a dealer service department or air conditioning shop that has the equipment to depressurize the system safely and recover the refrigerant. Never remove air conditioning components or hoses until the system has been depressurized.*

2   High temperatures under the hood can cause the deterioration of the rubber and plastic hoses used for engine, accessory and emission systems operation. Periodic inspection should be made for cracks, loose clamps, material hardening and leaks. Information specific to the cooling system hoses can be found in Section 10.

3   Some, but not all, hoses are secured to the fittings with clamps. Where clamps are used, check to be sure they haven't lost their tension, allowing the hose to leak. If clamps aren't used, make sure the hose hasn't expanded and/or hardened where it slips over the fitting, allowing it to leak.

Vacuum hoses

4   It's quite common for vacuum hoses, especially those in the emissions system, to be color-coded or identified by colored stripes molded into each hose. Various systems require hoses with different wall thicknesses, collapse resistance and temperature resistance. When replacing hoses, be sure the new ones are made of the same material.

5   Often the only effective way to check a hose is to remove it completely from the vehicle. If more than one hose is removed, be sure to label the hoses and fittings to ensure correct installation.

6   When checking vacuum hoses, be sure to include any plastic T-fittings in the check. Inspect the fittings for cracks and the hose where it fits over the fitting for distortion, which could cause leakage.

7   A small piece of vacuum hose (1/4-inch inside diameter) can be used as a stethoscope to detect vacuum leaks. Hold one end of the hose to your ear and probe around vacuum hoses and fittings, listening for the "hissing" sound characteristic of a vacuum leak. **Warning:** *When probing with the vacuum hose stethoscope, be careful not to allow your body or the hose to come into contact with moving engine components such as the drivebelt, cooling fan, etc.*

Fuel hose

Warning: *Gasoline is extremely flammable, so take extra precautions when you work on any part of the fuel system. Don't smoke or allow open flames or bare light bulbs near the work area, and don't work in a garage where a gas-type appliance (such as a water heater or clothes dryer) is present. Since gasoline is carcinogenic, wear fuel-resistant gloves when there's a possibility of being exposed to fuel, and, if you spill any fuel on your skin, rinse it off immediately with soap and water. Mop up any spills immediately and do not store fuel-soaked rags where they could ignite. When you perform any kind of work on the fuel system, wear safety glasses and have a Class B type fire extinguisher on hand. The fuel system is under pressure, so if any lines must be disconnected, the pressure in the system must be relieved first (see Chapter 4 for more information).*

8   Check all rubber fuel lines for deterioration and chafing. Check especially for cracks in areas where the hose bends and just before fittings, such as where a hose attaches to the fuel filter and fuel injection unit.

9   High quality fuel line, specifically designed for high-pressure fuel injection applications, must be used for fuel line replacement. Never, under any circumstances, use regular fuel line, unreinforced vacuum line, clear plastic tubing or water hose for fuel lines.

10   Spring-type clamps are commonly used on fuel lines. These clamps often lose their tension over a period of time, and can be "sprung" during the removal process. As a result, spring-type clamps should be replaced with screw-type clamps whenever a hose is replaced.

Metal lines

11   Sections of steel tubing are often used for fuel line between the fuel pump and fuel injection unit. Check carefully for cracks, kinks and flat spots in the line.

12   If a section of metal fuel line must be replaced, only seamless steel tubing should be used, since copper and aluminum tubing do not have the strength necessary to withstand normal engine vibration.

13   Check the metal brake lines where they enter the master cylinder and brake proportioning unit (if used) for cracks in the lines and loose fittings. Any sign of brake fluid leakage calls for an immediate, thorough inspection of the brake system.

12   Drivebelt and tensioner check and replacement (every 6000 miles or 6 months)

Drivebelt
Check

Refer to illustrations 12.2 and 12.4

1   A single serpentine drivebelt is located at the front of the engine and plays an impor-

1

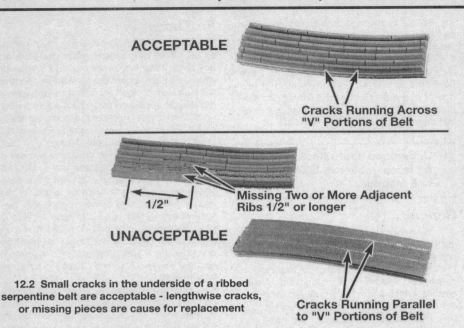

12.2 Small cracks in the underside of a ribbed serpentine belt are acceptable - lengthwise cracks, or missing pieces are cause for replacement

12.4 When the mark on the tensioner arm aligns with the mark on the tensioner body (arrows), replace the belt

tant role in the overall operation of the engine and its components. Due to its function and material make up, the belt is prone to wear and should be periodically inspected. The serpentine belt drives the alternator, power steering pump, water pump and air conditioning compressor.

2   With the engine off, open the hood and use your fingers (and a flashlight, if necessary), to move along the belt checking for cracks and separation of the belt plies. Also check for fraying and glazing, which gives the belt a shiny appearance **(see illustration)**. Both sides of the belt should be inspected, which means you will have to twist the belt to check the underside.

3   Check the ribs on the underside of the belt. They should all be the same depth, with none of the surface uneven.

4   The tension of the belt is maintained by the tensioner assembly and isn't adjustable. The belt should be checked at the specified mileage; if the belt shows noticeable damage

or wear during these checks it should be replaced **(see illustration)**.

Replacement

Refer to illustrations 12.5 and 12.6

5   Rotate the tensioner counterclockwise to release belt tension, then slip the belt from the pulleys **(see illustration)**.

6   To install the belt, guide it over the pulleys in the proper routing **(see illustration)**, rotate the tensioner counterclockwise and slip the belt onto the tensioner pulley.

Tensioner replacement

7   Remove the engine drivebelt as described previously.

8   Remove the tensioner retaining bolt and detach the tensioner assembly from the front of the engine.

9   Installation is the reverse of the removal procedure. Be sure to tighten the tensioner mounting bolt to the torque listed in this Chapter's Specifications.

13   Tire rotation (every 6000 miles or 6 months)

Refer to illustrations 13.2a and 13.2b

1   The tires should be rotated at the specified intervals and whenever uneven wear is noticed. Since the vehicle will be raised and the tires removed anyway, this is a good time to check the brakes (see Section 16).

2   Radial tires must be rotated in a specific pattern **(see illustrations)**. **Note:** *Most vehicles are sold with non-directional radial tires, but some replacement performance tires are available that are directional, and have a different rotation pattern. Directional tires have an arrow on the sidewall indicating the direction they must turn when mounted on the vehicle.*

3   See the information in *Jacking and towing* at the front of this manual for the proper procedures to follow when raising the vehicle and changing a tire; however, if the brakes are to be checked, don't apply the parking brake as stated. Make sure the tires are blocked to prevent the vehicle from rolling.

4   Preferably, the entire vehicle should be raised at the same time. This can be done on

12.5 Rotate the drivebelt tensioner counterclockwise to remove or install the belt, using a 3/8-inch square-drive tool (a ratchet is being used here)

12.6 A serpentine drivebelt routing diagram is located on the engine, directly above the belt

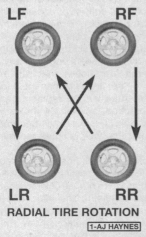

RADIAL TIRE ROTATION

1-AJ HAYNES

13.2a The recommended four-tire rotation pattern for *non-directional* radial tires

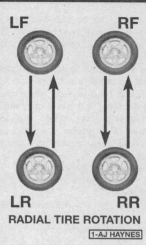

LF   RF

LR   RR

RADIAL TIRE ROTATION

1-AJ HAYNES

13.2b The recommended four-tire rotation pattern for *directional* radial tires

a hoist or by jacking up each corner of the vehicle and lowering it onto jackstands. Always use four jackstands and make sure the vehicle is safely supported.

5   After the tire rotation, check and adjust the tire pressures as necessary and be sure to check wheel lug nut tightness.

14 Seat belt check (every 6,000 miles or 6 months)

1   Check the seat belts, buckles, latch plates and guide loops for obvious damage and signs of wear.

2   See if the seat belt reminder light comes on when the key is turned to the Run or Start position. A chime should also sound.

3   The seat belts are designed to lock up during a sudden stop or impact, yet allow free movement during normal driving. Make sure the retractors return the belt against your chest while driving and rewind the belt

fully when the buckle is unlatched.

4   If any of the above checks reveal problems with the seat belt system, replace parts as necessary.

15 Steering, suspension and driveaxle boot check (every 15,000 miles or 12 months)

Note: *The steering linkage and suspension components should be checked periodically. Worn or damaged suspension and steering linkage components can result in excessive and abnormal tire wear, poor ride quality and vehicle handling, and reduced fuel economy. For detailed illustrations of the steering and suspension components, refer to Chapter 10.*

Strut/shock absorber check

Refer to illustration 15.6

1   Park the vehicle on level ground, turn the engine off and set the parking brake. Check the tire pressures.

2   Push down at one corner of the vehicle, then release it while noting the movement of the body. It should stop moving and come to rest in a level position within one or two bounces.

3   If the vehicle continues to move up-and-down or if it fails to return to its original position, a worn or weak strut assembly (front) or shock absorber (rear) is probably the reason.

4   Repeat the above check at each of the three remaining corners of the vehicle.

5   Raise the vehicle and support it securely on jackstands.

6   Check the struts (front) and shock absorbers (rear) for evidence of fluid leakage **(see illustration)**. A light film of fluid is no cause for concern. Make sure that any fluid noted is from the struts or shocks and not from some other source. If leakage is noted, replace the struts (front) or shocks (rear) as a pair.

15.6 Pull up the boot on front struts to check for signs of fluid leakage at the point where the shaft enters the cartridge

7   Check the struts/shocks to be sure that they are securely mounted and undamaged. Check the upper mounts for damage and wear. If damage or wear is noted, replace the struts/shocks as a set (front or rear). If the vehicle is equipped with Electronic Level Control (ELC), check the rear shock absorber boots for cracks, holes and general deterioration.

8   If the struts or shocks must be replaced, refer to Chapter 10 for the procedure.

Steering and suspension check

Refer to illustrations 15.9a, 15.9b, 15.10 and 15.12

9   Visually inspect the steering and suspension components (front and rear) for damage and distortion. Look for damaged seals, boots and bushings and leaks of any kind. At the front end, examine the bushings where the control arm meets the chassis, and at the rear where the axle's trailing arm is bushed **(see illustrations)**.

1

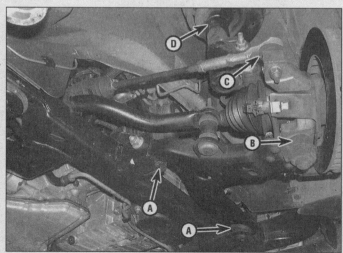

15.9a Examine the front suspension components

A   Control arm bushings
B   Balljoint
C   Tie-rod end
D   Strut/coil spring assembly

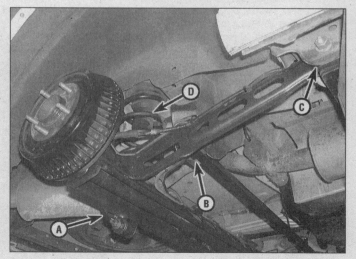

15.9b Examine the rear suspension components

A   Shock absorber
B   Track bar bushings
C   Trailing arm bushings
D   Coil spring

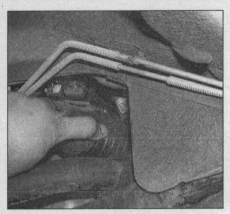

15.10 Flex the steering gear boots to check for cracks or signs of leakage

15.12 Check for tie-rod end play by moving the wheel/tire front and rear, and check for balljoint play by moving the top and bottom of the tire

10   Inspect the rack-and-pinion steering gear boots for signs of cracking or lubricant leakage **(see illustration)**. If the boots need replacing, refer to Chapter 10. **Note:** *Leakage would indicate defective rack seals, not simply a damaged boot.*

11   Clean the lower end of the steering knuckle. Have an assistant grasp the lower edge of the tire and move the wheel in-and-out while you look for movement at the steering knuckle-to-control arm balljoint. If there is any movement, the suspension balljoint(s) must be replaced.

12   Grasp each front tire at the front and rear edges, push in at the front, pull out at the rear, then reverse the motions and feel for play in the steering system components. If any freeplay is noted, check the tie-rod ends for looseness **(see illustration)**.

13   Additional steering and suspension system information and illustrations can be found in Chapter 10.

Driveaxle boot check

Refer to illustration 15.15

14   The driveaxle boots are very important because they prevent dirt, water and foreign material from entering and damaging the constant velocity (CV) joints. Oil and grease can cause the boot material to deteriorate

prematurely, so it's a good idea to wash the boots with soap and water. Because it constantly pivots back and forth following the steering action of the front hub, the outer CV boot wears out sooner and should be inspected regularly.

15   Inspect the boots for tears and cracks as well as loose clamps **(see illustration)**. If there is any evidence of cracks or leaking lubricant, they must be replaced as described in Chapter 8.

---

16   Brake check (every 15,000 miles or 12 months)

Warning: *The dust created by the brake system is harmful to your health. Never blow it out with compressed air and don't inhale any of it. An approved filtering mask should be worn when working on the brakes. Do not, under any circumstances, use petroleum-based solvents to clean brake parts. Use brake system cleaner only! Try to use non-asbestos replacement parts whenever possible.*

Note: *For detailed photographs of the brake system, refer to Chapter 9.*

1   In addition to the specified intervals, the brakes should be inspected every time the wheels are removed or whenever a defect is suspected.

2   Any of the following symptoms could indicate a potential brake system defect: The vehicle pulls to one side when the brake pedal is depressed; the brakes make squealing or dragging noises when applied; brake pedal travel is excessive; the pedal pulsates; or brake fluid leaks, usually onto the inside of the tire or wheel.

3   Loosen the wheel lug nuts.

4   Raise the vehicle and place it securely on jackstands.

5   Remove the wheels (see *Jacking and towing* at the front of this book, or your owner's manual, if necessary).

Disc brakes

Refer to illustrations 16.7a, 16.7b, 16.9 and 16.11

6   There are two pads (an outer and an inner) in each caliper. The pads are visible with the wheels removed.

7   Check the pad thickness by looking at each end of the caliper and through the inspection window in the caliper body **(see illustrations)**. If the lining material is less than the thickness listed in this Chapter's Specifications, replace the pads. **Note:** *Keep in mind that the lining material is riveted or bonded to a metal backing plate and the metal portion is not included in this measurement.*

8   If it is difficult to determine the exact thickness of the remaining pad material by the above method, or if you are at all concerned about the condition of the pads, remove the caliper(s), then remove the pads from the calipers for further inspection (refer to Chapter 9).

9   Once the pads are removed from the calipers, clean them with brake cleaner and re-measure them with a ruler or a vernier caliper **(see illustration)**.

10   Measure the disc thickness with a micrometer to make sure that it still has service life remaining. If either disc is thinner

15.15 Inspect the inner and outer driveaxle boots for loose clamps, cracks or signs of leaking lubricant (outer boot shown)

16.7a With the wheel off, check the thickness of the inner pad through the window in the caliper

16.7b The outer pad (arrow) is more easily checked at the edge of the caliper

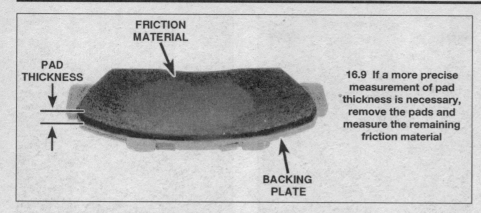

16.9 If a more precise measurement of pad thickness is necessary, remove the pads and measure the remaining friction material

16.11 Check the fitting at the caliper (A), look along the brake hose (B) for signs of cracking or fluid leakage, and check the fitting where the flexible brake hose meets the steel line on the chassis

than the specified minimum thickness, replace it (refer to Chapter 9). Even if the disc has service life remaining, check its condition. Look for scoring, gouging and burned spots. If these conditions exist, remove the disc and have it resurfaced (see Chapter 9).

11   Before installing the wheels, check all brake lines and hoses for damage, wear, deformation, cracks, corrosion, leakage, bends and twists, particularly in the vicinity of the rubber hoses at the calipers **(see illustration)**. Check the clamps for tightness and the connections for leakage. Make sure that all hoses and lines are clear of sharp edges, moving parts and the exhaust system. If any of the above conditions are noted, repair, reroute or replace the lines and/or fittings as necessary (see Chapter 9).

Drum brakes

Refer to illustrations 16.17 and 16.19

12   Raise the vehicle and support it securely on jackstands. Block the front tires to prevent the vehicle from rolling; however, don't apply the parking brake or it will lock the drums in place.

13   Remove the wheels, referring to *Jacking and towing* at the front of this manual if necessary.

14   Mark the hub so it can be reinstalled in the same position. Use a scribe, chalk, etc. on the drum, hub and backing plate.

15   Remove the brake drum (see Chapter 9 if necessary).

16   With the drum removed, carefully clean the brake assembly with brake system cleaner. **Warning:** *Don't blow the dust out with compressed air and don't inhale any of it.*

17   Note the thickness of the lining material on both front and rear brake shoes. If the material has worn away to within 1/16-inch of the recessed rivets or metal backing, the shoes should be replaced **(see illustration)**. The shoes should also be replaced if they're cracked, glazed (shiny areas), or covered with brake fluid.

18   Make sure all the brake assembly springs are connected and in good condition.

19   Check the brake components for signs of fluid leakage. With your finger or a small screwdriver, carefully pry back the rubber boots on the wheel cylinder located at the top of the brake shoes **(see illustration)**. Any leakage here is an indication that the wheel cylinders should be replaced immediately (see Chapter 9). Also, check all hoses, lines and connections for signs of leakage.

20   Clean the inside of the drum with brake system cleaner. Again, be careful not to

breathe the dust.

21   Check the inside of the drum for cracks, score marks, deep scratches and "hard spots" which will appear as small discolored areas. If imperfections cannot be removed with fine emery cloth, the drum must be taken to an automotive machine shop for resurfacing.

22   Repeat the procedure for the remaining wheel. If the inspection reveals that all parts are in good condition, reinstall the brake drums, install the wheels and lower the vehicle to the ground.

Brake booster check

23   Sit in the driver's seat and perform the following sequence of tests.

24   With the brake fully depressed, start the engine - the pedal should move down a little when the engine starts.

25   With the engine running, depress the brake pedal several times - the travel distance should not change.

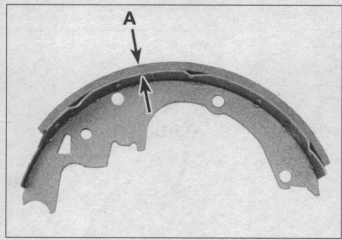

16.17 If the lining is bonded to the brake shoe, measure the lining thickness from the outer surface to the metal shoe, as shown here; if the lining is riveted to the shoe, measure from the lining outer surface to the rivet head

16.19 Check for fluid leakage at both ends of the wheel cylinder dust boots

26   Depress the brake, stop the engine and hold the pedal in for about 30 seconds - the pedal should neither sink nor rise.

27   Restart the engine, run it for about a minute and turn it off. Then firmly depress the brake several times - the pedal travel should decrease with each application.

28   If your brakes do not operate as described, the brake booster has failed. Refer to Chapter 9 for the replacement procedure.

Parking brake

29   One method of checking the parking brake is to park the vehicle on a steep hill with the parking brake set and the transmission in Neutral (be sure to remain in the driver's seat during this check!). If the parking brake cannot prevent the vehicle from rolling, it's in need of adjustment (see Chapter 9).

17   Exhaust system check (every 15,000 miles or 12 months)

Refer to illustrations 17.2a and 17.2b

1   With the engine cold (at least three hours after the vehicle has been driven), check the complete exhaust system from the engine to the end of the tailpipe. Ideally, the inspection should be done with the vehicle on a hoist to permit unrestricted access. If a hoist is not available, raise the vehicle and support it securely on jackstands.

2   Check the exhaust pipes and connections for evidence of leaks, severe corrosion and damage. Make sure that all brackets and hangers are in good condition and tight **(see illustrations)**.

3   At the same time, inspect the underside of the body for holes, corrosion, open seams, etc. which may allow exhaust gases to enter the interior. Seal all body openings with silicone or body putty.

4   Rattles and other noises can often be traced to the exhaust system, especially the mounts and hangers. Try to move the pipes, muffler and catalytic converter. If the compo-

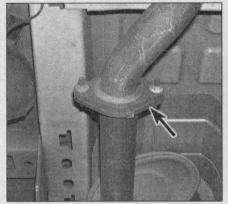

17.2a Check the flange connections for exhaust leaks - also check that the retaining nuts are securely tightened

nents can come in contact with the body or suspension parts, secure the exhaust system with new mounts.

5   This is also an ideal time to check the running condition of the engine by inspecting the very end of the tailpipe. The exhaust deposits here are an indication of engine state-of-tune. If the pipe is black and sooty or coated with white deposits, the engine may be in need of a tune-up (including a thorough fuel injection system inspection).

18   Wiper blade inspection and replacement (every 15,000 miles or 12 months)

Refer to illustrations 18.3, 18.5 and 18.6

1   The windshield wiper and blade assemblies should be inspected periodically for damage, loose components and cracked or worn blade elements.

2   Road film can build up on the wiper blades and affect their efficiency, so they should be washed regularly with a mild detergent solution.

17.2b Check the exhaust system hangers for damage and cracks

3   The action of the wiping mechanism can loosen the bolts, nuts and fasteners, so they should be checked and tightened, as necessary, at the same time the wiper blades are checked **(see illustration)**.

4   If the wiper blade elements (sometimes called inserts) are cracked, worn or warped, they should be replaced with new ones.

5   Lift the arm assembly away from the glass for clearance, press on the release lever, then slide the wiper blade assembly out of the hook in the end of the arm **(see illustration)**.

6   If the wiper blade has a metal clip on the end, use needle-nose pliers to compress the clip, then slide the element out of the frame and discard it **(see illustration)**. Some wiper blades don't have metal clips - simply squeeze the end of the element with your fingers and slide it out of the frame.

7   Compare the new element with the old for length, design, etc. Some replacement elements come in a three-piece design (two metal strips, one on either side of the rubber) that is held together by several small plastic sleeves. Keep the sleeves in place on this design until you start sliding the element into the frame. Remove each of the plastic

18.3 Gently pry off the trim cap and check the tightness of the wiper arm retaining nut

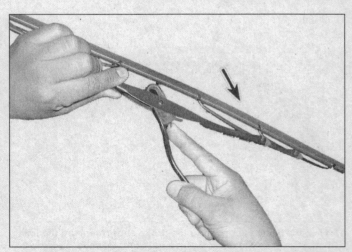

18.5 Press on the release tab (finger is on it here), then slide the blade assembly down and out of the hook in the arm

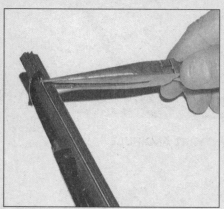

18.6 Use needle-nose pliers to compress the clip on the rubber element, then slide the element out - slide the new element in and lock the blade assembly fingers into the clip of the wiper element - on models with rubber prongs, the element can be pulled out by hand without pliers

19.2 Remove the cover from the rear of the glove box . . .

19.3 . . . remove the filter access door . . .

sleeves as needed when they reach the frame.

8   Slide the new element into the frame, notched end last and secure the clips into the notches of the frame.

9   Reinstall the blade assembly on the arm, wet the windshield and test for proper operation.

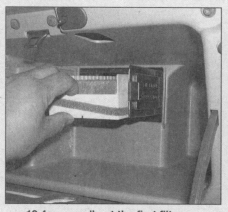

19.4a . . . pull out the first filter . . .

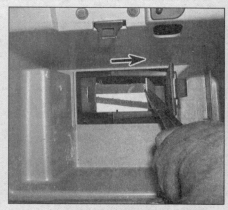

19.4b . . . slide the second filter to the right then remove it

19 Interior ventilation filter replacement (every 15,000 miles or 12 months)

Refer to illustrations 19.2, 19.3, 19.4a and 19.4b

1   These models are equipped with a pair of air filters that clean the air entering the vehicle through the ventilation system, as well as recirculated air.

2   Open the glove box door and remove the cover at the rear of the box **(see illustration)**.

3   Remove the filter access door **(see illustration)**.

4   Slide the filters out of the housing and replace them with new ones at the specified interval **(see illustrations)**.

5   Install the new filters by reversing the removal procedure.

20 Air filter replacement (every 30,000 miles or 24 months)

Refer to illustrations 20.1a and 20.1b

1   The air filter is located inside the air filter housing in the left (driver's) front corner of the engine compartment. To remove the air filter, release the clips **(see illustration)** that secure the two halves of the air cleaner housing together, then separate the cover halves and

remove the air filter element **(see illustration)**.

2   Inspect the outer surface of the filter element. If it is dirty, replace it. If it is only moderately dusty, it can be reused by blowing it clean from the back to the front surface with compressed air. Because it is a pleated paper type filter, it cannot be washed or oiled. If it cannot be cleaned satisfactorily with compressed air, discard and replace it. While the cover is off, be careful not to drop

anything down into the housing. **Caution:** *Never drive the vehicle with the air cleaner removed. Excessive engine wear could result and backfiring could even cause a fire under the hood.*

3   Wipe out the inside of the air cleaner housing.

4   Place the new filter into the air cleaner housing, making sure it seats properly.

5   Installation of the housing is the reverse of removal.

20.1a Release the clips and separate the halves of the air filter housing . . .

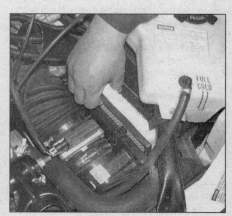

20.1b . . . then slide the element out of the housing

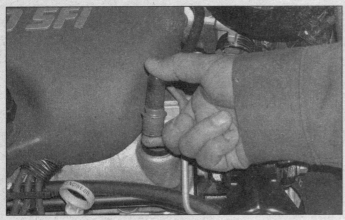

21.2 The PCV valve is located in the front valve cover - pull it out and check for vacuum with your finger with the engine idling

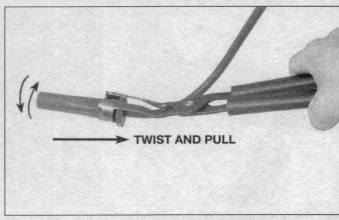

TWIST AND PULL

22.4 Using a spark plug boot puller tool like this one will make the job of removing the spark plug boots much easier

21   Positive Crankcase Ventilation (PCV) valve check and replacement (every 30,000 miles or 24 months)

Check

Refer to illustration 21.2

1   The PCV valve is located in the front valve cover.

2   With the engine idling at normal operating temperature, pull the valve (with hose attached) out of the rubber grommet in the valve cover **(see illustration)**.

3   Place your finger over the end of the valve. If there is no vacuum at the valve, check for a plugged hose, manifold port, or the valve itself. Replace any plugged or deteriorated hoses.

4   Turn off the engine and shake the PCV valve, listening for a rattle. If the valve doesn't rattle, replace it with a new one.

Replacement

5   To replace the valve, pull it out of the end of the hose, noting its installed position and direction.

6   When purchasing a replacement PCV valve, make sure it's for your particular vehicle, model year and engine size. Compare the old valve with the new one to make sure they are the same.

7   Push the valve into the end of the hose until it's seated.

8   Inspect the rubber grommet for damage and replace it with a new one if necessary.

9   Push the PCV valve and hose securely into position.

22   Spark plug wire check and replacement (every 30,000 miles or 24 months)

Refer to illustration 21.4

1   The spark plug wires should be checked and, if necessary, replaced at the same time new spark plugs are installed.

2   The easiest way to identify bad wires is to make a visual check while the engine is running. In a dark, well-ventilated garage, start the engine and look at each plug wire. Be careful not to come into contact with any moving engine parts. If there is a break in the wire, you will see arcing or a small spark at the damaged area. If arcing is noticed, make a note to obtain new wires.

3   The spark plug wires should be inspected one at a time, beginning with the spark plug for the number one cylinder (see the wire diagram at the beginning of this Chapter) to prevent confusion. Clearly label each plug wire with a piece of tape marked with the correct number. The plug wires must be reinstalled in the correct order to ensure proper engine operation.

4   Disconnect the plug wire from the first spark plug. A removal tool can be used, or you can grab the wire boot, twist it a half-turn and pull the boot free. Do not pull on the wire itself, only on the rubber boot **(see illustration)**. **Note:** *It will be necessary to rotate the engine forward and remove the alternator to gain access to the spark plugs in the rear (right) cylinder bank. Refer to Chapter 2A for the engine rotating procedure and Chapter 5 for the alternator removal procedure.*

5   Push the wire and boot back onto the end of the spark plug. It should fit snugly. If it doesn't, detach the wire and boot once more and use a pair of pliers to carefully crimp the metal connector inside the wire boot until it does.

6   Using a clean rag, wipe the entire length of the wire to remove built-up dirt and grease.

7   Once the wire is clean, check for burns, cracks and other damage. Do not bend the wire sharply or you might break the conductor.

8   Disconnect the wire from the coil pack. Pull only on the rubber boot. Check for corrosion on the coil pack towers and the plug wire ends, and that they fit tight. Reinstall the wire.

9   Inspect each of the remaining spark plug wires, making sure that each one is securely fastened on each end.

10   If new spark plug wires are required, purchase a set for your specific engine model. Pre-cut wire sets with the boots already installed are available. Remove and replace the wires one at a time to avoid mix-ups in the firing order. Should a mix up occur, refer to the Specifications at the beginning this Chapter.

23   Spark plug check and replacement (see maintenance schedule for service intervals)

Refer to illustrations 23.5, 23.8a, 23.8b, 23.11, 23.12 and 23.13

Caution: *The engine should be cool when the spark plugs are removed.*

1   Disconnect the cable from the negative terminal of the battery. **Caution:** *On models equipped with the Theftlock audio system, be sure you have the correct activation code before performing any procedure which requires disconnecting the battery (see the front of this manual).*

2   Rotate the engine forward (see Chapter 2A).

3   Remove the coil pack (see Chapter 5). This is necessary for access to the rear plugs.

4   A special plug wire removal tool is available for separating the wire boots from the spark plugs, and is a good idea on these models because the boots fit very tightly **(see illustration 22.4)**. Twist the boot one-half turn and remove it from the plug.

5   In most cases, the tools necessary for spark plug replacement include a spark plug socket which fits onto a ratchet (spark plug sockets are padded inside to prevent damage to the porcelain insulators on the new plugs), various extensions and a gap gauge to check and adjust the gaps on the new plugs **(see illustration)**. A torque wrench should be used to tighten the new plugs. It is a good idea to allow the engine to cool before removing or installing the spark plugs.

6   The best approach when replacing the spark plugs is to purchase the new ones in advance, adjust them to the proper gap and

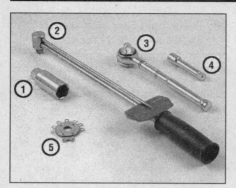

23.5 Tools required for changing spark plugs

1 **Spark plug socket** - *This will have special padding inside to protect the spark plug's porcelain insulator*
2 **Torque wrench** - *Although not mandatory, using this tool is the best way to ensure the plugs are tightened properly*
3 **Ratchet** - *Standard hand tool to fit the spark plug socket*
4 **Extension** - *Depending on model and accessories, you may need special extensions and universal joints to reach one or more of the plugs*
5 **Spark plug gap gauge** - *This gauge for checking the gap comes in a variety of styles. Make sure the gap for your engine is included*

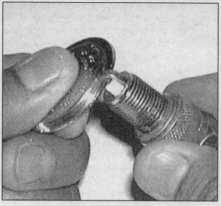

23.8a Spark plug manufacturers recommend using a tapered-thickness gauge when checking the gap - slide the thin side into the gap and turn until the gauge just fills the gap, then read the thickness on the gauge - do not force the tool into the gap or use the tapered portion to widen a gap

23.8b To change the gap, bend the side electrode only, using the adjuster hole in the tool, and be very careful not to crack or chip the porcelain insulator surrounding the center electrode

replace the plugs one at a time. When buying the new spark plugs, be sure to obtain the correct plug type for your particular engine. The plug type can be found in the Specifications at the front of this Chapter.

7 Allow the engine to cool completely before attempting to remove any of the plugs. While you are waiting for the engine to cool, check the new plugs for defects and adjust the gaps.

8 Check the gap by inserting the proper thickness gauge between the electrodes at the tip of the plug **(see illustration)**. The gap between the electrodes should be the same

as the one listed in this Chapter's Specifications. The gauge should slide between the electrodes with a slight amount of drag. If the gap is incorrect, use the adjuster on the gauge body to bend the curved side electrode slightly until the proper gap is obtained **(see illustration)**. If the side electrode is not exactly over the center electrode, bend it with the adjuster until it is. Check for cracks in the porcelain insulator (if any are found, the plug should not be used). **Note:** *Manufacturers recommend using a tapered thickness gauge when checking platinum-type spark plugs. Other types of gauges may scrape the thin platinum coating from the electrodes, thus dramatically shortening the life of the plugs.*

9 If compressed air is available, use it to blow any dirt or foreign material away from the spark plug hole. The idea here is to eliminate the possibility of debris falling into the cylinder as the spark plug is removed.

10 The rear spark plugs on these models are, for the most part, difficult to reach so a

spark plug socket incorporating a universal joint will be necessary.

11 Place the spark plug socket over the plug and remove it from the engine by turning it in a counterclockwise direction. When removing the spark plugs from the rear cylinder bank, work through the opening created by the removal of the coil pack **(see illustration)**.

12 Compare the spark plug with the chart shown on the inside back cover of this manual to get an indication of the general running condition of the engine. Before installing the new plugs, it is a good idea to apply a thin coat of anti-seize compound to the threads **(see illustration)**.

13 Thread one of the new plugs into the hole until you can no longer turn it with your fingers, then tighten it with a torque wrench (if available) or the ratchet. It's a good idea to slip a short length of rubber hose over the end of the plug to use as a tool to thread it into place **(see illustration)**. The hose will grip the plug well enough to turn it, but will start to slip if the plug begins to cross-thread in the hole - this will prevent damaged threads and the accompanying repair costs.

1

23.11 When removing the spark plugs from the rear cylinder bank, work through the opening that was created by removing the coil pack

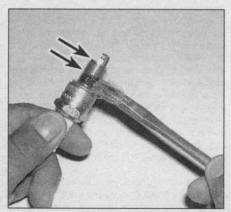

23.12 Apply a thin coat of anti-seize compound to the spark plug threads, being careful not to get any near the lower threads (arrows)

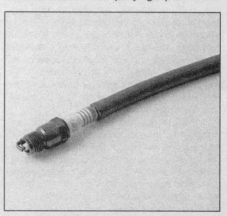

23.13 A length of snug-fitting rubber hose will save time and prevent damaged threads when installing the spark plugs

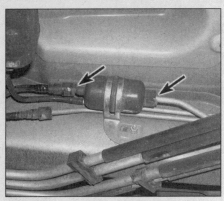

24.3 Squeeze the white plastic tabs (arrows) together and pull the lines away from the filter, then unbolt the filter mounting bracket to remove the fuel filter

14   Before pushing the spark plug wire onto the end of the plug, inspect it following the procedures outlined in Section 22. Attach the plug wire to the new spark plug, again using a twisting motion on the boot until it's seated on the spark plug.

15   Repeat the procedure for the remaining spark plugs, replacing them one at a time to prevent mixing up the spark plug wires.

16   Reinstall the coil pack (see Chapter 5).

24   Fuel filter replacement (every 30,000 miles or 24 months)

Refer to illustration 24.3

Warning: *Gasoline is extremely flammable, so take extra precautions when you work on any part of the fuel system. Don't smoke or allow open flames or bare light bulbs near the work area, and don't work in a garage where a gas-type appliance (such as a water heater or clothes dryer) is present. Since gasoline is carcinogenic, wear fuel-resistant gloves when there's a possibility of being exposed to fuel, and, if you spill any fuel on your skin, rinse it off immediately with soap and water. Mop up any spills immediately and do not store fuel-soaked rags where they could ignite. The fuel system is under constant pressure, so, if any fuel lines are to be disconnected, the fuel pressure in the system must be relieved first (see Chapter 4 for more information). When you perform any kind of work on the fuel system, wear safety glasses and have a Class B type fire extinguisher on hand.*

1   Relieve the fuel system pressure (see Chapter 4), then disconnect the cable from the negative terminal of the battery. **Caution:** *On models equipped with the Theftlock audio system, be sure you have the correct activation code before performing any procedure which requires disconnecting the battery (see the front of this manual).*

2   Raise the vehicle and support it securely on jackstands.

3   The fuel filter is mounted to the floorpan just in front of the fuel tank **(see illustration)**.

4   Twist the fuel line fittings 1/4-turn in either direction, then use compressed air to clean any dirt surrounding the fuel inlet and outlet line fittings.

5   Depress the white plastic tabs on the quick-connect fittings and detach the lines from the fuel filter **(see illustration 24.3)**. **Note:** *Have spare rags or a small container to catch or wipe up extra gasoline that will spill from the filter assembly.*

6   Detach the fuel filter mounting bracket bolt and remove the fuel filter.

7   Installation is the reverse of removal. Before attaching the fuel lines, lubricate each fitting with a thin film of engine oil. After reconnecting the lines, pull on them to make sure they are securely attached.

25   Fuel system check (every 30,000 miles or 24 months)

Warning: *Gasoline is extremely flammable, so take extra precautions when you work on any part of the fuel system. Don't smoke or allow open flames or bare light bulbs near the work area, and don't work in a garage where a gas-type appliance (such as a water heater or clothes dryer) is present. Since gasoline is carcinogenic, wear fuel-resistant gloves when there's a possibility of being exposed to fuel, and, if you spill any fuel on your skin, rinse it off immediately with soap and water. Mop up any spills immediately and do not store fuel-soaked rags where they could ignite. The fuel system is under constant pressure, so, if any fuel lines are to be disconnected, the fuel pressure in the system must be relieved first (see Chapter 4 for more information). When you perform any kind of work on the fuel system, wear safety glasses and have a Class B type fire extinguisher on hand.*

1   The fuel system is most easily checked with the vehicle raised on a hoist so the components underneath the vehicle are readily visible and accessible.

2   If the smell of gasoline is noticed while driving or after the vehicle has been in the sun, the system should be thoroughly inspected immediately.

3   Remove the fuel filler cap and check for damage, corrosion and an unbroken sealing imprint on the gasket. Replace the cap with a new one if necessary.

4   With the vehicle raised, inspect the fuel tank and filler neck for cracks and other damage. The connection between the filler neck and tank is especially critical. Sometimes a filler neck will leak due to cracks, problems a home mechanic can't repair. **Warning:** *Do not, under any circumstances, try to repair a fuel tank yourself (except rubber components).*

5   Carefully check all rubber hoses and metal lines leading away from the fuel tank. Check for loose connections, deteriorated hoses, crimped lines and other damage. Follow the lines to the front of the vehicle, carefully inspecting them all the way. Repair or replace damaged sections as necessary.

26   Brake fluid change (every 30,000 miles or 24 months)

Warning: *Brake fluid can harm your eyes and damage painted surfaces, so use extreme caution when handling or pouring it. Do not use brake fluid that has been standing open or is more than one year old. Brake fluid absorbs moisture from the air. Excess moisture can cause a dangerous loss of braking effectiveness.*

1   At the specified intervals, the brake fluid should be drained and replaced. Since the brake fluid may drip or splash when pouring it, place plenty of rags around the master cylinder to protect any surrounding painted surfaces.

2   Before beginning work, purchase the specified brake fluid (see *Recommended lubricants and fluids* at the beginning of this Chapter).

3   Remove the cap from the master cylinder reservoir.

4   Using a hand suction pump or similar device, withdraw the fluid from the master cylinder reservoir.

5   Add new fluid to the master cylinder until it rises to the base of the filler neck.

6   Bleed the brake system as described in Chapter 9 at all four brakes until new and uncontaminated fluid is expelled from the bleeder screw. Be sure to maintain the fluid level in the master cylinder as you perform the bleeding process. If you allow the master cylinder to run dry, air will enter the system.

7   Refill the master cylinder with fluid and check the operation of the brakes. The pedal should feel solid when depressed, with no sponginess. **Warning:** *Do not operate the vehicle if you are in doubt about the effectiveness of the brake system.*

27   Automatic transaxle fluid and filter change (every 60,000 miles or 48 months)

Refer to illustrations 27.7, 27.10a, 27.10b and 27.12

1   At the specified time intervals, the transaxle fluid should be drained and replaced. Since the fluid will remain hot long after driving, perform this procedure only after everything has cooled down completely.

2   Before beginning work, purchase the specified transaxle fluid (see *Recommended lubricants and fluids* at the front of this Chapter) and a new filter.

3   Other tools necessary for this job include jackstands to support the vehicle in a raised position, a drain pan capable of holding several quarts, newspapers and clean rags.

4   Raise and support the vehicle on jackstands.

5   With a drain pan in place, remove the front and side transaxle pan mounting bolts.

6   Loosen the rear pan bolts one turn.

27.7 After removing the front and side pan bolts, loosen the rear bolts and allow the fluid to drain, then remove the bolts and lower the pan from the vehicle

27.10a Pull the transaxle filter straight down and out of the transaxle - there are no fasteners

7   Carefully pry the transaxle pan loose with a screwdriver, allowing the fluid to drain **(see illustration)**.

8   Remove the remaining bolts, pan and gasket. Carefully clean the gasket surface of the transaxle to remove all traces of the old gasket and sealant.

9   Drain the fluid from the transaxle pan, clean the pan with solvent and dry it with compressed air. Be careful not to lose the magnet.

10   Remove the filter and pry out the seal **(see illustrations)**.

11   Push a new filter seal fully into its bore, then install the new filter.

12   Make sure the gasket surface on the transaxle pan is clean, then install the new gasket **(see illustration)**. Put the pan in place against the transaxle and install the bolts. Working around the pan, tighten each bolt a little at a time until the final torque figure is reached.

13   Lower the vehicle and add the specified amount of automatic transmission fluid (see Section 7).

14   With the shift lever in Park and the parking brake set, run the engine at a fast idle, but don't race it.

15   Move the shift lever through each gear and back to Park. Check the fluid level.

16   Check under the vehicle for leaks during the first few trips.

28   Cooling system servicing (draining, flushing and refilling) (every 60,000 miles or 48 months)

Warning: *Do not allow antifreeze to come in contact with your skin or painted surfaces of the vehicle. Flush contacted areas immediately with plenty of water. Do not store new coolant or leave old coolant lying around where it is easily accessible to children and pets, because they are attracted by its sweet smell. Ingestion of even a small amount can be fatal. Wipe up the garage floor and drip pan coolant spills immediately. Keep antifreeze containers covered and repair leaks in your cooling system immediately. Antifreeze is flammable - be sure to read the precautions on the container.*

Caution: *Never mix green-colored ethylene glycol anti-freeze and orange-colored "DEX-COOL" silicate-free coolant because doing so will destroy the efficiency of the "DEX-COOL"* coolant.

Note: *Non-toxic coolant is available at local auto parts stores. Although the coolant is non-toxic when fresh, proper disposal is still required.*

Draining

Refer to illustrations 28.3 and 28.4

1   Periodically, the cooling system should be drained, flushed and refilled to replenish the antifreeze mixture and prevent formation of rust and corrosion, which can impair the performance of the cooling system and cause engine damage. When the cooling system is serviced, all hoses and the radiator cap should be checked and replaced if necessary.

2   Apply the parking brake and block the wheels. **Warning:** *If the vehicle has just been driven, wait several hours to allow the engine to cool down before beginning this procedure.*

3   Move a large container under the radiator drain to catch the coolant. The drain valve is located on the lower left side of the radiator **(see illustration)**. Open the drain valve (a pair of pliers may be required to turn it). Remove the radiator cap.

27.10b Pry out the old seal, being careful not to damage the aluminum housing

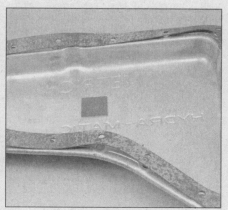

27.12 After cleaning the pan, place the magnet in position and install the gasket

28.3 Turn the drain valve (arrow) - the coolant will drain out of the hole in the radiator's lower left rubber mount

28.4 There's one cooling system bleed screw on the thermostat housing and one in the bypass pipe at the front of the engine, above the water pump

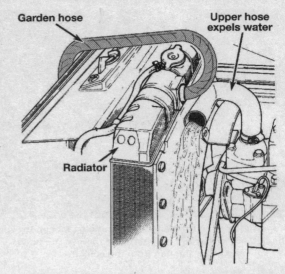

28.8 With the thermostat removed, disconnect the upper radiator hose and flush the radiator and block with a garden hose

4   Open the air bleed screws on the thermostat housing and in the bypass pipe located above the water pump **(see illustration)**. After the coolant has drained, temporarily tighten the bleed screws.

5   While the coolant is draining, check the condition of the radiator hoses, heater hoses and clamps (refer to Section 10 if necessary). Replace any damaged clamps or hoses. Remove the coolant reservoir (see Chapter 3) and rinse it out with clean water.

Flushing

Refer to illustration 28.8

6   Remove the thermostat from the engine (see Chapter 3), then reinstall the thermostat housing without the thermostat. This will allow the system to be thoroughly flushed.

7   Tighten the radiator drain valve. Turn your heating system controls to Hot, so that the heater core will be flushed at the same time as the rest of the cooling system.

8   Disconnect the upper radiator hose, then place a garden hose in the upper radiator inlet and flush the system until the water runs clear at the upper radiator hose **(see illustration)**.

9   In severe cases of contamination or clogging of the radiator, remove the radiator

(see Chapter 3) and have a radiator repair facility clean and repair it if necessary.

10   Many deposits can be removed by the chemical action of a cleaner available at auto parts stores. Follow the procedure outlined in the manufacturer's instructions. **Note:** *When the coolant is regularly drained and the system refilled with the correct antifreeze/water mixture, there should be no need to use chemical cleaners or descalers.*

Refilling

11   Install the coolant reservoir, reconnect the hoses and close the drain valve hand tight.

12   Open the bleed screws **(see illustration 28.4)** two or three turns and slowly add coolant to the radiator until it reaches the base of the filler neck.

13   Wait for a couple of minutes and make sure the coolant level is still up to the base of the filler neck; if it isn't, add coolant until it is.

14   Squeeze the upper radiator hose gently to make sure all remaining air is expelled, then add coolant until the level is up to the base of the radiator filler neck. Again, wait for a couple of minutes and check the level, adding as necessary to bring the level up to the base of the radiator filler neck.

15   Install the radiator cap, then close the bleed screw above the water pump, then the one on the thermostat housing, in that order (tighten them securely, but not excessively).

16   Fill the coolant reservoir with the same coolant mixture until the level is up to the COLD mark.

17   Run the engine until normal operating temperature is reached (allow the cooling fan to cycle on and off three times), then turn the engine off. Allow the engine to cool, then recheck the coolant level in the radiator, adding as necessary. **Caution:** *If the temperature indicator light comes on (or the temperature gauge indicates excessive temperature), turn off the engine and let it cool completely, then recheck the coolant level.*

18   Always refill the system with a mixture of antifreeze and water in the proportion called for on the antifreeze container, in this Chapter's Specifications or in your owner's manual. Chapter 3 also contains information on antifreeze mixtures.

19   Keep a close watch on the coolant level and the various cooling system hoses during the first few miles of driving. Tighten the hose clamps and add more coolant mixture as necessary.

Chapter 2 Part A
Engine

Contents

2A

Specifications

General

Displacement	204 cubic inches (3.4 liter)
Bore and stroke	3.62 x 3.31 inches
Cylinder numbers (drivebelt end-to-transaxle end)	
Front bank (radiator side)	2-4-6
Rear bank	1-3-5
Firing order	1-2-3-4-5-6

Torque specifications

Ft-lbs (unless otherwise indicated)

Camshaft sprocket bolt	
1997	81
1998 and later	103
Cylinder head bolts	
Step 1	37
Step 2	Rotate an additional 90-degrees (1/4-turn)
Driver's side engine mount-to-transaxle bracket nuts	35
Driver's side engine mount-to-frame nuts	35
Engine mount strut bracket-to-engine bolts	
Left side	52
Right side	37
Engine mount strut bracket-to-radiator support bolts	21
Engine mount strut through bolts	35
Exhaust manifold retaining nuts	144 in-lbs
Exhaust heat shield bolts	89 in-lbs
Exhaust crossover pipe nuts	18
Exhaust crossover pipe heat shield bolts	89 in-lbs
Driveplate-to-crankshaft bolts	
1997	61
1998 and later	52
Intake manifold bolts (lower)	115 in-lbs
Intake manifold bolts/studs (upper)	18

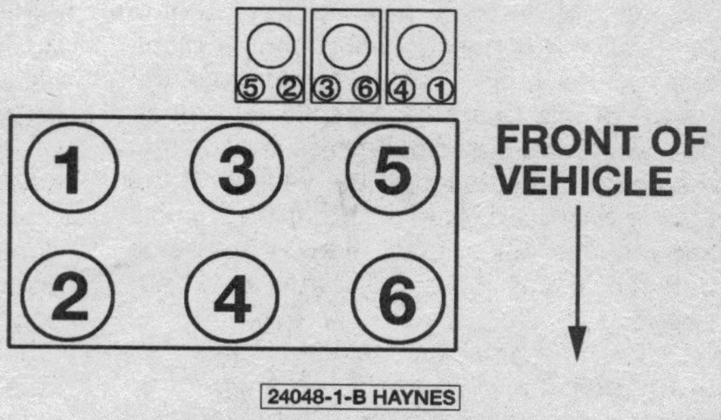

FRONT OF VEHICLE

24048-1-B HAYNES

Cylinder location and coil terminal identification diagram

Torque specifications   Ft-lbs (unless otherwise indicated)

Oil pan bolts/nuts
    To block 18
    Side bolts 37
Oil pump mounting bolt 30
Passenger side engine mount-to-engine mount bracket nuts 35
Passenger side engine mount bracket-to-oil pan bolts 43
Passenger side engine mount-to-frame nuts 32
Rocker arm bolts
    Step 1
        1997 .... 89 in-lbs
        1998 and later .... 168 in-lbs
    Step 2 .... Rotate an additional 30-degrees
Transaxle bracket bolts 70
Timing chain cover bolts
    1997
        Small 20
        Medium 35
        Large 41
    1998 and later
        Small 15
        Medium 35
        Large 41
Timing chain damper bolts 15
Valve cover-to-cylinder head bolts .... 89 in-lbs
Vibration damper bolt 76

1 General information

This Part of Chapter 2 is devoted to in-vehicle repair procedures for the 3.4L V6 engine. These engines utilize cast-iron blocks with six cylinders arranged in a "V" shape at a 60-degree angle between the two banks. The overhead valve aluminum cylinder heads are equipped with replaceable valve guides and seats. Hydraulic lifters actuate the valves through tubular pushrods.

The engines are easily identified by looking for the designations printed directly on top of the upper intake plenum.

All information concerning engine removal and installation and engine block and cylinder head overhaul can be found in Part B of this Chapter. The following repair procedures are based on the assumption that the engine is installed in the vehicle. If the engine has been removed from the vehicle and mounted on a stand, many of the steps outlined in this Part of Chapter 2 will not apply.

The Specifications included in this Part of Chapter 2 apply only to the procedures contained in this Part. Part B of Chapter 2 contains the Specifications necessary for cylinder head and engine block rebuilding.

2 Repair operations possible with the engine in the vehicle

Many major repair operations can be accomplished without removing the engine from the vehicle.

Clean the engine compartment and the exterior of the engine with some type of degreaser before any work is done. It'll make the job easier and help keep dirt out of the internal areas of the engine.

Depending on the components involved, it may be helpful to remove the hood to improve access to the engine as repairs are performed (refer to Chapter 11 if necessary). Cover the fenders to prevent damage to the paint. Special pads are available, but an old bedspread or blanket will also work.

If vacuum, exhaust, oil or coolant leaks develop, indicating a need for gasket or seal replacement, the repairs can generally be done with the engine in the vehicle. The intake and exhaust manifold gaskets, timing chain cover gasket, oil pan gasket, crankshaft oil seals and cylinder head gaskets are all accessible with the engine in place.

Exterior engine components, such as the intake and exhaust manifolds, the oil pan (and the oil pump), the water pump, the starter motor, the alternator and the fuel system components can be removed for repair with the engine in place.

Since the cylinder heads can be removed without pulling the engine, valve component servicing can also be accomplished with the engine in the vehicle. Replacement of the timing chain and sprockets is also possible with the engine in the vehicle, although camshaft removal can not be performed with the engine in the chassis (see Part B of this Chapter).

In extreme cases caused by a lack of necessary equipment, repair or replacement of piston rings, pistons, connecting rods and rod bearings is possible with the engine in the vehicle. However, this practice is not recommended because of the cleaning and preparation work that must be done to the components involved.

3 Top Dead Center (TDC) - locating

Refer to illustration 3.8

1 Top Dead Center (TDC) is the highest point in the cylinder each piston reaches as it travels up-and-down when the crankshaft turns. Each piston reaches TDC on the com-

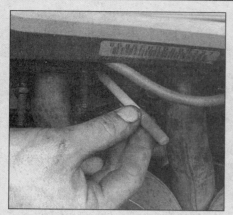

3.8 A plastic object inserted in the number one spark plug hole can be used to determine the highest point reached by that piston

4.2 Remove the engine cover (if equipped) by twisting out the oil filler neck, then pulling up and forward on the cover

4.6a The thermostat bypass pipe is secured to the engine by the hoses (A) and the bolt (B) on the water pump housing . . .

pression stroke and again on the exhaust stroke, but TDC generally refers to piston position on the compression stroke.

2 Positioning the piston(s) at TDC is an essential part of certain procedures such as timing chain/sprocket removal and camshaft removal.

3 Before beginning this procedure, be sure to place the transaxle in Park, apply the parking brake and block the rear wheels. Raise the front of the vehicle and support it securely on jackstands.

4 Remove the spark plugs (see Chapter 1). **Note:** *The engine must be rotated to the forward position during many procedures in this Chapter, including all procedures which require access to the right (rear) side of the engine. Many procedures that are associated with the left (front) side of the engine do not require the engine to be rotated. Only the components that are associated with the right cylinder head, valve cover, exhaust manifold, spark plugs, fuel, emission and electrical components from the centerline of the engine to firewall require the engine to be rotated.*

5 When looking at the drivebelt end of the engine, normal crankshaft rotation is clockwise. In order to bring any piston to TDC, the crankshaft must be turned with a socket and

ratchet attached to the bolt threaded into the center of the vibration damper on the crankshaft.

6 Have an assistant turn the crankshaft with a socket and ratchet as described above while you hold a finger over the number one spark plug hole. **Note:** *See the cylinder numbering diagram in the specifications for this Chapter.*

7 When the piston approaches TDC, air pressure will be felt at the spark plug hole. Instruct your assistant to turn the crankshaft slowly.

8 Insert a long blunt object into the spark plug hole **(see illustration)**. As the piston rises the object will be pushed out. Note the point where the object stops moving out - this is TDC. **Note:** *It is preferred, that a long plastic object be used during this procedure to ensure that object won't fall into the cylinder and will not scratch the cylinder walls. Always hold the object upright while the engine is being rotated so that the object will not get wedged as the piston travels upward.*

9 After the number one piston has been positioned at TDC on the compression stroke, TDC for any of the remaining pistons can be located by repeating the procedure described above and following the firing order.

2A

4 Valve covers - removal and installation

Removal

Refer to illustrations 4.2, 4.6a, 4.6b, 4.6c, 4.7 and 4.14

1 Disconnect the cable from the negative terminal of the battery. **Caution:** *On models equipped with the Theftlock audio system, be sure you have the correct activation code before disconnecting the battery (see the front of this manual).*

2 Remove the engine cover if equipped **(see illustration)**.

Front cover

3 Remove the air cleaner assembly (see Chapter 4).

4 Remove the spark plug wires from the spark plugs (see Chapter 1). Be sure each wire is labeled before removal to ensure correct reinstallation. Also detach the spark plug wire harness clamps from the coolant tube.

5 Remove the PCV tube from the valve cover.

6 Drain the coolant (see Chapter 1) and disconnect the coolant bypass pipe **(see illustrations)**. Also remove the passenger (right) side

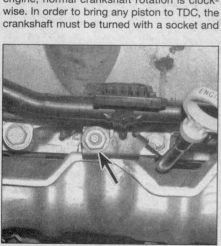

4.6b . . . and to the stud at the center (arrow) on the cylinder head

4.6c . . . and to the throttle body (A indicates two hose clamps, B indicates a support bracket retaining nut, C indicates the heater hose quick connect fitting to be removed

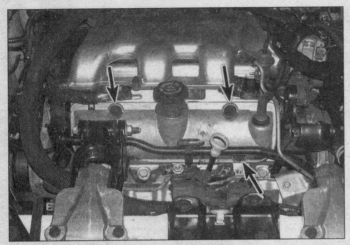

4.7 Loosen the valve cover mounting bolts (arrows indicate three) - the bolts will stay with the cover

4.14 The alternator bracket is retained by four bolts, three at the front (arrows) and one at the rear - use a ratchet and a long extension to reach the rear bolt

engine mount strut (see Section 18).

7   Loosen the valve cover mounting bolts **(see illustration)**.

8   Detach the valve cover. If the cover sticks to the cylinder head, use a block of wood and a hammer to dislodge it. If the cover still won't come loose, pry on it carefully, but don't distort the sealing flange. **Note:** *Although difficult, the left valve cover can be removed with the passenger side engine mount strut bracket still attached to the engine, it may be easier to remove the passenger side engine mount strut bracket from the engine to allow access to other components.*

Rear cover

9   Rotate the engine to the forward position (see Section 19).

10   Remove the ignition coil and module assembly (see Chapter 5), which also includes the solenoids for the vacuum canister and purge control (if equipped). Tag all disconnected wires and hoses.

11   Remove the spark plug wires from the spark plugs (see Chapter 1). Be sure each wire is labeled before removal to ensure correct reinstallation.

12   Detach the brake booster vacuum hose from the upper intake manifold. Also remove the crankcase breather hose from the rear valve cover.

13   Remove the serpentine drivebelt (see Chapter 1).

14   Remove the alternator (see Chapter 5) and the alternator support bracket **(see illustration)**.

15   Loosen the valve cover mounting bolts. **Note:** *Some models are equipped with Torx-head type bolts. Remove them with a Torx driver.*

16   Detach the valve cover. **Note:** *If the cover sticks to the cylinder head, use a block of wood and a hammer to dislodge it. If the cover still won't come loose, pry on it carefully, but don't distort the sealing flange.*

Installation

17   The mating surfaces of each cylinder head and valve cover must be perfectly clean when the covers are installed. Use a gasket scraper to remove all traces of sealant or old gasket material, then clean the mating surfaces with lacquer thinner or acetone (if there's sealant or oil on the mating surfaces when the cover is installed, oil leaks may develop). The valve covers are made of aluminum, so be extra careful not to nick or gouge the mating surfaces with the scraper.

18   Clean the mounting bolt threads with a wire brush if necessary to remove any corrosion and dirt on the threads. Use a tap to clean the threaded holes in the heads.

19   Apply a dab of RTV sealant to the two joints where the intake manifold and cylinder head meet.

20   Place the valve cover and new gasket in position, then install the bolts. Tighten the bolts in several steps to the torque listed in this Chapter's Specifications.

21   Complete the installation by reversing the removal procedure. Start the engine and check carefully for oil leaks at the valve cover-to-head joints.

5   Rocker arms and pushrods - removal, inspection and installation

Refer to illustrations 5.3 and 5.4

Removal

1   Disconnect the cable from the negative terminal of the battery. **Caution:** *On models equipped with the Theftlock audio system, be sure you have the correct activation code before disconnecting the battery (see the front of this manual).*

2   Remove the valve cover(s) (see Section 4). **Note:** *The engine must be rotated to the forward position during many procedures*

in this Chapter, including all procedures which require access to the right (rear) side of the engine. Many procedures that are associated with the left (front) side of the engine do not require the engine to be rotated. Only the components that are associated with the right cylinder head, valve cover, exhaust manifold, spark plugs, fuel, emission and electrical components from the centerline of the engine to firewall require the engine to be rotated.

3   Beginning at the drivebelt end of one cylinder head, remove the rocker arm mounting bolts one at a time and detach the rocker arms and pedestals **(see illustration)**. Store each set of rocker arm components separately in a marked plastic bag to ensure they're reinstalled in their original locations. **Note:** *The rocker arm bolt is "captured" to*

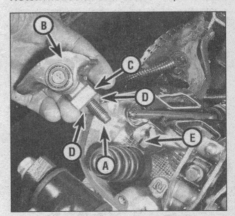

5.3 Rocker arm installation details - the rocker arms are kept as an assembly by a small sleeve between the bolt and the pedestal - note the projections on the pedestal; they fit into the grooves in the head

A   Rocker arm bolt
B   Rocker arm
C   Rocker arm pedestal
D   Pedestal projections
E   Grooves in the head

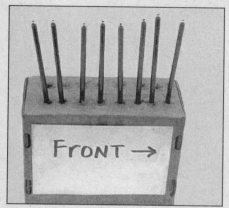

5.4 A perforated cardboard box can be used to store the pushrods to ensure they are reinstalled in their original locations - note the label indicating the front end of the engine

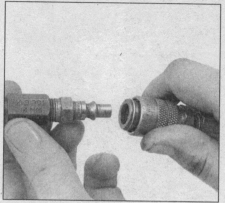

6.4 This is what the typical air hose adapter that threads into the spark plug hole looks like - they're commonly available at auto parts stores

6.6 While the valve spring tool is compressing the spring, remove the keepers with a small magnet or pliers

the pedestal mount by a metal sleeve inside. The components can be separated if necessary by tapping the bolt out of the pedestal, but normally all components for a particular valve will stay as an assembly.

4   Remove the pushrods and store them separately to make sure they don't get mixed up during installation **(see illustration)**. **Note:** *Intake and exhaust pushrods are different lengths. Intake pushrods are approximately 5 3/4 inches long, while exhausts are 6.0 inches long. They may also have color codes to easily tell them apart. OEM pushrods are typically color coded yellow for intake and green for exhaust.*

Inspection

5   Inspect each rocker arm for wear, cracks and other damage, especially where the pushrods and valve stems make contact.

6   Make sure the rollers operate freely as well.

7   Make sure the hole at the pushrod end of each rocker arm is open.

8   Inspect the pushrods for cracks and excessive wear at the ends. Roll each pushrod across a piece of plate glass to see if it's bent (if it wobbles, it's bent).

Installation

9   Lubricate the lower end of each pushrod with clean engine oil or moly-base grease and install them in their original locations. Make sure each pushrod seats completely in the lifter socket.

10   Apply moly-base grease to the ends of the valve stems and the upper ends of the pushrods.

11   Apply clean engine oil to the roller bearings on each rocker arm to prevent damage to the mating surfaces before engine oil pressure builds up. Install the rocker arms, pedestals and bolts and tighten them to the torque listed in this Chapter's Specifications. As the bolts are tightened, make sure the pushrods engage properly in the rocker arms

and that the projections on the bottom of the pedestals fit into the grooves on the head before tightening the bolts **(see illustration 5.3)**.

12   Install the valve covers. Start and run the engine, then check for oil leaks and unusual sounds coming from the valve cover area.

6   Valve springs, retainers and seals - replacement

Refer to illustrations 6.4, 6.6, 6.12 and 6.14

Note: *Broken valve springs and defective valve stem seals can be replaced without removing the cylinder head. Two special tools and a compressed air source are normally required to perform this operation, so read through this Section carefully and rent or buy the tools before beginning the job.*

1   Remove the valve cover(s) (see Section 4). **Note:** *The engine must be rotated to the forward position during many procedures in this Chapter, including all procedures, which require access to the right (rear) side of the engine. Many procedures that are associated with the left (front) side of the engine do not require the engine to be rotated. Only the components that are associated with the right (rear) cylinder head, valve cover, exhaust manifold, spark plugs, fuel, emission and electrical components from the centerline of the engine to firewall require the engine to be rotated.*

2   Remove the spark plugs from the cylinders which have the defective components. If all of the valve stem seals are being replaced, all of the spark plugs should be removed.

3   Turn the crankshaft until the piston in the affected cylinder is at top dead center (see Section 3). If you're replacing all of the valve stem seals, begin with cylinder number one and work on the valves for one cylinder at a time. Move from cylinder-to-cylinder following the firing order sequence (see this Chapter's Specifications).

4   Thread an adapter into the spark plug hole **(see illustration)** and connect an air hose from a compressed air source to it. Most auto parts stores can supply the air hose adapter. **Note:** *Many cylinder compression gauges utilize a screw-in fitting that may work with your air hose quick-disconnect fitting.*

5   Apply compressed air to the cylinder. **Warning:** *The piston may be forced down by compressed air, causing the crankshaft to turn suddenly. If the wrench used when positioning the number one piston at TDC is still attached to the bolt in the crankshaft nose, it could cause damage or injury when the crankshaft moves. The valves should be held in place by the air pressure. If the valve faces or seats are in poor condition, leaks may prevent air pressure from retaining the valves - a "valve job" is necessary to correct this problem.*

6   Stuff shop rags into the cylinder head holes above and below the valves to prevent parts and tools from falling into the engine, then use a valve spring compressor to compress the spring. Remove the keepers **(see illustration)** with small needle-nose pliers or a magnet.

7   Remove the spring retainer and valve spring, then remove the valve guide seal/spring seat.

8   Wrap a rubber band or tape around the top of the valve stem so the valve won't fall into the combustion chamber, then release the air pressure.

9   Inspect the valve stem for damage. Rotate the valve in the guide and check the end for eccentric movement, which would indicate the valve stem is bent.

10   Move the valve up-and-down in the guide and make sure it doesn't bind. If the valve stem binds, either the valve is bent or the guide is damaged. In either case, the head will have to be removed for repair.

11   Reapply air pressure to the cylinder to retain the valve in the closed position, then remove the tape or rubber band from the valve stem.

12   Lubricate the valve stem with engine oil and install a new valve guide seal/spring seat. An appropriate-size socket can be used to install the new seal, just don't force it once it bottoms **(see illustration)**.

13   Install the spring in position over the valve. **Note:** *The large end of the spring goes toward the cylinder head.*

14   Install the valve spring retainer. Compress the valve spring and carefully install the keepers in the groove. Apply a small dab of grease to the inside of each keeper to hold it in place if necessary **(see illustration)**. Remove the pressure from the spring tool and make sure the keepers are seated.

15   Disconnect the air hose and remove the adapter from the spark plug hole.

16   Install the spark plug(s) and hook up the wire(s).

17   Install the valve cover(s).

18   Start and run the engine, then check for oil leaks and unusual sounds coming from the valve cover area.

7   Intake manifold - removal and installation

Upper intake manifold (plenum)

Refer to illustration 7.8

1   Disconnect the cable from the negative terminal of the battery. **Caution:** *On models equipped with the Theftlock audio system, be sure you have the correct activation code before disconnecting the battery (see the front of this manual).*

2   Refer to Chapter 4 and relieve the fuel system pressure, then remove the air intake duct and detach the throttle cable and the cruise control cable from the throttle body. Label and disconnect the hoses and electrical connectors attached to the plenum and throttle body.

3   Rotate the engine to the forward position (see Section 19). This Step is not absolutely necessary, but it will be extremely helpful in allowing access to surrounding components.

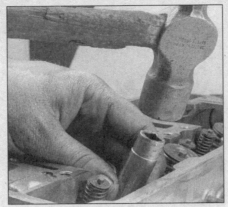

6.12 Tap the new seal in place on the guide with a socket

4   Detach the spark plug wires from the ignition coils and the spark plug wire clamps. Then position the plug wires aside, so that they will not interfere with the removal of the upper plenum. Remove the ignition coil and module assembly (see Chapter 5). Also remove the support braces from the rear of the alternator.

5   Referring to Chapter 6, remove the EGR valve and the MAP sensor.

6   Loosen the upper intake manifold bolts in the reverse order of the tightening sequence **(see illustration 7.8)** and remove the upper plenum with the throttle body attached.

7   To install the upper manifold, clean the mounting surfaces of the lower intake manifold and the upper plenum with lacquer thinner and remove all traces of the old gasket material or sealant.

8   Install the new gasket over the lower intake manifold, then install the upper plenum onto the lower intake manifold and tighten the bolts in the recommended tightening sequence **(see illustration)** to the torque listed in this Chapter's Specifications. The remainder of the installation is the reverse of removal.

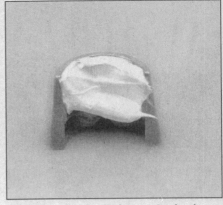

6.14 Keepers don't always stay in place, so apply a small dab of grease to each one as shown here before installation - the grease will hold the keepers in place on the valve stem

Lower intake manifold

Refer to illustrations 7.13a, 7.13b, 7.15, 7.19, 7.20 and 7.22

9   Remove the upper intake manifold (see Steps 1 through 6). Drain the cooling system (see Chapter 1).

10   Label and disconnect any remaining wires, fuel and vacuum lines from the lower intake manifold.

11   Refer to Chapter 4 and remove the fuel rail and injectors from the lower intake manifold.

12   Remove the valve covers and the coolant bypass pipe (see Section 4). Remove the power steering pump without disconnecting the hoses and set it aside (see Chapter 10).

13   Remove the heater pipe from the transaxle end of the lower intake manifold **(see illustrations)**.

14   Loosen the manifold mounting bolts/nuts in the reverse order of the tightening sequence in 1/4-turn increments until they can be removed by hand **(see illustration 7.22)**.

15   The manifold will probably be stuck to the cylinder heads and force may be required

7.8 Upper intake manifold TIGHTENING sequence

7.13a Remove the nut (arrow) securing the heater pipe bracket to the cylinder head . . .

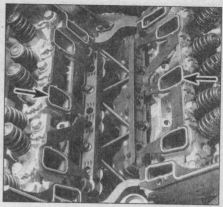

7.13b . . . and the quick connect fitting (arrow) from the heater pipe fitting on the thermostat housing/lower intake manifold, then pull it out the from the lower intake manifold - use a screwdriver to press inward on the tabs of the quick connect fitting to release it

7.15 Pry the manifold loose at a casting boss (arrow) - don't pry between the gasket surfaces!

7.19 Install the intake gaskets (arrows) against each cylinder head

to break the gasket seal **(see illustration)**. **Caution:** *Don't pry between the manifold and the heads or damage to the gasket sealing surfaces may occur, leading to vacuum leaks.*

16   Loosen the rocker arm bolts, rotate the rocker arms out of the way and remove the pushrods that go through the manifold gaskets (see Section 5).

17   Lift the old gaskets off. Use a gasket scraper to remove all traces of sealant and old gasket material, then clean the mating surfaces with lacquer thinner or acetone. **Note:** *The mating surfaces of the cylinder heads, block and manifold must be perfectly clean when the manifold is installed. Gasket removal solvents are available at most auto parts stores and may be helpful when removing old gasket material that's stuck to the heads and manifold (since the manifold is made of aluminum, aggressive scraping can cause damage). Be sure to follow the directions printed on the container. If there's old sealant or oil on the mating surfaces when*

the manifold is installed, oil or vacuum leaks may develop. Use a vacuum cleaner to remove any gasket material that falls into the intake ports or the lifter valley.

18   Use a tap of the correct size to chase the threads in the bolt holes, if necessary, then use compressed air (if available) to remove the debris from the holes. **Warning:** *Wear safety glasses or a face shield to protect your eyes when using compressed air!*

19   Place the intake manifold gaskets in position on the heads **(see illustration)**. Then install the pushrods and rocker arms (see Section 4).

20   Apply a 3/16-inch (5 mm) bead of RTV sealant to the front and rear ridges of the engine block between the heads **(see illustration)**.

21   Carefully lower the manifold into place and install the mounting bolts/nuts finger tight. **Note:** *Coat the bolt threads with pipe sealant before installing them.*

22   Tighten the four vertical bolts (1 through 4) at the center of the manifold in the recommended tightening sequence **(see illustration)** to the torque listed in this Chapter's Specifications.

23   Tighten the four angled bolts (5 through 8) at the ends of the manifold in the recommended tightening sequence to the torque listed in this Chapter's Specifications. **Caution:** *To prevent oil leaks, tighten the vertical bolts first to ensure that the lower manifold stays centered on the gaskets, then tighten the angled bolts.*

24   Install the remaining components in the reverse order of removal.

25   Change the oil and filter and refill the cooling system (see Chapter 1). Start the engine and check for leaks.

8   Exhaust manifolds - removal and installation

Removal

1   Disconnect the cable from the negative terminal of the battery. **Caution:** *On models equipped with the Theftlock audio system, be sure you have the correct activation code before disconnecting the battery (see the front of this manual).*

2   Remove the air cleaner assembly and the air intake duct (see Chapter 4).

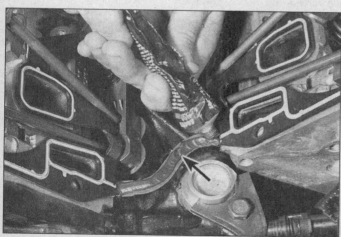

7.20 Apply a bead of sealant to the end ridges between the heads (arrow indicates ridge at transaxle end)

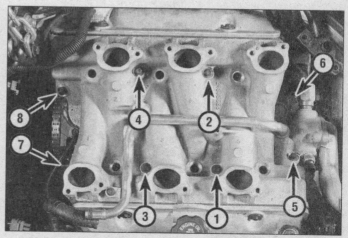

7.22 Intake manifold TIGHTENING sequence - make sure the bolts in the center (1 through 4) are completely tightened before tightening the end bolts (5 through 8)

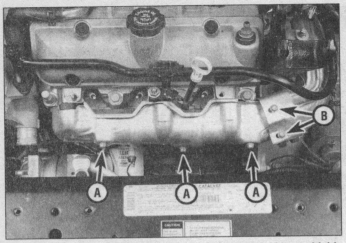

8.7 Remove the screws (A) and the exhaust manifold heat shield, then remove the exhaust crossover heat shield (B indicates the two front bolts, others are at the rear manifold)

8.8 Unbolt the crossover pipe where it joins the front manifold (arrows)

Front manifold

Refer to illustrations 8.7, 8.8 and 8.9

3   Allow the engine to cool completely, then drain the coolant (see Chapter 1).

4   Remove the upper radiator hose from the thermostat housing.

5   Remove the spark plug wires from the front spark plugs. Also remove the coolant by-pass pipe (see Section 4, Step 6).

6   Remove the engine mount struts and the passenger's side strut mount bracket from the engine (see Section 18).

7   Remove the crossover pipe heat shield and the manifold heat shield **(see illustration)**.

8   Unbolt the crossover pipe where it joins the front manifold **(see illustration)**. You should first apply penetrating oil to the fastener threads - they're usually rusted. **Note:** *After removing the three nuts, pull the crossover pipe back (the flexible joint toward the rear will allow some movement) and remove the three studs. There are hex portions on the studs. If the studs are not removed from the manifold, it is difficult to pull* the manifold from the cylinder head because the manifold is also mounted on studs.

9   Remove the mounting nuts and detach the manifold from the cylinder head **(see illustration)**.

Rear manifold

Refer to illustration 8.17

10   Remove the windshield wiper module cover (see Chapter 12). Also remove the engine cover if equipped **(see illustration 4.2)**.

11   Rotate the engine to the forward position (see Section 19).

12   Referring to Chapter 6, remove the EGR valve and the MAP sensor. After unbolting the EGR valve move the automatic transaxle dipstick tube aside.

13   Remove the ignition coil and module assembly (see Chapter 5) which also includes the solenoids for the vacuum canister and purge control (if equipped). Tag all disconnected wires and hoses, then detach the spark plug wires from the rear spark plugs and position the front plug wires aside, so they won't interfere with the removal of any remaining components.

14   Remove the crossover pipe heat shield and the manifold upper heat shield.

15   Unbolt the crossover pipe where it joins the rear manifold. You should first apply penetrating oil to the fastener threads - they're usually rusted.

16   Disconnect the electrical connector from oxygen sensor(s) and remove the EGR tube from the rear manifold (see Chapter 6). **Note:** *To help prevent possible damage to the oxygen sensor(s) it is recommended that the sensor(s) be removed from the exhaust manifold before the manifold is removed from the engine* (see Chapter 6).

17   Working under the vehicle, remove the exhaust pipe-to-manifold bolts and position the front exhaust pipe aside **(see illustration)**, then remove the manifold lower heat shield. **Note:** *You may have to apply penetrating oil to the fastener threads - they're usually corroded.*

18   Unbolt and remove the rear exhaust manifold.

8.9 Remove the six nuts (arrows indicate the upper three) from the exhaust manifold studs

8.17 Remove the nuts (arrows) holding the exhaust pipe to the rear manifold

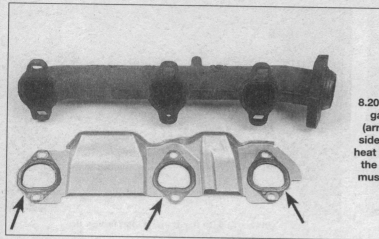

8.20 Examine the gasket areas (arrows) of both sides of the inner heat shield - if bad, the whole shield must be replaced

Installation (front or rear)

Refer to illustration 8.20

19   Clean the mating surfaces to remove all traces of old gasket material, then inspect the manifold for distortion and cracks. Warpage can be checked with a precision straightedge held against the mating flange. If a feeler gauge thicker than 0.030-inch can be inserted between the straightedge and flange surface, take the manifold to an automotive machine shop for resurfacing.

20   Remove the exhaust manifold inner heat shield (the gasket material is part of the inner heat shield) and examine the gasket areas for signs of corrosion or leakage **(see illustration)**. If the shield/gasket seems reusable, reinstall it, place the manifold in position and install the mounting bolts finger tight.

21   Starting in the middle and working out toward the ends, tighten the mounting bolts a little at a time until all of them are at the torque listed in this Chapter's Specifications.

22   Install the remaining components in the reverse order of removal.

23   Start the engine and check for exhaust leaks between the manifold and cylinder head and between the manifold and exhaust pipe.

9   Cylinder heads - removal and installation

Refer to illustrations 9.3, 9.11, 9.14a, 9.14b and 9.17

Removal

1   Disconnect the cable from the negative terminal of the battery. **Caution:** *On models equipped with the Theftlock audio system, be sure you have the correct activation code before disconnecting the battery (see the front of this manual).*

2   Remove the air cleaner assembly (see Chapter 4) and then remove the upper and lower intake manifold as described in Section 7. **Note:** *The engine must be rotated to the forward position during many procedures in this Chapter, including all procedures which*

require access to the right (rear) side of the engine. Many procedures that are associated with the left (front) side of the engine do not require the engine to be rotated. Only the components that are associated with the right cylinder head, valve cover, exhaust manifold, spark plugs, fuel, emission and electrical components from the centerline of the engine to firewall require the engine to be rotated.

3   If you're removing the front cylinder head, remove the oil dipstick tube mounting bolt **(see illustration)**.

4   Disconnect all wires and vacuum hoses from the cylinder head(s). Be sure to label them to simplify reinstallation.

5   Detach the exhaust manifold from the cylinder head being removed (see Section 8).

6   Remove the rocker arms and pushrods (see Section 5).

7   Using the new head gasket, outline the cylinders and bolt pattern on a piece of cardboard. Be sure to indicate the front (drivebelt end) of the engine for reference. Punch holes at the bolt locations. Loosen each of the cylinder head mounting bolts 1/4-turn at a time until they can be removed by hand - work from bolt-to-bolt in a pattern that's *reverse* of the tightening sequence **(see illustration 9.17)**. **Caution:** *The engine must be completely cool before loosening the cylinder*

head bolts. Store the bolts in the cardboard holder as they're removed - this will ensure they are reinstalled in their original locations, which is absolutely essential. Note which ones are studs and their location.

8   Lift the head(s) off the engine. If resistance is felt, don't pry between the head and block as damage to the mating surfaces will result. Recheck for head bolts that may have been overlooked, then use a hammer and block of wood to tap up on the head and break the gasket seal. Be careful because there are locating dowels in the block which position each head. As a last resort, pry each head up at the rear corner only and be careful not to damage anything. After removal, place the head on blocks of wood to prevent damage to the gasket surfaces.

9   Refer to Chapter 2, Part B, for cylinder head disassembly, inspection and valve service procedures.

Installation

10   The mating surfaces of each cylinder head and block must be perfectly clean when the head is installed.

11   Use a gasket scraper to remove all traces of carbon and old gasket material **(see illustration)**, then clean the mating surfaces with lacquer thinner or acetone. If there's oil on the mating surfaces when the head is installed, the gasket may not seal correctly and leaks may develop. When working on the block, it's a good idea to cover the lifter valley with shop rags to keep debris out of the engine. Use a shop rag or vacuum cleaner to remove any debris that falls into the cylinders.

12   Check the block and head mating surfaces for nicks, deep scratches and other damage. If damage is slight, it can be removed with a file; if it's excessive, machining may be the only alternative.

13   Use a tap of the correct size to chase the threads in the head bolt holes. Dirt, corrosion, sealant and damaged threads will affect torque readings.

14   Position the new gasket over the dowel pins in the block. Some gaskets are marked

2A

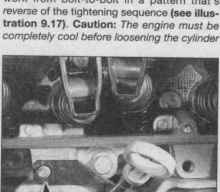

9.3 Remove the bolt (arrow) holding the oil dipstick tube to the front cylinder head

9.11 Remove the old gasket and carefully scrape off all old gasket material and sealant

9.14a Position the new gasket over the dowel pins (arrows) . . .

THIS SIDE UP

9.14b . . . with the correct side facing up

TOP or THIS SIDE UP to ensure correct installation **(see illustrations)**.

15 Carefully position the head on the block without disturbing the gasket.

16 Clean the bolt threads and install the bolts in the correct locations - two different lengths are used. Here's where the cardboard holder comes in handy.

17 Tighten the bolts, using the recommended sequence **(see illustration)**, to the torque listed in this Chapter's Specifications. Then, using the same sequence, turn each bolt the amount of angle listed in this Chapter's Specifications.

18 The remaining installation steps are the reverse of removal.

19 Change the engine oil and filter (see Chapter 1).

9.17 Cylinder head bolt TIGHTENING sequence

10 Crankshaft pulley - removal and installation

Refer to illustrations 10.5, 10.6, and 10.7

1 Disconnect the cable from the negative terminal of the battery. **Caution:** *On models equipped with the Theftlock audio system, be sure you have the correct activation code before disconnecting the battery (see the front of this manual).*

2 With the parking brake applied and the shifter in Park (automatic) or in gear (manual), loosen the lug nuts from the right front wheel, then raise the front of the vehicle and support it securely on jackstands.

3 Remove the right front wheel and the right splash shield from the wheelwell.

4 Remove the drivebelt (see Chapter 1).

5 Remove the bolt from the front of the crankshaft **(see illustration)**. The bolt is normally very tight, so use a large breaker bar and a six-point socket to remove it. **Note 1:** *Remove the driveplate cover and position a large screwdriver in the ring gear teeth to keep the crankshaft from turning while an assistant removes the crankshaft pulley bolt.* **Note 2:** *It will be necessary to support the right side of the engine subframe with a floor jack. Loosen the right side subframe bolts and lower the subframe to allow clearance for*

the removal of the crankshaft pulley and the pulley bolt.

6 Using a puller that bolts to the crankshaft hub, remove the crankshaft pulley/balancer from the crankshaft **(see illustration)**. **Caution:** *On these engines a rubber sleeve connects the inertia weight to the balancer hub. Take care when working on the crankshaft pulley/balancer that you do not accidentally shift the inertia weight's position relative to the sleeve or balancer hub, as this will upset the tuning of the balancer.*

7 Position the crankshaft pulley/balancer on the crankshaft and slide it on as far as it will go. Note that the slot (keyway) in the hub must be aligned with the Woodruff key in the end of the crankshaft **(see illustration)**.

8 Using a crankshaft balancer installation tool, press the crankshaft pulley/balancer onto the crankshaft. Note that the crankshaft bolt can also be used to press the crankshaft balancer into position, but when doing so, use a liberal amount of clean engine oil on the bolt threads to prevent galling.

10.5 Remove the crankshaft bolt (arrow) - it's very tight, so use a six-point socket and a breaker bar

10.6 Use a puller that bolts to the crankshaft pulley hub; jaw-type pullers will damage the crankshaft pulley

10.7 The pulley keyway must be aligned with the Woodruff key (arrow) in the crankshaft nose

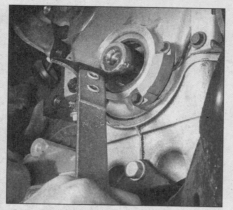

11.2 Carefully pry the old seal out of the timing chain cover - don't damage the crankshaft in the process

11.3 Drive the new seal into place with a large socket and hammer

9   Tighten the crankshaft bolt to the torque listed in this Chapter's Specifications.
10   The remaining installation steps are the reverse of removal.

11   Crankshaft front oil seal - removal and installation

Refer to illustrations 11.2, 11.3 and 11.4

1   Remove the crankshaft pulley (see Section 10).
2   Note how the seal is installed - the new one must be installed to the same depth and facing the same way. Carefully pry the oil seal out of the cover with a seal puller or a large screwdriver **(see illustration)**. Be very careful not to distort the cover or scratch the crankshaft! Wrap electrician's tape around the tip of the screwdriver to avoid damage to the crankshaft.
3   Apply clean engine oil or multi-purpose grease to the outer edge of the new seal, then install it in the cover with the lip (spring side) facing IN. Drive the seal into place **(see illustration)** with a large socket and a hammer (if a large socket isn't available, a piece of pipe will also work). Make sure the seal enters the bore squarely and stop when the front face is flush with the timing cover.
4   Check the surface on the pulley hub that the oil seal rides on. if the surface has been grooved from long time contact with the seal, a press on sleeve may be available to renew the sealing surface **(see illustration)**. This sleeve is pressed into place with a hammer and a block of wood and is commonly available at auto parts stores for various applications.
5   Lubricate the pulley hub with clean engine oil and reinstall the crankshaft pulley. Use a vibration damper installation tool to press the pulley onto the crankshaft.
6   Install the crankshaft pulley retaining bolt and tighten it to the torque listed in this Chapter's Specifications.
7   The remainder of installation is the reverse of the removal.

12   Timing chain and sprockets - removal, inspection and installation

Removal

Refer to illustrations 12.7, 12.9a, 12.9b, 12.12a, 12.12b and 12.14

1   Disconnect the cable from the negative terminal of the battery. **Caution:** *On models equipped with the Theftlock audio system, be sure you have the correct activation code before disconnecting the battery (see the front of this manual).*
2   Drain the coolant and engine oil (see Chapter 1).
3   Loosen, but do not remove, the water pump pulley bolts, then remove the serpentine drivebelt (see Chapter 1).
4   Remove the water pump pulley (see Chapter 3).
5   Remove the crankshaft pulley (see Section 10).
6   Disconnect the electrical connector at the crankshaft position sensor and detach the wiring harness brackets from the front cover (see Chapter 6).
7   Unbolt the drivebelt tensioner and idler

11.4 If the sealing surface of the pulley hub has a wear groove from contact with the seal, repair sleeves are available at most auto parts stores

pulley **(see illustration)**.
8   Unbolt the power steering pump and tie it aside (see Chapter 10). Leave the hoses connected.
9   Disconnect the coolant hoses from the bypass pipe and water pump housing, and remove the coolant bypass pipe from the front cover **(see illustrations)**.

2A

12.7 The drivebelt tensioner is secured to the timing chain cover by a bolt (arrow)

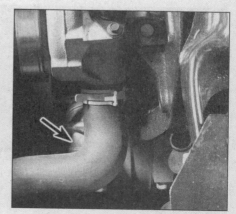

12.9a Disconnect the radiator hose (arrow) from the water pump housing

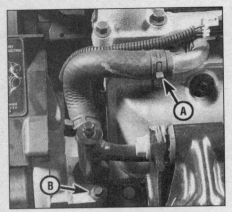

12.9b Disconnect the hose at the intake manifold pipe (A), then remove the bolt (B) at the bypass and pull the bypass from the front cover

12.12a Timing chain cover bolt locations (arrows), upper . . .

10   Remove the starter (see Chapter 5).
11   Remove the oil pan (see Section 14). **Note:** *The front cover can be removed with the oil pan in place, but the pan must be removed for a good installation to seal against the bottom of the front cover.*
12   Remove the timing chain cover-to-engine block bolts **(see illustrations)**.
13   Separate the cover from the engine. If it's stuck, tap it with a soft-face hammer, but don't try to pry it off.
14   Temporarily install the crankshaft pulley bolt and turn the crankshaft with the bolt to align the timing marks on the crankshaft and camshaft sprockets. When aligned at TDC for number 1 piston, the crankshaft sprocket timing mark should align with the mark on the bottom of the chain tensioner plate, and the small hole in the camshaft sprocket should be at the 6 o'clock position, aligned with the timing mark in the top of the chain tensioner plate **(see illustration)**.
15   Remove the camshaft sprocket bolt. Do not turn the camshaft in the process (if you do, realign the timing marks before the bolt is removed).
16   Use two large screwdrivers to carefully pry the camshaft sprocket off the camshaft

dowel pin. Slip the timing chain and camshaft sprocket off the engine.

Inspection

Refer to illustration 12.18

17   The timing chain should be replaced with a new one if the engine has high mileage, the chain has visible damage, or total freeplay midway between the sprockets exceeds one-inch. Failure to replace a worn timing chain may result in erratic engine performance, loss of power and decreased fuel mileage. Loose chains can "jump" timing. In the worst case, chain "jumping" or breakage will result in severe engine damage. Always replace the timing chain and sprockets in sets. If you intend to install a new timing chain, remove the crankshaft sprocket with a puller and install a new one. Be sure to align the key in the crankshaft with the keyway in the sprocket during installation.
18   Inspect the timing chain damper (guide) for cracks and wear and replace it if necessary. The damper is held to the engine block by two bolts **(see illustration)**. The damper should be reinstalled before installing the new timing chain and sprockets.
19   Clean the timing chain and sprockets with solvent and dry them with compressed air (if available). **Warning:** *Wear eye protection when using compressed air.*

20   Inspect the components for wear and damage. Look for teeth that are deformed, chipped, pitted and cracked.

Installation

21   If the camshaft has turned at all since removal of the sprocket, turn the camshaft to position the dowel pin at 3 o'clock. Mesh the timing chain with the camshaft sprocket, then engage it with the crankshaft sprocket. The timing marks should be aligned as shown in **illustration 12.14. Note:** *If the crankshaft has been disturbed, turn it until the "O" stamped on the crankshaft sprocket is exactly at the top.*
22   Install the camshaft sprocket bolt (make sure the dowel hole in the sprocket is aligned

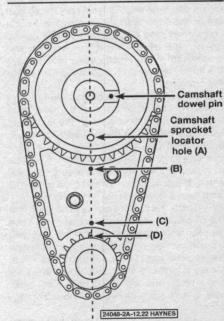

Camshaft dowel pin
Camshaft sprocket locator hole (A)
(B)
(C)
(D)

24048-2A-12.22 HAYNES

12.14 The timing marks on the sprockets should align as shown - a straight line should pass through the center of the camshaft, camshaft sprocket locator hole (A), the upper mark on the tensioner (B), the lower mark on the tensioner (C), the crankshaft sprocket timing mark (D) and the center of the crankshaft

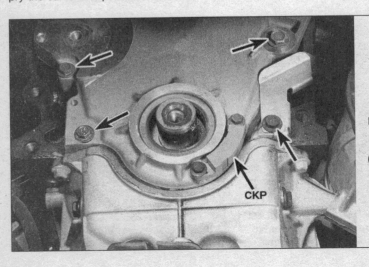

CKP

12.12b . . . and lower (arrows) - the crankshaft position sensor (CKP) should be unbolted and laid aside

12.18 The timing chain damper (guide) is retained by two bolts (arrows)

13.5 Remove the bolts (A) and pull up the roller lifter guides (B)

with the dowel pin in the camshaft) and tighten to the torque listed in this Chapter's Specifications.

23 Lubricate the chain and sprocket with clean engine oil.

24 Use a gasket scraper to remove all traces of old gasket material and sealant from the cover and engine block. The cover is made of aluminum, so be careful not to nick or gouge it. Clean the gasket sealing surfaces with lacquer thinner or acetone.

25 Apply a thin layer of anaerobic sealant to both sides of the new gasket, then position the gasket on the engine block (the dowel pins should keep it in place). Apply sealant to the bottom of the gasket, where it meets the oil pan.

26 Attach the cover to the engine and install the bolts. Follow a criss-cross pattern when tightening the fasteners and work up to the torque listed in this Chapter's Specifications in three steps.

27 The remainder of installation is the reverse of removal. Refer to Section 14 for oil pan installation.

28 Add oil and coolant, start the engine and check for leaks.

13 Valve lifters - removal, inspection and installation

1 A noisy valve lifter can be isolated when the engine is idling. Hold a mechanic's stethoscope or a length of hose near the location of each valve while listening at the other end. Another method is to remove the valve cover and, with the engine idling, touch each of the valve spring retainers, one at a time. If a valve lifter is defective, it'll be evident from the shock felt at the retainer each time the valve seats.

2 The most likely causes of noisy valve lifters are dirt trapped inside the lifter and lack of oil flow, viscosity or pressure. Before condemning the lifters, check the oil for fuel contamination, correct level, cleanliness and correct viscosity.

Removal

Refer to illustrations 13.5, 13.6a, 13.6b and 13.7

3 Remove the valve cover(s) and intake manifold as described in Sections 4 and 7.

4 Remove the rocker arms and pushrods

(see Section 5).

5 Remove the bolts holding the roller lifter guide to the block, and remove the two roller lifter guides **(see illustration)**. Mark the guides as to which side they came from.

6 There are several ways to extract the lifters from the bores. A special tool designed to grip and remove lifters is manufactured by many tool companies and is widely available, but it may not be required in every case. On newer engines without a lot of varnish buildup, the lifters can often be removed with a small magnet or even with your fingers. A machinist's scribe with a bent end can be used to pull the lifters out by positioning the point under the retainer ring in the top of each lifter **(see illustrations)**. **Caution:** *Don't use pliers to remove the lifters unless you intend to replace them with new ones (along with the camshaft). The pliers may damage the precision machined and hardened lifters, rendering them useless.*

7 Before removing the lifters, arrange to store them in a clearly labeled box to ensure they're reinstalled in their original locations. Remove the lifters and store them where they won't get dirty **(see illustration)**.

2A

13.6a A magnetic pick-up tool . . .

13.6b . . . or a scribe can be used to remove the lifters

13.7 Store the lifters in order to ensure installation in their original locations

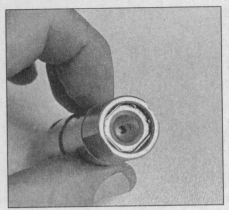

13.10a Check the pushrod seat in the top of each lifter for wear

13.10b The roller on the roller lifters must turn freely - check for wear and excessive play as well

14.3 Disconnect the oil level sensor connector (arrow) if equipped

Inspection and installation

Refer to illustrations 13.10a and 13.10b

8   Parts for valve lifters are not available separately. The work required to remove them from the engine again if cleaning is unsuccessful outweighs any potential savings from repairing them.

9   Clean the lifters thoroughly with solvent and dry them thoroughly, without mixing them up.

10   Check each lifter wall and plunger seat for scuffing, score marks or uneven wear **(see illustration)**. Check the rollers carefully for wear or damage and make sure they turn freely without excessive play **(see illustration)**. If the lifters walls are worn (not very likely), inspect the lifter bores in the block. If the pushrod seats are worn, inspect the pushrods also.

11   When reinstalling used lifters, make sure they're replaced in their original bores. Coat all lifters with moly-base grease or engine assembly lube prior to installation.

12   Install the push rods and the rocker arms (see Section 5).

13   The remaining installation steps are the reverse of removal.

14   Run the engine and check for oil leaks.

14   Oil pan - removal and installation

Note: *This procedure requires an engine support fixture to secure the engine from above when the engine mounts are removed. Make sure you have these tools or rent them before beginning the procedure.*

Removal

Refer to illustrations 14.3, 14.10, 14.15, 14.16a, 14.16b and 14.17

1   Disconnect the cable from the negative terminal of the battery. **Caution:** *On models equipped with the Theftlock audio system, be sure you have the correct activation code before disconnecting the battery (see the front of this manual).*

2   Remove the engine mount torque struts (see Section 18).

3   Raise the front of the vehicle and place it securely on jackstands. Apply the parking brake and block the rear wheels to keep it from rolling off the stands. Remove the lower splash pan and drain the engine oil (refer to Chapter 1 if necessary). Disconnect the oil-level sensor connector from the sensor **(see illustration)**.

4   Refer to Chapter 3 and unbolt the air conditioning compressor and set it aside without disconnecting the refrigerant lines.

5   Remove the front exhaust pipe.

6   Detach the lower ball joints from the steering knuckles (see Chapter 10). Disconnect the clips securing the ABS sensor wiring harness and let the lower control arms hang down.

7   Remove the steering gear mounting bolts (see Chapter 10). Also detach the power steering lines from the clips on the engine subframe.

8   Remove the flywheel/driveplate lower cover.

9   Remove the starter (see Chapter 5).

10   Remove the hood (see Chapter 11) and support the engine with a support fixture **(see illustration)**.

11   Refer to Section 18 and remove the lower retaining nuts from the driver's and passenger side engine mounts, then remove the passenger side mount and bracket from the oil pan.

12   Place a floor jack under the right side of the engine subframe.

13   Loosen the left side subframe bolts - DO

14.10 Attach chains to the front and rear engine lifting eyes and support the engine with an engine support fixture

14.15 Remove these bolts (arrows) at the pan and transmission, then remove the transmission-to-engine brace if equipped

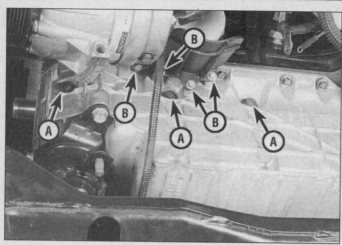

14.16a Remove the oil pan side bolts (A indicates the three bolts on the radiator side) - also remove the oil filter shield bolts (B) if equipped

14.16b The side bolts on the rear side of the oil pan are more difficult to remove, but a box-end wrench with an offset bend in it can remove them

NOT REMOVE THEM!

14   Remove the right side subframe bolts and lower the right side of the subframe. Remove the serpentine drivebelt and the crankshaft pulley.

15   At the rear side of the oil pan, remove the bolts and the brace (if equipped) from the transaxle-to-engine **(see illustration).**

16   Remove the three side bolts (connecting the sides of the cast aluminum oil pan to the main cap supports) on each side of the oil pan **(see illustrations).** Also remove the oil filter shield bolted to the top front of the pan and any wiring harness retaining clips that are attached to the oil pan.

17   Remove the remaining 12 oil pan-to-block bolts, then carefully separate the oil pan from the block **(see illustration).** Don't pry between the block and the pan or damage to the sealing surfaces could occur and oil leaks may develop. Instead, tap the pan with a soft-face hammer to break the gasket seal.

Installation

Refer to illustration 14.19

18   Clean the pan with solvent and remove all old sealant and gasket material from the block and pan mating surfaces. Clean the mating surfaces with lacquer thinner or acetone and make sure the bolt holes in the block are clear.

19   Apply a bead of RTV sealant to the front of the gasket, where it contacts the front cover, and a short bead (9/32-inch wide) to either side of the rear main cap where it meets the block, then install the new one-piece oil pan gasket **(see illustration).**

20   Place the oil pan in position on the block and install the nuts/bolts.

21   After the pan-to-block fasteners are installed, tighten them to the torque listed in this Chapter's Specifications. Starting at the center, follow a criss-cross pattern and work up to the final torque in three steps.

22   After all the pan-to-block bolts have been torqued, install the oil pan side bolts and tighten them to Specifications.

23   The remaining steps are the reverse of the removal procedure.

24   Refill the engine with oil, run it until normal operating temperature is reached and check for leaks.

15   Oil pump - removal and installation

2A

Refer to illustration 15.2

1   Remove the oil pan (see Section 14).

2   Unbolt the oil pump and lower it from the engine **(see illustration).** **Note:** *The oil pump driveshaft will come out with the pump as you lower it. It's a rod with a flat-sided portion at each end.*

3   If the pump is defective, replace it with a new one - don't reuse the original or attempt to rebuild it. Inspect the ends of the oil pump driveshaft and the plastic collar that retains the driveshaft to the oil pump. If there are signs of wear on the shaft or if the plastic collar is cracked or missing, replace the shaft with a new one. **Note:** *The plastic collar centers the oil pump driveshaft over the oil pump shaft. If the collar is not used or is missing, damage to the oil pump driveshaft and the oil*

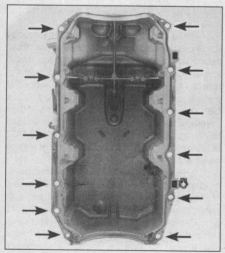

14.17   Remove the 12 oil pan-to-block bolts (arrows) - pan removed for clarity

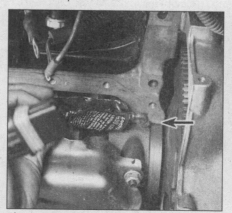

14.19 Apply a bead of RTV sealant on either side of the rear main cap, where the pan gasket will meet it (arrow)

15.2 Oil pump mounting bolt location (arrow)

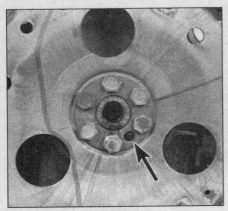

16.2a Most driveplates have locating dowels (arrow) - if the one you're working on doesn't have one, make some marks to ensure proper alignment on reassembly

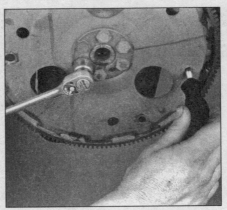

16.2b A large screwdriver wedged in one of the holes in the driveplate can be used to keep the driveplate from turning as the mounting bolts are removed

17.4 Carefully pry the old seal out

pump will occur. A new plastic collar is usually included with a new oil pump or driveshaft.

4   Prime the pump by pouring clean engine oil into the pick-up screen while turning the pump driveshaft.

5   To install the pump, turn the flat on the driveshaft so it mates with the slot in the oil pump shaft. Make sure the plastic collar is fitted over the oil pump-to-oil pump driveshaft joint, then install the oil pump and driveshaft assembly into the block while engaging the upper end of the oil pump driveshaft into the oil pump drive.

6   Install the pump mounting bolt and tighten it to the torque listed in this Chapter's Specifications.

7   The remainder of assembly is the reverse of the removal procedure.

16   Driveplate - removal and installation

Removal

Refer to illustrations 16.2a and 16.2b

1   Raise the vehicle and support it securely on jackstands, then refer to Chapter 7 and remove the transaxle.

2   Remove the bolts that secure the driveplate to the crankshaft **(see illustration)**. If the crankshaft turns, insert a screwdriver through one of the holes in the driveplate **(see illustration)**. **Note:** *If there is a retaining ring between the bolts and the driveplate, note which side faces the driveplate when removing it.*

3   Remove the driveplate from the crankshaft. Be sure to support it while removing the last bolt. **Warning:** *Wear gloves to protect your fingers - the edges of the ring gear teeth may be sharp.*

4   Clean the driveplate to remove grease and oil. Inspect the surface for cracks, and check for cracked and broken ring gear teeth. Lay the driveplate on a flat surface to check for warpage.

5   Clean and inspect the mating surfaces of the driveplate and the crankshaft. If the crankshaft rear seal is leaking, replace it before reinstalling the driveplate (see Section 17).

Installation

6   Position the driveplate against the crankshaft. Be sure to align the marks made during removal. Note that some engines have an alignment dowel or staggered bolt holes to ensure correct installation. Before installing the bolts, apply thread locking compound to the threads and place the retaining ring in position on the flywheel/driveplate.

7   Prevent the driveplate from turning as you tighten the bolts to the torque listed in this Chapter's Specifications. If the front pump seal/O-ring on the transaxle is leaking, now would be a very good time to replace it.

8   The remainder of installation is the reverse of the removal procedure.

17   Rear main oil seal - replacement

Refer to illustration 17.4

1   Remove the transaxle (see Chapter 7).

2   Remove the driveplate (see Section 16).

3   Inspect the oil seal, as well as the oil pan and engine block surface for signs of leakage. Sometimes an oil pan gasket leak can appear to be a rear oil seal leak.

4   Pry the oil seal from the block with a screwdriver **(see illustration)**. Be careful not to nick or scratch the crankshaft or the seal bore. Thoroughly clean the seal bore in the block with a shop towel. Remove all traces of oil and dirt.

5   Lubricate the lips of the new seal with engine oil or multi-purpose grease. Install the seal over the end of the crankshaft (make sure the lips of the seal point toward the engine) and carefully tap it into place. A special aftermarket tool may be available at your local auto parts store. The tool just fits the diameter of the seal and, used with a ham-

mer, drives the seal in. **Note:** *Do not drive it in any further than the original seal was installed.*

6   Install the driveplate (see Section 16).

7   Install the transaxle (see Chapter 7).

18   Powertrain mounts - check and replacement

1   Powertrain mounts seldom require attention, but broken or deteriorated mounts should be replaced immediately or the added strain placed on the driveline components may cause damage or wear. The 3.4L engine is equipped with two powertrain mounts and two torque struts. The driver's side mount attaches the transaxle to the engine subframe, while the passenger side mount attaches the front of the oil pan to the engine subframe. The torque struts are mounted on the side of the engine (at the front of the engine compartment) to control rotational torque and limit the engine's movement.

Check

2   During the check, the engine must be raised slightly to remove the weight from the mounts.

3   Raise the vehicle and support it securely on jackstands. Support the engine from above using an engine support fixture (available at rental yards). If the special support fixture is unavailable, position a jack under the engine oil pan. Place a large wood block between the jack head and the oil pan, then carefully raise the engine just enough to take the weight off the mounts. **Warning:** *DO NOT place any part of your body under the engine when it's supported only by a jack!*

4   Check the mounts to see if the rubber is cracked, hardened or separated from the metal plates. Sometimes the rubber will split right down the center.

5   Check for relative movement between the mount plates and the engine or frame (use a large screwdriver or pry bar to attempt to move the mounts). If movement is noted, lower the engine and tighten the mount fasteners.

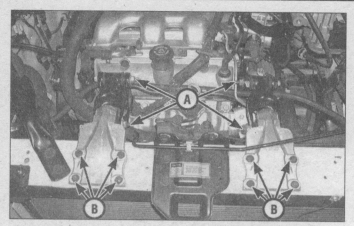

18.7 Engine mount torque strut retaining bolts (A) and the radiator side strut-bracket bolts (B)

18.8a Removing the passenger side strut bracket bolts (arrow indicates upper bolt)

Replacement

Refer to illustrations 18.7, 18.8a, 18.8b, 18.12a, 18.12b, 18.12c and 18.12d

6   Disconnect the cable from the negative terminal of the battery. **Caution:** *On models equipped with the Theftlock audio system, be sure you have the correct activation code before disconnecting the battery (see the front of this manual).*

Engine mount torque struts and brackets

7   To remove the engine mount torque struts, simply remove the retaining bolts and detach the struts from the strut brackets **(see illustration)**.

8   To remove the torque strut brackets, remove the bolts from the engine or the radiator support and remove the brackets from the vehicle **(see illustrations)**. On the driver's side bracket it will be necessary to remove the thermostat housing cover first (see Chapter 3).

9   Installation is the reverse of removal. Tighten the bolts to torque listed in this Chapter's Specifications.

Engine and transaxle mounts

10   The transaxle mount is located on the driver's side of the vehicle and the engine mount is located on the passenger's side of the vehicle. Loosen the front wheel lug nuts from the side in which you want to change the mount. Raise the front of the vehicle and support it securely on jackstands. Remove the wheel and the lower splash shield from the wheelwell.

11   Remove air intake duct from the throttle body. Also remove the front exhaust pipe from the rear exhaust manifold (see Chapter 4).

12   Raise the engine slightly with a jack or hoist. If you're using a floor jack, make sure to place a block of wood between the jack and the oil pan to prevent damage. Remove the bolts holding the mount bracket to the engine or to the transaxle, then remove the lower nuts securing the mount to the subframe **(see illustrations)**.

13   Raise the engine until you can remove the mount, then remove the mount bracket from the old mount and install the bracket onto the new mount.

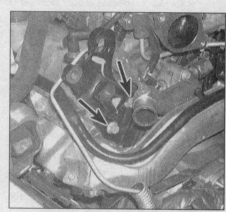

18.8b Driver's side strut bracket bolts (arrows indicate the two upper bolts, lower bolt not visible)

14   Installation is the reverse of removal. Use thread-locking compound on the mount bolts and be sure to tighten them securely to this Chapter's Specifications.

18.12a The engine mount (A) is located between the front of the oil pan and the chassis on the passenger side of the vehicle - with the engine supported from above remove the bolts (arrows) holding the bracket to the oil pan . . .

18.12b . . . and the nuts (arrows) securing the mount to the subframe from below, then unbolt the mount from the engine bracket and install the new mount

2A

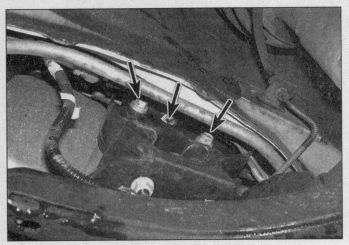

18.12c Transaxle mount bracket bolts (arrows) . . .

18.12d . . . and the transaxle mount-to-subframe nuts (arrows)

19   Rotating the engine

Refer to illustration 19.4

1   Block the rear wheels, place the transaxle in neutral and disconnect the cable from the negative terminal of the battery. **Caution:** *On models equipped with the Theft-lock audio system, be sure you have the correct activation code before disconnecting the battery (see the front of this manual).*

2   Remove the air cleaner duct and air cleaner. Also remove the accelerator cable and the cruise control cable from the throttle body (see Chapter 4).

3   Remove the two bolts and detach the driver's side torque strut from the vehicle **(see illustration 18.7)**. Remove one bolt from the radiator side of the passenger side torque strut and pivot the passenger side torque strut towards the engine.

4   Attach a ratcheting strap to the front the radiator support and to the engine lifting eye

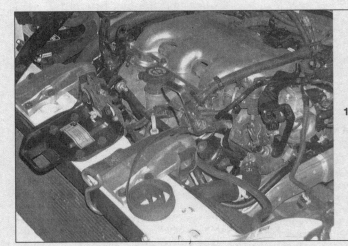

19.4 Rotate the engine forward with a ratcheting strap

on the driver's side strut bracket, then ratchet the strap to tilt the engine toward the radiator side **(see illustration)**.

5   Reverse the procedure when you have completed the task that required rotating the engine. Tighten the engine torque struts to the torque listed in this Chapter's Specifications.

Chapter 2 Part B
General engine overhaul procedures

Contents

Specifications

General

VIN code	E
Displacement	204 cubic inches (3.4 liters)
Bore and stroke	3.62 x 3.31 inches
Cylinder numbers (drivebelt end-to-transaxle end)	
Front bank (radiator side)	2-4-6
Rear bank	1-3-5
Firing order	1-2-3-4-5-6
Cylinder compression pressure	100 psi minimum
Maximum variation between cylinders	30-percent
Oil pressure	15 psi at 1100 rpm

Cylinder head

Warpage limit	0.005 inch*

*If more than 0.010 inch must be removed, replace the head

Valves and related components

Valve face angle.. 45-degrees
Valve seat angle (intake and exhaust) 45-degrees
Valve margin width, minimum
    Intake.. 0.083 inch
    Exhaust... 0.106 inch
Valve stem-to-guide clearance... 0.0010 to 0.0027 inch
Valve spring free length (intake and exhaust)...................... 1.89 inches
Installed height .... 1.701 inches

Crankshaft and connecting rods

Connecting rod journal
    Diameter.. 1.9987 to 1.9994 inches
    Bearing oil clearance... 0.0007 to 0.0024 inch
Connecting rod side clearance (endplay) .... 0.007 to 0.017 inch
Main bearing journal
    Diameter.. 2.6473 to 2.6483 inches
    Bearing oil clearance... 0.0008 to 0.0025 inch
    Taper/out-of-round limit... 0.0002 inch
Crankshaft endplay (at thrust bearing) .... 0.0024 to 0.0083 inch

Engine block

Cylinder bore
    Out-of-round limit.. 0.0003 inch
    Taper limit (thrust side)... 0.0004 inch
    Diameter.. 3.6228 to 3.6235 inches
Block deck warpage limit .... If more than 0.010 inch must be removed, replace the block

Pistons and rings

Piston-to-bore clearance.. 0.0013 to 0.0027 inch
Piston ring end gap
    Top compression ring .... 0.006 to 0.014 inch
    Second compression ring .... 0.0197 to 0.0280 inch
    Oil control ring .... 0.0098 to 0.050 inch
Piston ring side clearance
    Compression ring .... 0.002 to 0.0033 inch
    Oil control ring .... 0.008 inch

Camshaft

Bearing journal diameter.. 1.868 to 1.869 inches
Bearing oil clearance .... 0.001 to 0.0039 inch
Lobe lift .... 0.2727 inch

Torque specifications**   **Ft-lbs (unless otherwise indicated)**

Main bearing caps, bolts/studs
    Step 1 37
    Step 2 .... Tighten an additional 77 degrees
Connecting rod caps
    Step 1 15
    Step 2 .... Tighten an additional 75 degrees
Camshaft thrust plate screw.. 89 in-lbs

**Note:* Refer to Part A for additional torque specifications.*

1   General information - engine overhaul

Included in this portion of Chapter 2 are the general overhaul procedures for the cylinder head and internal engine components.

The information ranges from advice concerning preparation for an overhaul and the purchase of replacement parts to detailed, step-by-step procedures covering removal and installation of internal engine components and the inspection of parts.

The following Sections have been written based on the assumption that the engine has been removed from the vehicle. For information concerning in-vehicle engine repair, as well as removal and installation of the external components necessary for the overhaul, see Chapter 2A and Section 8 of this Chapter.

The Specifications included in this Part are only those necessary for the inspection and overhaul procedures which follow. Refer to Chapter 2, Part A for additional Specifications.

It's not always easy to determine when, or if, an engine should be completely overhauled, as a number of factors must be considered.

High mileage is not necessarily an indication that an overhaul is needed, while low mileage doesn't preclude the need for an overhaul. Frequency of servicing is probably the most important consideration. An engine that's had regular and frequent oil and filter changes, as well as other required maintenance, will most likely give many thousands of miles of reliable service. Conversely, a neglected engine may require an overhaul very early in its life.

Excessive oil consumption is an indication that piston rings, valve seals and/or valve guides are in need of attention. Make sure that oil leaks aren't responsible before deciding that the rings and/or guides are bad. Perform a cylinder compression check to determine the extent of the work required (see Section 3). Also check the vacuum readings under various conditions (see Section 4).

Loss of power, rough running, knocking or metallic engine noises, excessive valve train noise and high fuel consumption rates may also point to the need for an overhaul, especially if they're all present at the same time. If a complete tune-up doesn't remedy the situation, major mechanical work is the only solution.

An engine overhaul involves restoring the internal parts to the specifications of a new engine. During an overhaul, the piston rings are replaced and the cylinder walls are reconditioned (re-bored and/or honed). If a re-bore is done by an automotive machine shop, new oversize pistons will also be installed. The main bearings, connecting rod bearings and camshaft bearings are generally replaced with new ones and, if necessary, the crankshaft may be reground to restore the journals. Generally, the valves are serviced as

well, since they're usually in less-than-perfect condition at this point. While the engine is being overhauled, other components, such as the starter and alternator, can be rebuilt as well. The end result should be a like new engine that will give many trouble free miles. **Note:** *Critical cooling system components such as the hoses, drivebelts, thermostat and water pump should be replaced with new parts when an engine is overhauled. The radiator should be checked carefully to ensure that it isn't clogged or leaking (see Chapter 3). If you purchase a rebuilt engine or short block, some rebuilders will not warranty their engines unless the radiator has been professionally flushed. Also, we don't recommend overhauling the oil pump - always install a new one when an engine is rebuilt.*

Before beginning the engine overhaul, read through the entire procedure to familiarize yourself with the scope and requirements of the job. Overhauling an engine isn't difficult, but it is time-consuming. Plan on the vehicle being tied up for a minimum of two weeks, especially if parts must be taken to an automotive machine shop for repair or reconditioning. Check on availability of parts and make sure that any necessary special tools and equipment are obtained in advance. Most work can be done with typical hand tools, although a number of precision measuring tools are required for inspecting parts to determine if they must be replaced. Often an automotive machine shop will handle the inspection of parts and offer advice concerning reconditioning and replacement. **Note:** *Always wait until the engine has been completely disassembled and all components, especially the engine block, have been inspected before deciding what service and repair operations must be performed by an automotive machine shop. Since the block's condition will be the major factor to consider when determining whether to overhaul the original engine or buy a rebuilt one, never purchase parts or have machine work done on other components until the block has been thoroughly inspected.* As a general rule, time is the primary cost of an overhaul, so it doesn't pay to install worn or substandard parts.

As a final note, to ensure maximum life and minimum trouble from a rebuilt engine, everything must be assembled with care in a spotlessly-clean environment.

2   Oil pressure check

Refer to illustration 2.2

1   Low engine oil pressure can be a sign of an engine in need of rebuilding. A "low oil pressure" indicator (often called an "idiot light") is not a test of the oiling system. Such indicators only come on when the oil pressure is dangerously low. Even a factory oil pressure gauge in the instrument panel is only a relative indication, although much better for driver information than a warning light.

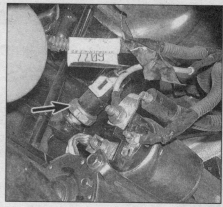

2.2 The oil pressure sending unit (arrow) is located next to the oil filter

A better test is with a mechanical (not electrical) oil pressure gauge. When used in conjunction with an accurate tachometer, an engine's oil pressure performance can be compared to the manufacturer's Specifications.

2   Find the oil pressure indicator sending unit **(see illustration)**.

3   Remove the oil pressure sending unit and install a fitting which will allow you to directly connect your hand-held, mechanical oil pressure gauge. Use Teflon tape or sealant on the threads of the adapter and the fitting on the end of your gauge's hose.

4   Connect an accurate tachometer to the engine, according to the tachometer manufacturer's instructions.

5   Check the oil pressure with the engine running (full operating temperature) at the specified engine speed, and compare it to this Chapter's Specifications. If it's extremely low, the bearings and/or oil pump are probably worn out.

3   Cylinder compression check

Refer to illustration 3.6

1   A compression check will tell you what mechanical condition the upper end (pistons, rings, valves, head gaskets) of the engine is in. Specifically, it can tell you if the compression is down due to leakage caused by worn piston rings, defective valves and seats or a blown head gasket. **Note:** *The engine must be at normal operating temperature and the battery must be fully charged for this check.*

2   Begin by cleaning the area around the spark plugs before you remove them. Compressed air should be used, if available, otherwise a small brush will work. The idea is to prevent dirt from getting into the cylinders as the compression check is being done.

3   Remove all of the spark plugs from the engine (see Chapter 1).

4   Block the throttle wide open.

5   Disable the ignition system by disconnecting the wires to the ignition control module (see Chapter 5). Also, disable the fuel injection system by unplugging the electrical

2B

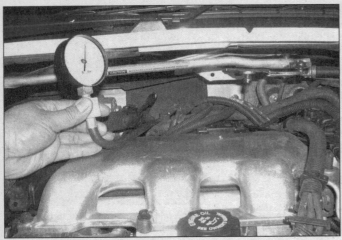

3.6 A compression gauge with a threaded fitting for the spark plug hole is preferred over the type that requires hand pressure to maintain the seal - be sure to open the throttle valve as far as possible during the compression check

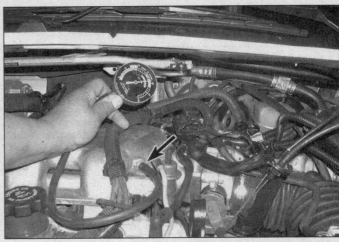

4.4 A simple vacuum gauge, attached to a manifold vacuum port (arrow) can be very useful when trying to diagnose an engine's condition

connector to the injector wiring harness or by removing the fuel pump fuse.

6   Install the compression gauge in the number one spark plug hole **(see illustration)**.

7   Crank the engine over at least seven compression strokes and watch the gauge. The compression should build up quickly in a healthy engine. Low compression on the first stroke, followed by gradually increasing pressure on successive strokes, indicates worn piston rings. A low compression reading on the first stroke, which doesn't build up during successive strokes, indicates leaking valves or a blown head gasket (a cracked head could also be the cause). Deposits on the undersides of the valve heads can also cause low compression. Record the highest gauge reading obtained.

8   Repeat the procedure for the remaining cylinders, turning the engine over for the same length of time for each cylinder, and compare the results to this Chapter's Specifications.

9   If the readings are below normal, add some engine oil (about three squirts from a plunger-type oil can) to each cylinder, through the spark plug hole, and repeat the test.

10   If the compression increases after the oil is added, the piston rings are definitely worn. If the compression doesn't increase significantly, the leakage is occurring at the valves or head gasket. Leakage past the valves may be caused by burned valve seats and/or faces or warped, cracked or bent valves.

11   If two adjacent cylinders have equally low compression, there's a strong possibility the head gasket between them is blown. The appearance of coolant in the combustion chambers or the crankcase would verify this condition.

12   If one cylinder is about 20-percent lower than the others, and the engine has a slightly rough idle, a worn exhaust lobe on the

camshaft could be the cause.

13   If the compression is unusually high, the combustion chambers are probably coated with carbon deposits. If that's the case, the cylinder heads should be removed and decarbonized.

14   If compression is way down or varies greatly between cylinders, it would be a good idea to have a leak-down test performed by an automotive repair shop. This test will pinpoint exactly where the leakage is occurring and how severe it is.

15   Installation of the fuses and the remaining components is the reverse of removal.

4   Vacuum gauge diagnostic checks

Refer to illustrations 4.4 and 4.6

1   A vacuum gauge provides valuable information about what is going on in the engine at a low cost. You can check for worn rings or cylinder walls, leaking head or intake manifold gaskets, incorrect air/fuel adjustments, restricted exhaust, stuck or burned valves, weak valve springs, improper ignition or valve timing and ignition problems.

2   Unfortunately, vacuum gauge readings are easy to misinterpret, so they should be used in conjunction with other tests to confirm the diagnosis.

3   Both the gauge readings and the rate of needle movement are important for accurate interpretation. Most gauges measure vacuum in inches of mercury (in-Hg). As vacuum increases (or atmospheric pressure decreases), the reading will increase. Also, for every 1,000-foot increase in elevation above sea level, the gauge readings will decrease about one inch of mercury.

4   Connect the vacuum gauge directly to intake manifold vacuum, not to ported (above the plate) vacuum **(see illustration)**. Be sure

no hoses are left disconnected during the test or false readings will result.

5   Before you begin the test, allow the engine to warm up completely. Block the wheels and set the parking brake. With the transmission in Park, start the engine and allow it to run at normal idle speed.

6   Read the vacuum gauge; an average, healthy engine should normally produce about 17 to 22 inches of vacuum with a fairly steady needle. Refer to the following vacuum gauge readings and what they indicate about the engine's condition **(see illustration)**.

7   A low, steady reading usually indicates a leaking gasket between the intake manifold and carburetor or throttle body, a leaky vacuum hose, late ignition timing or incorrect camshaft timing. Eliminate all other possible causes, utilizing the tests provided in this Chapter before you remove the timing chain cover to check the timing marks.

8   If the reading is three to eight inches below normal and it fluctuates at that low reading, suspect an intake manifold gasket leak at an intake port.

9   If the needle has regular drops of about two to four inches at a steady rate, the valves are probably leaking. Perform a compression or leak-down test to confirm this.

10   An irregular drop or down-flick of the needle can be caused by a sticking valve or an ignition misfire. Perform a compression or leak-down test and read the spark plugs.

11   A rapid vibration of about four inches-Hg at idle combined with exhaust smoke indicates worn valve guides. Perform a leak-down test to confirm this. If the rapid vibration occurs with an increase in engine speed, check for a leaking intake manifold gasket or head gasket, weak valve springs, burned valves or ignition misfire.

12   A slight fluctuation, say one inch up and down, may mean ignition problems. Check all the usual tune-up items and, if necessary, run the engine on an ignition analyzer.

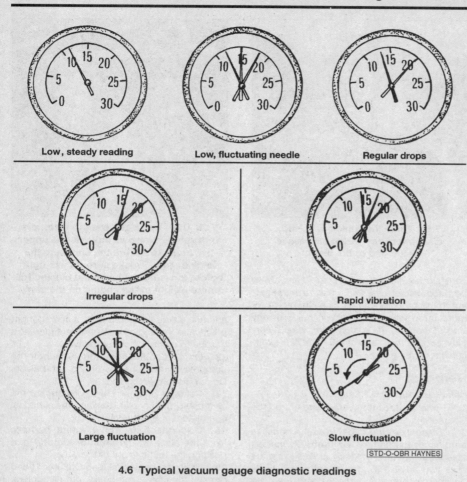

Low, steady reading

Low, fluctuating needle

Regular drops

Irregular drops

Rapid vibration

Large fluctuation

Slow fluctuation

STD-O-OBR HAYNES

4.6 Typical vacuum gauge diagnostic readings

13   If there is a large fluctuation, perform a compression or leak-down test to look for a weak or dead cylinder or a blown head gasket.

14   If the needle moves slowly through a wide range, check for a clogged PCV system, incorrect idle fuel mixture, throttle body or intake manifold gasket leaks.

15   Check for a slow return after revving the engine by quickly snapping the throttle open until the engine reaches about 2,500 rpm and let it shut. Normally the reading should drop to near zero, rise above normal idle reading (about 5 in-Hg over) and then return to the previous idle reading. If the vacuum returns slowly and doesn't peak when the throttle is snapped shut, the rings may be worn. If there is a long delay, look for a restricted exhaust system (often the muffler or catalytic converter). An easy way to check this is to temporarily disconnect the exhaust ahead of the suspected part and re-test.

5   Engine rebuilding alternatives

The home mechanic is faced with a number of options when performing an engine overhaul. The decision to replace the engine block, piston/connecting rod assem-blies and crankshaft depends on a number of factors, with the number one consideration being the condition of the block. Other considerations are cost, access to machine shop facilities, parts availability, time required to complete the project and the extent of prior mechanical experience.

Some of the rebuilding alternatives include:

Individual parts - If the inspection procedures reveal the engine block and most engine components are in reusable condition, purchasing individual parts may be the most economical alternative. The block, crankshaft and piston/connecting rod assemblies should all be inspected carefully. Even if the block shows little wear, the cylinder bores should be surface-honed.

Short-block - A short-block consists of an engine block with a crankshaft and piston/connecting rod assemblies already installed. All new bearings are incorporated and all clearances will be correct. The existing camshaft, valve train components, cylinder heads and external parts can be bolted to the short block with little or no machine shop work necessary. Some rebuilding companies include a new timing chain, camshaft and lifters with their short-block assemblies.

Long-block - A long-block consists of a short block plus an oil pump, oil pan, cylinder heads, rocker arm covers, camshaft and valve train components, timing sprockets and chain and timing chain cover. All components are installed with new bearings, seals and gaskets incorporated throughout. The installation of manifolds and external parts is all that's necessary. Give careful thought to which alternative is best for you and discuss the situation with local automotive machine shops, auto parts dealers and experienced rebuilders before ordering or purchasing replacement parts.

6   Engine removal - methods and precautions

If you've decided the engine must be removed for overhaul or major repair work, several preliminary steps should be taken. Locating a suitable place to work is extremely important. Adequate work space, along with storage space for the vehicle, will be needed.

Cleaning the engine compartment and engine before beginning the removal procedure will help keep tools clean and organized. An engine hoist will also be necessary. Safety is of primary importance, considering the potential hazards involved in removing the engine from this vehicle.

If the engine is being removed by a novice, a helper should be available. Advice and aid from someone more experienced would also be helpful. There are many instances when one person cannot simultaneously perform all of the operations required when lifting the engine out of the vehicle.

Plan the operation ahead of time. Arrange for or obtain all of the tools and equipment you'll need prior to beginning the job. Some of the equipment necessary to perform engine removal and installation safely and with relative ease in addition to a hydraulic jack, jack stands and an engine hoist) are a complete sets of wrenches and sockets as described in the front of this manual, wooden blocks and plenty of rags and cleaning solvent for mopping up spilled oil, coolant and gasoline.

Plan for the vehicle to be out of use for quite a while. A machine shop will be required to perform some of the work which the do-it-yourselfer can't accomplish without special equipment. These shops often have a busy schedule, so it would be a good idea to consult them before removing the engine in order to accurately estimate the amount of time required to rebuild or repair components that may need work.

Always be extremely careful when removing and installing the engine. Serious injury can result from careless actions. Plan ahead, take your time and a job of this nature, although major, can be accomplished successfully. **Note:** *Because it may be some time before you reinstall the engine, it is very helpful to make sketches or take photos of various accessory mountings and wiring hookups before removing the engine.*

2B

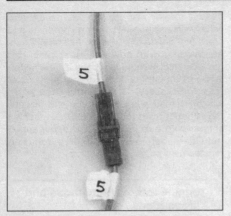

7.6a Label each wire before unplugging the connector

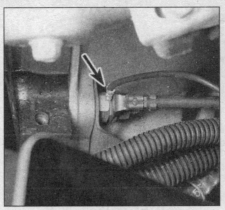

7.6b While the vehicle is raised, disconnect any wiring harnesses attached to the block

7.28 Use long, high strength fasteners with spacers (arrows indicate the upper two bolts) to secure the engine to the engine stand - make sure they're tight before lowering the hoist and placing the entire weight of the engine on the stand

7   Engine - removal and installation

Note: *Engine/transaxle removal on these vehicles is a difficult job, especially for the do-it-yourself mechanic working at home in the driveway. Because of the vehicle's design, the engine and transaxle must be removed from the bottom of the vehicle, not the top, and the front suspension subframe must come down with them. With just a floor jack and jackstands, the vehicle can't be raised high enough for the engine/transaxle/subframe to slide out the front. Also a special jack that supports the subframe should be used to guide the drivetrain out without the engine tipping over. The factory recommends that the engine removal be performed only when there is access to a vehicle hoist. Once the front wheels are removed, the vehicle can be lowered until the subframe rests on a wooden pallet, preferably with caster wheels. When everything is disconnected from the vehicle, it can be raised up, leaving the engine/transaxle/subframe on a moveable, working platform.*

Warning 1: *The air conditioning system is under high pressure. DO NOT loosen any fittings or remove any components until after the system has been discharged. Air conditioning refrigerant should be properly discharged into an EPA-approved container at a dealer service department or an automotive air conditioning repair facility. Always wear eye protection when disconnecting air conditioning system fittings.*

Warning 2: *Gasoline is extremely flammable, so take extra precautions when you work on any part of the fuel system. Don't smoke or allow open flames or bare light bulbs near the work area, and don't work in a garage where a natural gas-type appliance (such as a water heater or a clothes dryer) with a pilot light is present. Since gasoline is carcinogenic, wear latex gloves when there's a possibility of being exposed to fuel, and, if you spill any fuel on your skin, rinse it off immediately with soap and water. Mop up any spills immediately and do not store fuel-soaked rags where they could ignite. The fuel system is under*

constant pressure, so, if any fuel lines are to be disconnected, the fuel pressure in the system must be relieved first (see Chapter 4 for more information). When you perform any kind of work on the fuel system, wear safety glasses and have a Class B type fire extinguisher on hand.

Removal

Refer to illustrations 7.6a, 7.6b and 7.28

1   Relieve the fuel system pressure (see Chapter 4).

2   Disconnect the cable from the negative terminal of the battery. **Caution:** *On models equipped with the Theftlock audio system, be sure you have the correct activation code before disconnecting the battery (see the front of this manual).*

3   Cover the fenders and cowl and remove the hood and windshield wiper motor cover (see Chapter 11). Special pads are available to protect the fenders, but an old bedspread or blanket will also work.

4   Remove the air cleaner assembly (see Chapter 4).

5   Drain the cooling system (see Chapter 1).

6   Label the vacuum lines, emissions system hoses, electrical connectors, ground straps and fuel lines that would interfere with engine removal, to ensure correct reinstallation, then detach them. Pieces of masking tape with numbers or letters written on them work well **(see illustration)**. If there's any possibility of confusion, make a sketch of the engine compartment and clearly label the lines, hoses and wires. Don't overlook ground wires that may be bolted to the engine **(see illustration)**.

7   Label and detach all coolant hoses from the engine.

8   Remove the cooling fan assembly and radiator (see Chapter 3).

9   Remove the drivebelt(s) (see Chapter 1).

10   Disconnect the accelerator cable and cruise control cable (if equipped) from the engine (see Chapter 4). Also remove the engine mount struts (see Chapter 2A).

11   Unbolt the power steering pump (see Chapter 10). Leave the lines/hoses attached

and make sure the pump is kept in an upright position in the engine compartment (use wire or rope to restrain it out of the way).

12   On air-conditioned models, unbolt the compressor (see Chapter 3) and set it aside. Do not disconnect the hoses.

13   Refer to Chapter 7 and disconnect the shift cable, fluid cooler lines and the electrical connectors at the transaxle.

14   Disconnect the main wiring harness from the clips on the radiator support and position the harness out of the way.

15   Drain the engine oil (see Chapter 1) and remove the filter. On models with oil coolers, disconnect the oil cooler hoses and remove the oil cooler (see Chapter 3).

16   Remove the starter motor (see Chapter 5).

17   Remove the alternator (see Chapter 5).

18   Unbolt the exhaust system from the engine (see Part A and Chapter 4).

19   Turn the steering wheel to the straight-ahead position and lock the column by removing the key.

20   Raise the vehicle on the hoist and remove the front wheels and the splash shields from each wheelwell. Refer to Chapter 10 and disconnect the intermediate shaft from the steering gear.

21   Remove the links from the front stabilizer bar and separate the tie-rods and lower suspension arms from the steering knuckles (see Chapter 10).

22   Refer to Chapter 8 and remove the left and right driveaxles.

23   Either use a subframe jack to support the subframe/engine/transaxle, or lower the vehicle hoist until the subframe is supported on something sturdy like a wooden pallet.

24   Remove the four subframe-to-body bolts and raise the vehicle up, leaving the subframe and drivetrain on the wooden pallet. Move the pallet and drivetrain assembly out from under the vehicle, then remove the engine-to transaxle bolts and the driveplate bolts (see Chapter 7).

25 Attach a standard engine-lifting hoist (available at most tool rental facilities and equipment rental yards) to lifting hooks on the engine and raise the engine/transaxle slightly, enough to remove the engine mounts.

26 Raise the engine slightly. Carefully work it forward to separate it from the transaxle. Be sure the torque converter stays in the transaxle (clamp a pair of vise-grips to the transaxle housing to keep the converter from sliding out). Slowly raise the engine out of the subframe. Check carefully to make sure nothing is hanging up.

27 Remove the driveplate (see Part A or B of this Chapter).

28 Mount the engine on an engine stand **(see illustration)**.

29 Once the engine is removed, support the transmission with blocks of wood on the subframe.

Installation

30 Check the powertrain mounts. If they're worn or damaged, replace them.

31 Carefully lower the engine into the subframe - make sure the engine mounts line up.

32 Guide the torque converter into the crankshaft following the procedure outlined in Chapter 7. Don't pull the converter away from the transaxle; let the engine move back against the transaxle.

33 Install the transaxle-to-engine bolts and tighten them securely. **Caution:** *DO NOT use the bolts to force the transaxle and engine together!*

34 Install the engine mounts between the engine and the subframe.

35 Lower the vehicle hoist until the subframe can be raised close enough to the body to insert the four subframe bolts. Reinstall the remaining components in the reverse order of removal. Don't forget to install the torque converter-to-driveplate nuts.

36 Add coolant and oil as needed. Run the engine and check for leaks and proper operation of all accessories, then install the hood and test drive the vehicle.

9.2 A small plastic bag, with an appropriate label, can be used to store the valve train components so they can be kept together and reinstalled in the original positions

8 Engine overhaul - disassembly sequence

1 It's much easier to disassemble and work on the engine if it's mounted on a portable engine stand. A stand can often be rented quite cheaply from an equipment rental yard. Before it's mounted on a stand, the flywheel/driveplate should be removed from the engine.

2 If a stand isn't available, it's possible to disassemble the engine with it blocked up on the floor. Be extra careful not to tip or drop the engine when working without a stand.

3 If you're going to obtain a rebuilt engine, all external components must come off first, to be transferred to the replacement engine, just as they will if you're doing a complete engine overhaul yourself. These include:

Alternator and brackets
Emissions control components
Ignition coil/module assembly, spark
    plug wires and spark plugs
Thermostat and housing cover
Water pump
Engine front cover
Fuel injection components
Intake/exhaust manifolds
Valve covers
Oil filter
Engine mounts
Flywheel/driveplate

Note: *When removing the external components from the engine, pay close attention to details that may be helpful or important during installation. Note the installed position of gaskets, seals, spacers, pins, brackets, washers, bolts and other small items.*

4 If you're obtaining a short-block, then the cylinder heads, oil pan and oil pump will have to be removed as well. See *Engine rebuilding alternatives* for additional information regarding the different possibilities to be considered.

5 If you're planning a complete overhaul, the engine must be disassembled and the

9.3 Use a valve spring compressor to compress the spring, then remove the keepers from the valve stem

internal components removed in the following general order:

Rocker arms and pushrods
Valve lifters
Cylinder heads
Timing chain cover
Timing chain and sprockets
Camshaft
Oil pan
Oil pump
Piston/connecting rod assemblies
Crankshaft and main bearings

6 Before beginning the disassembly and overhaul procedures, make sure the following items are available. Also, refer to *Engine overhaul - reassembly sequence* for a list of tools and materials needed for engine reassembly.

Common hand tools
Small cardboard boxes or plastic bags
    for storing parts
Gasket scraper
Ridge reamer
Engine balancer puller
Micrometers
Telescoping gauges
Dial indicator set
Valve spring compressor
Cylinder surfacing hone
Piston ring groove-cleaning tool
Electric drill motor
Tap and die set
Wire brushes
Oil gallery brushes
Cleaning solvent

9 Cylinder head - disassembly

Refer to illustrations 9.2, 9.3 and 9.4

Note: *New and rebuilt cylinder heads are commonly available for most engines at dealerships and auto parts stores. Due to the fact that some specialized tools are necessary for the disassembly and inspection procedures, and replacement parts aren't always readily available, it may be more practical and economical for the home mechanic to purchase replacement heads rather than taking the time to disassemble, inspect and recondition the originals.*

1 Cylinder head disassembly involves removal of the intake and exhaust valves and related components. It is already assumed that the rocker arm components are removed from the cylinder head. If they're not already removed, label the parts and store them separately so they can be reinstalled in their original locations.

2 Before the valves are removed, arrange to label and store them, along with their related components, so they can be kept separate and reinstalled in their original locations **(see illustration)**.

3 Compress the springs on the first valve with a spring compressor and remove the keepers **(see illustration)**. Carefully release the valve spring compressor and remove the retainer, the spring and the spring seat (if used).

9.4 If the valve won't pull through the guide, deburr the edge of the stem end and the area around the top of the keeper groove with a file or whetstone

10.12 Check the cylinder head gasket surface for warpage by trying to slip a feeler gauge under the straightedge (see this Chapter's Specifications for the maximum warpage allowed and use a feeler gauge of that thickness)

4   Pull the valve out of the head, then remove the oil seal from the guide. If the valve binds in the guide (won't pull through), push it back into the head and deburr the area around the keeper groove with a fine file or whetstone **(see illustration)**.

5   Repeat the procedure for the remaining valves. Remember to keep all the parts for each valve together so they can be reinstalled in the same locations.

6   Once the valves and related components have been removed and stored in an organized manner, the heads should be thoroughly cleaned and inspected. If a complete engine overhaul is being done, finish the engine disassembly procedures before beginning the cylinder head cleaning and inspection process.

---

10   Cylinder head - cleaning and inspection

---

1   Thorough cleaning of the cylinder heads and related valve train components, followed by a detailed inspection, will enable you to decide how much valve service work must be done during the engine overhaul. **Note:** *If the engine was severely overheated, the cylinder head is probably warped* (see Step 12).

Cleaning

2   Scrape all traces of old gasket material and sealant off the head gasket, intake manifold and exhaust manifold mating surfaces. Be very careful not to gouge the cylinder head. Special gasket-removal solvents that soften gaskets and make removal much easier are available at auto parts stores.

3   Remove all built-up scale from the coolant passages.

4   Run a stiff wire brush through the various holes to remove deposits that may have formed in them.

5   Run an appropriate-size tap into each of

the threaded holes to remove corrosion and thread sealant that may be present. If compressed air is available, use it to clear the holes of debris produced by this operation. **Warning:** *Wear eye protection when using compressed air!*

6   Clean the cylinder head with solvent and dry it thoroughly.

7   Compressed air will speed the drying process and ensure that all holes and recessed areas are clean. **Note:** *Decarbonizing chemicals are available and may prove very useful when cleaning cylinder heads and valve train components. They're very caustic and should be used with caution. Be sure to follow the instructions on the container.*

8   Clean the rocker arms, roller bearings, bolts and pushrods with solvent and dry them thoroughly (don't mix them up during the cleaning process). Compressed air will speed the drying process and can be used to clean out the oil passages.

9   Clean all the valve springs, keepers and retainers with solvent and dry them thoroughly. Do the components from one valve at a time to avoid mixing up the parts.

10   Scrape off any heavy deposits that may have formed on the valves, then use a motorized wire brush to remove deposits from the valve heads and stems. Again, make sure the valves don't get mixed up.

Inspection

Note: *Be sure to perform all of the following inspection procedures before concluding machine shop work is required. Make a list of the items that need attention.*

Cylinder head

Refer to illustrations 10.12 and 10.14

11   Inspect the head very carefully for cracks, evidence of coolant leakage and other damage. If cracks are found, check with an automotive machine shop concerning repair. If repair isn't possible, a new cylinder head must be obtained.

12   Using a straightedge and feeler gauge, check the head gasket mating surface for warpage **(see illustration)**. If the warpage exceeds the limit in this Chapter's Specifications, it can be resurfaced at an automotive machine shop. **Note:** *If the heads are resurfaced, the intake manifold flanges may also require machining.*

13   Examine the valve seats in each of the combustion chambers. If they're pitted, cracked or burned, the head will require valve service that's beyond the scope of the home mechanic.

14   Check the valve stem-to-guide clearance by measuring the lateral movement of the valve stem with a dial indicator attached securely to the head **(see illustration)**. The valve must be in the guide and approximately 1/16-inch off the seat. The total valve stem movement indicated by the gauge needle must be divided by two to obtain the actual clearance. After this is done, if there's still some doubt regarding the condition of the valve guides, they should be checked by an

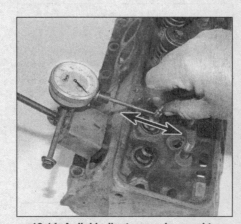

10.14 A dial indicator can be used to determine the valve stem-to-guide clearance (move the valve stem as indicated by the arrows)

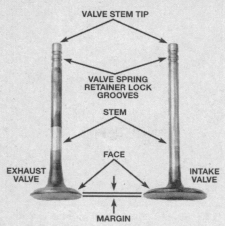

10.15 Check for valve wear at the points shown here

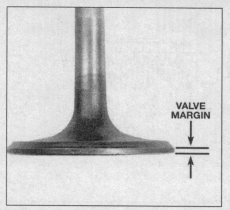

10.16 The margin width on the valve must be as specified (if no margin exists, the valve cannot be re-used)

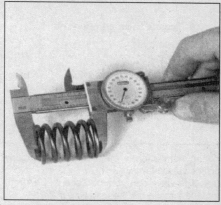

10.17 Measure the free length of each valve spring with a dial or vernier caliper

2B

automotive machine shop (the cost should be minimal).

Valves

Refer to illustrations 10.15 and 10.16

15   Carefully inspect each valve face for uneven wear, deformation, cracks, pits and burned areas. Check the valve stem for scuffing and galling and the neck for cracks. Rotate the valve and check for any obvious indication that it's bent. Look for pits and excessive wear on the end of the stem. The presence of any of these conditions **(see illustration)** indicates the need for valve service by an automotive machine shop.

16   Measure the margin width on each valve **(see illustration)**. Any valve with a margin narrower than specified in this Chapter will have to be replaced with a new one.

Valve components

Refer to illustrations 10.17 and 10.18

17   Check each valve spring for wear (on the ends) and pits. Measure the free length and compare it to this Chapter's Specifications **(see illustration)**. Any springs that are shorter than specified have sagged and shouldn't be re-used. The tension of all springs should be checked with a special fix-

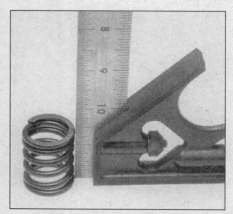

10.18 Check each valve spring for squareness

ture before deciding they're suitable for use in a rebuilt engine (take the springs to an automotive machine shop for this check).

18   Stand each spring on a flat surface and check it for squareness **(see illustration)**. If any of the springs are distorted or sagged, replace all of them with new parts. **Note:** *These engines are equipped with conical type valve springs which are smaller at the top. On these models it will be necessary to place the square along both sides of the spring (180 degrees apart) and note the measurements between the top of the spring and the square. If the spring is square the measurement will be the same on both sides.*

19   Check the spring retainers and keepers for obvious wear and cracks. Any questionable parts should be replaced with new ones, as extensive damage will occur if they fail during engine operation.

Valve actuating components

20   Refer to Chapter 2A and inspect the rocker arms, pushrods and the valve lifters.

All components

21   If the inspection process indicates the valve components are in generally poor condition and worn beyond the limits specified, which is usually the case in an engine that's being overhauled, reassemble the valves in the cylinder head (see Section 11 for valve servicing recommendations).

11   Valves - servicing

1   Because of the complex nature of the job and the special tools and equipment needed, servicing of the valves, the valve seats and the valve guides, commonly known as a valve job, should be done by a professional.

2   The home mechanic can remove and disassemble the head, do the initial cleaning and inspection, then reassemble and deliver it to an automotive machine shop for the actual service work. Doing the inspection will enable you to see what condition the head

and valvetrain components are in and will ensure that you know what work and new parts are required when dealing with an automotive machine shop.

3   The automotive machine shop, will remove the valves and springs, recondition or replace the valves and valve seats, recondition the valve guides, check and replace the valve springs, spring retainers and keepers (as necessary), replace the valve seals with new ones, reassemble the valve components and make sure the installed spring height is correct. The cylinder head gasket surface will also be resurfaced if it's warped.

4   After the valve job has been performed by a professional, the head will be in like new condition. When the head is returned, be sure to clean it again before installation on the engine to remove any metal particles and abrasive grit that may still be present from the valve service or head resurfacing operations. Use compressed air, if available, to blow out all the oil holes and passages.

12   Cylinder head - reassembly

Refer to illustrations 12.6 and 12.7

1   Regardless of whether or not the head was sent to an automotive repair shop for valve servicing, make sure it's clean before beginning reassembly.

2   If the head was sent out for valve servicing, the valves and related components will already be in place. Begin the reassembly procedure with Step 8.

3   Beginning at one end of the head, lubricate and install the first valve. Apply moly-base grease or clean engine oil to the valve stem.

4   Install the spring seat and shims, if originally installed, before the valve seals.

5   Install new seals on each of the valve guides. Gently tap each seal into place until it's completely seated on the guide. Many seal sets come with a plastic installer, but use hand pressure. Do not hammer on the seals or they could be driven down too far and subsequently leak. Don't twist or cock the seals

12.6 Typical valve components

1 *Keepers*
2 *Retainer or rotator*
3 *Oil seal*
4 *Spring*
5 *Valve*
6 *Valve spring seat*

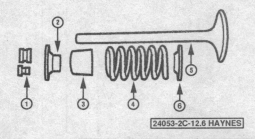

24053-2C-12.6 HAYNES

during installation or they won't seal properly on the valve stems.

6   The valve components **(see illustration)** may be installed in the following order:

> *Valves*
> *Valve spring seat*
> *Valve stem seals*
> *Valve spring shims (if any)*
> *Valve springs*
> *Retainers*
> *Keepers*

7   Compress the springs with a valve spring compressor and carefully install the keepers in the groove, then slowly release the compressor and make sure the keepers seat properly. Apply a small dab of grease to each keeper to hold it in place if necessary **(see illustration)**. Tap the valve stem tips with a plastic hammer to seat the keepers, if necessary.

8   Repeat the procedure for the remaining valves. Be sure to return the components to their original locations - don't mix them up!

9   Check the installed valve spring height with a ruler graduated in 1/32-inch increments or a dial caliper. If the head was sent out for service work, the installed height should be correct (but don't automatically assume it is). The measurement is taken from the top of each spring seat or top shim to the bottom of the retainer. If the height is greater than specified in this Chapter, shims can be added under the springs to correct it. **Caution:** *Do not, under any circumstances, shim the springs to the point where the installed height is less than specified.*

10   Apply moly-base grease to the rocker arm faces and the pivots, then install the rocker arms and pivots on the cylinder heads. Tighten the bolts finger-tight.

13   Camshaft - removal and inspection

Removal

Refer to illustrations 13.1 and 13.3

1   Remove the bolt and clamp holding the oil pump drive and pull the oil pump drive straight up and out of the block **(see illustration)**.

2   Refer to Chapter 2A and remove the timing chain and sprockets (lifters should already be removed and stored in a marked container).

3   Remove the bolts holding the camshaft thrust plate to the block **(see illustration)**.

4   Slide the camshaft straight out of the engine, using a long bolt (with the same thread as the camshaft sprocket bolt) screwed into the front of the camshaft as a "handle". Support the shaft near the block and be careful not to scrape or nick the bearings.

Inspection

Refer to illustrations 13.6a and 13.6b

5   After the camshaft has been removed, clean it with solvent and dry it, then inspect the bearing journals for uneven wear, pitting and evidence of seizure. If the journals are damaged, the camshaft bearings are probably damaged as well. Both the shaft and bearings will have to be replaced.

6   Measure the bearing journals with a

12.7 Apply a small dab of grease to each keeper as shown here before Installation - it'll hold them in place on the valve stem as the spring is released

13.1 Remove the bolt (arrow) and pull out the oil pump drive

micrometer **(see illustration)** to determine whether they are excessively worn or out-of-round. Measure the camshaft lobes also to check for wear. Measure the camshaft lobes at their highest point, then subtract the measurement of the lobe at it's smallest diameter - the difference is the lobe lift **(see illustration)**.

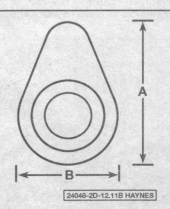

24048-2D-12.11B HAYNES

13.6b Measure the camshaft lobe maximum diameter (A) and the minimum (B) - subtract (B) from (A), the difference is the lobe lift

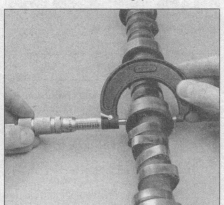

13.3 Remove the retaining bolts and the camshaft thrust plate

13.6a Measure the camshaft bearing journals with a micrometer

14.1 A ridge reamer is required to remove the ridge from the top of each cylinder - do this before removing the pistons!

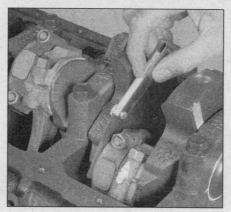

14.3 Check the connecting rod side clearance with a feeler gauge as shown

14.4 Mark the rod bearing caps in order from the front of the engine to the rear (one mark for the front cap, two for the second one and so on)

7   Inspect the camshaft lobes for heat discoloration, score marks, chipped areas, pitting and uneven wear. If the lobes are in good condition and if the lobe lift measurements are as specified, you can reuse the camshaft.

8   Check the camshaft bearings in the block for wear and damage. Look for galling, pitting and discolored areas.

9   The inside diameter of each bearing can be determined with a small hole gauge and outside micrometer or an inside micrometer. Subtract the camshaft bearing journal diameter(s) from the corresponding bearing inside diameter(s) to obtain the bearing oil clearance. If it's excessive, new bearings or housings will be required regardless of the condition of the originals.

10   Camshaft bearing replacement requires special tools and expertise that place it outside the scope of the home mechanic. Take the block to an automotive machine shop to ensure the job is done correctly.

14 Pistons and connecting rods - removal

Refer to illustrations 14.1, 14.3, 14.4 and 14.6

Note: *Prior to removing the piston/connecting rod assemblies, remove the cylinder heads, the oil pan and the oil pump by referring to the appropriate Sections in Chapter 2 Part A.*

1   Use your fingernail to feel if a ridge has formed at the upper limit of ring travel (about 1/4-inch down from the top of each cylinder). If carbon deposits or cylinder wear have produced ridges, they must be completely removed with a special tool **(see illustration)**. Follow the manufacturer's instructions provided with the tool. Failure to remove the ridges before attempting to remove the piston/connecting rod assemblies may result in piston breakage.

2   After the cylinder ridges have been removed, turn the engine upside-down so the crankshaft is facing up. Remove the oil baffle plate bolted to the main caps.

3   Before the connecting rods are removed, check the endplay with feeler gauges. Slide them between the first connecting rod and the crankshaft throw until the play is removed **(see illustration)**. The endplay is equal to the thickness of the feeler gauge(s). If the endplay exceeds the service limit, new connecting rods will be required. If new rods (or a new crankshaft) are installed, the endplay may fall under the minimum specified in this Chapter (if it does, the rods will have to be machined to restore it - consult an automotive machine shop for advice if necessary). Repeat the procedure for the remaining connecting rods.

4   Check the connecting rods and caps for identification marks. If they aren't plainly marked, use a small center-punch **(see illustration)** to make the appropriate number of indentations on each rod and cap (1, 2, 3, etc., depending on the cylinder they're associated with).

5   Loosen each of the connecting rod cap nuts 1/2-turn at a time until they can be removed by hand. Remove the number one connecting rod cap and bearing insert. Don't drop the bearing insert out of the cap.

6   Slip a short length of plastic or rubber hose over each connecting rod cap bolt to protect the crankshaft journal and cylinder wall as the piston is removed **(see illustration)**.

7   Remove the bearing insert and push the connecting rod/piston assembly out through the top of the engine. Use a wooden or plastic hammer handle to push on the upper bearing surface in the connecting rod. If resistance is felt, double-check to make sure all of the ridge was removed from the cylinder.

8   Repeat the procedure for the remaining cylinders.

9   After removal, reassemble the connecting rod caps and bearing inserts in their respective connecting rods and install the cap nuts finger tight. Leaving the old bearing inserts in place until reassembly will help prevent the connecting rod bearing surfaces

from being accidentally nicked or gouged.

10   Don't separate the pistons from the connecting rods.

15 Crankshaft - removal

Refer to illustrations 15.3 and 15.4

Note: *The crankshaft can be removed only after the engine has been removed from the vehicle. It's assumed the flywheel/driveplate, timing chain, oil pan, oil pump and piston/connecting rod assemblies have already been removed.*

1   Before the crankshaft is removed, check the endplay. Mount a dial indicator with the stem in line with the crankshaft and touching one of the crank throws.

2   Push the crankshaft all the way to the rear and zero the dial indicator. Next, pry the crankshaft to the front as far as possible and check the reading on the dial indicator. The distance it moves is the endplay. If it's greater than listed in this Chapter's Specifications, check the crankshaft thrust surfaces for wear. If no wear is evident, new main bearings should correct the endplay.

14.6 To prevent damage to the crankshaft journals and cylinder walls, slip sections of rubber or plastic hose over the rod bolts before removing the pistons/rods

3   If a dial indicator isn't available, feeler gauges can be used. Gently pry or push the crankshaft all the way to the front of the engine. Slip feeler gauges between the crankshaft and the front face of the thrust main bearing to determine the clearance **(see illustration)**. **Note:** *The thrust bearing is located at the number three main bearing cap.*

4   Check the main bearing caps to see if they're marked to indicate their locations. They should be numbered consecutively from the front of the engine to the rear. If they aren't, mark them with number stamping dies or a center-punch. Main bearing caps generally have a cast-in arrow, which points to the front of the engine **(see illustration)**. Loosen the main bearing cap bolts 1/4-turn at a time each, until they can be removed by hand. Note if any stud bolts are used and make sure they're returned to their original locations when the crankshaft is reinstalled.

5   Gently tap the caps with a soft-face hammer, then separate them from the engine block. If necessary, use the bolts as levers to remove the caps. Try not to drop the bearing inserts if they come out with the caps.

6   Carefully lift the crankshaft straight out of the engine. It may be a good idea to have an assistant available, since the crankshaft is quite heavy. With the bearing inserts in place in the engine block and main bearing caps, return the caps to their respective locations on the engine block and tighten the bolts finger tight.

16   Engine block - cleaning

Refer to illustrations 16.4a, 16.4b, 16.8 and 16.10

1   Remove the main bearing caps and separate the bearing inserts from the caps and the engine block. Tag the bearings, indicating which cylinder they were removed from and whether they were in the cap or the block, then set them aside.

2   Using a gasket scraper, remove all traces of gasket material from the engine block. Be very careful not to nick or gouge the gasket sealing surfaces.

3   Remove all of the covers and threaded oil gallery plugs from the block. The plugs are usually very tight - they may have to be drilled out and the holes retapped. Use new plugs when the engine is reassembled.

4   Remove the core plugs from the engine block. To do this, knock one side of the plugs into the block with a hammer and punch, then grasp them with large pliers and pull them out **(see illustrations)**.

5   If the engine is extremely dirty, it should be taken to an automotive machine shop to be cleaned. **Note:** *If the block is cleaned in a caustic-solution hot tank, this will ruin any bearing inserts left in the block, such as the camshaft bearings. If the engine is being rebuilt, these bearings should be replaced anyway.*

6   After the block is returned, clean all oil

15.3 Checking crankshaft endplay with a feeler gauge

15.4 The arrow on the main bearing cap indicates the front of the engine

16.4b Pull the core plugs from the block with pliers

16.4a A hammer and large punch can be used to knock the core plugs sideways in their bores

holes and oil galleries one more time. Brushes specifically designed for this purpose are available at most auto parts stores. Flush the passages with warm water until the water runs clear, dry the block thoroughly and wipe all machined surfaces with a light, rust preventive oil. If you have access to compressed air, use it to speed the drying process and blow out all the oil holes and galleries. **Warning:** *Wear eye protection when using compressed air!*

7   If the block isn't extremely dirty or sludged up, you can do an adequate cleaning job with hot soapy water and a stiff brush. Take plenty of time and do a thorough job. Regardless of the cleaning method used, be sure to clean all oil holes and galleries very thoroughly, dry the block completely and coat all machined surfaces with light oil.

8   The threaded holes in the block must be clean to ensure accurate torque readings during reassembly. Run the proper size tap into each of the holes to remove rust, corrosion, thread sealant or sludge and restore damaged threads **(see illustration)**. If possible, use compressed air to clear the holes of debris produced by this operation. Now is a good time to clean the threads on the head bolts and the main bearing cap bolts as well.

9   Reinstall the main bearing caps and tighten the bolts finger tight.

10   After coating the sealing surfaces of the new core plugs with a non-hardening sealant (such as Permatex no. 2), install them in the engine block **(see illustration)**. Make sure they're driven in straight and seated properly or leakage could result. Special tools are available for this purpose, but a large socket, with an outside diameter that will just slip into

16.8 All bolt holes in the block - particularly the main bearing cap and head bolt holes - should be cleaned and restored with a tap (be sure to remove debris from the holes after this is done)

16.10 A large socket on an extension can be used to drive the new core plugs into the bores

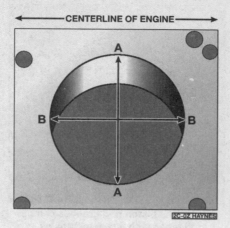

17.4a Measure the diameter of each cylinder at a right angle to the engine centerline (A), and parallel to the engine centerline (B) - out-of-round is the difference between A and B; taper is the difference between the diameter at the top of the cylinder and the diameter at the bottom of the cylinder

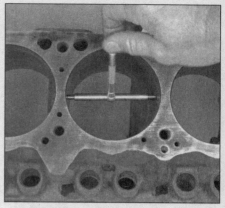

17.4b The ability to "feel" when the telescoping gauge is at the correct point will be developed over time, so work slowly and repeat the check until you're satisfied the bore measurement is accurate

the core plug, a 1/2-inch drive extension and a hammer will work just as well.

11 Apply non-hardening sealant (such as Permatex no. 2 or Teflon pipe sealant) to the new oil gallery plugs and thread them into the holes in the block. Make sure they're tightened securely.

12 If the engine isn't going to be reassembled right away, cover it with a large plastic trash bag to keep it clean.

17 Engine block - inspection

Refer to illustrations 17.4a, 17.4b and 17.4c
Note: *The manufacturer recommends checking the block deck for warpage and the main bearing bore concentricity and alignment. Since special measuring tools are needed, the checks should be done by an automotive machine shop.*

1 Before the block is inspected, it should be cleaned as described in Section 16.

2 Visually check the block for cracks, rust and corrosion. Look for stripped threads in the threaded holes. It's also a good idea to have the block checked for hidden cracks by an automotive machine shop that has the special equipment to do this type of work. If defects are found, have the block repaired, if possible, or replaced.

3 Check the cylinder bores for scuffing and scoring.

4 Check the cylinders for taper and out-of-round conditions as follows **(see illustrations)**:

5 Measure the diameter of each cylinder at the top (just under the ridge area), center and bottom of the cylinder bore, parallel to the crankshaft axis.

6 Next, measure each cylinder's diameter at the same three locations perpendicular to the crankshaft axis.

7 The taper of each cylinder is the difference between the bore diameter at the top of the cylinder and the diameter at the bottom. The out-of-round specification of the cylinder bore is the difference between the parallel and perpendicular readings. Compare your

results to this Chapter's Specifications.

8 If the cylinder walls are badly scuffed or scored, or if they're out-of-round or tapered beyond the limits given in this Chapter's Specifications, have the engine block rebored and honed at an automotive machine shop.

9 If a rebore is done, oversize pistons and rings will be required.

10 Using a precision straightedge and feeler gauge, check the block deck (the surface the cylinder heads mate with) for distortion as you did with the cylinder heads (see Section 10). If it's distorted beyond the specified limit, the block decks can be resurfaced by an automotive machine shop.

11 If the cylinders are in reasonably good condition and not worn to the outside of the limits, and if the piston-to-cylinder clearances can be maintained properly, they don't have to be rebored. Honing is all that's necessary (see Section 18).

18 Cylinder honing

Refer to illustrations 18.3a and 18.3b

1 Prior to engine reassembly, the cylinder bores must be honed so the new piston rings will seat correctly and provide the best possible combustion chamber seal. **Note:** *If you don't have the tools or don't want to tackle the honing operation, most automotive machine shops will do it for a reasonable fee.*

2 Before honing the cylinders, install the main bearing caps and tighten the bolts to the torque listed in this Chapter's Specifications.

3 Two types of cylinder hones are commonly available - the flex hone or "bottle brush" type and the more traditional surfacing hone with spring-loaded stones. Both will do the job, but for the less experienced mechanic the "bottle brush" hone will probably be easier to use. You'll also need some honing oil (kerosene will work if honing oil isn't available), rags and an electric drill motor. Proceed as follows:

a) Mount the hone in the drill motor, compress the stones and slip it into the first cylinder **(see illustration)**. *Be sure to wear safety goggles or a face shield!*

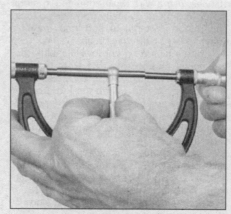

17.4c The gauge is then measured with a micrometer to determine the bore size

18.3a A "bottle brush" hone will produce a better cross hatch pattern when using a drill motor to hone the cylinders

2B

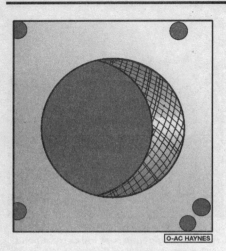

18.3b The cylinder hone should leave a smooth, crosshatch pattern with the lines intersecting at approximately a 60-degree angle

19.4a The piston ring grooves can be cleaned with a special tool, as shown here . . .

19.4b . . . or a section of broken ring

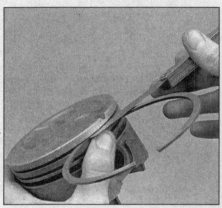

19.10 Check the ring side clearance with a feeler gauge at several points around the groove

b) *Lubricate the cylinder with plenty of honing oil, turn on the drill and move the hone up-and-down in the cylinder at a pace that will produce a fine crosshatch pattern on the cylinder walls, and with the drill square and centered with the bore. Ideally, the crosshatch lines should intersect at approximately a 45-60-degree angle* **(see illustration)**. *Be sure to use plenty of lubricant and don't take off any more material than is absolutely necessary to produce the desired finish.* **Note:** *Piston ring manufacturers may specify a different crosshatch angle - read and follow any instructions included with the new rings.*

c) *Don't withdraw the hone from the cylinder while it's running. Instead, shut off the drill and continue moving the hone up-and-down in the cylinder until it comes to a complete stop, then compress the stones and withdraw the hone. If you're using a "bottle brush" type hone, stop the drill motor, then turn the chuck in the normal direction of rotation while withdrawing the hone from the cylinder.*

d) *Wipe the oil out of the cylinder and repeat the procedure for the remaining cylinders.*

4   After the honing job is complete, chamfer the top edges of the cylinder bores with a small file so the rings won't catch when the pistons are installed. Be very careful not to nick the cylinder walls with the end of the file.

5   The entire engine block must be washed again very thoroughly with warm, soapy water to remove all traces of the abrasive grit produced during the honing operation. **Note:** *The bores can be considered clean when a lint-free white cloth - dampened with clean engine oil - used to wipe them out doesn't pick up any more honing residue, which will show up as gray areas on the cloth. Be sure to run a brush through all oil holes and gal-*leries and flush them with running water.

6   After rinsing, dry the block and apply a coat of light rust preventive oil to all machined surfaces. Wrap the block in a plastic trash bag to keep it clean and set it aside until reassembly.

19   Pistons and connecting rods - inspection

Refer to illustrations 19.4a, 19.4b, 19.10 and 19.11

1   Before the inspection process can be carried out, the piston/connecting rod assemblies must be cleaned and the original piston rings removed from the pistons. **Note:** *Always use new piston rings when the engine is reassembled.*

2   Using a piston ring installation tool, carefully remove the rings from the pistons. Be careful not to nick or gouge the pistons in the process.

3   Scrape all traces of carbon from the top of the piston. A hand-held wire brush or a piece of fine emery cloth can be used once the majority of the deposits have been scraped away. Do not, under any circumstances, use a wire brush mounted in a drill motor to remove deposits from the pistons. The piston material is soft and may be eroded away by the wire brush.

4   Use a piston ring groove-cleaning tool to remove carbon deposits from the ring grooves. If a tool isn't available, a piece broken off the old ring will do the job. Be very careful to remove only the carbon deposits - don't remove any metal and do not nick or scratch the sides of the ring grooves **(see illustrations)**.

5   Once the deposits have been removed, clean the piston/rod assemblies with solvent and dry them with compressed air (if available). **Warning:** *Wear eye protection. Make sure the oil return holes in the back sides of the ring grooves are clear.*

6   If the pistons and cylinder walls aren't damaged or worn excessively, and if the engine block isn't rebored, new pistons won't be necessary. Normal piston wear appears as even vertical wear on the piston thrust surfaces and slight looseness of the top ring in its groove. New piston rings, however, should always be used when an engine is rebuilt.

7   Carefully inspect each piston for cracks around the skirt, at the pin bosses and at the ring lands.

8   Look for scoring and scuffing on the thrust faces of the skirt, holes in the piston crown and burned areas at the edge of the crown. If the skirt is scored or scuffed, the engine may have been suffering from overheating and/or abnormal combustion, which caused excessively high operating temperatures. The cooling and lubrication systems should be checked thoroughly. A hole in the piston crown is an indication that abnormal combustion (preignition) was occurring. Burned areas at the edge of the piston crown are usually evidence of spark knock (detonation). If any of the above problems exist, the causes must be corrected or the damage will occur again. The causes may include intake air leaks, incorrect fuel/air mixture, low octane fuel, ignition timing and EGR system malfunctions.

9   Corrosion of the piston, in the form of small pits, indicates coolant is leaking into the combustion chamber and/or the

19.11 Measure the piston diameter at a 90-degree angle to the piston pin and at the specified distance from the centerline of the piston pin bore

20.1 The oil holes should be chamfered so sharp edges don't gouge or scratch the new bearings

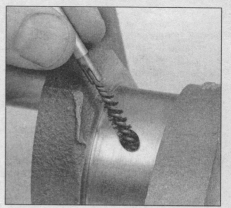

20.2 Use a wire or stiff plastic bristle brush to clean the oil passages in the crankshaft

20.5 Measure the diameter of each crankshaft journal at several points to detect taper and out-of-round conditions

20.7 If the seals have worn grooves in the crankshaft journals, or if the seal contact surfaces are nicked or scratched, the new seals will leak

crankcase. Again, the cause must be corrected or the problem may persist in the rebuilt engine.

10   Measure the piston ring side clearance by laying a new piston ring in each ring groove and slipping a feeler gauge in beside it **(see illustration)**. Check the clearance at three or four locations around each groove. Be sure to use the correct ring for each groove - they are different. If the side clearance is greater than specified in this Chapter, new pistons will have to be used.

11   Check the piston-to-bore clearance by measuring the bore (see Section 17) and the piston diameter. Make sure the pistons and bores are correctly matched. Measure the piston across the skirt, at a 90-degree angle to the piston pin **(see illustration)**. The measurement must be taken at a specific point to be accurate: The pistons are measured 0.51-inch below the centerline of the piston pin bore and at right angles to the piston pin. Measure the cylinder bore 2.5-inches from the top for comparison with the piston measurement.

12   Subtract the piston diameter from the bore diameter to obtain the clearance. If it's greater than specified, the block will have to be rebored and new pistons and rings installed.

13   Check the piston-to-rod clearance by twisting the piston and rod in opposite directions. Any noticeable play indicates excessive wear, which must be corrected. The piston/connecting rod assemblies should be taken to an automotive machine shop to have the pistons and rods re-sized and new pins installed.

14   If the pistons must be removed from the connecting rods for any reason, they should be taken to an automotive machine shop. While they are there, have the connecting rods checked for bend and twist, since automotive machine shops have special equipment for this purpose. **Note:** *Unless new pistons and/or connecting rods must be installed, do not disassemble the pistons and connecting rods.*

15   Check the connecting rods for cracks and other damage. Temporarily remove the rod caps, lift out the old bearing inserts, wipe the rod and cap bearing surfaces clean and inspect them for nicks, gouges and scratches. After checking the rods, replace the old bearings, slip the caps into place and tighten the nuts finger tight. **Note:** *If the engine is being rebuilt because of a connecting rod knock, be sure to install new or remanufactured connecting rods.*

20   Crankshaft - inspection

Refer to illustrations 20.1, 20.2, 20.5 and 20.7

1   Remove all burrs from the crankshaft oil holes with a stone, file or scraper **(see illustration)**.

2   Clean the crankshaft with solvent and dry it with compressed air (if available). **Warning:** *Wear eye protection when using compressed air.* Be sure to clean the oil holes with a stiff brush **(see illustration)** and flush them with solvent.

3   Check the main and connecting rod bearing journals for uneven wear, scoring, pits and cracks.

4   Check the rest of the crankshaft for cracks and other damage. It should be Magnafluxed to reveal hidden cracks - an automotive machine shop will handle the procedure.

5   Using a micrometer, measure the diameter of the main and connecting rod journals and compare the results to this Chapter's Specifications **(see illustration)**. By measuring the diameter at a number of points around each journal's circumference, you'll be able to determine whether or not the journal is out-of-round. Take the measurement at each end of the journal, near the crank throws, to determine if the journal is tapered.

6   If the crankshaft journals are damaged, tapered, out-of-round or worn beyond the limits given in the Specifications, have the crankshaft reground by an automotive machine shop. Be sure to use the correct-size bearing inserts if the crankshaft is reconditioned.

7   Check the oil seal journals at each end of the crankshaft for wear and damage. If the seal has worn a groove in the journal, or if it's nicked or scratched **(see illustration)**, the new seal may leak when the engine is reassembled. In some cases, an automotive

2B

machine shop may be able to repair the journal by pressing on a thin sleeve. If repair isn't feasible, a new or different crankshaft should be installed.

8   Examine the main and rod bearing inserts (see Section 21).

21   Main and connecting rod bearings - inspection and selection

Refer to illustration 21.1

1   Even though the main and connecting rod bearings should be replaced with new ones during the engine overhaul, the old bearings should be retained for close examination, as they may reveal valuable information about the condition of the engine **(see illustration)**.

2   Bearing failure occurs because of lack of lubrication, the presence of dirt or other foreign particles, overloading the engine and corrosion. Regardless of the cause of bearing failure, it must be corrected before the engine is reassembled to prevent it from happening again.

3   When examining the bearings, remove them from the engine block, the main bearing caps, the connecting rods and the rod caps and lay them out on a clean surface in the same general position as their location in the engine. This will enable you to match any bearing problems with the corresponding crankshaft journal.

4   Dirt and other foreign particles get into the engine in a variety of ways. It may be left in the engine during assembly, or it may pass through filters or the PCV system. It may get into the oil, and from there into the bearings. Metal chips from machining operations and normal engine wear are often present. Abrasives are sometimes left in engine components after reconditioning, especially when parts aren't thoroughly cleaned using the proper cleaning methods. Whatever the source, these foreign objects often end up embedded in the soft bearing material and are easily recognized. Large particles won't embed in the bearing and will score or gouge the bearing and journal. The best prevention for this cause of bearing failure is to clean all parts thoroughly and keep everything spotlessly clean during engine assembly. Frequent and regular engine oil and filter changes are also recommended.

5   Lack of lubrication (or lubrication breakdown) has a number of interrelated causes. Excessive heat (which thins the oil), overloading (which squeezes the oil from the bearing face) and oil leakage or throw off (from excessive bearing clearances, worn oil pump or high engine speeds) all contribute to lubrication breakdown. Blocked oil passages, which usually are the result of misaligned oil holes in a bearing shell, will also oil starve a bearing and destroy it. When lack of lubrication is the cause of bearing failure, the bearing material is wiped or extruded from the steel backing of the bearing. Temperatures may increase to the point where the steel backing turns blue from overheating.

6   Driving habits can have a definite effect on bearing life. Low speed operation in too high a gear (lugging the engine) puts very high loads on bearings, which tends to squeeze out the oil film. These loads cause the bearings to flex, which produces fine cracks in the bearing face (fatigue failure). Eventually the bearing material will loosen in pieces and tear away from the steel backing. Short trip driving leads to corrosion of bearings because insufficient engine heat is produced to drive off the condensed water and corrosive gases. These products collect in the engine oil, forming acid and sludge. As the oil is carried to the engine bearings, the acid attacks and corrodes the bearing material.

7   Incorrect bearing installation during engine assembly will lead to bearing failure as well. Tight-fitting bearings leave insufficient oil clearance and will result in oil starvation. Dirt or foreign particles trapped behind a bearing insert result in high spots on the bearing which lead to failure.

22   Engine overhaul - reassembly sequence

1   Before beginning engine reassembly, make sure you have all the necessary new parts, gaskets and seals as well as the following items on hand:

Common hand tools
Torque wrench (1/2-inch drive) with
   angle-torque gauge
Piston ring Installation tool
Piston ring compressor
Crankshaft balancer Installation tool
Short lengths of rubber or plastic hose
   to fit over connecting rod bolts
Plastigage
Feeler gauges
Fine-tooth file
New engine oil
Engine assembly lube or moly-base
   grease
Gasket sealant
Thread locking compound

2   In order to save time and avoid problems, engine reassembly must be done in the following general order:

Crankshaft and main bearings
Piston/connecting rod assemblies
Rear main oil seal
Camshaft
Oil pump drive assembly
Timing chain and sprockets
Cylinder heads
Valve lifters
Rocker arms and pushrods
Timing chain cover
Oil pump
Oil pan
Driveplate

Assembled after engine installation

Intake and exhaust manifolds
Valve covers

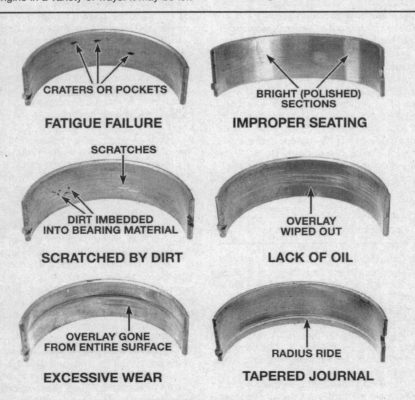

CRATERS OR POCKETS

FATIGUE FAILURE

BRIGHT (POLISHED) SECTIONS

IMPROPER SEATING

SCRATCHES

DIRT IMBEDDED INTO BEARING MATERIAL

SCRATCHED BY DIRT

OVERLAY WIPED OUT

LACK OF OIL

OVERLAY GONE FROM ENTIRE SURFACE

EXCESSIVE WEAR

RADIUS RIDE

TAPERED JOURNAL

21.1 Typical bearing failures

23.3 When checking piston ring end gap, the ring must be square in the cylinder bore (this is done by pushing the ring down with the top of a piston as shown)

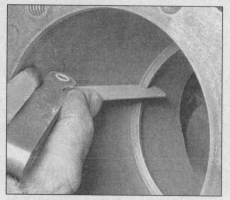

23.4 With the ring square in the cylinder, measure the end gap with a feeler gauge

23.5 If the end gap is too small, clamp a file in a vise and file the ring ends (from the outside in only) to enlarge the gap slightly

23 Piston rings - installation

Refer to illustrations 23.3, 23.4, 23.5, 23.9a, 23.9b and 23.12

1   Before installing the new piston rings, the ring end gaps must be checked. It's assumed the piston ring side clearance has been checked and verified correct (see Section 19).

2   Lay out the piston/connecting rod assemblies and the new ring sets so the ring sets will be matched with the same piston and cylinder during the end gap measurement and engine assembly.

3   Insert the top (number one) ring into the first cylinder and square it up with the cylinder walls by pushing it in with the top of the piston **(see illustration)**. The ring should be near the bottom of the cylinder, at the lower limit of ring travel.

4   To measure the end gap, slip feeler gauges between the ends of the ring until a gauge equal to the gap width is found **(see illustration)**. The feeler gauge should slide between the ring ends with a slight amount of drag. Compare the measurement to this Chapter's Specifications. If the gap is larger or smaller than specified, double-check to make sure you have the correct rings before proceeding.

5   If the gap is too small, it must be enlarged or the ring ends may come in contact with each other during engine operation, which can cause serious engine damage. The end gap can be increased by filing the ring ends very carefully with a fine file. Mount the file in a vise equipped with soft jaws, slip the ring over the file with the ends contacting the file teeth and slowly move the ring to remove material from the ends. When performing this operation, file only from the outside in **(see illustration)**. **Note:** *When you have the end gap correct, remove any burrs from the filed ends of the rings with a whetstone.*

6   Excess end gap isn't critical unless it's greater than 0.040-inch. Again, double-check to make sure you have the correct rings for the engine. If the engine block has been bored oversize, necessitating oversize pistons, matching oversize rings are required.

7   Repeat the procedure for each ring that will be installed in the first cylinder and for each ring in the remaining cylinders. Remember to keep rings, pistons and cylinders matched up.

8   Once the ring end gaps have been checked/corrected, the rings can be installed on the pistons.

9   The oil control ring (lowest one on the piston) is usually installed first. It's composed of three separate components. Slip the spacer/expander into the groove **(see illustration)**. If an anti-rotation tang is used, make sure it's inserted into the drilled hole in the ring groove. Next, install the lower side rail. Don't use a piston ring installation tool on the oil ring side rails, as they may be damaged. Instead, place one end of the side rail into the groove between the spacer/expander and the ring land, hold it firmly in place and slide a finger around the piston while pushing the rail into the groove **(see illustration)**. Next, install the upper side rail in the same manner.

10   After the three oil ring components have been installed, check to make sure both the upper and lower side rails can be turned smoothly in the ring groove.

11   The number two (middle) ring is installed next. It's usually stamped with a mark, which must face up, toward the top of the piston. **Note:** *Always follow the instructions printed on the ring package or box - different manufacturers may require different approaches. Don't mix up the top and middle rings, as they have different cross-sections.*

12   Use a piston ring installation tool and make sure the identification mark is facing the top of the piston, then slip the ring into the middle groove on the piston **(see illustration)**. Don't expand the ring any more than

2B

23.9a Installing the spacer/expander in the oil control ring groove

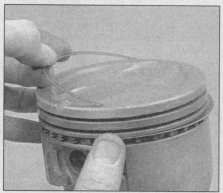

23.9b DO NOT use a piston ring installation tool when installing the oil ring side rails

23.12 Installing the compression rings with a ring expander - the mark (arrow) must face up

necessary to slide it over the piston.

13   Install the number one (top) ring in the same manner. Make sure the mark is facing up. Be careful not to confuse the number one and number two rings.

14   Repeat the procedure for the remaining pistons and rings.

24   Crankshaft - installation and main bearing oil clearance check

1   Crankshaft installation is the first step in engine reassembly. It's assumed at this point that the engine block and crankshaft have been cleaned, inspected and repaired or reconditioned.

2   Position the engine with the bottom facing up.

3   Remove the main bearing cap bolts and lift out the caps. Lay them out in the proper order to ensure correct installation.

4   If they're still in place, remove the original bearing inserts from the block and the main bearing caps. Wipe the bearing surfaces of the block and caps with a clean, lint-free cloth. They must be kept spotlessly clean.

Main bearing oil clearance check

Refer to illustrations 24.11 and 24.15

Note: *Don't touch the faces of the new bearing inserts with your fingers. Oil and acids from your skin can etch the bearings.*

5   Clean the back sides of the new main bearing inserts and lay one in each main bearing saddle in the block. If one of the bearing inserts from each set has a large groove in it, make sure the grooved insert is installed in the block. Lay the other bearing from each set in the corresponding main bearing cap. Make sure the tab on the bearing insert fits into the recess in the block or cap, neither higher than the cap's edge nor lower. **Caution:** *The oil holes in the block must line up with the oil holes in the bearing inserts. Do not hammer the bearing into place and don't nick or gouge the bearing faces. No lubrication should be used at this time.*

6   The flanged thrust bearing must be installed in the number three main cap. **Caution:** *Some engines may have a oversize rear main bearing. Check your crankshaft for a marking on the last counterweight, and check the backside of the old bearing insert for a similar marking. If they are marked oversize, an oversize rear bearing will be required.*

7   Clean the faces of the bearings in the block and the crankshaft main bearing journals with a clean, lint-free cloth.

8   Check or clean the oil holes in the crankshaft, as any dirt here can go only one way - straight through the new bearings.

9   Once you're certain the crankshaft is clean, carefully lay it in position in the main bearings.

10   Before the crankshaft can be perma-

24.11 Lay the Plastigage strips (arrow) on the main bearing journals, parallel to the crankshaft centerline

nently installed, the main bearing oil clearance must be checked.

11   Cut several pieces of the appropriate size Plastigage (they should be slightly shorter than the width of the main bearings) and place one piece on each crankshaft main bearing journal, parallel with the journal axis **(see illustration)**.

12   Clean the faces of the bearings in the caps and install the caps in their original locations (don't mix them up) with the arrows pointing toward the front of the engine. Don't disturb the Plastigage.

13   Starting with the center main and working out toward the ends, tighten the main bearing cap bolts to the torque listed in this Chapter's Specifications in three steps. Don't rotate the crankshaft at any time during this operation, and do not tighten one cap completely - tighten all caps equally. Before tightening, the main caps should be seated using light taps with a brass or plastic mallet.

14   Remove the bolts/studs and carefully lift off the main bearing caps. Keep them in order. Don't disturb the Plastigage or rotate the crankshaft. If any of the main bearing caps are difficult to remove, tap them gently from side-to-side with a soft-face hammer to loosen them.

15   Compare the width of the crushed Plastigage on each journal to the scale printed on the Plastigage envelope to obtain the main bearing oil clearance **(see illustration)**. Check the Specifications to make sure it's correct.

16   If the clearance is not as specified, the bearing inserts may be the wrong size (which means different ones will be required). Before deciding different inserts are needed, make sure no dirt or oil was between the bearing inserts and the caps or block when the clearance was measured. If the Plastigage was wider at one end than the other, the journal may be tapered (see Section 20).

17   Carefully scrape all traces of the Plastigage material off the main bearing journals and/or the bearing faces. Use your fingernail or the edge of a credit card - don't nick or scratch the bearing faces.

24.15 Measuring the width of the crushed Plastigage to determine the main bearing oil clearance (be sure to use the correct scale - standard and metric ones are included)

Final crankshaft installation

18   Carefully lift the crankshaft out of the engine.

19   Clean the bearing faces in the block, then apply a thin, uniform layer of moly-base grease or engine assembly lube to each of the bearing surfaces. Be sure to coat the thrust faces as well as the journal face of the thrust bearing.

20   Make sure the crankshaft journals are clean, then lay the crankshaft back in place in the block.

21   Clean the faces of the bearings in the caps, then apply lubricant to them.

22   Install the caps in their original locations with the arrows pointing toward the front of the engine. **Note:** *Apply a small amount of RTV sealant between the rear main cap and engine block sealing surfaces.*

23   With all caps in place and bolts just started, tap the ends of the crankshaft forward and backward with a lead or brass hammer to line up the main bearing and crankshaft thrust surfaces.

24   Following the procedures outlined in Step 13, retighten all main bearing cap bolts to the torque listed in this Chapter's Specifications, starting with the center main and working out toward the ends.

25   Rotate the crankshaft a number of times by hand to check for any obvious binding.

26   The final step is to check the crankshaft endplay with feeler gauges or a dial indicator as described in Section 15. The endplay should be correct if the crankshaft thrust faces aren't worn or damaged and new bearings have been installed.

25   Camshaft - installation

Refer to illustration 25.1

1   Lubricate the camshaft bearing journals and cam lobes with a special camshaft installation lubricant **(see illustration)**.

2   Slide the camshaft into the engine,

25.1 Coat the camshaft lobes and journals with assembly lube before installation

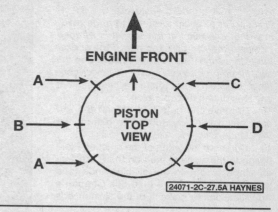

27.5 Ring end gap positions

A   Oil ring rail gaps
B   Second compression ring gap
C   Oil ring spacer gap (position between marks)
D   Top compression ring gap

using a long bolt (the same thread as the camshaft sprocket bolt) screwed into the front of the camshaft as a "handle." Support the cam near the block and be careful not to scrape or nick the bearings. Install the camshaft retainer plate and tighten the bolts to the torque listed in this Chapter's Specifications.

3   Dip the gear portion of the oil pump drive in engine oil and insert it into the block. It should be flush with its mounting boss before inserting the retaining bolt. **Note:** *Position a new O-ring on the oil pump driveshaft before installation.*

4   Complete the installation of the timing chain and sprockets by referring to Chapter 2A.

26   Rear main oil seal - replacement

Refer to Chapter 2A for the rear main seal replacement procedure.

27   Pistons and connecting rods - installation and rod bearing oil clearance check

1   Before installing the piston/connecting rod assemblies, the cylinder walls must be perfectly clean, the top edge of each cylinder must be chamfered, and the crankshaft must be in place.

2   Remove the cap from the end of the number one connecting rod (check the marks made during removal). Remove the original bearing inserts and wipe the bearing surfaces of the connecting rod and cap with a clean, lint-free cloth. They must be kept spotlessly clean.

Piston installation and rod bearing oil clearance check

Refer to illustrations 27.5, 27.11, 27.13 and 27.17

3   Clean the back side of the new upper bearing insert, then lay it in place in the connecting rod. Make sure the tab on the bearing

fits into the recess in the rod. Don't hammer the bearing insert into place and be very careful not to nick or gouge the bearing face. Don't lubricate the bearing at this time.

4   Clean the back side of the other bearing insert and install it in the rod cap. Again, make sure the tab on the bearing fits into the recess in the cap, and don't apply any lubricant. It's critically important that the mating surfaces of the bearing and connecting rod are perfectly clean and oil free when they're assembled.

5   Stagger the piston ring gaps around the piston (**see illustration**).

6   Slip a section of plastic or rubber hose over each connecting rod cap bolt.

7   Lubricate the piston and rings with clean engine oil and attach a piston ring compressor to the piston. Leave the skirt protruding about 1/4-inch to guide the piston into the cylinder. The rings must be compressed until they're flush with the piston.

8   Rotate the crankshaft until the number one connecting rod journal is at BDC (bottom dead center) and apply a coat of engine oil to the cylinder walls.

9   With the mark or notch on top of the piston facing the front of the engine, gently insert the piston/connecting rod assembly into the number one cylinder bore and rest the bottom edge of the ring compressor on the engine block.

10   Tap the top edge of the ring compressor

to make sure it's contacting the block around its entire circumference.

11   Gently tap on the top of the piston with the end of a wooden or plastic hammer handle (**see illustration**) while guiding the end of the connecting rod into place on the crankshaft journal. The piston rings may try to pop out of the ring compressor just before entering the cylinder bore, so keep some pressure down on the ring compressor. Work slowly, and if any resistance is felt as the piston enters the cylinder, stop immediately. Find out what's hanging up and fix it before proceeding. Do not, for any reason, force the piston into the cylinder - you might break a ring and/or the piston.

12   Once the piston/connecting rod assembly is installed, the connecting rod bearing oil clearance must be checked before the rod cap is permanently bolted in place.

13   Cut a piece of the appropriate size Plastigage slightly shorter than the width of the connecting rod bearing and lay it in place on the number one connecting rod journal, parallel with the journal axis (**see illustration**).

14   Clean the connecting rod cap bearing face, remove the protective hoses from the connecting rod bolts and install the rod cap. Make sure the mating mark on the cap is on the same side as the mark on the connecting rod.

15   Install the nuts and tighten them to the torque listed in this Chapter's Specifications.

2B

27.11 Drive the piston into the cylinder bore with the end of a wooden or plastic hammer handle

27.13 Lay the Plastigage strips on each rod bearing journal, parallel to the crankshaft centerline

Work up to it in three steps. **Note:** *Use a thin-wall socket to avoid erroneous torque readings that can result if the socket is wedged between the rod cap and nut. If the socket tends to wedge itself between the nut and the cap, lift up on it slightly until it no longer contacts the cap. Do not rotate the crankshaft at any time during this operation.*

16   Remove the nuts and detach the rod cap, being very careful not to disturb the Plastigage.

17   Compare the width of the crushed Plastigage to the scale printed on the Plastigage envelope to obtain the oil clearance **(see illustration)**. Compare it to this Chapter's Specifications to make sure the clearance is correct.

18   If the clearance is not as specified, the bearing inserts may be the wrong size (which means different ones will be required). Before deciding different inserts are needed, make sure no dirt or oil was between the bearing inserts and the connecting rod or cap when the clearance was measured. Also, recheck the journal diameter. If the Plastigage was wider at one end than the other, the journal may be tapered (see Section 20).

Final connecting rod installation

19   Carefully scrape all traces of the Plastigage material off the rod journal and/or bearing face. Be very careful not to scratch the bearing - use your fingernail or the edge of a credit card.

20   Make sure the bearing faces are perfectly clean, then apply a uniform layer of clean moly-base grease or engine assembly lube to both of them. You'll have to push the piston into the cylinder to expose the face of the bearing insert in the connecting rod - be sure to slip the protective hoses over the rod bolts first.

21   Slide the connecting rod back into place on the journal, remove the protective hoses from the rod cap bolts, install the rod cap and tighten the nuts to the torque listed in this Chapter's Specifications. Again, work up to the torque in three steps.

22   Repeat the entire procedure for the remaining pistons/connecting rods.

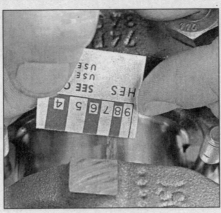

27.17 Measuring the width of the crushed Plastigage to determine the rod bearing oil clearance (be sure to use the correct scale - standard and metric ones are included)

23   The important points to remember are:
a) *Keep the back sides of the bearing inserts and the insides of the connecting rods and caps perfectly clean when assembling them.*
b) *Make sure you have the correct piston/rod assembly for each cylinder.*
c) *The arrow or mark on the piston must face the front of the engine.*
d) *Lubricate the cylinder walls with clean oil.*
e) *Lubricate the bearing faces when installing the rod caps after the oil clearance has been checked.*

24   After all the piston/connecting rod assemblies have been properly installed, rotate the crankshaft a number of times by hand to check for any obvious binding.

25   As a final step, the connecting rod endplay must be checked (see Section 14).

26   Compare the measured endplay to this Chapter's Specifications to make sure it's correct. If it was correct before disassembly and the original crankshaft and rods were reinstalled, it should still be right. If new rods or a new crankshaft were installed, the endplay may be inadequate. If so, the rods will have to be removed and taken to an automotive machine shop for re-sizing.

28   Initial start-up and break-in after overhaul

Warning: *Have a fire extinguisher handy when starting the engine for the first time.*

1   Once the engine has been installed in the vehicle, double-check the oil and coolant levels.

2   With the spark plugs out of the engine, disable the ignition system by disconnecting the wires to the ignition control module (see Chapter 5). Also, disable the fuel injection system by unplugging the electrical connector to the injector wiring harness or by removing the fuel pump fuse. Crank the engine until oil pressure registers on the gauge or the light goes out.

3   Install the spark plugs, hook up the plug wires and install the fuses.

4   Start the engine. It may take a few moments for the fuel system to build up pressure, but the engine should start without a great deal of effort. **Note:** *If the engine keeps backfiring, recheck the valve timing and spark plug wire routing.*

5   After the engine starts, it should be allowed to warm up to normal operating temperature. While the engine is warming up, make a thorough check for fuel, oil and coolant leaks.

6   Shut the engine off and recheck the engine oil and coolant levels.

7   Drive the vehicle to an area with no traffic, accelerate from 30 to 50 mph, then allow the vehicle to slow to 30 mph with the throttle closed. Repeat the procedure 10 or 12 times. This will load the piston rings and cause them to seat properly against the cylinder walls. Check again for oil and coolant leaks.

8   Drive the vehicle gently for the first 500 miles (no sustained high speeds) and keep a constant check on the oil level. It isn't unusual for an engine to use oil during the break-in period.

9   At approximately 500 to 600 miles, change the oil and filter.

10   For the next few hundred miles, drive the vehicle normally. Don't pamper it or abuse it.

11   After 2000 miles, change the oil and filter again and consider the engine broken in.

Chapter 3
Cooling, heating and air conditioning systems

Contents

Specifications

General

Coolant capacity	See Chapter 1
Radiator cap pressure rating	15 psi
Thermostat opening temperature	195-degrees F
Refrigerant type	R-134a
Refrigerant capacity	
Front air conditioning only	2.38 pounds
Front and rear air conditioning	2.9 pounds

Torque specifications

	Ft-lbs (unless otherwise indicated)
Transaxle oil cooler lines	33
Thermostat housing nuts/bolts	18
Water pump attaching bolts	89 in-lbs
Water pump pulley bolts	18

1 General information

All vehicles covered by this manual employ a pressurized engine cooling system with thermostatically controlled coolant circulation. Coolant is drawn from the radiator by an impeller-type water pump mounted at the front of the block. The coolant is then circulated through the engine block, intake manifold and the cylinder head(s) before it's redirected back into the radiator.

A wax pellet type thermostat is located in the thermostat housing on the engine. During warm up, the closed thermostat prevents coolant from circulating through the radiator. When the engine reaches normal operating temperature, the thermostat opens and allows hot coolant to travel through the radiator, where it is cooled before returning to the engine.

The cooling system is pressurized by a spring-loaded radiator cap, which, by maintaining pressure, increases the boiling point of the coolant. If the coolant temperature goes above this increased boiling point, the extra pressure in the system forces the radiator cap valve off its seat and allows the coolant to escape through the overflow tube into the coolant reservoir. When the system cools, the excess coolant is automatically drawn from the reservoir back into the radiator.

The coolant reservoir serves as both the point at which fresh coolant is added to the cooling system to maintain the proper fluid level and as a holding tank for overheated coolant.

The heating system works by directing air through the heater core mounted in the dash and then to the interior of the vehicle by a system of ducts. Temperature is controlled by mixing heated air with fresh air, using a system of doors in the ducts, and a blower motor.

The air conditioning system consists of an evaporator core located under the dash, a condenser in front of the radiator, an accumulator in the engine compartment and a belt-driven compressor mounted at the front of the engine.

Also available as an option is a rear mounted auxiliary heating/air conditioning system. In this system, the driver has controls on the dashboard for both the front and rear heating/air conditioning systems and the rear passengers have over-head controls for the rear heating and air conditioning system only. A second heater core, air conditioning evaporator core and blower motor are located at the rear of the vehicle behind the left rear interior panel.

2 Antifreeze - general information

Refer to illustration 2.4
Warning: *Do not allow antifreeze to come in contact with your skin or painted surfaces of* the vehicle. Rinse off spills immediately with plenty of water. Antifreeze is highly toxic if ingested. Never leave antifreeze lying around in an open container or in puddles on the floor; children and pets are attracted by it's sweet smell and may drink it. Check with local authorities about disposing of used antifreeze. Many communities have collection centers which will see that antifreeze is disposed of safely. Never dump used anti-freeze on the ground or pour it into drains.
Caution: *The manufacturer recommends using only DEX-COOL coolant for these systems. DEX-COOL is a long-lasting coolant designed for 100,000 miles or 5 years. Never mix green-colored ethylene glycol anti-freeze and orange-colored "DEX-COOL" silicate-free coolant because doing so will destroy the efficiency of the "DEX-COOL".*

The cooling system should be filled with a water/ethylene glycol based antifreeze solution which will prevent freezing down to at least -20-degrees F (even lower in cold climates). It also provides protection against corrosion and increases the coolant boiling point.

The cooling system should be drained, flushed and refilled at least every other year (see Chapter 1). The use of antifreeze solutions for periods of longer than two years is likely to cause damage and encourage the formation of rust and scale in the system. However, these models are filled with a new, long-life "DEX-COOL coolant," which the manufacturer claims is good for five years.

Before adding antifreeze to the system, check all hose connections. Antifreeze can leak through very minute openings.

The exact mixture of antifreeze to water which you should use depends on the relative weather conditions. The mixture should contain at least 50-percent antifreeze, but should never contain more than 70-percent antifreeze. Consult the mixture ratio chart on the antifreeze container before adding coolant. Hydrometers are available at most auto parts stores to test the coolant **(see illustration)**. Always use antifreeze which meets the vehicle manufacturer's specifications.

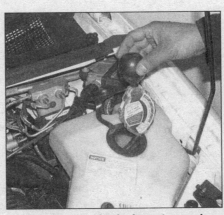

2.4 An inexpensive hydrometer can be used to test the condition of your coolant

3 Thermostat - check and replacement

Warning: *The engine must be completely cool when this procedure is performed.*

Check

1   Before assuming the thermostat is to blame for a cooling system problem, check the coolant level, drivebelt tension (see Chapter 1) and temperature gauge (or light) operation.
2   If the engine seems to be taking a long time to warm up (based on heater output or temperature gauge operation), the thermostat is probably stuck open. Replace the thermostat with a new one.
3   If the engine runs hot, use your hand to check the temperature of the upper radiator hose. If the hose isn't hot, but the engine is, the thermostat is probably stuck closed, preventing the coolant inside the engine from escaping to the radiator. Replace the thermostat. **Caution:** *Don't drive the vehicle without a thermostat. The computer may stay in open loop and emissions and fuel economy will suffer.*
4   If the upper radiator hose is hot, it means the coolant is flowing and the thermostat is open. Consult the *Troubleshooting* Section at the front of this manual for cooling system diagnosis.

Replacement

Refer to illustrations 3.8, 3.10, 3.11, 3.12 and 3.13
5   Disconnect the cable from the negative terminal of the battery. **Caution:** *On models equipped with the Theftlock audio system, be sure you have the correct activation code before disconnecting the battery (see the front of this manual).* Partially drain the cooling system. If the coolant is relatively new or in good condition, save it and reuse it. If it is to be replaced, see Section 2 for cautions about proper handling of used antifreeze.
6   Remove the air cleaner and duct (see Chapter 4). Also remove the exhaust crossover pipe (see the exhaust manifold removal procedure in Chapter 2A).
7   Follow the upper radiator hose to the engine to locate the thermostat housing cover. The thermostat is located at the end of the lower intake manifold on the driver's side of the engine compartment.
8   Loosen the hose clamp, then detach the hose from the thermostat housing cover **(see illustration)**. If the hose sticks, grasp it near the end with a pair of adjustable pliers and twist it to break the seal, then pull it off. If the hose is old or deteriorated, cut it off and install a new one.
9   If the outer surface of the cover fitting that mates with the hose is deteriorated (corroded, pitted, etc.) it may be damaged further by hose removal. If it is, the thermostat housing cover will have to be replaced.
10   Remove the bolts/nuts and detach the thermostat cover **(see illustration)**. If the

3.8 Upper radiator hose clamp (arrow) at the thermostat housing cover

3.10 Thermostat housing cover bolts (arrows)

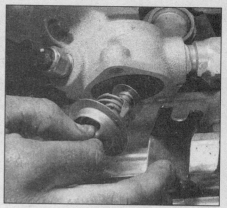

3.11 Note how the thermostat is installed, then remove it from the intake manifold

3.12 If the thermostat comes out without its rubber seal (arrow), pry it out of the housing with a small screwdriver

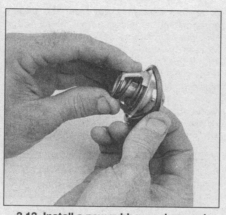

3.13 Install a new rubber seal around the thermostat

4.1 Disconnect the electrical connector from the fan and apply fused battery power and ground to test the fan

3

cover is stuck, tap it with a soft-face hammer to jar it loose. Be prepared for some coolant to spill as the gasket seal is broken.

11   Note how it's installed (which end is facing up), then remove the thermostat **(see illustration)**.

12   If the thermostat comes out without the rubber seal, pry the old seal out of the lower intake manifold **(see illustration)**.

13   Place a new rubber seal around the thermostat **(see illustration)** and install the

thermostat into lower intake manifold, making sure the correct end faces out - the spring is directed toward the engine.

14   Reattach the thermostat housing cover to the thermostat housing and tighten the bolts to the torque listed in this Chapter's Specifications. Now may be a good time to check and replace the hoses and clamps (see Chapter 1).

15   The remaining steps are the reverse of the removal procedure.

16   Refer to Chapter 1 and refill the system, then run the engine and check carefully for leaks.

17   Repeat steps 1 through 4 to be sure the repairs corrected the previous problem(s).

---

4   Engine cooling fans and circuit - check and component replacement

Warning: *Keep hands, tools and clothing away from the fan. To avoid injury or damage DO NOT operate the engine with a damaged fan. Do not attempt to repair fan blades - replace a damaged fan with a new one.*

Check

Refer to illustrations 4.1 and 4.2

1   To test a fan motor, unplug the electrical connector at the motor and use fused jumper wires to connect battery power and ground directly to the fan **(see illustration)**. If the fan still doesn't work, replace the motor.

2   If the motor tests OK, check the cooling fan fuses and relays, located in the underhood fuse/relay panel **(see illustration)**.

3   Remove the cooling fan relays and test them as described in Chapter 12.

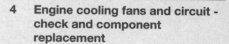

4.2 The cooling fan fuses (A) and relays (B) are easily identifiable by viewing the decal on the inside of the underhood fuse/relay box cover - note that the No.1 fuse and relay control the low-speed operation of the fans and the No. 2 fuse and relay control the high-speed operation of the fans

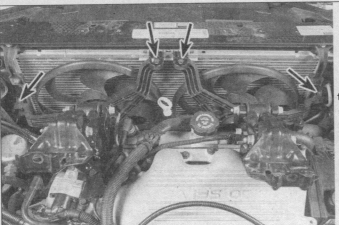

4.11 Detach the bolts (arrows) securing the fans to the radiator (1998 and earlier shown, 1999 and later have three mounting bolts) - note that the bottom legs of the fans on early models or the cooling fan shroud on later models simply slip over the tangs on the lower radiator support

4.13 Remove the nut (arrow) securing the fan blade to the fan motor

4   If the relays and the fan motor are good, check the engine coolant temperature sensor for proper operation (see Chapter 6).

5   If the relays, the fan motor and the engine coolant temperature sensor are good, check the wiring from the relays to the PCM (computer) for open or short circuits. Refer to the wiring schematics at the end of Chapter 12.

6   If the circuit checks out OK but the fan still does not come on, have the Powertrain Control Module (PCM) diagnosed at a dealer service department or other qualified repair facility.

Replacement

Refer to illustrations 4.11 and 4.13
Warning: *Keep hands, tools and clothing away from the fan. To avoid injury or damage DO NOT operate the engine with a damaged fan. Do not attempt to repair fan blades - replace a damaged fan with a new one.*

7   Disconnect the cable from the negative terminal of the battery. **Caution:** *On models equipped with the Theftlock audio system, be sure you have the correct activation code before disconnecting the battery (see the front of this manual).* Remove the air cleaner assembly (see Chapter 4).

8   Remove the bolts securing the engine mount torque strut brackets to the radiator support and rotate the engine torque struts, with the radiator brackets attached, towards the engine (see Chapter 2A). Loosen the through-bolts in the strut mounts first to avoid damage to the rubber bushings.

9   Disconnect the electrical connectors from the fan motors. Detach the wiring harness from the clips on the radiator support and position the wiring harness aside.

10   On 1999 and later vehicles, detach the transaxle oil cooler lines from the clips at the bottom of the cooling fan shroud.

11   Remove the bolts securing fan shroud to the radiator **(see illustration)**. **Note:** *On 1999 and later models the cooling fan and shroud assembly must be removed as a complete unit, unlike earlier models where either cooling fan can be removed separately.*

12   Pull the fan assembly outward to dislodge it from the radiator, then guide the fan or shroud assembly out from the engine compartment, making sure that all wiring clips are disconnected. Be careful not to contact the radiator cooling fins.

13   If the fan is damaged, remove the nut holding the fan blade to the motor **(see illustration)**. **Note:** *On some models, the fan motor can be separated from the plastic mount for replacement, on others it is sold as an assembly.*

14   Installation is the reverse of removal.

5   Radiator and coolant reservoir - removal and installation

Warning: *The engine must be completely cool when this procedure is performed.*

Radiator

Removal

Refer to illustrations 5.6, 5.8, 5.9a and 5.9b

1   Disconnect the cable from the negative terminal of the battery. **Caution:** *On models equipped with the Theftlock audio system, be sure you have the correct activation code before disconnecting the battery (see the front of this manual).*

2   Drain the cooling system (see Chapter 1). If the coolant is relatively new or in good condition, save it and reuse it. Refer to the coolant **Warning** in Section 2.

3   Remove the air cleaner assembly (see Chapter 4).

4   Remove the bolts securing the engine mount torque strut brackets to the radiator support and rotate the engine torque struts, with the radiator brackets attached, towards the engine (see Chapter 2A). Loosen the through-bolts in the strut mounts first to avoid damage to the rubber bushings.

5   Refer to Section 4 and remove the engine cooling fans.

6   Disconnect the electrical connector from the low-coolant sensor in the right radiator tank. Disconnect the cooler lines from the radiator, then cap the ends to prevent excessive fluid loss and contamination. Use a drip pan to catch spilled fluid. Also disconnect the coolant reservoir hose from the radiator neck **(see illustration)**.

7   Loosen the hose clamps, then detach the radiator hoses from the fittings. If they're stuck, grasp each hose near the end with a pair of adjustable pliers and twist it to break the seal, then pull it off - be careful not to distort the radiator fittings. If the hoses are old or deteriorated, cut them off and install new ones.

8   Remove the bolt holding the transmission cooler lines to the bottom of the radiator **(see illustration)**.

5.6 Remove the following components from the right side of the radiator

A   *Coolant recovery hose*
B   *Upper transaxle cooler line*
C   *Coolant level sensor connector*
D   *Lower radiator hose*
E   *Lower transaxle cooler line*

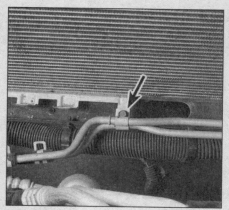

5.8 Remove the bolt (arrow) retaining the transmission lines to the radiator

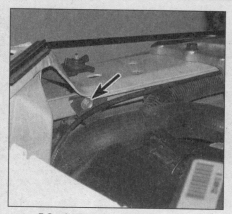

5.9a Left side radiator bracket

5.9b Right side radiator bracket

5.13 The rubber isolators (arrows) must be in place before installing the radiator

9   Remove the bolts from the upper radiator mounting brackets **(see illustrations)**.
10   Tilt the radiator back toward the engine and lift it out of the engine compartment, making sure not to hit the delicate aluminum core on any engine or body parts.
11   With the radiator removed, it can be inspected for leaks and damage. If it needs repair, have a radiator shop or dealer service department perform the work, as special techniques are required.
12   Bugs and dirt can be removed from the radiator with compressed air and a soft

brush. Don't bend the cooling fins as this is done.

Installation

Refer to illustrations 5.13 and 5.14
13   Installation is the reverse of the removal procedure. Be sure that the radiator mounting insulators are in place and in good condition before installing the radiator **(see illustration)**.
14   If the radiator is to be replaced, remove the low coolant sensor from the old radiator and attach it with the clips to the new radia-

tor, using a new O-ring lubricated with clean coolant **(see illustration)**.
15   After installation, fill the cooling system with the proper mixture of antifreeze and water. Be sure to bleed the system of air (see Chapter 1).
16   Start the engine and check for leaks. Allow the engine to reach normal operating temperature, indicated by the upper radiator hose becoming hot. Recheck the coolant level and add more if required.
17   Check and add automatic transmission fluid as needed.

Coolant reservoir

Refer to illustration 5.19
18   Disconnect the radiator overflow hose from the top of the radiator **(see illustration 5.6)**.
19   Remove the mounting clips and lift the coolant reservoir from the vehicle **(see illustration)**.
20   Prior to installation make sure the reservoir is clean and free of debris which could be drawn into the radiator (wash it with soapy water and a brush if necessary, then rinse thoroughly).
21   Installation is the reverse of removal.
Note: *Be sure the plastic tab on the reservoir is inserted into the notch on the inner fenderwell, then clip the reservoir to the engine compartment brace and install the clip on the radiator support.*

---

6   Water pump - check and replacement

Warning: *Wait until the engine is completely cool before starting this procedure.*

Check

Refer to illustration 6.2
1   Water pump failure can cause overheating and serious damage to the engine. There are three ways to check the operation of the water pump while it is installed on the engine. If any one of the following quick-checks indicates water pump problems, it should be replaced immediately.

5.14 Remove the low coolant sensor (arrow) by prying back the two spring clips - use a new O-ring when reinstalling the sensor

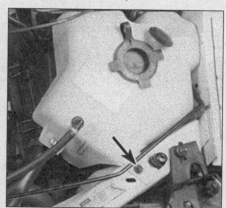

5.19 Remove the clip (arrow) securing the reservoir to the radiator support, then pull upward on the reservoir to detach it from the engine compartment brace

3

6.2   The weep hole (arrow) is located on the top of the water pump (pump removed for clarity)

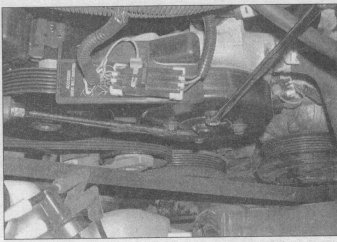

6.9 Use a pry bar or long screwdriver to hold the pulley in place while loosening the water pump pulley bolts

2   A seal protects the water pump impeller shaft bearing from contamination by engine coolant. If this seal fails, a weep hole in the water pump snout will leak coolant **(see illustration)** (an inspection mirror can be used to look at the underside of the pump if the hole isn't on top). If the weep hole is leaking, shaft bearing failure will follow. Replace the water pump immediately.

3   The water pump impeller shaft bearing can also prematurely wear out. When the bearing wears out, it emits a high-pitched squealing sound. If such a noise is coming from the water pump during engine operation, the shaft bearing has failed - replace the water pump immediately. **Note:** *Do not confuse belt noise with bearing noise.*

4   To identify excessive bearing wear, grasp the water pump pulley and try to force it up-and-down or from side-to-side. If the pulley can be moved either horizontally or vertically, the bearing is nearing the end of its service life. Replace the water pump. Don't mistake drivebelt slippage, which causes a squealing sound, for water pump bearing failure.

5   It is possible for a water pump to be bad, even if it doesn't howl or leak water. Sometimes the fins on the back of the impeller can corrode away until the pump is no longer effective. The only way to check for this is to remove the pump for examination.

Replacement

Refer to illustrations 6.9, 6.11 and 6.13

6   Disconnect the cable from the negative terminal of the battery. **Caution:** *On models equipped with the Theftlock audio system, be sure you have the correct activation code before disconnecting the battery (see the front of this manual).*

7   Drain the coolant (see Chapter 1).

8   Remove the serpentine drivebelt (see Chapter 1).

9   Loosen the bolts on the water pump pulley, using a prybar to hold it **(see illustration)**.

10   Remove the small belt guard just above the water pump (if equipped).

11   Remove the bolts/nuts and detach the water pump from the engine **(see illustration). Note:** *Most models have a locating mark at the top of the pump. If yours doesn't have one, make a mark yourself for help in orienting the pump during reassembly (if the same pump is to be reinstalled).*

12   Clean the fastener threads and any threaded holes in the engine to remove corrosion and sealant.

13   Compare the new pump to the old one to make sure they're identical. If using the existing pump, inspect the back of the pump for a broken or corroded impeller **(see illustration)**.

14   Remove all traces of old gasket material from the engine with a gasket scraper.

15   Clean the engine and water pump mating surfaces with lacquer thinner or acetone.

16   Carefully attach the pump and new gasket to the engine and start the bolts/nuts finger tight. Make sure the alignment mark is at the top.

17   Tighten the fasteners in 1/4-turn increments to the torque figure listed in this Chapter's Specifications. Don't overtighten them

or the pump may be distorted.

18   Reinstall all parts removed for access to the pump.

19   Refill and bleed the cooling system (see Chapter 1). Run the engine and check for leaks.

7   Coolant temperature gauge sending unit - check and replacement

Check

1   The coolant temperature indicator system is composed of a temperature gauge or warning light mounted in the dash and a coolant temperature sensor mounted on the engine. This coolant temperature sensor doubles as an information sensor for the fuel and emissions systems (see Chapter 6) and as a sending unit for the temperature gauge.

2   If an overheating indication occurs, check the coolant level in the system and then make sure the wiring between the gauge and the sending unit is secure and all fuses are intact.

3   Check the operation of the coolant tem-

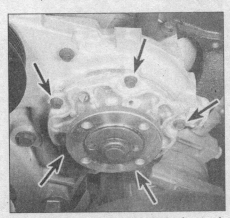

6.11 Water pump retaining bolts (arrows)

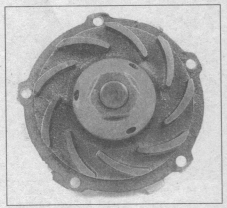

6.13 Inspect the impeller for damage and corrosion

8.4   Connect a voltmeter to the heater blower motor connector by backprobing the connector using pins, and check the running voltage at each blower switch position

BLOWER MOTOR CONNECTOR

BLOWER RESISTOR CONNECTOR

perature sensor (see Chapter 6). If the sensor is defective, replace it with a new part of the same specification.

4   If the coolant temperature sensor is good, have the temperature gauge checked by a dealer service department. This test will require a scan tool to access the information as it is processed by the On Board computer.

Replacement

5   Refer to Chapter 6 for the engine coolant temperature sensor replacement procedure.

38036-3-8.8A HAYNES

8.8a   Blower resistor connector terminal guide

A   Blower switch position No. 2 or M1
B   Blower switch position No. 1 or Low
C   Blower switch position No. 4 or M3
D   Blower switch position No. 3 or M2
E   Ground terminal
F   Blower switch position No. 5 or High
G   Blower relay power terminal (hot at all times)

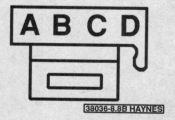

38036-8.8B HAYNES

8.8b   Rear auxiliary blower resistor connector terminal guide

A   Not used
B   Rear auxiliary switch position No. 3
C   Rear auxiliary switch position No. 1
D   Rear auxiliary switch position No. 2

8   Blower motor and circuit - check

Refer to illustrations 8.4, 8.8a, 8.8b and 8.9
Warning: *The models covered by this manual are equipped with a Supplemental Inflatable Restraint (SIR) system, more commonly known as airbags. Always disable the airbag system before working in the vicinity of any airbag system components to avoid the possibility of accidental deployment of the airbags, which could cause personal injury (see Chapter 12).*
Note: *This procedure applies to the front blower motor and circuit on all models covered by this manual. Some models are equipped with rear auxiliary heating and air conditioning which can be tested in a similar manner, except that the driver's side rear trim panel must be removed to access the rear blower motor (see Chapter 11) and the fuse for the rear blower motor is marked RR HVAC. The rear blower resistor is also different but, it can be tested by simply checking for continuity between all three terminals of the resistor. When testing a rear blower motor and circuit be aware that the passenger's rear blower switch will not operate unless the rear blower switch on the instrument panel is set to the "R" position. When the rear blower switch on the instrument panel is set to the "R" position, it applies a ground signal to a relay in the passenger's rear blower switch, allowing the rear passenger's switch to operate the blower and temperature controls.*

1   Check the fuse (marked HVAC) and all connections in the circuit for looseness and corrosion. Make sure the battery is fully charged. **Note:** *The front blower relay is located on the blower resistor under the right side of the dash and the HVAC fuse are located in the fuse panel under the dash.*
2   With the transaxle in Park, set the parking brake securely, turn the ignition switch to the Run position. It isn't necessary to start the vehicle.
3   Remove the lower right dash insulator panel (below the glove box) for access to the blower motor.
4   Backprobe the blower motor electrical connector with two straight pins and connect a voltmeter to the blower motor connector and ground **(see illustration)**.
5   Move the blower switch through each of its positions and note the voltage readings. Changes in voltage indicate that the motor speeds will also vary as the switch is moved to the different positions.
6   If there is voltage present, but the blower motor does not operate, the blower motor is probably faulty. Disconnect the blower motor connector, then hook one side of the blower motor terminals to a chassis ground and the other to a fused source of battery voltage. If the blower doesn't operate, it is faulty.
7   If there was no voltage present at the blower motor, follow the blower motor ground wire from the motor to the chassis and check the ground terminal for continuity to ground against the chassis metal. If there was no voltage present at the blower motor at one or more speeds, and the motor itself tested OK, check the blower motor resistor.
8   Disconnect the electrical connector from the blower motor resistor **(see illustration 8.4)**. Check for voltage at each of the terminals in the connector as the blower speed switch is moved to the different positions with the ignition On **(see illustrations)**. If the voltmeter responds correctly to the switch and the blower is known to be good then the resistor is probably faulty.
9   Check for continuity between terminals A, B, C and D on the blower resistor, then check for continuity between terminal C on the blower resistor and terminal 1 of the blower motor connector **(see illustration)**. If continuity does not exist, replace the blower resistor/relay assembly.

3

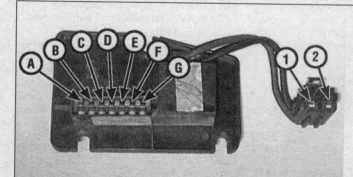

8.9   Front blower motor resistor/relay terminal guide

9.3 Front blower motor mounting details

A Electrical connector
B Cooling hose
C Mounting screws

9.5 Remove the retaining clip to detach the fan from the blower motor

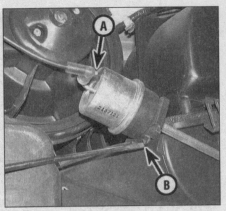

9.10 Remove the vacuum hose (A), unsnap the retaining tab (B) and disengage the mode actuator from its mount - let the mode actuator hang down on the actuating arm

10   Also test the blower motor relay for correct operation. Disconnect the connector from the blower motor. Detach the screws and remove the blower resistor/blower motor relay assembly from the heating/air conditioning module. Apply positive battery power to terminal F, and ground terminal E, and test for continuity between terminal G and terminal 1 on the blower motor connector. There should now be continuity; if not, replace the relay/blower resistor assembly. **Note:** *Rear auxiliary heating /air conditioning systems are equipped with a relay in the passenger's rear control switch only. See the wiring diagrams at the end of this manual for specific details.*

11   If there is no voltage present from the switch, then the switch, control panel or related wiring is probably faulty. Refer to the wiring diagrams at the end of this manual and check the switch for continuity between the appropriate terminals with the switch in different positions. If the switch is Ok, check the wiring between the blower resistor connector and the fuse panel for opens and shorts.

9   Blower motor - removal and installation

Warning: *The models covered by this manual are equipped with a Supplemental Inflatable Restraint (SIR) system, more commonly known as airbags. Always disable the airbag system before working in the vicinity of any airbag system components to avoid the possibility of accidental deployment of the airbags, which could cause personal injury (see Chapter 12).*

Front blower motor

Refer to illustrations 9.3 and 9.5

1   Remove the lower right dash insulator panel (below the glove box) for access to the blower motor (see Chapter 11).
2   Remove the blower motor cooling hose.
3   Disconnect the electrical connector from the blower motor and remove the three

screws from the blower housing **(see illustration).**
4   Pull the blower motor and fan straight down.
5   If you're replacing the blower motor with a new one, remove the clip and detach the fan from the blower motor **(see illustration).**
6   Install the fan onto the new motor and install the blower motor into the heater housing.
7   Installation is the reverse of the removal procedure.

Rear blower motor

Refer to illustrations 9.10 and 9.11

8   Some models have an auxiliary heating air conditioning system located in the rear of the vehicle, behind the left rear interior trim panel. The rear blower motor and resistor can be checked in the same manner as the front system (see Section 8).
9   To access the rear auxiliary blower motor, remove the left rear quarter trim panel (see Chapter 11).
10   Detach the mode actuator and set it aside to allow rear blower motor removal **(see illustration).**
11   Disconnect the electrical connector and detach the blower motor from the housing **(see illustration).**
12   Installation is the reverse of removal.

10   Heater and air conditioning control assembly - removal and installation

Warning: *The models covered by this manual are equipped with a Supplemental Inflatable Restraint (SIR) system, more commonly known as airbags. Always disable the airbag system before working in the vicinity of any airbag system components to avoid the possibility of accidental deployment of the airbags, which could cause personal injury (see Chapter 12).*

Removal

Refer to illustrations 10.3a, 10.3b and 10.3c

1   Disconnect the cable from the negative terminal of the battery. **Caution:** *On models equipped with the Theftlock audio system, be sure you have the correct activation code before disconnecting the battery (see the front of this manual).*
2   Remove the center trim panel from the instrument panel to allow access to the heater/air conditioning control mounting screws (see Chapter 11).
3   Remove the control assembly retaining screws and pull the unit from the dash. It can be pulled out just far enough to allow disconnecting the electrical connections and vacuum harness from the control head. Use a small screwdriver to release the clips and the vacuum harness **(see illustrations).**

Installation

4   To install the control assembly, reverse the removal procedure. **Caution:** *When reconnecting vacuum harness to the control*

9.11 Lift the retaining tab (A) and rotate the rear blower motor counterclockwise to release it from the blower housing - (B) indicates the location of the rear blower resistor

10.3a Remove the screws (arrows) retaining the heater/air conditioning control assembly to the instrument panel - the lower two screws secure the rear heating/air conditioning control panel (if equipped)

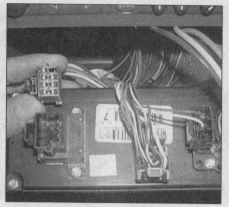

10.3b Pull the control assembly outward and disconnect the electrical connectors . . .

10.3c . . . and the vacuum harness

assembly, do not use any lubricant to make them slip on easier; it can affect vacuum operation. If necessary, use a drop of plain water to make reconnection easier.

11   Heater core - removal and installation

Warning 1: The models covered by this manual are equipped with a Supplemental Inflatable Restraint (SIR) system, more commonly known as airbags. Always disable the airbag system before working in the vicinity of any airbag system components to avoid the possibility of accidental deployment of the airbags, which could cause personal injury (see Chapter 12).

Warning 2: The air conditioning system is under high pressure. DO NOT loosen any fittings or remove any components until after the system has been discharged. Air conditioning refrigerant should be properly discharged into an EPA-approved container at a dealership service department or an automotive air conditioning facility. Always wear eye protection when disconnecting air conditioning system fittings.

Front heater core

Refer to illustrations 11.5, 11.7, 11.8, 11.9, 11.10a, 11.10b, 11.11 and 11.12

1   Disconnect the cable at the negative terminal of the battery. **Caution:** On models equipped with the Theftlock audio system, be sure you have the correct activation code before disconnecting the battery (see the front of this manual).

2   Drain the cooling system (see Chapter 1).

3   Remove the air cleaner and the air intake duct assembly (see Chapter 4).

4   Remove the driver's side wiper linkage to allow access to the heater hoses on the firewall.

5   Disconnect the heater hoses at the

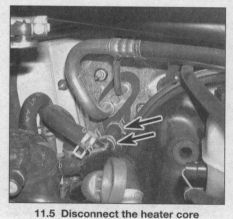

11.5 Disconnect the heater core hoses (arrows) at the engine compartment firewall

heater core inlet and outlet on the engine side of the firewall (see illustration) and plug the open fittings. If the hoses are stuck to the pipes, cut them off and replace them with new ones upon installation.

6   From the inside of the car, remove the lower right sound insulator panel from below the glove box, the lower left sound insulator panel and the knee bolster from below the steering column. Then remove the center

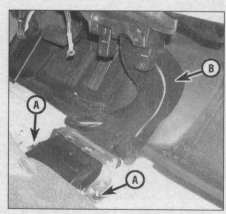

11.8 Remove the floor duct brace (A) and the floor duct (B)

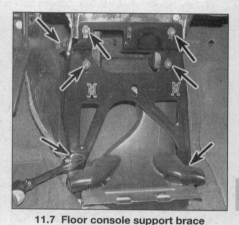

11.7 Floor console support brace retaining bolts (arrows)

floor console (see Chapter 11 if necessary).

7   Remove the center floor console support brace (see illustration).

8   Remove the floor air duct from below the heater case (see illustration).

9   Remove the heater core outlet cover (see illustration).

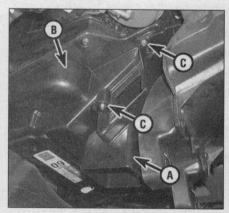

11.9 The heater core outlet cover (A) must be removed before the heater core cover (B) - (C) indicates two left side screws securing the outlet cover, the two right side screws are not visible in this photo

3

11.10a Heater core cover retaining screws (arrows) - left side

11.10b Heater core cover retaining screws (arrow) - right side

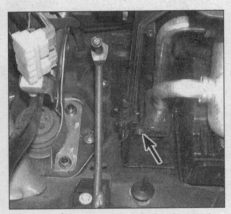

11.11 Remove the screw (arrow) securing the heater core pipe clamp to the brace on the firewall

11.12 Detach the heater core clamp (arrow) and remove the heater core from the housing

11.16 The auxiliary rear heating/air conditioning unit is mounted behind the left rear trim panel

10   Remove the heater core cover **(see illustrations)**.

11   Remove the heater core pipe retaining clamp screw **(see illustration)**.

12   Remove the heater core clamp screw and clamp **(see illustration)**, then slide the heater core out carefully.

13   Installation is the reverse of removal. **Note:** *When reinstalling the heater core, make sure any original insulating/sealing materials are in place around the heater core pipes and around the core.*

14   Refill the cooling system (see Chapter 1).

15   Start the engine and check for proper operation.

Rear heater core

Refer to illustrations 11.16, 11.19, 11.22 and 11.23

16   Some models may be equipped with an optional rear heater/air conditioning system. the unit is located behind the left-rear interior trim panel (behind the left rear wheel housing). It includes a blower motor, heater core and evaporator core **(see illustration)**.

17   Drain the cooling system (see Chapter 1).

18   Raise and suitably support the vehicle on jackstands, to access the hose connec-

tions under the rear of the vehicle chassis.

19   Detach the heater hoses from the heater core tubes and drain the remaining coolant from the lines into a suitable container **(see illustration)**. Be prepared for excess coolant to expel from the lines as the hoses are disconnected. If the coolant is relatively new or in good condition, save it and reuse it. Refer

to the coolant **Warning** in Section 2.

20   Lower the vehicle.

21   Refer to Chapter 11 for removal of the left rear quarter trim panel and the rear seats.

22   Remove the heater core tube retaining bracket and the bolt securing the heater core tube flange to the heater core **(see illustration)**. Push downward on the tubes to sepa-

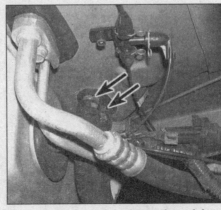

11.19 Depress the tabs on the quick connect fittings to detach the heater hoses from the rear heater core tubes

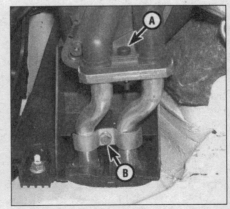

11.22 Rear heater core tube flange retaining bolt (A) and the tube retaining bracket (B)

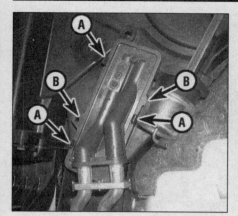

11.23 Rear heater core retaining tabs (A) - some models may have retaining screws at locations (B)

12.1 Check that the evaporator housing drain tube (arrow) at the firewall is clear of any blockage - the view here is from below the engine looking up through the right wheelwell

12.9 Insert a thermometer in the center duct while operating the air conditioning system - the output air should be 35-40 degrees F less than the ambient temperature, depending on humidity (but not lower than 40-degrees F)

rate the tubes from the rear heater core.

23 Remove the screws and/or depress the release tabs securing the heater core to the housing, then remove the heater core **(see illustration)**. Note: *Some models may have retaining screws and release tabs, while other models may have provisions for retaining screws but were not originally installed at the factory. Regardless, all models have three retaining tabs which must be released before the heater core can be separated from the heater core housing.*

24 Installation is the reverse of the removal procedure.

25 Refill the cooling system (see Chapter 1).

26 Start the engine and check for proper operation.

12 Air conditioning and heating system - check and maintenance

Air conditioning system

Refer to illustration 12.1

Warning: *The air conditioning system is under high pressure. Do not loosen any hose fittings or remove any components until after the system has been discharged. Air conditioning refrigerant should be properly discharged into an EPA-approved recovery/recycling unit at a dealer service department or an automotive air conditioning repair facility. Always wear eye protection when disconnecting air conditioning system fittings.*

Caution 1: *All models covered by this manual use environmentally friendly R-134a. This refrigerant (and its appropriate refrigerant oils) are not compatible R-12 refrigerant system components and must never be mixed or the components will be damaged.*

Caution 2: *When replacing entire components, additional refrigerant oil should be added equal to the amount that is removed with the component being replaced. Be sure to read the can before adding any oil to the*

system, to make sure it is compatible with the R-134a system.

1 The following maintenance checks should be performed on a regular basis to ensure that the air conditioning continues to operate at peak efficiency.

a) *Inspect the condition of the compressor drivebelt. If it is worn or deteriorated, replace it (see Chapter 1).*

b) *Check the drivebelt tension and, if necessary, adjust it (see Chapter 1).*

c) *Inspect the system hoses. Look for cracks, bubbles, hardening and deterioration. Inspect the hoses and all fittings for oil bubbles or seepage. If there is any evidence of wear, damage or leakage, replace the hose(s).*

d) *Inspect the condenser fins for leaves, bugs and any other foreign material that may have embedded itself in the fins. Use a "fin comb" or compressed air to remove debris from the condenser.*

e) *Make sure the system has the correct refrigerant charge.*

f) *If you hear water sloshing around in the dash area or have water dripping on the carpet, check the evaporator housing drain tube* **(see illustration)** *and insert a piece of wire into the opening to check for blockage.*

2 It's a good idea to operate the system for about ten minutes at least once a month. This is particularly important during the winter months because long term non-use can cause hardening, and subsequent failure, of the seals. Note that using the Defrost function operates the compressor.

3 If the air conditioning system is not working properly, proceed to Step 6 and perform the general checks outlined below.

4 Because of the complexity of the air conditioning system and the special equipment necessary to service it, in-depth troubleshooting and repairs, beyond checking the refrigerant charge and the compressor clutch operation, are not included in this

manual. However, simple checks and component replacement procedures are provided in this Chapter. For more complete information on the air conditioning system, refer to the *Haynes Automotive Heating and Air Conditioning Manual.*

5 The most common cause of poor cooling is simply a low system refrigerant charge. If a noticeable drop in system cooling ability occurs, one of the following quick checks will help you determine whether the refrigerant level is low. Should the system lose its cooling ability, the following procedure will help you pinpoint the cause.

Check

Refer to illustration 12.9

6 Warm the engine up to normal operating temperature.

7 Place the air conditioning temperature selector at the coldest setting and put the blower at the highest setting. Open the doors (to make sure the air conditioning system doesn't cycle off as soon as it cools the passenger compartment).

8 After the system reaches operating temperature, feel the two pipes connected to the evaporator at the firewall.

9 The outlet pipe should be cold (the tubing that leads back to the compressor). If the evaporator outlet is warm, the system probably needs a charge. Insert a thermometer in the center air distribution duct **(see illustration)** while operating the air conditioning system at its maximum setting - the temperature of the output air should be 35 to 40 degrees F below the ambient air temperature (down to approximately 40 degrees F). If the ambient (outside) air temperature is very high, say 110 degrees F, the duct air temperature may be as high as 60 degrees F, but generally the air conditioning is 35 to 40 degrees F cooler than the ambient air.

10 If the air isn't as cold as it used to be, the system probably needs a charge.

3

11   If the air is warm and the system doesn't seem to be operating properly, check the operation of the compressor clutch.

12   Have an assistant switch the air conditioning On while you observe the front of the compressor. The clutch will make an audible click and the center of the clutch should rotate.

13   If the clutch does not operate, check the appropriate fuses in the interior fuse panel.

14   Remove the compressor clutch (AC) relay from the engine compartment relay panel and test it (see Chapter 12). With the relay out and the ignition On, check for battery power at two of the relay terminal sockets (refer to the wiring diagrams for wire color designations to determine which terminals to check). There should be battery power with the key On, at the terminals for the relay control and power circuits.

15   Using a jumper wire, connect the terminals in the relay box from the relay power circuit to the terminal that leads to the compressor clutch (refer to the wiring diagrams for wire color designations to determine which terminals to connect). Listen for the clutch to click as you make the connection. If the clutch doesn't respond, disconnect the clutch connector at the compressor and check for battery voltage at the compressor clutch connector. Check for continuity to ground on the black wire terminal of the compressor clutch connector. If power and ground are available and the clutch doesn't operate when connected, the compressor clutch is defective.

16   If the compressor clutch, relay and related circuits are good and the system is fully charged with refrigerant and the compressor does not operate under normal conditions, have the PCM and related circuits checked by a dealer service department or other properly equipped repair facility.

17   Further inspection or testing of the system is beyond the scope of the home mechanic and should be left to a professional.

Adding refrigerant

Refer to illustrations 12.18 and 12.21

Caution: *Make sure any refrigerant, refrigerant oil or replacement component your purchase is designated as compatible with environmentally friendly R-134a systems.*

18   Purchase an R-134a automotive charging kit at an auto parts store **(see illustration)**. A charging kit includes a 12-ounce can of refrigerant, a tap valve and a short section of hose that can be attached between the tap valve and the system low side service valve. Because one can of refrigerant may not be sufficient to bring the system charge up to the proper level, it's a good idea to buy an additional can. **Warning:** *Never add more than two cans of refrigerant to the system.*

19   Hook up the charging kit by following the manufacturer's instructions. **Warning:** *DO NOT hook the charging kit hose to the system high side!* The fittings on the charging kit are designed to fit **only** on the low side of the system.

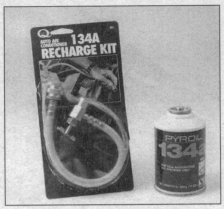

12.18 A basic charging kit for 134a systems is available at most auto parts stores - it must say 134a (not R-12) and so should the can of refrigerant

20   Back off the valve handle on the charging kit and screw the kit onto the refrigerant can, making sure first that the O-ring or rubber seal inside the threaded portion of the kit is in place. **Warning:** *Wear protective eyewear when dealing with pressurized refrigerant cans.*

21   Remove the dust cap from the low-side charging and attach the quick-connect fitting on the kit hose **(see illustration)**.

22   Warm up the engine and turn On the air conditioning. Keep the charging kit hose away from the fan and other moving parts. **Note:** *The charging process requires the compressor to be running. If the clutch cycles off, you can put the air conditioning switch on High and leave the car doors open to keep the clutch on and compressor working.*

23   Turn the valve handle on the kit until the stem pierces the can, then back the handle out to release the refrigerant. You should be able to hear the rush of gas. Add refrigerant to the low side of the system, keeping the can upright at all times, but shaking it occasionally. Allow stabilization time between each addition. **Note:** *The charging process will go faster if you wrap the can with a hot-water-soaked shop rag to keep the can from freezing up.*

24   If you have an accurate thermometer, you can place it in the center air conditioning duct inside the vehicle and keep track of the output air temperature **(see illustration 12.9)**. A charged system that is working properly should cool down to approximately 40-degrees F. If the ambient (outside) air temperature is very high, say 110 degrees F, the duct air temperature may be as high as 60 degrees F, but generally the air conditioning is 30-40 degrees F cooler than the ambient air.

25   When the can is empty, turn the valve handle to the closed position and release the connection from the low-side port. Replace the dust cap.

26   Remove the charging kit from the can and store the kit for future use with the piercing valve in the UP position, to prevent inadvertently piercing the can on the next use.

12.21 Attach the refrigerant kit to the low-side charging port (arrow) - it's between the engine and the radiator - the cap should be marked with an "L"

Heating systems

27   If the carpet under the heater core is damp, or if antifreeze vapor or steam is coming through the vents, the heater core is leaking. Remove it (see Section 12) and install a new unit (most radiator shops will not repair a leaking heater core).

28   If the air coming out of the heater vents isn't hot, the problem could stem from any of the following causes:

a) *The thermostat is stuck open, preventing the engine coolant from warming up enough to carry heat to the heater core. Replace the thermostat (see Section 3).*

b) *There is a blockage in the system, preventing the flow of coolant through the heater core. Feel both heater hoses at the firewall. They should be hot. If one of them is cold, there is an obstruction in one of the hoses or in the heater core, or the heater control valve is shut. Detach the hoses and back flush the heater core with a water hose. If the heater core is clear but circulation is impeded, remove the two hoses and flush them out with a water hose.*

c) *If flushing fails to remove the blockage from the heater core, the core must be replaced (see Section 11).*

Eliminating air conditioning odors

Refer to illustration 12.32

29   Unpleasant odors that often develop in air conditioning systems are caused by the growth of a fungus, usually on the surface of the evaporator core. The warm, humid environment there is a perfect breeding ground for mildew to develop.

30   The evaporator core on most vehicles is difficult to access, and factory dealerships have a lengthy, expensive process for eliminating the fungus by opening up the evaporator case and using a powerful disinfectant and rinse on the core until the fungus is gone. You can service your own system at home,

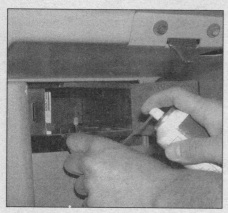

12.32 With the interior compartment air filter removed, spray the disinfectant at the evaporator core

but it takes something much stronger than basic household germ-killers or deodorizers.

31   Aerosol disinfectants for automotive air conditioning systems are available in most auto parts stores, but remember when shopping for them that the most effective treatments are also the most expensive. The basic procedure for using these sprays is to start by running the system in the RECIRC mode for ten minutes with the blower on its highest speed. Use the highest heat mode to dry out the system and keep the compressor from engaging by disconnecting the wiring connector at the compressor (see Section 14).

32   The disinfectant can usually comes with a long spray hose. Remove the interior ventilation filters (see Chapter 1), point the nozzle towards the evaporator core, and spray according to the manufacturer's recommendations **(see illustration)**. Try to cover the whole surface of the evaporator core, by aiming the spray up, down and sideways. Follow the manufacturer's recommendations for the length of spray and waiting time between applications.

33   Once the evaporator has been cleaned, the best way to prevent the mildew from coming back again is to make sure your evaporator housing drain tube is clear **(see illustration 12.1)**.

13   Air conditioning accumulator/drier - removal and installation

Warning: *The air conditioning system is under high pressure. DO NOT loosen any fittings or remove any components until after the system has been discharged. Air conditioning refrigerant should be properly discharged into an EPA-approved container at a dealership service department or an automotive air conditioning repair facility. Always wear eye protection when disconnecting air conditioning system fittings.*
Note: *This procedure applies to 2000 and earlier models only. 2001 models are equipped with a receiver/drier that is mounted to the front of the condenser. On 2001 models, it will be necessary to remove the condenser and detach the receiver/drier from the condenser after the condenser is removed from the vehicle (see Section 15).*

Removal

Refer to illustration 13.3

1   Have the air conditioning system discharged (see **Warning** above). Disconnect the cable from the negative terminal of the battery. **Caution:** *On models equipped with the Theftlock audio system, be sure you have the correct activation code before disconnecting the battery (see the front of this manual).*

2   Remove the air cleaner cover and the air intake duct (see Chapter 4).

3   Disconnect the refrigerant inlet and outlet lines **(see illustration)**, using back-up wrenches if necessary. Cap or plug the open lines immediately to prevent the entry of dirt or moisture.

4   Loosen the clamp bolt on the mounting bracket and slide the accumulator/drier assembly up and out of the compartment. **Note:** *It may be helpful to remove the air cleaner housing from the inner fenderwell to allow better access to the accumulator clamp bolt.*

Installation

5   If you are replacing the accumulator/drier with a new one, add one ounce of fresh refrigerant oil to the new unit (oil must be R-134a compatible).

6   Place the new accumulator/drier into position in the bracket.

7   Install the inlet and outlet lines, using clean refrigerant oil on the new O-rings. Tighten the mounting bolt securely.

8   Connect the cable to the negative terminal of the battery.

9   Have the system evacuated, recharged and leak tested by a dealership service department or an automotive air conditioning repair facility.

14   Air conditioning compressor - removal and installation

Warning: *The air conditioning system is under high pressure. DO NOT loosen any fittings or remove any components until after the system has been discharged. Air conditioning refrigerant should be properly discharged into an EPA-approved container at a dealership service department or an automotive air conditioning repair facility. Always wear eye protection when disconnecting air conditioning system fittings.*
Note 1: *The accumulator/drier or receiver/drier (see Section 13) should be replaced whenever the compressor is replaced.*
Note 2: *Whenever the compressor is replaced because of internal damage, the expansion (orifice) tube (2000 and earlier models) or the refrigerant filter (2001 models) should also be replaced (see Section 16 or 17).*

Removal

Refer to illustrations 14.8, 14.9a and 14.9b

1   Have the air conditioning system discharged (see **Warning** above). Disconnect the cable from the negative terminal of the battery. **Caution:** *On models equipped with the Theftlock audio system, be sure you have the correct activation code before disconnecting the battery (see the front of this manual).*

2   Remove the serpentine drivebelt (see Chapter 1).

3   Remove the passenger's side engine mount strut and the strut bracket from the engine (see Chapter 2A).

4   Remove the engine cooling fans (see Section 4).

5   Raise the vehicle and support it securely on jackstands.

6   Working below the vehicle, clean the compressor thoroughly around the refrigerant line fittings.

7   Disconnect the electrical connector from the air conditioning compressor.

8   Disconnect the suction and discharge lines from the compressor. Both lines are mounted to the back of the compressor with a plate secured by one bolt. Plug the open fit-

3

13.3 Accumulator mounting details

A   Inlet line
B   Outlet line
C   Retaining clamp bolt

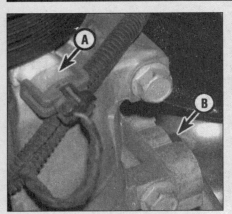

14.8 Disconnect the electrical connector (A) and the retaining bolt (B) securing the refrigerant lines to the back of the compressor

14.9a Compressor upper mounting bolts (arrows)

14.9b Compressor lower mounting bolt (arrow)

tings to prevent the entry of dirt and moisture, and discard the seals between the plate and compressor **(see illustration)**.

9   Remove the compressor mounting bolts **(see illustrations)**. Detach the compressor from the mounting bracket and let it rest on the engine crossmember.

10   Lower the vehicle and remove the compressor through the top of the engine compartment.

Installation

11   If a new compressor is being installed, pour the oil from the old compressor into a graduated container and add that exact amount of new refrigerant oil to the new compressor. Also follow any directions included with the new compressor. **Note:** *Some replacement compressors come with refrigerant oil in them. Follow the directions with the compressor regarding the draining of excess oil prior to installation.* **Caution:** *The oil used must be labeled as compatible with R-134a refrigerant systems.*

12   Installation is the reverse of the disassembly. When installing the line fitting bolt to the compressor, use new seals lubricated with clean refrigerant oil, and tighten the bolt securely.

13   Reconnect the cable to the negative terminal of the battery.

14   Have the system evacuated, recharged and leak tested by a dealership service department or an automotive air conditioning repair facility.

---

15   Air conditioning condenser - removal and installation

Warning: *The air conditioning system is under high pressure. DO NOT loosen any fittings or remove any components until after the system has been discharged. Air conditioning refrigerant should be properly discharged into an EPA-approved container at a dealership service department or an automotive air conditioning repair facility. Always wear eye protection when disconnecting air conditioning system fittings.*

Removal

Refer to illustrations 15.2 and 15.4

1   Have the air conditioning system discharged and recovered (see **Warning** above). Disconnect the cable from the negative terminal of the battery. **Caution:** *On models equipped with a Theftlock audio system, be sure the lockout feature is turned off before performing any procedure which requires disconnecting the battery.*

2   Disconnect the refrigerant line fittings from the left side of the condenser and cap the open fittings to prevent the entry of dirt and moisture. **(see illustration)**.

3   Remove the cooling fans (see Section 4) and the radiator (see Section 5).

4   Pull the condenser toward the engine, wiggling it until it is free of the upper and lower rubber insulators, then withdraw it carefully from the vehicle **(see illustration)**. **Caution:** *The condenser is made of aluminum - be careful not to damage it during removal.*

15.2 The condenser lines (arrows) are located just to the left of the radiator

15.4 Pull the condenser core back carefully until it is free of the rubber insulators (arrows)

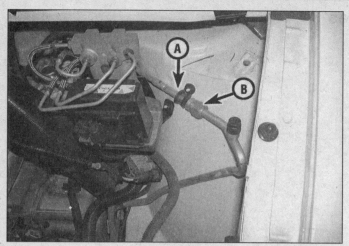

16.3 Working on the driver's side of the engine compartment, use a set of back up wrenches to detach the pipe fitting (A) - (B) indicates the orifice tube location

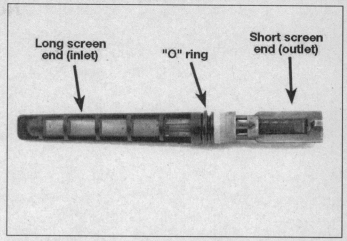

16.5 The expansion tube is equipped with a tapered mesh screen that must be cleaned and not have any holes or damage

Installation

5   Installation is the reverse of removal. Be sure to use new, R134a compatible O-rings on the refrigerant line fittings, lubricated with clean refrigerant oil. If a new condenser is installed, add 1 ounce of new refrigerant oil to the system (R-134a compatible).

6   Have the system evacuated, recharged and leak tested by a dealership service department or an automotive air conditioning repair facility.

16 Air conditioning expansion (orifice) tube - removal and installation

Refer to illustrations 16.3 and 16.5

Warning: *The air conditioning system is under high pressure. DO NOT loosen any fittings or remove any components until after the system has been discharged. Air conditioning refrigerant should be properly discharged into an EPA-approved container at a dealership service department or an automotive air conditioning repair facility. Always wear eye protection when disconnecting air conditioning system fittings.*

Note: *This procedure applies to 2000 and earlier models only. 2000 and earlier models are equipped with an accumulator/drier and a expansion orifice tube, while 2001 models are equipped with a receiver/drier, a thermal expansion valve and a refrigerant line filter.*

1   Have the air conditioning system discharged and the refrigerant recovered (see **Warning** above). Disconnect the cable from the negative terminal of the battery. **Caution:** *On models equipped with the Theftlock audio system, be sure you have the correct activa-*tion code before disconnecting the battery *(see the front of this manual).*

2   Remove the air cleaner cover and the air intake duct (see Chapter 4).

3   Disconnect the refrigerant high-pressure line at the orifice tube **(see illustration)**.

4   The expansion tube is a tube with a fixed-diameter orifice and a mesh filter at each end. When you separate the pipe at the fitting you will see one end of the orifice tube inside the pipe leading to the evaporator. Use needle-nose pliers to remove the orifice tube.

5   The orifice tube acts to meter the refrigerant, changing it from high-pressure liquid to low-pressure liquid. It is possible to reuse the orifice tube if **(see illustration):**

a) *The screens aren't plugged with grit or foreign material*
b) *Neither screen is torn*
c) *The plastic housing over the screens is intact*
d) *The brass orifice inside the plastic housing is unrestricted*

6   Installation is the reverse of removal. Be sure to insert the expansion tube with the shorter end in first, toward the evaporator. **Caution:** *Always use a new O-ring when installing the expansion (orifice) tube.*

7   Retighten the fitting and refrigerant line, then have the system evacuated, recharged and leak-tested by the shop that discharged it.

17 Air conditioning refrigerant filter - removal and installation

Warning: *The air conditioning system is under high pressure. DO NOT loosen any fittings or remove any components until after* the system has been discharged. Air conditioning refrigerant should be properly discharged into an EPA-approved container at a dealership service department or an automotive air conditioning repair facility. Always wear eye protection when disconnecting air conditioning system fittings.

Note: *This procedure applies to 2001 models only. 2000 and earlier models are equipped with an expansion orifice tube (see Section 16).*

1   Have the air conditioning system discharged and the refrigerant recovered (see **Warning** above). Disconnect the cable from the negative terminal of the battery. **Caution:** *On models equipped with the Theftlock audio system, be sure you have the correct activation code before disconnecting the battery (see the front of this manual).*

2   Raise the front of the vehicle and support it securely on jackstands.

3   Remove the plastic air baffle from below the radiator.

4   Using a back up wrench, loosen the two flare nuts securing the refrigerant filter to the evaporator tube.

5   Remove the refrigerant filter from the evaporator tube. Cap or plug the open lines immediately to prevent the entry of dirt or moisture.

6   Remove the caps or plugs from the evaporator tube and install a new filter with the arrow pointing towards the evaporator core.

7   Retighten the fittings on the refrigerant line, then have the system evacuated, recharged and leak-tested by the shop that discharged it.

3

Notes

Chapter 4
Fuel and exhaust systems

Contents

Specifications

General

Fuel pressure (key On, engine Off)	
1999 and earlier	41 to 47 psi
2000 and later	52 to 59 psi
Fuel injector resistance	11.4 to 12.6 ohms
Fuel level sending unit resistance	
1997	
Empty	1.0 ohm
Full	88 ohms
1998 and later	
Empty	40 ohms
Full	250 ohms

Torque specifications

	Ft-lbs (unless otherwise indicated)
Fuel rail mounting bolts	89 in-lbs
Fuel pressure regulator mounting bolt	76 in-lbs
Fuel tank mounting strap bolts	35
Throttle body mounting bolts	18
Upper intake manifold bolts	18

1.1 Typical fuel system components

1	Fuel pump relay (inside Underhood Electrical Center)	
2	Throttle body	
3	Accelerator cable	
4	Air filter housing	
5	Fuel pressure regulator, fuel rail and injectors (under upper intake manifold)	

1   General information

Refer to illustration 1.1
Warning: *Gasoline is extremely flammable, so take extra precautions when you work on any part of the fuel system. Don't smoke or allow open flames or bare light bulbs near the work area, and don't work in a garage where a gas-type appliance (such as a water heater or a clothes dryer) is present. Since gasoline is carcinogenic, wear latex gloves when there's a possibility of being exposed to fuel, and, if you spill any fuel on your skin, rinse it off immediately with soap and water. Mop up any spills immediately and do not store fuel-soaked rags where they could ignite. The fuel system is under constant pressure, so, if any fuel lines are to be disconnected, the fuel pressure in the system must be relieved first. When you perform any kind of work on the fuel system, wear safety glasses and have a Class B type fire extinguisher on hand.*

All models covered by this manual are equipped with a Sequential Multi Port Fuel Injection (SFI) system **(see illustration)**. This system uses timed impulses to sequentially inject the fuel directly into the intake ports of each cylinder. The injectors are controlled by the Powertrain Control Module (PCM). The PCM monitors various engine parameters and delivers the exact amount of fuel, in the correct sequence, into the intake ports.

All models are equipped with an electric fuel pump, mounted in the fuel tank. It is necessary to remove the fuel tank for access to the fuel pump. The fuel level sending unit is an integral component of the fuel pump module and it must be removed from the fuel tank in the same manner.

The exhaust system consists of exhaust manifolds, catalytic converter, exhaust pipes and a muffler. Each of these components is replaceable. For further information regarding the catalytic converter, refer to Chapter 6.

2   Fuel pressure relief procedure

Warning: *See the* **Warning** *in Section 1.*
Note: *After the fuel pressure has been relieved, it's a good idea to lay a shop towel over any fuel connection to be disassembled, to absorb the residual fuel that may leak out when servicing the fuel system.*

1   Before servicing any fuel system component, you must relieve the fuel pressure to minimize the risk of fire or personal injury.
2   Remove the fuel filler cap - this will relieve any pressure built up in the tank.
3   Disconnect the cable from the negative battery terminal. **Caution:** *On models equipped with the Theftlock audio system, be sure the lockout feature is turned off before performing any procedure which requires disconnecting the battery (see the front of this manual).*
4   Locate the test port on the fuel rail (see Section 3). Remove the cap and connect a fuel pressure gauge, equipped with a bleed-off valve and drain tube, to the test port. Relieve the fuel pressure by bleeding the fuel through the bleed-off valve and into an approved fuel container.
5   Place shop towels around the fuel fitting to be disconnected to absorb any residual fuel that may spill out.

3   Fuel pump/fuel pressure - check

Warning: *See the* **Warning** *in Section 1.*

Preliminary check

1   If you suspect insufficient fuel delivery,

first inspect all fuel lines to ensure that the problem is not simply a leak in a line.
2   Set the parking brake and have an assistant turn the ignition switch to the On position while you listen to the fuel pump (inside the fuel tank). You should hear a "whirring" sound, lasting for approximately two seconds indicating the fuel pump is operating. If the fuel pump is operating, proceed to the pressure check.
3   If there is no sound, check the fuel pump circuit, referring to Chapter 12 and the wiring diagrams. Check the related fuses and the fuel pump relay. If the fuses and relay are good, check the fuel pump relay control circuit from the electrical center to the PCM. If the circuit is good and the PCM fails to energize the fuel pump relay, have the PCM diagnosed by a dealer service department or other qualified repair shop.
4   Disconnect the electrical connector from the fuel pump module at the fuel tank (see Section 7). Using a test light or voltmeter, cycle the ignition key On and Off and check for power at the gray wire terminal of the harness connector. Using a continuity tester or ohmmeter, check for continuity to a good chassis ground at the black wire terminal. If power is not indicated on the gray wire terminal or the ground circuit is open, repair the wiring harness.
5   If power is present at the connector, the ground circuit is good and the fuel pump does not operate when connected, replace the fuel pump (see Section 7).

Pressure check

Refer to illustration 3.6
Note: *In order to perform the fuel pressure test, you will need a fuel pressure gauge capable of measuring high fuel pressure. The fuel gauge must be equipped with the proper fitting required to attach it to the test port. To*

3.6 Fuel pressure test port location

test the fuel pressure regulator, a fuel shut off valve must be installed in the fuel return line with the necessary adapters.

6   Remove the cap from the fuel pressure test port and attach a fuel pressure gauge **(see illustration)**.

7   Turn the ignition key On; the fuel pump should run for approximately two seconds then shut off. Note the pressure indicated on the gauge and compare your reading with the pressure listed in this Chapter's Specifications. Cycle the ignition key On and Off several times, if necessary, to obtain the highest reading.

8   If the fuel pressure is lower than specified, turn the ignition key Off and relieve the fuel system pressure. Install a fuel shut-off valve in the fuel return line and close the valve. **Caution:** *Do not pinch the flexible fuel line shut or damage the fuel line may occur.* Turn the ignition key On and note the fuel pressure. **Caution:** *Do not allow the fuel pressure to rise above 65 psi or damage to the fuel pressure regulator may occur.* If the fuel pressure is now above the specified pressure, replace the fuel pressure regulator (see Section 14). If the fuel pressure is lower than specified, check the fuel lines and the fuel filter for restrictions. If no restriction is found, remove the fuel pump module (see Section 7) and check the fuel strainer for restrictions, check the fuel flex pipe for leaks and check the fuel pump wiring for high resistance. If no problems are found, replace the fuel pump.

9   If the fuel pressure recorded in Step 7 is higher than specified, check the fuel return line for restrictions. If no restrictions are found, replace the fuel pressure regulator (see Section 14).

10   If the fuel pressure is within specifications, start the engine. **Warning:** *Make sure the fuel pressure gauge hose is positioned away from the engine drivebelt before starting the engine.* With the engine running, the fuel pressure should be 3 to 10 psi below the pressure recorded in Step 7. If it isn't, remove the vacuum hose from the fuel pressure regulator and verify there is 12 to 14 in-Hg of vacuum present at the hose. If vacuum is not present at the hose, check the hose for a

restriction or a broken hose. If vacuum is present, reconnect the hose to the fuel pressure regulator. If the fuel pressure regulator does not decrease the fuel pressure with vacuum applied, replace the fuel pressure regulator.

11   Turn the engine off and monitor the fuel pressure for five minutes. The fuel pressure should not drop more than 5 psi within ten minutes. If it does, there is a leak in the fuel line, a fuel injector is leaking or the fuel pump module check valve is defective. To determine if the fuel injectors are leaking, cycle the ignition key On and Off several times to obtain the highest fuel pressure reading, then immediately shut-off both the fuel supply and return lines. If the pressure drops below 5 psi within ten minutes, a fuel injector (or injectors) is leaking (or the fuel line or fuel rail may be leaking, but such a leak would be very apparent). If the fuel injectors hold pressure, the main fuel line is leaking or the fuel pump is defective.

4   Fuel lines and fittings - repair and replacement

Refer to illustrations 4.2, 4.11a, 4.11b and 4.11c
Warning: *See the* **Warning** *in Section 1.*

1   Always relieve the fuel pressure before servicing fuel lines or fittings (see Section 2).

2   Metal fuel supply and vapor lines extend from the fuel tank to the engine compartment. The lines are secured to the underbody or frame with plastic retainers **(see illustration)**. Flexible hose connects the metal lines to the fuel tank, fuel filter and fuel rail. Fuel lines must be occasionally inspected for leaks or damage.

3   In the event of any fuel line damage, metal lines may be repaired with steel tubing of the same diameter, provided the correct fittings are used. Flexible lines, on the other hand, must be replaced with factory replacement parts; others may fail from the high pressures of this system. Never repair a damaged section of steel line with rubber hose and hose clamps.

4   If evidence of contamination is found in the system or fuel filter during disassembly, the line should be disconnected and blown out. Check the fuel strainer on the fuel pump module for damage and deterioration.

5   Don't route fuel line or hose within four inches of any part of the exhaust system or within ten inches of the catalytic converter. Fuel line must never be allowed to chafe against the engine, body or frame. A minimum of 1/4-inch clearance must be maintained around a fuel line.

6   When replacing a fuel line, remove all fasteners attaching the fuel line to the vehicle body.

7   Because fuel lines used on fuel-injected vehicles are under high pressure, they require special consideration.

Steel tubing

8   If replacement of a steel fuel line or emission line is called for, use steel tubing meeting the manufacturers specification.

9   Don't use copper or aluminum tubing to replace steel tubing. These materials cannot withstand normal vehicle vibration.

10   Some fuel lines have threaded fittings with O-rings. Any time the fittings are loosened to service or replace components:

a)   *Use a flare-nut wrench on the fitting nut and a backup wrench on the stationary portion of the fitting while loosening and tightening the fittings.*

b)   *Check all O-rings for cuts, cracks and deterioration. Replace any that appear hardened, worn or damaged.*

c)   *If the lines are replaced, always use original equipment parts, or parts that meet the original equipment standards.*

Flexible hose with quick-connect fitting

11   There are various methods of disconnecting the fittings, depending upon the type of quick-connect fitting installed on the fuel line **(see illustrations)**. Clean any debris from around the fitting. Disconnect the fitting and carefully remove the fuel line from the vehicle.

4

4.2 The fuel lines are secured to the underbody with retainers (arrow)

4.11a To disconnect a plastic collar two-tab type fitting, squeeze the two tabs together (arrows) and pull the lines apart

Caution: *The quick-connect fittings are not serviced separately. Do not attempt to repair these types of fuel lines in the event the fitting or line becomes damaged. Replace the entire fuel line as an assembly.*

12   Installation is the reverse of removal with the following additions:

a) *Clean the quick-connect fittings with a lint-free cloth and apply clean engine oil the fittings.*

b) *After connecting a quick-connect fitting, check the integrity of the connection by attempting to pull the lines apart.*

c) *Use new O-rings at the threaded fittings (if equipped).*

d) *Cycle the ignition key On and Off several times and check for leaks at the fitting, before starting the engine.*

5   Fuel tank - removal and installation

Refer to illustrations 5.6, 5.8, 5.9 and 5.10
Warning: *See the* **Warning** *in Section 1.*
Note: *If necessary, clean the fuel tank and areas surrounding the fuel lines and hoses to prevent contaminating the fuel system.*

1   Disconnect the cable from the negative battery terminal. **Caution:** *On models equipped with the Theftlock audio system, be sure you have the correct activation code before disconnecting the battery (see the front of this manual).*

2   Remove the fuel tank filler cap to relieve fuel tank pressure.

3   Relieve the fuel system pressure (see Section 2).

4   Using a siphoning kit (available at most auto parts stores), siphon the fuel into an approved gasoline container. **Warning:** *Do not start the siphoning action by mouth!*

5   Raise the vehicle and support it securely on jackstands.

6   Disconnect the fuel supply and return lines (see Section 4) and the EVAP hose from

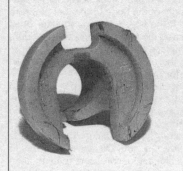

4.11b A special tool (available at most auto parts stores) is required to disconnect the metal collar type fitting

4.11c To disconnect a metal collar type fitting (arrow), place the tool over the fuel line, insert it squarely into the fitting and pull the lines apart (the tool is not required to connect the lines)

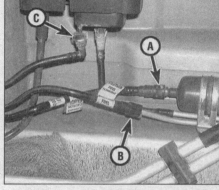

5.6 Disconnect the fuel supply line (A), return line (B) and the EVAP hose (C)

the EVAP canister **(see illustration)**.

7   Disconnect the fuel tank vent hose from the fuel tank.

8   Loosen the hose clamp and disconnect the fuel filler hose from the fuel tank **(see illustration)**.

9   Position a transmission jack under the fuel tank and support the tank. Remove the

fuel tank strap bolts and pivot the straps down **(see illustration)**.

10   Lower the tank slightly and disconnect the electrical connectors from the fuel pump module **(see illustration)**.

11   Lower the jack and remove the tank from the vehicle.

12   Installation is the reverse of removal.

5.8 Loosen the hose clamp and disconnect the fuel filler hose (arrow) from the fuel tank

5.9 Remove the fuel tank strap bolts (arrows) and swing the straps down

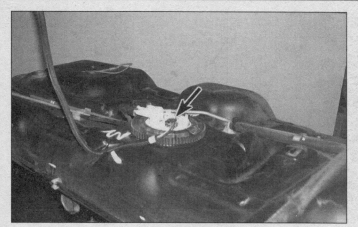

5.10 Lower the fuel tank and disconnect the fuel pump/fuel level sending unit electrical connector from the fuel pump module

7.4 Disconnect the fuel hoses from the fuel pump module fittings

7.5 Loosen the fuel pump module retaining ring by rotating it counterclockwise

7.6 Carefully remove the fuel pump module from the tank and drain the fuel from the reservoir

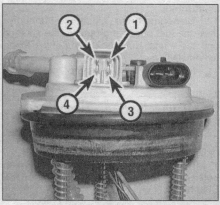

8.2 Fuel pump module connector terminal identification

1   Fuel level sending unit signal
2   Fuel pump 12-volt supply (from fuel pump relay)
3   Ground
4   Fuel level sending unit ground

6   Fuel tank cleaning and repair - general information

1   The fuel tanks installed in the vehicles covered by this manual are not repairable. If the fuel tank becomes damaged, it must be replaced.

2   Cleaning the fuel tank (due to fuel contamination) should be performed by a professional with the proper training to carry out this critical and potentially dangerous work. Even after cleaning and flushing, explosive fumes may remain inside the fuel tank.

3   If the fuel tank is removed from the vehicle, it should not be placed in an area where sparks or open flames could ignite the fumes coming out of the tank. Be especially careful inside a garage where a gas-type appliance is located.

7   Fuel pump module - removal and installation

Refer to illustrations 7.4, 7.5 and 7.6
Warning: *See the* **Warning** *in Section 1.*

1   Disconnect the cable from the negative battery terminal. **Caution:** *On models*

equipped with the Theftlock audio system, be sure you have the correct activation code before disconnecting the battery (see the front of this manual).

2   Relieve the fuel system pressure (see Section 2).

3   Remove the fuel tank from the vehicle (see Section 5).

4   Disconnect the fuel lines and EVAP line from the fuel pump module **(see illustration)**.

5   Using a suitable tool, rotate the fuel pump module retaining ring counterclockwise until it's loose **(see illustration)**.

6   Remove the fuel pump module from the tank **(see illustration)**. Angle the assembly slightly to avoid damaging the fuel level sending unit float. **Warning:** *Some fuel may remain the module reservoir and spill as the module is removed. Have several shop towels ready and a drain pan nearby to place the module in.*

7   The electric fuel pump is not serviced separately. In the event of failure, the complete assembly must be replaced. Transfer the fuel pressure sensor (if equipped) and fuel level sending unit to the new fuel pump module assembly, if necessary (see Section 8).

8   Clean the fuel tank sealing surface and install a new O-ring on the fuel tank.

9   Install the fuel pump module, aligning the fuel line fittings with the fuel lines.

10   Press the fuel pump module down until seated and install the retaining ring.

11   The remainder of installation is the reverse of removal.

8   Fuel level sending unit - check and replacement

Warning: *See the* **Warning** *in Section 1.*

Check

Refer to illustration 8.2

1   Remove the fuel tank and the fuel pump module (see Sections 5 and 7).

2   Connect the probes of an ohmmeter to the two fuel level sensor terminals (1 and 4) of the fuel pump module electrical connector **(see illustration)**.

3   Position the float in the down (empty) position and note the reading on the ohmmeter.

4

4   Move the float up to the full position while watching the meter. Compare your measurements with the values listed in this Chapter's Specifications.

5   If the fuel level sending unit resistance is incorrect or does not change smoothly as the float travels from empty to full, replace the fuel level sending unit assembly.

Replacement

Refer to illustrations 8.7, 8.8 and 8.9

6   Remove the fuel tank and the fuel pump module (see Sections 5 and 7).

7   Disconnect the fuel level sending unit electrical connector from the module cover **(see illustration)**.

8   Remove the sending unit retaining clip **(see illustration)**.

9   Pinch the tabs together and slide the fuel level sending unit off the module **(see illustration)**.

10   Disconnect the electrical connector from the fuel pump and remove the sending unit and wiring. Note the routing of the wiring for installation.

11   Installation is the reverse of removal.

9   Air filter housing - removal and installation

Refer to illustrations 9.4, 9.5, 9.6 and 9.7

1   Remove the coolant reservoir mounting bolt and position the reservoir aside (see Chapter 3).

2   Remove the fender support brace.

3   Disconnect the electrical connectors from the Mass Airflow sensor and Intake Air Temperature sensor.

4   Disconnect the air intake duct from the throttle body. Loosen the Mass Airflow sensor hose clamp at the air filter cover and remove the air intake duct and Mass Airflow sensor **(see illustration)**. **Caution:** *Handle the mass airflow sensor carefully, damage to the sensor will effect the operation of the fuel injection system.*

5   Unsnap the latches and remove the cover and the air filter element **(see illustration)**.

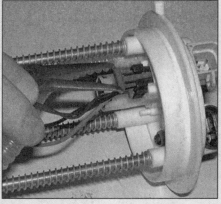

8.7 Disconnect the fuel pump/fuel level sending unit electrical connector from the fuel pump module

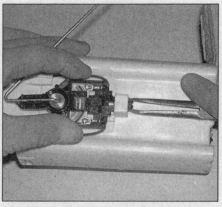

8.9 Pinch the tabs together and remove the fuel level sending unit from module

6   Unsnap the latch and remove the upper cover **(see illustration)**. Carefully remove the PCM, without disconnecting the electrical connectors, and position the PCM aside.

7   Remove the air filter housing mounting bolts and remove the housing **(see illustration)**.

8   Installation is the reverse of removal.

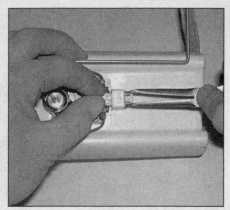

8.8 Remove the sending unit retaining clip

9.4 Loosen the hose clamp (arrow) and disconnect the MAF sensor and air intake duct from the air filter cover

10   Accelerator cable - replacement

Refer to illustrations 10.3, 10.4 and 10.5

1   Disconnect the cable from the negative battery terminal. **Caution:** *On models equipped with the Theftlock audio system, be sure you have the correct activation code before disconnecting the battery (see the front of this manual).*

9.5 Loosen the latches (arrows) and remove the air filter housing cover

9.6 Loosen the latch and remove the upper cover

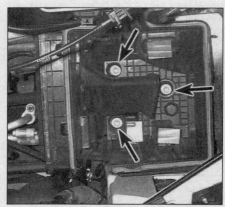

9.7 Remove the bolts (arrows) and remove the air filter housing

10.3 Rotate the throttle lever and pass the cable through the slot in the throttle lever

10.4 Depress the locking tabs and remove the cable from the bracket

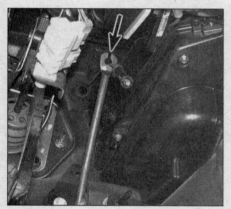

10.5 Pull the accelerator cable retainer out of the pedal and slide the cable through the slot

2   Remove the throttle lever shield, if equipped.

3   Rotate the throttle lever and separate the accelerator cable end from the throttle lever **(see illustration)**.

4   Depress the locking tabs on the cable housing and push the cable through the bracket **(see illustration)**. Detach the cable from the cable retainers.

5   Remove the trim panel from under the dash and detach the cable from the accelerator pedal **(see illustration)**.

6   Depress the locking tabs on the cable housing and push the cable through the firewall and into the engine compartment.

7   Remove the cable from the engine compartment.

8   Installation is the reverse of removal.

11   Fuel injection system - general information

The Sequential Multi Port Fuel Injection (SFI) system consists of three sub-systems: air intake, engine control and fuel delivery. The system uses a Powertrain Control Mod-

ule (PCM) along with the sensors (coolant temperature sensor, throttle position sensor, mass airflow sensor, oxygen sensor, etc.) to determine the proper air/fuel ratio under all operating conditions.

The fuel injection system and the engine control system are closely linked in function and design. For additional information on the engine control system and sensors, refer to Chapter 6.

Air intake system

The air intake system consists of the air filter, the air intake ducts, the throttle body, the air intake plenum and the intake manifold.

When the engine is idling, the air/fuel ratio is controlled by the idle air control system, which consists of the Powertrain Control Module (PCM) and the Idle Air Control valve. This idle air control regulates the amount of airflow past the throttle plate and into the intake manifold, thus increasing or decreasing the engine idle speed. The PCM receives information from the sensors (vehicle speed, coolant temperature, air conditioning, power steering mode etc.) and adjusts the idle according to the demands of the engine and driver. Refer to Chapter 6 for information on the Idle Air Control valve.

Emissions and engine control system

The emissions and engine control system is described in detail in Chapter 6.

Fuel delivery system

The fuel delivery system consists of the fuel tank, fuel lines, fuel pump, fuel pressure regulator, fuel rail and fuel injectors.

The fuel pump is an electric type. Fuel is drawn through an inlet screen into the pump, flows through the one-way valve, passes through the fuel filter and is delivered to the fuel rail and injectors. The pressure regulator maintains a constant fuel pressure to the injectors. Excess fuel is routed back to the fuel tank through the fuel pressure regulator.

The fuel pump relay is located in the engine compartment electrical center. The PCM controls the relay by supplying battery voltage to the relay coil. When energized, the fuel pump relay connects battery voltage to the fuel pump. If the PCM does not detect a signal from the camshaft or crankshaft sensors (as with the engine not running or cranking), the PCM will de-energize the relay.

The injectors are solenoid-actuated pintle types consisting of a solenoid, plunger, needle valve and housing. When current is applied to the solenoid coil, the needle valve raises and pressurized fuel sprays out the nozzle. The injection quantity is determined by the length of time the valve is open (the length of time during which current is supplied to the solenoid coils).

12   Fuel injection system - check

Refer to illustrations 12.7, 12.8 and 12.10
Note: *The following procedure is based on the assumption that the fuel pressure is adequate* (see Section 3).

1   Check all electrical connectors that are related to the system. Check the ground wire connections for tightness. Loose connectors and poor grounds can cause many problems that resemble more serious malfunctions.

2   Check to see that the battery is fully charged, as the control unit and sensors depend on an accurate supply voltage in order to properly meter the fuel.

3   Check the air filter element - a dirty or partially blocked filter will severely impede performance and economy (see Chapter 1).

4   Check the related fuses. If a blown fuse is found, replace it and see if it blows again. If it does, search for a wire shorted to ground in the harness.

5   Check the air intake duct from the air filter housing to the throttle body for leaks, which will result in an excessively lean mixture. Also check the condition of all vacuum hoses connected to the intake manifold and/or throttle body.

4

12.7 Use a stethoscope to determine if the injectors are working properly - they should make a steady clicking sound that rises and falls with engine speed changes

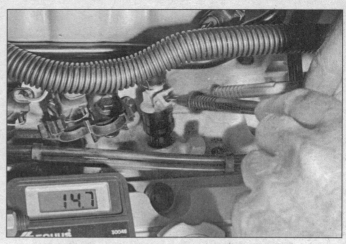

12.8 Measure the resistance of each injector across the two terminals of the injector

6   Remove the air intake duct from the throttle body and check for dirt, carbon or other residue build-up on the throttle bore and throttle plate. If it's dirty, clean it with carburetor cleaner spray, a toothbrush and a shop towel. **Caution:** *Do not use a solvent containing Methyl Ethyl Ketone or damage to the throttle body may occur.*

7   Start the engine and place an automotive stethoscope against each injector, one at a time, and listen for a clicking sound, indicating operation **(see illustration)**. If you don't have a stethoscope, place the tip of a screwdriver against the injector and listen through the handle.

8   Disconnect the injector electrical connectors and measure the resistance of each injector **(see illustration)**. Compare the measurements with the resistance values listed in this Chapter's Specifications. **Note:** *Follow the wiring harness from the fuel injectors to locate the fuel injector harness main connector and perform the tests there. Refer to the wiring diagrams at the end of Chapter 12 to determine the terminals for testing by wire color.*

9   Turn the ignition key On and check for battery voltage at the pink wire terminal of one of the injector harness connectors. If battery voltage is not present, check the fuel injector fuse and related wiring (see Chapter 12).

10   Install an injector test light ("noid" light) into each injector electrical connector, one at a time **(see illustration)**. Crank the engine over. Confirm that the light flashes evenly on each connector. This tests the PCM control of the injectors. If the light does not flash, have the PCM checked at a dealer service department or other properly equipped repair facility. **Note:** *Follow the wiring harness from the fuel injectors to locate the fuel injector harness main connector and perform the tests there. Refer to the wiring diagrams at the end of Chapter 12 to determine the terminals for testing by wire color.*

11   The remainder of the engine control system checks can be found in Chapter 6.

13   Throttle body - removal and installation

Refer to illustration 13.8

Warning: *Wait until the engine is completely cool before beginning this procedure.*

1   Disconnect the cable from the negative battery terminal. **Caution:** *On models equipped with the Theftlock audio system, be sure you have the correct activation code before disconnecting the battery (see the front of this manual).*

2   Partially drain the cooling system (see Chapter 1).

3   Remove the air intake duct.

4   Disconnect the electrical connectors from the throttle body.

5   Label and detach the vacuum hoses from the throttle body.

6   Detach the accelerator cable (see Section 10) and if equipped, the cruise control cable. Remove the accelerator cable bracket.

7   Detach the coolant hoses from the throttle body. Remove the nut and the coolant pipe bracket from the stud.

8   Remove the mounting bolts and remove the throttle body and gasket **(see illustration)**.

9   Remove all traces of old gasket material from the throttle body and intake manifold and install a new gasket. **Caution:** *Do not use solvent or a sharp tool to clean the throttle body gasket surface or damage to the throttle body may occur.*

10   Install the throttle body and tighten the bolts to the torque listed in this Chapter's Specifications.

11   The remainder of installation is the reverse of removal.

12   Refill the cooling system (see Chapter 1).

14   Fuel pressure regulator - replacement

Refer to illustrations 14.6 and 14.8

Warning: *See the* **Warning** *in Section 1.*

1   Disconnect the cable from the negative battery terminal. **Caution:** *On models equipped with the Theftlock audio system, be*

12.10 Install the "noid" light (available at most auto parts stores) into each injector electrical connector and confirm that it blinks when the engine is cranking

13.8 Throttle body mounting bolts (arrows)

14.6 Remove the fuel pressure regulator mounting bolt (arrow)

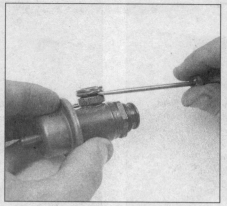

14.8 Replace the fuel pressure regulator-to-fuel rail O-ring

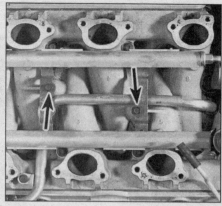

15.7 Remove the fuel rail mounting bolts (arrows)

sure you have the correct activation code before disconnecting the battery (see the front of this manual).

2   Relieve the fuel system pressure (see Section 2).

3   Remove the upper intake manifold (see Chapter 2A).

4   Detach the vacuum hose from the port on the regulator.

5   Detach the fuel return line from the fuel pressure regulator.

6   Remove the pressure regulator retaining bolt and pull the fuel pressure regulator from the fuel rail with a twisting motion **(see illustration)**. **Note:** *Place a shop towel under the fuel pressure regulator to catch the fuel.*

7   Check the filter screen for contamination and clean it as necessary.

8   Be sure to replace the fuel pressure regulator O-ring seal, lubricating it with a light film of engine oil **(see illustration)**.

9   Install the fuel return line before tightening the fuel pressure regulator mounting bolt, otherwise a dangerous fuel leak may develop.

10   The remainder of installation is the reverse of removal.

15 Fuel rail and injectors - removal and installation

Warning: *See the **Warning** in Section 1.*
Note: *When replacing components of the fuel rail/injector assembly, refer to the identification numbers on the fuel rail and injectors. Fuel injectors are calibrated with different flow rates and must not be interchanged with injectors from a different application.*

Removal

Refer to illustrations 15.7, 15.8a and 15.8b

1   Relieve the fuel pressure (see Section 2).

2   Disconnect the cable from the negative battery terminal. **Caution:** *On models equipped with the Theftlock audio system, be sure you have the correct activation code before disconnecting the battery (see the front of this manual).*

3   Remove the upper intake manifold (see Chapter 2A). Cover the lower intake manifold ports to prevent any foreign objects from entering the engine.

4   Clearly label and remove any vacuum hoses or electrical wiring that will interfere with the fuel rail removal. Detach any wiring harness retainers from the fuel rail.

5   Disconnect the fuel injector electrical connectors and position the harness aside. **Note:** *Apply a numbered tag to each connector with the corresponding cylinder number.*

6   Disconnect the fuel inlet line from the fuel rail (see Section 4). Before separating the fuel line from the fuel rail, remove any fuel line bracket fasteners. Disconnect the fuel return line from the fuel pressure regulator (see Section 14).

7   Clean any debris from around the injectors. Remove the fuel rail mounting nuts/bolts **(see illustration)**. Gently rock the fuel rail and injectors to loosen the injectors. Remove the fuel rail and fuel injectors as an assembly.

8   Remove the retaining clip and remove the injector(s) from the fuel rail assembly **(see illustrations)**. Remove and discard the O-rings and seals. **Note:** *Whether you're replacing an injector or a leaking O-ring, it's a good idea to remove all the injectors from the fuel rail and replace all the O-rings.*

Installation

9   Coat the new seal rings (if equipped) with clean engine oil and slide them onto the injectors.

10   Coat the new O-rings with clean engine oil and install them on the injector(s), then insert each injector into its corresponding bore in the fuel rail. Install the injector retaining clip.

11   Install the injector and fuel rail assembly on the intake manifold. Fully seat the injectors, then tighten the fuel rail mounting nuts to the torque listed in this Chapter's Specifications.

12   Connect the fuel feed and return lines. Loosen the fuel pressure regulator mounting screw before tightening the fuel return line or a fuel leak may develop. Make sure the fuel lines are securely installed and install the fuel line bracket fasteners, as required.

13   Connect the electrical connectors to each injector, referring to the numbered tags.

14   The remainder of installation is the reverse of removal.

15   After the injector/fuel rail assembly installation is complete, turn the ignition switch to On, but don't operate the starter (this activates the fuel pump for about two seconds, which builds up fuel pressure in the fuel lines and the fuel rail). Repeat this about

15.8a Remove the fuel injector retaining clip and carefully withdraw the injector from the fuel rail

15.8b Remove the injector O-rings and replace them with new ones

4

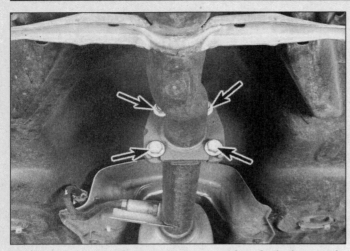

16.2a Inspect the exhaust system connections for leakage and make sure the fasteners (arrows) are tight

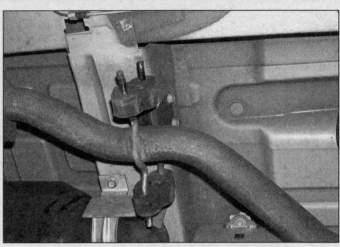

16.2b Inspect the rubber insulators for damage

two or three times, then check the fuel lines, fuel rail and injectors for fuel leakage.

16 Exhaust system servicing - general information

Warning: *Inspection and repair of exhaust system components should be done only after enough time has elapsed after driving the vehicle to allow the system components to cool completely. Also, when working under the vehicle, make sure it is securely supported on jackstands.*

1   The exhaust system consists of the exhaust manifolds, catalytic converters, muffler, resonators, the tailpipe and all connecting pipes, brackets, hangers and clamps. The exhaust system is attached to the body with mounting brackets and rubber hangers. If any of the parts are improperly installed, excessive noise and vibration will be transmitted to the body.

Muffler and pipes

Refer to illustrations 16.2a and 16.2b

2   Conduct regular inspections of the exhaust system to keep it safe and quiet.

Look for any damaged or bent parts, open seams, holes, loose connections, excessive corrosion or other defects which could allow exhaust fumes to enter the vehicle **(see illustrations)**. Also check the catalytic converter when you inspect the exhaust system (see below). Deteriorated exhaust system components should not be repaired; they should be replaced with new parts.

3   If the exhaust system components are extremely corroded or rusted together, welding equipment will probably be required to remove them. The convenient way to accomplish this is to have a muffler repair shop remove the corroded sections with a cutting torch. If, however, you want to save money by doing it yourself (and you don't have a welding outfit with a cutting torch), simply cut off the old components with a hacksaw. If you have compressed air, special pneumatic cutting chisels can also be used. If you do decide to tackle the job at home, be sure to wear safety goggles to protect your eyes from metal chips and work gloves to protect your hands.

4   Here are some simple guidelines to follow when repairing the exhaust system:

a) *Work from the back to the front when removing exhaust system components.*

b) *Apply penetrating oil to the exhaust system component fasteners to make them easier to remove.*

c) *Use new gaskets, hangers and clamps when installing exhaust systems components.*

d) *Apply anti-seize compound to the threads of all exhaust system fasteners during reassembly.*

e) *Be sure to allow sufficient clearance between newly installed parts and all points on the underbody to avoid overheating the floor pan and possibly damaging the interior carpet and insulation. Pay particularly close attention to the catalytic converter and heat shield.*

Catalytic converter

Warning: *The converter gets very hot during operation. Make sure it has cooled down before you touch it.*

Note: *See Chapter 6 for additional information on the catalytic converter.*

5   Periodically inspect the heat shield for cracks, dents and loose or missing fasteners.

6   Inspect the converter for cracks or other damage.

7   If the catalytic converter requires replacement, refer to Chapter 6.

Chapter 5
Engine electrical systems

Contents

Specifications

General

Battery voltage
Engine off .... 12.0 to 12.6 volts
Engine running .... 13.5 to 14.7 volts

Torque specifications   Ft-lbs
Alternator mounting bolts 37
Starter mounting bolts 35

1   General information and precautions

General information

Refer to illustration 1.1

The engine electrical systems include all ignition, charging and starting components **(see illustration)**. Because of their engine-related functions, these components are discussed separately from body electrical devices such as the lights, the instruments, etc. (which are included in Chapter 12).

Precautions

Always observe the following precautions when working on the electrical system:

a) *Be extremely careful when servicing engine electrical components. They are easily damaged if checked, connected or handled improperly.*

b) *Never leave the ignition switched on for long periods of time when the engine is not running.*

c) *Never disconnect the battery cables while the engine is running.*

d) *Maintain correct polarity when connecting battery cables from another vehicle during jump starting - see the "Booster battery (jump) starting" section at the front of this manual.*

1.1 Typical engine electrical system components

1	Ignition coils and ignition control module	3	Battery
2	Spark plug wires	4	Underhood fuse/relay panel
		5	Alternator

5

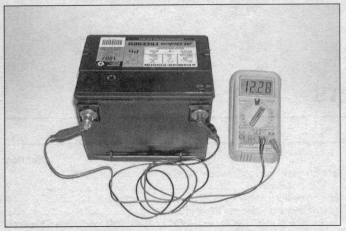

3.2 To test the open circuit voltage of the battery, connect a voltmeter to the battery - a fully charged battery should measure at least 12.4 volts (depending on outside air temperature)

3.3 Connect a battery load tester to the battery and check the battery condition under load following the tool manufacturers instructions

e) *Always disconnect the negative battery cable before working on the electrical system.*

It's also a good idea to review the safety-related information regarding the engine electrical systems located in the *"Safety first!"* section at the front of this manual, before beginning any operation included in this Chapter.

Battery disconnection

Caution: *On models equipped with the Theft-lock audio system, be sure you have the correct activation code before disconnecting the battery (see the front of this manual).*

Several systems on the vehicle require battery power to be available at all times, either to ensure their continued operation (such as the clock) or to maintain control unit memories (such as that in the engine management system's Powertrain Control Module) which would be wiped out if the battery were to be disconnected. Therefore, whenever the battery is to be disconnected, first note the following to ensure that there are no unforeseen consequences of this action:

a) *First, on any vehicle with power door locks, it is a wise precaution to remove the key from the ignition and to keep it with you, so that it does not get locked inside if the power door locks should engage accidentally when the battery is reconnected!*

b) *The engine management system's PCM will lose the information stored in its memory when the battery is disconnected. This includes idling and operating values, and any fault codes detected (see Chapter 6). Whenever the battery is disconnected, the information relating to idle speed control and other operating values will have to be re-programmed into the unit's memory. The PCM does this by itself, but until then, there may be surging, hesitation, erratic idle and a generally inferior level of performance. To allow the PCM to relearn these values, start the*

engine and run it as close to idle speed as possible until it reaches its normal operating temperature, then run it for approximately two minutes at 1200 rpm. Next, drive the vehicle as far as necessary - approximately 5 miles of varied driving conditions is usually sufficient - to complete the relearning process.

Devices known as "memory-savers" can be used to avoid some of the above problems. Precise details vary according to the device used. Typically, it is plugged into the cigarette lighter, and is connected by its own wires to a spare battery; the vehicle's own battery is then disconnected from the electrical system, leaving the "memory-saver" to pass sufficient current to maintain audio unit security codes and PCM memory values, and also to run permanently live circuits such as the clock, all the while isolating the battery in the event of a short-circuit occurring while work is carried out. **Warning:** *Some of these devices allow a considerable amount of current to pass, which can mean that many of the vehicle's systems are still operational when the main battery is disconnected. If a "memory-saver" is used, ensure that the circuit concerned is actually "dead" before carrying out any work on it!*

The battery is located at the right front corner of the engine compartment, under the fuse/relay panel. To disconnect the negative battery cable from the battery, remove the screw retaining the fuse/relay panel to the radiator support (see Section 3) and rotate the fuse/relay panel up on the fender brace. Using the appropriate size box end-wrench or socket, unscrew the battery cable terminal from the negative battery post and position the cable aside.

2   Battery - emergency jump starting

Refer to the Booster battery (jump) starting procedure at the front of this manual.

3   Battery - check and replacement

Warning: *Hydrogen gas is produced by the battery, so keep open flames and lighted cigarettes away from it at all times. Always wear eye protection when working around a battery. Rinse off spilled electrolyte immediately with large amounts of water.*

Check

Refer to illustrations 3.2 and 3.3

1   The battery's surface charge must be removed before accurate voltage measurements can be made. Turn On the high beams for ten seconds, then turn them Off, let the vehicle stand for two minutes. Remove the battery from the vehicle (see Steps 4 through 10).

2   Check the battery state of charge. Visually inspect the indicator eye on the top of the battery, if the indicator eye is clear, charge the battery as described in Chapter 1. Next perform an open voltage circuit test using a digital voltmeter **(see illustration)**. With the engine and all accessories Off, connect the negative probe of the voltmeter to the negative terminal of the battery and the positive probe to the positive terminal of the battery. The battery voltage should be 12.4 volts or more. If the battery is less than the specified voltage, charge the battery before proceeding to the next test. Do not proceed with the battery load test unless the battery charge is correct.

3   Perform a battery load test. An accurate check of the battery condition can only be performed with a load tester (available at most auto parts stores). This test evaluates the ability of the battery to operate the starter and other accessories during periods of heavy amperage draw (load). Install a special battery load testing tool onto the terminals **(see illustration)**. Load test the battery according to the tool manufacturer's instructions. This tool utilizes a carbon pile to increase the load demand (amperage draw)

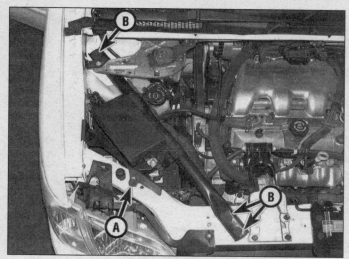

3.5 To access the battery, remove the fuse/relay panel retaining bolt (A) and rotate the panel up - after disconnecting the cable from the negative battery terminal, detach the panel from the fender brace, remove the fender brace bolts (B) and remove the fender brace

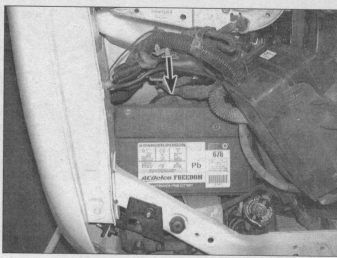

3.7 Remove the battery retainer (arrow) and lift out the battery

on the battery. Maintain the load on the battery for 15 seconds or less and observe that the battery voltage does not drop below 9.6 volts. If the battery condition is weak or defective, the tool will indicate this condition immediately. **Note:** *Cold temperatures will cause the minimum voltage requirements to drop slightly. Follow the chart given in the tool manufacturer's instructions to compensate for cold climates. Minimum load voltage for freezing temperatures (32 degrees F) should be approximately 9.1 volts.*

Replacement

Refer to illustrations 3.5, 3.7 and 3.9
Caution: *On models equipped with the Theft-lock audio system, be sure you have the correct activation code before disconnecting the battery (see the front of this manual).*

4   Remove the windshield wiper motor cover.
5   Remove the screw retaining the underhood fuse/relay panel to the radiator support and rotate the panel up on the fender brace **(see illustration)**. Disconnect the cable from the negative battery terminal.
6   Detach the fuse/relay panel from the fender brace and position it aside. Remove the fender brace. Disconnect the cable from the positive battery terminal.
7   Remove the battery retainer bolt and retainer **(see illustration)**.
8   Remove the battery and place it on a workbench. Remove the battery insulator. **Note:** *Battery handling tools are available at most auto parts stores for a reasonable price. They make it easier to remove and carry the battery.*
9   While the battery is removed, inspect the tray, retainer brackets and related fasteners for corrosion or damage **(see illustration)**.
10   If corrosion is evident, remove the bat-

3.9 Inspect the tray, retainer brackets and related fasteners for corrosion or damage - if necessary, remove the bolts (arrows) and the battery tray

tery tray and use a baking soda/water solution to clean the corroded area to prevent further oxidation. Repaint the area as necessary using rust resistant paint.
11   Clean and service the battery and cables (see Chapter 1).
12   If you are replacing the battery, make sure you purchase one that is identical to yours, with the same dimensions, amperage rating, cold cranking amps rating, etc. Make sure it is fully charged prior to installation in the vehicle.
13   Installation is the reverse of removal. Connect the positive cable first and the negative cable last.
14   After connecting the cables to the battery, apply a light coating of petroleum jelly or grease to the connections to help prevent corrosion.

---

4   Battery cables - replacement

Refer to illustrations 4.4a and 4.4b
Caution: *On models equipped with the Theft-*

lock audio system, be sure you have the correct activation code before disconnecting the battery (see the front of this manual).
1   Periodically inspect the entire length of each battery cable for damage, cracked or burned insulation and corrosion. Poor battery cable connections can cause starting problems and decreased engine performance.
2   Check the cable-to-terminal connections at the ends of the cables for cracks, loose wire strands and corrosion. The presence of white, fluffy deposits under the insulation at the cable terminal connection is a sign that the cable is corroded and should be replaced. Check the terminals for distortion, missing mounting bolts and corrosion.
3   When removing the cables, always disconnect the negative cable first and hook it up last or the battery may be shorted by the tool used to loosen the cable clamps. Even if only the positive cable is being replaced, be sure to disconnect the negative cable first (see Chapter 1 for further information regarding battery cable maintenance).
4   Refer to Section 3 and disconnect the

5

cables from the battery, then disconnect them at the opposite end. Detach the cables from the starter solenoid, underhood electrical center and ground terminals, as necessary **(see illustrations)**. Note the routing of each cable to ensure correct installation.

5   If you are replacing either or both of the battery cables, take them with you when buying new cables. It is vitally important that you replace the cables with identical parts. Cables have characteristics that make them easy to identify: positive cables are usually red and larger in cross-section; ground cables are usually black and smaller in cross-section.

6   Clean the threads of the starter solenoid or ground connection with a wire brush to remove rust and corrosion. Apply a light coat of battery terminal corrosion inhibitor or petroleum jelly to the threads to prevent future corrosion.

7   Attach the cable to the terminal and tighten the mounting nut/bolt securely.

8   Before connecting a new cable to the battery, make sure that it reaches the battery without having to be stretched.

5   Ignition system - general information

All models are equipped with a distributorless ignition system (DIS). The ignition system consists of the battery, ignition coils, ignition control module, spark plug wires, spark plugs, camshaft position sensor, crankshaft position sensor and the Powertrain Control Module (PCM). The ignition control module and PCM control the ignition timing and spark advance characteristics for the engine. The ignition timing is not adjustable.

The DIS ignition systems use a "waste spark" method of spark distribution. Each cylinder is paired with its opposing cylinder in the firing order (1-4, 2-5, 3-6) so one cylinder under compression fires simultaneously with its opposing cylinder, where the piston is on the exhaust stroke. Since the cylinder on the exhaust stroke requires very little of the available voltage to fire its plug, most of the voltage is used to fire the plug of the cylinder on the compression stroke. Conventional ignition coils have one end of the secondary winding connected to the engine ground. On DIS, neither end of the secondary winding is grounded - instead, one end of the coils secondary winding is directly attached to the spark plug and the other end is attached to the spark plug of the companion cylinder.

The crankshaft position sensor produces a signal voltage to indicate crankshaft position and crankshaft speed. This signal is used by the Ignition Control Module (ICM) during start up and passed on to the Powertrain Control Module (PCM) to control ignition timing.

The DIS system is also integrated with a knock sensor system. The system uses a knock sensor in conjunction with the Power-

4.4a The negative cable is fastened to the transaxle bellhousing

train Control Module (PCM) to control spark timing. The knock sensor system allows the engine to use maximum spark advance without spark knock, which improves driveability and fuel economy.

6   Ignition system - check

Refer to illustrations 6.4, 6.6, 6.7, 6.8 and 6.9
Warning 1: *Because of the high voltage generated by the ignition system, extreme care should be taken whenever an operation is performed involving ignition components. This not only includes the ignition coil, but related components and test equipment.*
Warning 2: *The following procedure requires the engine to be cranked during testing, make sure the meter leads, loose clothing, long hair, etc. are away from the moving parts of the engine (drivebelt, cooling fan, etc.) before cranking the engine.*

1   Before proceeding with the ignition system, check the following items:

a) *Make sure the battery cable clamps, where they connect to the battery, are clean and tight.*

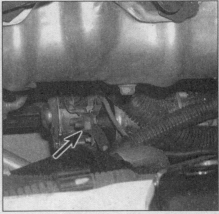

4.4b Disconnect the positive cable from the starter (one branch of the positive cable is connected to the underhood electrical center)

b) *Test the condition of the battery (see Section 3). If it does not pass all the tests, replace it with a new battery.*
c) *Check the ignition coil and ignition control module external wiring and connections.*
d) *Check the related fuses inside the underhood electrical center (see Chapter 12). If they're burned, determine the cause and repair the circuit.*

2   If the engine turns over but won't start or has a severe misfire, make sure there is sufficient secondary ignition voltage to fire the spark plugs.

3   Disable the fuel system by removing the fuel pump fuse from the underhood fuse/relay box (see Chapter 12).

4   Disconnect a spark plug wire from one of the spark plugs and attach a calibrated ignition system tester (available at most auto parts stores) to the spark plug boot. Connect the clip on the tester to a bolt or metal bracket on the engine **(see illustration)**. Crank the engine and watch the end of the tester to see if a bright blue, well-defined spark occurs (weak spark or intermittent spark is the same as no spark).

6.4 To use a calibrated ignition tester; disconnect a spark plug wire, connect the tester to the spark plug boot and clip the tester to a convenient ground - crank the engine over; if there's enough power to fire the plug, bright blue sparks will be visible between the electrode tip and the tester body (weak sparks or intermittent sparks are the same as no spark)

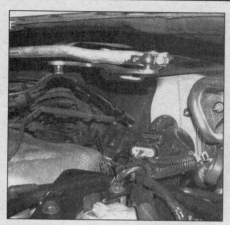

6.6 Check the ignition coil secondary resistance across the two coil towers

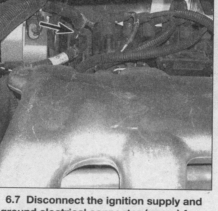

6.7 Disconnect the ignition supply and ground electrical connector (arrow) from the ignition control module and check for battery voltage at the pink wire terminal

6.8 Disconnect the crankshaft position sensor electrical connector from the ignition control module and check for a crankshaft position sensor signal as the engine is cranked

A Electronic spark control connector
B Crankshaft position sensor connector

5   If spark occurs, sufficient voltage is reaching the plug to fire it (repeat the check at the remaining spark plug wires to verify that the spark plug wires and ignition coils are good). If the ignition system is operating properly the problem lies elsewhere; i.e. a mechanical or fuel system problem. However, the spark plugs may be fouled, so remove and check them as described in Chapter 1.

6   If no spark occurs at one or more wires, remove the suspected spark plug wire from the ignition coil and check the terminals at both ends for damage. Using an ohmmeter, check the wire for an open or high resistance. The resistance of a good spark plug wire should be approximately 7000 ohms. If the spark plug wires are good, remove both spark plug wires from the suspected coil and using an ohmmeter, measure the secondary resistance across the coil towers (see illustration). Ignition coil secondary resistance should be approximately 5,000 to 7,000 ohms. If it isn't, replace the defective ignition coil.

7   If the engine won't start due to no spark, check for battery voltage to the ignition module from the ignition switch. Attach a 12 volt test light to the battery negative (-) terminal or other good ground. Disconnect the ignition power/ground electrical connector from the

module and check for power at the pink wire terminal (see illustration). Battery voltage should be available with the ignition key On. If there is no battery voltage present, check the wiring and/or circuit between the underhood fuse/relay box and ignition control module (don't forget to check the fuses). Also check the black wire terminal for continuity to battery ground. Note: Refer to the wiring diagrams at the end of Chapter 12 for wire color identification for testing and additional information on the circuits.

8   Check for a crankshaft position sensor signal. Disconnect the crankshaft position sensor connector (purple and yellow wires) from the ignition control module (see illustration). Connect a digital voltmeter to the terminals in the connector (harness side) and set the meter to read AC volts. Crank the engine and note the voltage. The 7X crankshaft position sensor should produce a minimum of 200 millivolts with the engine cranking. If a crankshaft position sensor signal is not present, check the circuits from the ignition control module to the 7X crankshaft position sensor. If the circuits are good, replace the 7X crankshaft position sensor (see Chapter 6).

9   Check for a trigger signal from the ignition control module. Remove one of the ignition coils from the ignition control module. Attach the lead of a test light to one of the coil terminals at the ignition control module and touch the probe of the test light to the other terminal (see illustration). Crank the engine. The test light should blink with the engine cranking if a trigger signal is present. If a trigger signal is present at the coil, the ignition control module and 7X crankshaft position sensor are functioning properly; check the ignition coils as described previously. Check each pair of coil terminals, if necessary. If a trigger signal is not present at one or more of the coil terminal pairs and the 7X crankshaft position sensor is good, replace the ignition control module.

10   If all the components are good and there is no spark, have the PCM checked by a dealer service department or other qualified repair shop.

7   Ignition coils and ignition control module - removal and installation

Removal

Refer to illustrations 7.4 and 7.5

1   Disconnect the cable from the negative battery terminal. Caution: On models equipped with the Theftlock audio system, be sure you have the correct activation code before disconnecting the battery (see the front of this manual).

2   Remove the engine cover and rotate the engine forward (see Chapter 2A).

3   Label the spark plug wires corresponding to the cylinder numbers and remove them from the ignition coils. Disconnect the electrical connectors from the ignition module.

4   Remove the ignition coil/module mount-

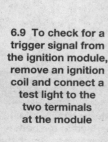

6.9 To check for a trigger signal from the ignition module, remove an ignition coil and connect a test light to the two terminals at the module

5

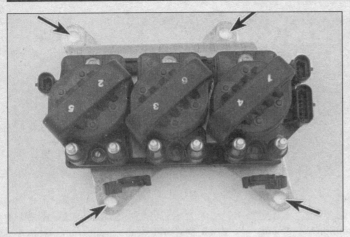

7.4 Remove the ignition coil/module bracket mounting bolts (arrows show bolt locations; coil/module removed for clarity)

7.5 Ignition coil mounting screws (arrows)

ing nuts/bolts and remove the assembly from the engine **(see illustration)**.

5   Remove the ignition coil mounting screws and remove the ignition coils from the module **(see illustration)**.

Installation

6   Align the ignition coil with the blade terminals on the module and press the coil on until it's seated.

7   Install the mounting screws and tighten them securely.

8   Install the coil/module assembly onto the engine and tighten the fasteners securely. Connect the ignition module electrical connectors and install the spark plug wires in their proper locations.

9   The remainder of installation is the reverse of removal.

8   Charging system - general information and precautions

The main components of the charging system are alternator (with an integral voltage regulator), the battery and the wiring connecting the components. The components work together to supply electrical power for the electrical system and maintain the battery in a charged condition. The alternator is driven by the drivebelt at the front of the engine.

Alternators should be considered non-serviceable and, if defective, exchanged as cores for new or rebuilt units. An identification number and amperage rating is stamped on the alternator housing. Refer to these numbers to obtain the correct replacement alternator, if necessary.

The purpose of the voltage regulator is to limit the alternator voltage output to a preset value. This prevents power surges and circuit overloads during peak voltage output. On all models with which this manual is concerned, the voltage regulator is integral with the alternator.

The charging system doesn't ordinarily require periodic maintenance. However, the drivebelt, battery and wires and connections should be inspected at the intervals outlined in Chapter 1.

The instrument panel warning light should come on when the ignition key is turned to START, then go off immediately after the engine has started. If the warning light stays on or comes on when the engine is running, a charging system problem has occurred (see Section 9).

Be very careful when making electrical circuit connections to a vehicle equipped with an alternator and note the following:

a) *When reconnecting wires to the alternator from the battery, be sure to note the polarity.*
b) *Before using arc welding equipment to repair any part of the vehicle, disconnect the wires from the alternator and the battery terminals.* **Caution:** *On models equipped with the Theftlock audio system, be sure the lockout feature is turned off before performing any procedure which requires disconnecting the battery (see the front of this manual).*
c) *Never start the engine with a battery charger connected.*
d) *Always disconnect both battery leads before using a battery charger.*
e) *The alternator is turned by an engine drivebelt which could cause serious injury if your hands, hair or clothes become entangled in it with the engine running.*
f) *Because the alternator is connected directly to the battery, it could arc or cause a fire if overloaded or shorted out.*
g) *Wrap a plastic bag over the alternator and secure it with rubber bands before steam cleaning the engine.*

9   Charging system - check

Refer to illustration 9.2
Note: *These vehicles are equipped with an On-Board Diagnostic (OBD) system that is useful for detecting charging system prob-*

lems. *Refer to Chapter 6 for the list of diagnostic codes and procedures for obtaining the codes.*

1   If a malfunction occurs in the charging circuit, do not immediately assume that the alternator is causing the problem. First check the following items:

a) *The battery cables where they connect to the battery. Make sure the connections are clean and tight.*
b) *The battery electrolyte specific gravity (by observing the charge indicator on the battery). If it is low, charge the battery.*
c) *Check the external alternator wiring and connections.*
d) *Check the drivebelt condition and tension (see Chapter 1).*
e) *Check the alternator mounting bolts for tightness.*
f) *Run the engine and check the alternator for abnormal noise.*

2   Normally the test connections would be made at the battery terminals on the battery. But, since the battery is difficult to access,

9.2 To measure battery voltage, attach the positive voltmeter lead to the battery terminal at the fuse/relay panel; attach the negative lead to the ground point on the inner fender

10.5 Remove the nut and wire terminal from the output terminal (A) and disconnect the alternator electrical connector (B) - if equipped, remove the rear brace bolt (C)

10.6 Remove the alternator mounting bolts (arrows)

connect the positive lead of a voltmeter to the positive battery terminal at the underhood fuse/relay panel and connect the negative lead of the voltmeter to the ground point on the inner fender **(see illustration)**. Check the battery voltage with the engine off. It should be approximately 12.4 to 12.6 volts, if the battery is fully charged.

3   Start the engine and check the battery voltage again. It should now be greater than the voltage recorded in Step 2, but not more than 14.7 volts.

4   If the indicated voltage reading is less or more than the specified charging voltage, have the charging system checked at a dealer service department or other properly equipped repair facility. **Note:** Many auto parts stores will bench test an alternator off the vehicle. Refer to your local auto parts store regarding their policy, many will perform this service free of charge.

10   Alternator - removal and installation

Refer to illustrations 10.5 and 10.6

1   Disconnect the cable from the negative battery terminal. **Caution:** On models equipped with the Theftlock audio system, be sure you have the correct activation code before disconnecting the battery (see the front of this manual).

2   Remove the drivebelt (see Chapter 1).

3   Remove the windshield wiper module cover and detach the wiper arm linkage from the wiper motor crank arm (see Chapter 12). Position the linkage aside.

4   Remove the engine cover and rotate the engine forward (see Chapter 2A).

5   Disconnect the output wire and the electrical connector from the alternator **(see illustration)**.

6   Remove the alternator mounting bolts **(see illustration)**. On 1997 and 1998 models, remove the front and rear braces.

7   On 1997 and 1998 models, place a floor jack centered under the front of the subframe. Remove the front subframe bolts and lower the subframe approximately three inches. **Caution:** Do not allow the subframe to contact the front bumper cover or damage to the cover may result. Remove the alternator from the engine compartment.

8   On 1999 and later models, remove the alternator from it's mounting bracket and rest the alternator on the driveaxle. Remove the drivebelt tensioner (see Chapter 1). Detach the power steering line clamps, remove the power steering pump mounting bolts and position the power steering pump aside, without disconnecting the hoses from the pump (see Chapter 9). Remove the alternator from the engine compartment.

9   If you are replacing the alternator, take the old one with you when purchasing a replacement unit. Make sure the new/rebuilt unit looks identical to the old alternator. Look at the terminals - they should be the same in number, size and location as the terminals on the old alternator. Finally, look at the identification numbers - they will be stamped into the housing. Make sure the numbers are the same on both alternators.

10   Many new/rebuilt alternators do not have a pulley installed, so you may have to switch the pulley from the old unit to the new/rebuilt one. When buying an alternator, find out the shop's policy regarding pulleys; some shops will perform this service free of charge.

11   Installation is the reverse of removal. Tighten the alternator mounting bolts to the torque listed in this Chapter's Specifications. On 1997 and 1998 models, raise the subframe into position, install NEW mounting bolts and tighten the bolts to the torque listed in the Chapter 10 Specifications). **Caution:** Anytime the subframe mounting bolts are loosened or removed, the bolts must be replaced with new original equipment replacement bolts.

12   Install the drivebelt (see Chapter 1).

13   Check the charging voltage to verify proper operation of the alternator (see Section 9).

11   Starting system - general information and precautions

The starter motor assembly is a permanent magnet, gear drive starter motor. The starter motor assembly is serviced as a complete unit. If any component of the starter motor fails, including the solenoid, the entire assembly must be replaced.

The starting system consists of the battery, starter motor assembly and the wiring connecting the components.

When the ignition key is turned to the START position, the starter solenoid is actuated through the starter control circuit. The starter solenoid then connects the battery to the starter motor. The battery supplies the electrical energy to the starter motor, which does the actual work of cranking the engine.

Always observe the following precautions when working on the starting system:

a) Excessive cranking of the starter motor can overheat it and cause serious damage. Never operate the starter motor for more than 15 seconds at a time without pausing to allow it to cool for at least two minutes.

b) The starter is connected directly to the battery and could arc or cause a fire if mishandled, overloaded or shorted.

c) Always detach the cable from the negative terminal of the battery before working on the starting system.

12   Starter motor and circuit - check

Refer to illustration 12.4

1   If a malfunction occurs in the starting circuit, do not immediately assume that the starter is causing the problem. First, check the following items:

a) Make sure the battery cable clamps, where they connect to the battery, are clean and tight.

b) Check the condition of the battery cables (see Section 4). Replace any defective battery cables with new parts.

c) Test the condition of the battery (see Section 3). If it does not pass all the tests, replace it with a new battery.

d) Check the starter motor wiring and connections.

e) Check the starter motor mounting bolts for tightness.

f) Check the related fuses in the engine compartment fuse box (see Chapter 12). If they're blown, determine the cause and repair the circuit.

g) Check the ignition switch circuit for correct operation (see Chapter 12).

h) Check the starter relay (located in the underhood electrical center) for proper operation (see Chapter 12).

i) Check the operation of the clutch start switch (manual transmission) or the Park/Neutral position switch (automatic transmission) (see Chapter 8 or 7B).

5

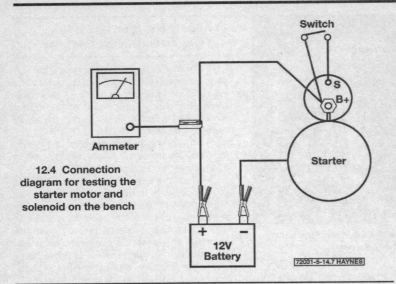

12.4 Connection diagram for testing the starter motor and solenoid on the bench

Switch

S
B+

Ammeter

Starter

12V Battery

72031-5-14.7 HAYNES

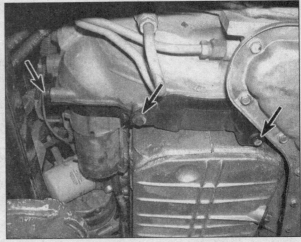

13.3 Remove the bolts (arrows) and the driveplate/torque converter cover

These systems must operate correctly to provide battery voltage to the starter relay.

2   If the starter does not activate when the ignition switch is turned to the start position, check for battery voltage to the starter solenoid. This will determine if the solenoid is receiving the correct voltage from the starter relay. Install a 12-volt test light or a voltmeter to the starter solenoid terminal (purple wire). While an assistant turns the ignition switch to the start position, observe the test light or voltmeter. The test light should shine brightly or battery voltage should be indicated on the voltmeter. If voltage is not available to the starter solenoid, refer to the wiring diagrams in Chapter 12 and check the fuses, ignition switch, starter relay and related wiring in series with the starting system. If voltage is available but there is no movement from the starter motor, remove the starter from the engine (see Section 14) and bench test the starter (see Step 4).

3   If the starter turns over slowly, check the starter cranking voltage and the current draw from the battery. This test must be performed with the starter assembly on the engine. Crank the engine over (for 10 seconds or less) and observe the battery voltage. It should not drop below 8.5 volts. Also, observe the current draw using an amp meter. Typically a starter amperage draw should not exceed 350 amps. If the starter motor amperage draw is excessive, have it tested by a dealer service department or other qualified repair shop. There are several conditions that may affect the starter cranking potential. The battery must be in good condition and the battery cold-cranking rating must not be under-rated for the particular application. Be sure to check the battery specifications carefully. The battery terminals and cables must be clean and not corroded. Also, in cases of extreme cold temperatures, make sure the battery and/or engine block is warmed before performing the tests.

4   If the starter is receiving voltage but

does not operate, remove the starter motor from the vehicle and check it on the bench. Most likely the starter motor or solenoid is defective, but in some rare cases the engine may be seized, so be sure to rotate the crankshaft pulley to verify the engine is not seized before proceeding (see Chapter 2A). Clamp the starter motor firmly in a bench mounted vise. Install a jumper cable from the positive terminal of a test battery to the B+ terminal on the starter (**see illustration**). Install another jumper cable from the negative terminal of the battery to the body of the starter. Install a starter switch between the positive battery terminal and the solenoid S terminal. Operate the switch. **Caution:** *Do not energize the starter for longer than 10 seconds without stopping and allowing it to cool or damage to the starter motor may occur.* The solenoid plunger, shift lever and overrunning clutch should extend and rotate the pinion drive at approximately 3,000 to 4,000 rpm. If the solenoid plunger extends and rotates the pinion drive, the starter assembly is operating properly. If the solenoid clicks but the pinion drive does not extend, or if the pinion drive extends but does not rotate (or rotates slowly), the solenoid and/or starter motor is defective.

13 Starter motor - removal and installation

Refer to illustrations 13.3, 13.4 and 13.5

1   Disconnect the cable from the negative battery terminal. **Caution:** *On models equipped with the Theftlock audio system, be sure you have the correct activation code before disconnecting the battery (see the front of this manual).*

2   Raise the vehicle and support it securely on jackstands.

3   Remove the transaxle driveplate/torque converter cover (**see illustration**).

4   Disconnect the wires from the terminals

on the starter motor solenoid (**see illustration**).

5   Remove the starter mounting bolts and remove the starter from the vehicle (**see illustration**).

6   Installation is the reverse of removal.

13.4 Remove the nuts and disconnect the battery cable and the solenoid terminal from the starter motor

13.5 Remove the starter mounting bolts (arrows)

Chapter 6
Emissions and engine control systems

Contents

1   General information

Refer to illustrations 1.1 and 1.7

To prevent pollution of the atmosphere from incompletely burned and evaporating gases, and to maintain good driveability and fuel economy, a number of emission control systems are incorporated **(see illustration)**. They include the:

Electronic engine control system
Crankcase ventilation system
Exhaust gas recirculation system
Evaporative emissions control system
Secondary air injection system (2000 and later models)
Catalytic converter

All of these systems are linked, directly or indirectly, to the emissions and engine control systems.

The Sections in this Chapter include general descriptions, checking procedures within the scope of the home mechanic (when possible) and component replacement procedures for each of the systems listed above.

Before assuming that an emissions control system is malfunctioning, check the fuel and ignition systems carefully. The diagnosis of some emission control devices requires specialized tools, equipment and training. If checking and servicing become too difficult or if a procedure is beyond your ability, consult a dealer service department or other properly equipped repair facility. Remember, the most frequent cause of emissions problems is simply a loose or broken vacuum hose or wire, so always check the hose and wiring connections first.

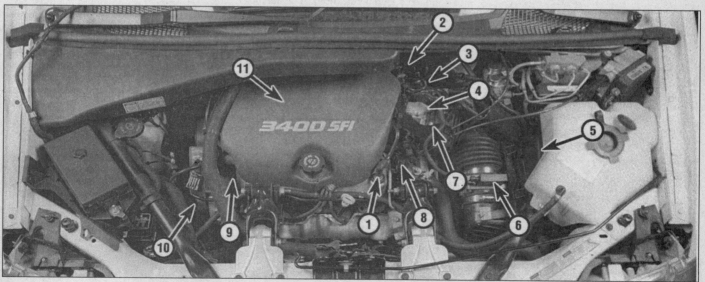

1.1 Typical emission and engine control system components

1   *Positive Crankshaft Ventilation (PCV) valve*
2   *Evaporative emissions system (EVAP) purge valve*
3   *Exhaust Gas Recirculation (EGR) valve*
4   *Idle Air Control (IAC) valve and Throttle Position Sensor (TPS)*
     (mounted on throttle body)
5   *Powertrain Control Module (PCM)*

6   *Mass Airflow (MAF) sensor*
7   *Intake Air Temperature (IAT) sensor*
8   *Engine Coolant Temperature (ECT) sensor*
9   *Camshaft Position (CMP) sensor*
10   *Crankshaft Position (CKP) sensor*
11   *Manifold Absolute Pressure (MAP) sensor (under cover)*

6

1.7 The Vehicle Emission Control Information (VECI) label is located in the engine compartment and contains information on the emission devices on your vehicle, vacuum line routing, etc.

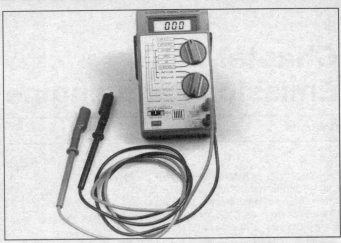

2.1 Digital multimeters can be used for testing all types of circuits; because of their high impedance, they are much more accurate than analog meters for measuring low-voltage computer circuits

This doesn't mean, however, that emission control systems are particularly difficult to maintain and repair. You can quickly and easily perform many checks and do most of the regular maintenance at home with common tune-up and hand tools. **Note:** *Because of a Federally mandated warranty which covers the emission control system components, check with your dealer about warranty coverage before working on any emissions-related systems. Once the warranty has expired, you may wish to perform some of the component checks and/or replacement procedures in this Chapter to save money.*

Pay close attention to any special precautions outlined in this Chapter. It should be noted that the illustrations of the various systems may not exactly match the system installed on the vehicle you're working on because of changes made by the manufacturer during production or from year-to-year.

A Vehicle Emissions Control Information (VECI) label is located in the engine compartment **(see illustration)**. This label contains important emissions specifications and adjustment information, as well as a vacuum hose schematic with emissions components identified. When servicing the engine or emissions systems, the VECI label in your particular vehicle should always be checked for up-to-date information.

2 On-Board Diagnostic (OBD) system and trouble codes

Diagnostic tool information
Refer to illustrations 2.1, 2.2 and 2.3

1 A digital multimeter is necessary for checking fuel injection and emission related components **(see illustration)**. A digital multimeter is preferred over the older style analog multimeter for several reasons. The analog multimeter cannot display the volts, ohms or amps measurement in hundredths and thousandths increments. When working with electronic circuits which are often very low voltage, this accurate reading is most important. Another good reason for the digital multimeter is the high impedance circuit. The digital multimeter is equipped with a high resistance internal circuitry (10 million ohms). Because a voltmeter is hooked up in parallel with the circuit when testing, it is vital that none of the voltage being measured should be allowed to travel the parallel path set up by the meter itself. This dilemma does not show itself when measuring larger amounts of voltage (9 to 12 volt circuits) but if you are measuring a low voltage circuit such as the oxygen sensor signal voltage, a fraction of a volt may be a significant amount when diagnosing a problem. However, there are several exceptions where using an analog voltmeter may be necessary to test certain sensors.

2 Hand-held scanners are the most powerful and versatile tools for analyzing engine management systems used on later model vehicles **(see illustration)**. Each brand scan tool must be examined carefully to match the year, make and model of the vehicle you are working on. Often interchangeable cartridges are available to access the particular manufacturer (Ford, GM, Chrysler, etc.). Some

2.2 Scanners like the Actron Scantool and the AutoXray XP240 are powerful diagnostic aids - programmed with comprehensive diagnostic information, they can tell you just about anything you want to know about your engine management system

2.3 Code readers like the Actron OBD-II diagnostic tester simplify the task of extracting trouble codes

manufacturers will specify by continent (Asia, Europe, USA, etc.). With the arrival of the Federally mandated emission control system (OBD-II), a specially designed scanner has been developed. Several tool manufacturers have released OBD-II scan tools for the home mechanic. Ask the parts salesman at a local auto parts store for additional information concerning availability and cost.

3   An OBD-II code reader may be available at auto parts stores, as well **(see illustration)**. This tool simplifies the procedure for extracting codes from the engine management computer and are less expensive than a scan tool but are not equipped with the scan tool diagnostic functions.

On-Board Diagnostic system general description

4   All models described in this manual are equipped with the second generation On-Board Diagnostic (OBD-II) system. The system consists of an onboard computer, known as the Powertrain Control Module (PCM), information sensors and output actuators.

5   The information sensors monitor various functions of the engine and send data to the PCM. Based on the data and the information programmed into the computer's memory, the PCM generates output signals to control various engine functions via control relays, solenoids and other output actuators. The PCM is specifically calibrated to optimize the emissions, fuel economy and driveability of the vehicle.

6   Because of a Federally mandated warranty which covers the emissions system components and because any owner-induced damage to the PCM, the sensors and/or the control devices may void the warranty, it isn't a good idea to attempt diagnosis or replacement of the system components while the vehicle is under warranty. Take the vehicle to a dealer service department if the PCM or a system component malfunctions.

Information sensors

7   **Camshaft Position (CMP) sensor** - The Camshaft Position sensor provides information on camshaft position. The PCM uses this information, along with the Crankshaft Position sensor information, to control fuel injection synchronization.

8   **Crankshaft Position (CKP) sensor** - The Crankshaft Position sensor senses crankshaft position (TDC) during each engine revolution. The PCM uses this information to control ignition timing and fuel injection synchronization.

9   **Engine Coolant Temperature (ECT) sensor** - The Engine Coolant temperature sensor senses engine coolant temperature. The PCM uses this information to control fuel injection duration and ignition timing.

10   **Intake Air Temperature (IAT) sensor** - The Intake Air temperature sensor senses the temperature of the air entering the intake manifold. The PCM uses this information to control fuel injection duration.

11   **Knock Sensor (KS)** - The knock sensor is a piezoelectric element that detects the sound of engine detonation, or "pinging". The PCM uses the input signal from the knock sensor to recognize detonation and retard spark advance to avoid engine damage.

12   **Manifold Absolute Pressure (MAP) sensor** - The manifold absolute pressure sensor monitors intake manifold pressure and ambient barometric pressure. The PCM uses this input signal to determine engine load and adjusts fuel injection duration accordingly.

13   **Mass Airflow (MAF) sensor** - The mass airflow sensor measures the amount of air passing through the sensor body and ultimately entering the engine. The PCM uses this information to control fuel delivery.

14   **Oxygen (O2) sensor** - The oxygen sensors generate a voltage signal that varies with the varying oxygen content of the exhaust gas. The PCM uses this information to determine if the fuel system is running rich or lean and make adjustments accordingly.

15   **Throttle Position Sensor (TPS)** - The throttle position sensor senses throttle movement and position. This signal enables the PCM to determine when the throttle is closed, in a cruise position, or wide open. The PCM uses this information to control fuel delivery and ignition timing.

16   **Vehicle Speed Sensor (VSS)** - The vehicle speed sensor provides information to the PCM to indicate vehicle speed.

17   **Miscellaneous PCM inputs** - In addition to the various sensors, the PCM monitors various switches and circuits to determine vehicle operating conditions. The switches and circuits include:

a)   *Air conditioning system*
b)   *Battery voltage*
c)   *Brake On/Off switch*
d)   *Cruise control system*
e)   *EGR valve position*
f)   *Engine oil level and pressure*
g)   *EVAP system*
h)   *Fuel level and fuel tank pressure*
i)   *Ignition switch*
j)   *Park/neutral position switch*
k)   *Sensor signal and ground circuits*
l)   *Transaxle control system*

Output actuators

18   **Air conditioning clutch relay** - The PCM controls the operation of the air conditioning compressor clutch with the air conditioning clutch relay.

19   **Check Engine light** - The PCM will illuminate the Check Engine light if a malfunction in the electronic engine control system occurs.

20   **Cruise control module** - The cruise control system operation is controlled by the PCM.

21   **Engine cooling fan relay** - The engine cooling fan is controlled by the PCM according to information received from the Engine Coolant temperature sensor.

22   **EGR valve** - The electronic EGR valve is controlled by the PCM. Ideal EGR flow is determined by the PCM and the EGR valve pintle position is adjusted accordingly.

23   **EVAP canister purge and vent valve solenoids** - The evaporative emission canister purge and vent valve solenoids are operated by the PCM to purge the fuel vapor canister and route fuel vapor to the intake manifold for combustion.

24   **Secondary Air Injection (AIR) pump** - The PCM operates the secondary air injection pump to inject fresh air into the exhaust stream, lower emission levels under certain operating conditions.

25   **Fuel injectors** - The PCM opens the fuel injectors individually in firing order sequence. The PCM also controls the time the injector is held open (pulse width). The pulse width of the injector (measured in milliseconds) determines the amount of fuel delivered. For more information on the fuel delivery system and the fuel injectors, including injector replacement, refer to Chapter 4.

26   **Fuel pump relay** - The fuel pump relay is activated by the PCM with the ignition switch in the Start or Run position. When the ignition switch is turned on, the relay is activated to supply initial line pressure to the system. For more information on fuel pump check and replacement, refer to Chapter 4.

27   **Idle Air Control valve (IAC)** - The idle air control valve controls the amount of air allowed to bypass the throttle plate when the throttle valve is closed or at idle position. The more air allowed to bypass the throttle plate, the higher the idle speed. The idle air control valve opening and the resulting idle speed is controlled by the PCM.

28   **Ignition coils/control module** - The PCM controls ignition timing through the ignition coils/control module depending on engine operation conditions. Refer to Chapter 5 for more information on the ignition coils or ignition control module.

Obtaining diagnostic trouble codes

Refer to illustration 2.30

Note: *The diagnostic trouble codes on all models can only be extracted from the Powertrain Control Module (PCM) using a specialized scan tool. Have the vehicle diagnosed by a dealer service department or other qualified automotive repair facility if the proper scan tool is not available.*

29   The PCM will illuminate the SERVICE ENGINE SOON light (USA) or the CHECK ENGINE light (Canada) (also known as the Malfunction Indicator Lamp) on the dash if it recognizes a fault in the system. The light will remain illuminated until the problem is repaired and the code is cleared or the PCM does not detect any malfunction for several consecutive drive cycles.

30   The diagnostic codes for the On-Board Diagnostic (OBD) system can only be extracted from the PCM using a scan tool. The scan tool is programmed to interface

6

2.30 The diagnostic connector is typically located under the instrument panel

with the OBD system by plugging into the diagnostic connector **(see illustration)**. When used, the scan tool has the ability to diagnose in-depth driveability problems and it allows freeze frame data to be retrieved from the PCM stored memory. Freeze frame data is an OBD II PCM feature that records all related sensor and actuator activity on the PCM data stream whenever an engine control or emissions fault is detected and a trouble code is set. This ability to look at the circuit conditions and values when the malfunction occurs provides a valuable tool when trying to diagnose intermittent driveability problems. If the tool is not available and intermittent driveability problems exist, have the vehicle checked at a dealer service department or other qualified repair shop.

Clearing diagnostic trouble codes

31   After the system has been repaired, the codes must be cleared from the PCM memory. The preferred method is with a scan tool, but the codes can be cleared by disconnecting battery power from the PCM for a minimum of thirty seconds. Battery power can be disconnected from the PCM by removing the PCM fuse, disconnecting the PCM power connector near the positive battery terminal (if equipped) or by disconnecting the negative battery cable from the battery. **Caution:** *On models equipped with the Theftlock audio system, be sure the lockout feature is turned off before performing any procedure which requires disconnecting the battery (see the front of this manual).*

32   Always clear the codes from the PCM before starting the engine after a new electronic emission control component is installed onto the engine. The PCM stores the operating parameters of each sensor. The PCM may set a trouble code if a new sensor is allowed to operate before the parameters from the old sensor have been erased.

Diagnostic trouble code identification

33   The accompanying list of diagnostic trouble codes is a compilation of all the codes that may be encountered using a generic scan tool. Additional trouble codes may be available with the use of the manufacturer specific scan tool. Not all codes pertain to all models and not all codes will illuminate the Check Engine light when set. All models require a scan tool to access the diagnostic trouble codes.

Code	Code Identification
P0101	Mass air flow sensor circuit, range or performance problem
P0102	Mass air flow sensor circuit, low input
P0103	Mass air flow sensor circuit, high input
P0105	Manifold absolute pressure sensor or throttle position sensor circuit malfunction
P0106	Manifold absolute pressure sensor circuit, range or performance problem
P0107	Manifold absolute pressure sensor circuit, low input
P0108	Manifold absolute pressure sensor circuit, high input
P0112	Intake air temperature circuit, low input
P0113	Intake air temperature circuit, high input
P0117	Engine coolant temperature circuit, low input
P0118	Engine coolant temperature circuit, high input
P0121	Throttle position sensor circuit, range or performance problem
P0122	Throttle position sensor circuit, low input
P0123	Throttle position sensor circuit, high input
P0125	Insufficient coolant temperature for closed loop fuel control
P0131	Oxygen sensor circuit, low voltage (upstream sensor)
P0132	Oxygen sensor circuit, high voltage (upstream sensor)
P0133	Oxygen sensor circuit, slow response (upstream sensor)
P0134	Oxygen sensor circuit - no activity detected (upstream sensor)
P0135	Oxygen sensor heater circuit malfunction (upstream sensor no)
P0137	Oxygen sensor circuit, low voltage (downstream sensor)
P0138	Oxygen sensor circuit, high voltage (downstream sensor)
P0140	Oxygen sensor circuit - no activity detected (downstream sensor)
P0141	Oxygen sensor heater circuit malfunction (downstream sensor)
P0171	System too lean
P0172	System too rich

Code	Code Identification
P0200	Injector circuit malfunction
P0201	Injector circuit malfunction - cylinder no. 1
P0202	Injector circuit malfunction - cylinder no. 2
P0203	Injector circuit malfunction - cylinder no. 3
P0204	Injector circuit malfunction - cylinder no. 4
P0205	Injector circuit malfunction - cylinder no. 5
P0206	Injector circuit malfunction - cylinder no. 6
P0218	Transaxle fluid over temperature
P0230	Fuel pump primary circuit malfunction
P0300	Random/multiple cylinder misfire detected
P0301	Cylinder no. 1 misfire detected
P0302	Cylinder no. 2 misfire detected
P0303	Cylinder no. 3 misfire detected
P0304	Cylinder no. 4 misfire detected
P0305	Cylinder no. 5 misfire detected
P0306	Cylinder no. 6 misfire detected
P0325	Knock sensor circuit malfunction
P0327	Knock sensor circuit, low input
P0335	Crankshaft position sensor circuit malfunction
P0336	Crankshaft position sensor circuit, range or performance problem
P0341	Camshaft position sensor circuit, range or performance problem
P0342	Camshaft position sensor circuit, low input
P0401	Exhaust gas recirculation, insufficient flow detected
P0403	Exhaust gas recirculation circuit malfunction
P0404	Exhaust gas recirculation circuit, range or performance problem
P0405	Exhaust gas recirculation sensor circuit low
P0410	Secondary air injection system
P0412	Secondary air injection solenoid control circuit
P0418	Secondary air injection pump relay control circuit
P0420	Catalyst system efficiency below threshold
P0440	Evaporative emission control system malfunction
P0441	EVAP system no flow detected
P0442	Evaporative emission control system, small leak detected
P0443	Evaporative emission control system, purge control circuit malfunction
P0446	Evaporative emission control system, vent system performance
P0449	Evaporative emission control system, vent control circuit malfunction
P0452	Evaporative emission control system, pressure sensor low input
P0453	Evaporative emission control system, pressure sensor high input
P0460	Fuel level sensor circuit malfunction
P0461	Fuel level sensor circuit, range or performance problem
P0462	Fuel level sensor circuit, low input
P0463	Fuel level sensor circuit, high input
P0480	Cooling fan control circuit malfunction
P0481	Cooling fan control circuit malfunction
P0502	Vehicle speed sensor circuit low output
P0503	Vehicle speed sensor signal intermittent

6

Code	Code Identification
P0506	Idle control system, rpm lower than expected
P0507	Idle control system, rpm higher than expected
P0530	Air conditioning refrigerant pressure sensor, circuit malfunction
P0560	System voltage malfunction
P0562	System voltage low
P0563	System voltage high
P0601	Internal control module, memory error
P0602	Control module, programming error
P0620	Charging system performance
P0650	Malfunction Indicator Light (MIL) control circuit
P0654	Tachometer control circuit
P0705	Transmission range sensor, circuit malfunction (PRNDL input)
P0706	Transaxle range switch performance
P0711	Fluid temperature sensor circuit out-of-range
P0712	Fluid temperature sensor circuit low input
P0713	Fluid temperature sensor circuit high input
P0716	Input speed sensor circuit out-of-range
P0717	Input speed sensor circuit no signal
P0719	Torque converter clutch brake switch circuit low
P0724	Torque converter clutch brake switch circuit high
P0730	Incorrect gear ratio
P0741	Torque converter clutch system stuck off
P0740	Torque converter clutch circuit
P0742	Torque converter clutch system stuck on
P0748	Pressure control solenoid valve circuit
P0751	1-2 shift solenoid performance
P0753	1-2 shift solenoid circuit
P0756	2-3 shift solenoid performance
P0757	2-3 shift valve performance
P0758	2-3 shift solenoid circuit
P1106	Manifold absolute pressure sensor circuit intermittent high voltage
P1107	Manifold absolute pressure sensor circuit intermittent low voltage
P1111	Intake air temperature sensor circuit intermittent high voltage
P1112	Intake air temperature sensor circuit intermittent low voltage
P1114	Engine coolant temperature sensor circuit intermittent low voltage
P1115	Engine coolant temperature sensor circuit intermittent high voltage
P1121	Throttle position sensor circuit intermittent high voltage
P1122	Throttle position sensor circuit intermittent low voltage
P1133	Oxygen sensor insufficient switching (upstream sensor)
P1134	Oxygen sensor transition time ratio (upstream sensor)
P1171	Fuel system lean during acceleration
P1200	Fuel injector control circuit
P1336	Crankshaft position sensor system variation not learned
P1350	By-pass line monitor
P1351	Ignition control circuit open
P1352	Ignition by-pass circuit open

Code	Code Identification
P1361	Ignition control circuit not switching
P1362	Ignition by-pass circuit shorted
P1374	Crankshaft position sensor 3X reference circuit
P1380	Electronic brake control module rough road sensing error
P1381	No serial data from electronic brake control module
P1404	EGR valve closed pintle position
P1406	EGR valve pintle position circuit
P1441	EVAP system flow during non-purge
P1442	EVAP vacuum switch circuit
P1483	Engine cooling system performance
P1546	Air conditioning clutch relay control circuit
P1554	Cruise control status circuit
P1571	Traction control torque request circuit
P1573	Serial data communication failure with electronic brake and traction control module
P1585	Cruise control inhibit circuit
P1601	Serial communication malfunction
P1602	Serial data communication failure with electronic brake control module
P1610	Serial data communication failure with body function controller
P1621	PCM memory performance
P1626	Serial data communication failure with vehicle theft deterrent controller (no password)
P1629	Theft deterrent system fuel enable circuit
P1630	Theft deterrent PCM in learn mode
P1631	Theft deterrent password incorrect
P1632	Theft deterrent fuel disabled
P1635	5-volt reference circuit
P1639	5-volt reference circuit
P1641	Malfunction indicator light control circuit
P1651	Electric cooling fan relay control circuit
P1652	Electric cooling fan relay control circuit
P1654	Air conditioning relay control circuit
P1655	Evaporative emission control system, purge valve solenoid control circuit
P1662	Cruise control inhibit control circuit
P1663	Charge indicator lamp control circuit
P1665	Evaporative emission control system, vent valve solenoid control circuit
P1671	Malfunction indicator light control circuit
P1672	Low engine oil indicator control circuit
P1673	Engine temperature indicator control circuit
P1675	Evaporative emission control system, vent solenoid control circuit
P1676	Evaporative emission control system, purge valve solenoid control circuit
P1810	Pressure switch assembly malfunction
P1811	Long shift time
P1814	Torque converter overstressed
P1860	Torque converter clutch pulse width modulator solenoid circuit
P1870	Transaxle component slipping
P1887	Torque converter clutch release switch malfunction

6

3.4 Remove these bolts (arrows) and the fender brace for access to the PCM

3.5 Release the latch (arrow) and remove the PCM cover

3.6 Loosen the bolts (arrows) and disconnect the electrical connectors from the PCM

3 Powertrain Control Module (PCM) - removal and installation

Refer to illustrations 3.4, 3.5 and 3.6
Caution: *Avoid static electricity damage to the Powertrain Control Module (PCM) by grounding yourself to the body of the vehicle before touching the PCM and using a special anti-static pad to store the PCM on, once it is removed.*
Note 1: *Anytime the PCM is replaced with a new unit the PCM must be reprogrammed by a dealership service department with special equipment. A Crankshaft Position sensor variation relearn procedure and a vehicle anti-theft system password relearn procedure must be performed, as well. The following procedure pertains to removal and installation of the original PCM only. If the PCM must be replaced with a new unit, take the vehicle to a dealership service department.*
Note 2: *Anytime the battery is disconnected stored operating parameters may be lost from the PCM causing the engine to run rough for sometime while the PCM relearns the information.*
1   Disconnect the cable from the negative battery terminal. **Caution:** *On models equipped with the Theftlock audio system, be sure you have the correct activation code*

4.2 Throttle Position Sensor (TPS) location

before disconnecting the battery (see the front of this manual).
2   Remove the coolant reservoir and position it aside (see Chapter 3).
3   Remove the cruise control module from its mounting bracket and position it aside. Remove the bracket.
4   Remove the left fender brace **(see illustration)**.
5   Detach the PCM cover latch and remove the cover **(see illustration)**.
6   Remove the PCM from the air filter housing and carefully disconnect the electrical connectors from the PCM **(see illustration)**.
7   Installation is the reverse of removal.

4 Throttle Position Sensor (TPS) - check and replacement

1   The Throttle Position Sensor (TPS) is a variable potentiometer connected to the end of the throttle shaft on the throttle body. By monitoring the output voltage from the TPS, the PCM can determine fuel delivery based on throttle valve angle (driver demand). A broken or loose TPS can cause intermittent bursts of fuel from the injectors and an unstable idle because the PCM thinks the throttle is moving.

Check

Refer to illustrations 4.2, 4.3 and 4.4
Note: *Performing the following test will set a diagnostic trouble code and illuminate the SERVICE ENGINE SOON or CHECK ENGINE light. Clear the diagnostic trouble code after performing the tests and making the necessary repairs (see Section 2).*
2   The Throttle Position Sensor (TPS) is located on the side of the throttle body **(see illustration)**. Check the terminals in the connector for corrosion and tightness. Check the wiring harness leading to the sensor for damage. Repair as required.
3   Before checking the TPS, check the voltage supply and ground circuits from the PCM. Disconnect the electrical connector

from the TPS and connect the positive lead of a voltmeter to the gray wire terminal and the negative lead to the black wire terminal at the harness connector **(see illustration)**. Turn the ignition key On - the voltage should read approximately 5.0 volts. If the voltage is incorrect, check the wiring from the TPS to the PCM. If the circuits are good, have the PCM checked at a dealer service department or other properly equipped repair facility.
4   To check the TPS operation, reconnect the connector to the TPS and using a suitable probe, backprobe the dark blue wire terminal of the TPS connector **(see illustration)** (see Chapter 12 for additional information on how to backprobe a connector). Connect the positive lead of a voltmeter to the probe and the negative lead to a good engine ground point. Turn the ignition key On - with the throttle fully closed the voltage should read approximately 0.5 volt. Gradually open the throttle - the voltage should increase smoothly to approximately 4.5 volts at wide-open throttle. If the test results are incorrect, replace the TPS.

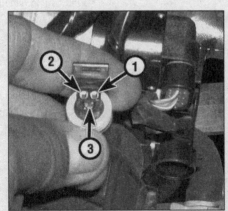

4.3 Disconnect the electrical connector from the TPS and check the voltage supply and ground circuits from the PCM at the harness connector

1   5-volt supply
2   Sensor ground
3   Throttle position sensor signal

4.4 To check the TPS, backprobe the dark blue wire terminal of the TPS connector with a voltmeter

4.7 Remove the TPS mounting screws (arrows)

5.2 MAP sensor location

Replacement

Refer to illustration 4.7

5   Remove the air intake duct from the throttle body (see Chapter 4).

6   Disconnect the electrical connector from the TPS.

7   Remove the TPS mounting screws and remove the TPS from the throttle body **(see illustration)**.

8   Install a new O-ring on the TPS. With the throttle in the closed position, align the TPS with the throttle shaft and install the TPS. Tighten the screws securely.

9   The remainder of installation is the reverse of removal.

5   Manifold Absolute Pressure (MAP) sensor - check and replacement

1   The Manifold Absolute Pressure (MAP) sensor monitors the intake manifold pressure changes resulting from changes in engine load and speed and converts the information into a voltage output. The PCM receives information as a varying voltage signal from closed throttle (high vacuum) to wide open throttle (low vacuum). The PCM uses the MAP sensor to control fuel delivery and ignition timing.

Check

Refer to illustrations 5.2 and 5.3

Note: *Performing the following test will set a diagnostic trouble code and illuminate the SERVICE ENGINE SOON or CHECK ENGINE light. Clear the diagnostic trouble code after performing the tests and making the necessary repairs (see Section 2).*

2   The MAP sensor is located on the upper intake manifold plenum **(see illustration)**. Check the terminals in the connector for corrosion and tightness. Check the wiring harness leading to the sensor for damage. Repair as required.

3   Before checking the MAP sensor, check the voltage supply and ground circuits from the PCM. Disconnect the electrical connector from the MAP sensor and connect the positive lead of a voltmeter to the gray wire terminal and the negative lead to the orange/black or black wire terminal at the harness connector **(see illustration)**. Turn the ignition key On - the voltage should read approximately 5.0 volts. If the voltage is incorrect, check the wiring from the MAP sensor to the PCM. If the circuits are good, have the PCM checked at a dealer service department or other properly equipped repair facility.

4   To check the MAP sensor operation, reconnect the connector to the MAP sensor and using a suitable probe, backprobe the light green wire terminal of the MAP sensor

connector (see Chapter 12 for additional information on how to backprobe a connector). Connect the positive lead of a voltmeter to the probe and the negative lead to a good engine ground point. Turn the ignition key On (engine off) - the voltage should read 4.0 to 5.0 volts. Start the engine and allow it to idle - the voltage should decrease to approximately 0.5 to 2.0 volts. If the test results are incorrect, replace the MAP sensor.

Replacement

Refer to illustration 5.7

5   Remove the intake manifold cover.

6   Disconnect the electrical connector and the vacuum line from the MAP sensor.

7   Detach the retaining screws and remove the MAP sensor **(see illustration)**.

8   Installation is the reverse of removal.

6   Mass Airflow (MAF) sensor - check and replacement

1   The MAF sensor measures the amount of air passing through the sensor body and ultimately entering the engine through the throttle body. The PCM uses this information to control fuel delivery - the more air entering the engine (acceleration), the more fuel required.

5.3 Disconnect the electrical connector from the MAP sensor and check the voltage supply and ground circuits from the PCM at the harness connector

1   Sensor ground
2   MAP sensor signal
3   5-volt supply

5.7 Remove the screws (arrows) and remove the MAP sensor from the upper intake manifold

6

6.2 The Mass Airflow (MAF) sensor is attached to the air filter housing

6.3 Disconnect the electrical connector from the MAF sensor and check the voltage supply and ground circuits at the harness connector

1   *MAF sensor signal*
2   *Ground*
3   *12-volt supply*

6.6 Loosen the hose clamps (arrows) and remove the Mass Airflow sensor

Check

Refer to illustrations 6.2 and 6.3

2   The Mass Airflow sensor (MAF) is located on the air filter housing **(see illustration)**. A scan tool is necessary to check the output of the MAF sensor (see Section 2). The scan tool displays the sensor output in grams per second. With the engine idling at normal operating temperature, the display should read approximately 4.0 to 6.0 grams per second. When the engine is accelerated the values should rise quickly and remain steady at a steady engine speed.

3   Before checking the MAF sensor operation, check the voltage supply and ground circuits. Disconnect the electrical connector from the MAF sensor and connect the positive lead of a voltmeter to the pink wire terminal and the negative lead to the black/white wire terminal at the harness connector **(see illustration)**. Turn the ignition key On - the voltage should read approximately 12.0 volts. If the voltage is incorrect, check the circuits from the MAP sensor to the power distribution center and engine ground point (don't forget to check the fuses first). If the power and ground circuits are good, check the MAF sensor operation with a scan tool. If the MAF sensor does not respond as described in Step 2, replace the MAF sensor.

Replacement

Refer to illustration 6.6

4   Disconnect the electrical connector from the MAF sensor.

5   Loosen the hose clamp securing the air intake duct to the MAF sensor and remove the duct.

6   Loosen the hose clamp retaining the MAF sensor to the air filter cover and remove the sensor **(see illustration)**. **Caution:** *Handle the MAF sensor with care. Damage to this sensor will affect the operation of the entire fuel injection system.*

7   Installation is the reverse of removal.

7   Intake Air Temperature (IAT) sensor - check and replacement

1   The Intake Air Temperature (IAT) sensor is a thermistor (a resistor which varies the value of its resistance in accordance with temperature changes). The change in the resistance values will directly affect the voltage signal from the sensor to the PCM. As the sensor temperature INCREASES, the resistance values will DECREASE and vice versa.

Check

Refer to illustrations 7.2, 7.3 and 7.4

Note: *Performing the following test will set a diagnostic trouble code and illuminate the SERVICE ENGINE SOON or CHECK ENGINE light. Clear the diagnostic trouble code after performing the tests and making the necessary repairs (see Section 2).*

2   The Intake Air temperature sensor is located in the air intake duct between the air filter housing and the throttle body **(see illustration)**. Check the terminals in the connector for corrosion and tightness. Check the wiring harness leading to the sensor for dam-

age. Repair as required.

3   Before checking the Intake Air temperature sensor, check the voltage supply and ground circuits from the PCM. Disconnect the electrical connector from the Intake Air temperature sensor and connect the positive lead a voltmeter to the tan wire terminal and the negative lead to the black wire terminal at the harness connector **(see illustration)**. Turn the ignition key On - the voltage should read approximately 5.0 volts. If the voltage is incorrect, check the wiring from the sensor to the PCM. If the circuits are good, have the PCM checked at a dealer service department or other properly equipped repair facility.

4   With the ignition switch OFF, disconnect the electrical connector from the Intake Air temperature sensor. Using an ohmmeter, measure the resistance between the two Intake Air temperature sensor terminals on the sensor while it is completely cold (50 to 80-degrees F). Reconnect the electrical connector to the sensor, start the engine and warm it up until it reaches operating temperature (180 to 200-degrees F), disconnect the connector and check the resistance again.

7.2 Intake air temperature sensor location

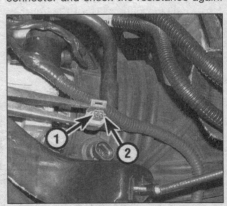

7.3 Disconnect the electrical connector from the Intake Air temperature sensor and check the voltage supply and ground circuits from the PCM at the harness connector

1   *Intake air temperature sensor signal*
2   *Sensor ground*

Temperature (degrees-F)	Resistance (ohms)
212	176
194	240
176	332
158	458
140	668
122	972
112	1182
104	1458
95	1800
86	2238
76	2795
68	3520
58	4450
50	5670
40	7280
32	9420

7.4 Intake air temperature sensor and Engine Coolant temperature sensor approximate temperature vs. resistance values

8.2 Engine Coolant Temperature sensor location

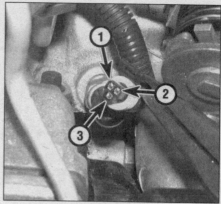

8.3 Disconnect the electrical connector from the Engine Coolant temperature sensor and check the voltage supply and ground circuits from the PCM at the harness connector

1   ECT sensor signal
2   Sensor ground
3   Temperature gauge (not all models)

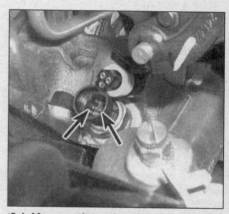

8.4 Measure the resistance of the Engine coolant temperature sensor

Compare your measurements to the resistance chart **(see illustration)**. If the sensor resistance test results are incorrect, replace the Intake Air temperature sensor. **Note:** *A more accurate check may be performed by removing the sensor and warming it with a hair dryer or heat gun while you monitor the resistance of the sensor.*

Replacement

5   Disconnect the electrical connector from the sensor.
6   Carefully remove the sensor from the air intake duct.
7   Installation is the reverse of removal.

8   Engine Coolant Temperature (ECT) sensor - check and replacement

1   The Engine Coolant Temperature (ECT) sensor is a thermistor (a resistor which varies the value of its resistance in accordance with temperature changes). The change in the resistance values will directly affect the voltage signal from the sensor to the PCM. As the sensor temperature INCREASES, the resistance values will DECREASE and vice versa.

Check

Refer to illustrations 8.2, 8.3 and 8.4
Note: *Performing the following test will set a diagnostic trouble code and illuminate the SERVICE ENGINE SOON or CHECK ENGINE light. Clear the diagnostic trouble code after performing the tests and making the necessary repairs (see Section 2).*
2   The Engine Coolant temperature sensor threads into a coolant passage in the intake manifold **(see illustration)**. Check the terminals in the connector for corrosion and tightness. Check the wiring harness leading to the sensor for damage. Repair as required.
3   Before checking the Engine Coolant temperature sensor, check the voltage sup-

ply and ground circuits from the PCM. Disconnect the electrical connector from the Engine Coolant temperature sensor and connect the positive lead a voltmeter to the yellow wire terminal and the negative lead to the orange black or black wire terminal of the harness connector **(see illustration)**. Turn the ignition key On - the voltage should read approximately 5.0 volts. If the voltage is incorrect, check the wiring from the Engine Coolant temperature sensor to the PCM. If the circuits are good, have the PCM checked at a dealer service department or other properly equipped repair facility.
4   With the ignition switch OFF, disconnect the electrical connector from the Engine Coolant temperature sensor. Using an ohmmeter, measure the resistance between the signal and ground terminals on the sensor while it is completely cold (50 to 80-degrees F) **(see illustration)**. Reconnect the electrical connector to the sensor, start the engine and warm it up until it reaches operating temperature (180 to 200-degrees F), disconnect the connector and check the resistance again. Compare your measurements to the resistance chart **(see illustration 7.4)**. If the sensor resistance test results are incorrect, replace the Engine Coolant temperature sensor. **Note:** *A more accurate check may be performed by removing the sensor and suspending the tip of the sensor in a container of water. Heat the water on the stove while you monitor the resistance of the sensor.*

Replacement

Warning: *Wait until the engine is completely cool before beginning this procedure.*
5   Drain the cooling system (see Chapter 1).
6   Remove the air intake duct.
7   Disconnect the electrical connector from the sensor and carefully unscrew the sensor.
8   Before installing the new sensor, wrap the threads with Teflon sealing tape to prevent leakage and thread corrosion.
9   Installation is the reverse of removal.

9   Crankshaft Position (CKP) sensor - check and replacement

1   The Crankshaft Position sensor provides the ignition module and PCM with a crankshaft position signal. The ignition module uses the signal to determine the spark sequence (firing order) for each cylinder. The PCM uses the signal to precisely control ignition timing and calculate engine speed (RPM). The signal is also used by the Onboard Diagnostic system for misfire detection. 3.4L V6 engines are equipped with two Crankshaft Position sensors; a 7X Crankshaft Position sensor and a 24X Crankshaft Position sensor. The 7X Crankshaft Position sensor is a magnetic inductive sensor triggered by seven slots cut into a reluctor ring on the crankshaft. The sensor tip is positioned approximately 0.050 inch from the reluctor ring. As the notches pass the sensor the magnetic field is altered, producing a pulsating voltage signal seven times per crankshaft revolution. The 24X Crankshaft Position sen-

6

9.2 7X Crankshaft Position sensor location

9.4 24X Crankshaft Position sensor location

9.5a 24X Crankshaft Position sensor electrical connector location

sor is a Hall effect device triggered by an interrupter ring behind the crankshaft pulley. The 24X Crankshaft Position sensor produces on-off pulses as the 24 blades and windows of the interrupter pass through the sensor's magnetic field. The ignition system will not operate if the PCM does not receive a 7X Crankshaft Position sensor input.

Check

Note: *Performing the following test will set a diagnostic trouble code and illuminate the SERVICE ENGINE SOON or CHECK ENGINE light. Clear the diagnostic trouble code after performing the tests and making the necessary repairs (see Section 2).*

7X Crankshaft Position sensor

Refer to illustration 9.2

2   The 7X Crankshaft Position sensor is located on the rear (firewall) side of the engine block **(see illustration)**. Check the terminals in the connector for corrosion and tightness. Check the wiring harness leading to the sensor for damage. Repair as required.
3   Disconnect the electrical connector from the 7X Crankshaft Position sensor. Connect a voltmeter to the two terminals of the sensor and set the meter to read AC volts. **Note:** *The test connection can be made at the ignition control module electrical connector purple and yellow wire terminals, if desired.* Crank the engine and note the voltage. The 7X Crankshaft Position sensor should produce a minimum of 200 millivolts with the engine cranking. If a Crankshaft Position sensor signal is not present, replace the 7X Crankshaft Position sensor.

24X Crankshaft Position sensor

Refer to illustrations 9.4, 9.5a and 9.5b

4   The 24X Crankshaft Position sensor is located on the front of the engine behind the crankshaft pulley **(see Illustration)**. Check the terminals in the connector for corrosion and tightness. Check the wiring harness leading to the sensor for damage. Repair as required.
5   Before checking the Crankshaft Position sensor, check the voltage supply and ground

circuits from the PCM. Disconnect the electrical connector and connect the positive lead of a voltmeter to the red/white (1997) or yellow/black (1998 and later) wire terminal and the negative lead to the black (1997) or light green (1998 and later) wire terminal at the harness connector **(see illustrations)**. Turn the ignition key On - the voltage should read approximately 12.0 volts. If the voltage is incorrect, check the wiring from the Crankshaft Position sensor to the PCM. If the circuits are good, have the PCM checked at a dealer service department or other properly equipped repair facility.
6   To check the 24X Crankshaft Position sensor operation, reconnect the connector to the Crankshaft Position sensor and using a suitable probe, backprobe the light blue/black wire terminal of the Crankshaft Position sensor connector (see Chapter 12 for additional information on how to backprobe a connector). Connect the positive lead of a voltmeter to the probe and the negative lead to a good engine ground point. Turn the ignition key On. The meter should indicate approximately 10.0 volts. Rotate the engine slowly with a breaker bar and socket attached to the crankshaft pulley center bolt while watching the meter. The voltage should fluctuate between 10.0 volts and zero as the blades and windows in the interrupter pass the sensor. If the test results are incorrect, replace the 24X Crankshaft Position sensor. **Note:** *Rotate the engine slowly. Removing the spark plugs from the engine will make the crankshaft much easier to turn.*

Replacement

Note: *Anytime a Crankshaft Position sensor is disturbed, A Crankshaft Position Sensor Variation Learning Procedure should be performed or a false misfire diagnostic trouble code may be set. If after replacing the sensor, a false diagnostic trouble codes is set, take the vehicle to a dealership service department for the procedure.*

7X Crankshaft Position sensor

Refer to illustration 9.9

7   Loosen the right front wheel lug nuts,

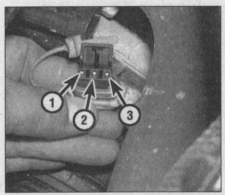

9.5b Disconnect the 24X Crankshaft Position sensor electrical connector (arrow) and check the voltage supply and ground circuits at the harness side of the connector

1   12-volt supply
2   Sensor signal
3   Sensor ground

raise the vehicle and support it securely on jackstands.
8   Remove the right front wheel and the inner fender lining.
9   Remove the engine block-to-transaxle bracket **(see illustration)**.
10   Disconnect the 7X Crankshaft Position sensor wiring harness connector.
11   Remove the 7X Crankshaft Position sensor heat shield.
12   Remove the 7X Crankshaft Position sensor mounting bolt and withdraw the sensor from the engine block.
13   Replace the O-ring and lightly lubricate it with clean engine oil.
14   Installation is the reverse of removal.

24X Crankshaft Position sensor

15   Remove the drivebelt (see Chapter 1).
16   Loosen the right front wheel lug nuts, raise the vehicle and support it securely on jackstands.
17   Remove the right front wheel and the inner fender lining.
18   Remove the crankshaft pulley (see Chapter 2A).

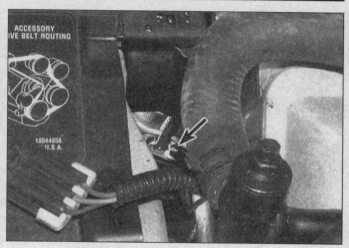

9.9 To access the 7X Crankshaft Position sensor, remove the bolts (arrows) and the transaxle bracket

10.2 Camshaft position sensor location

19   Remove the bolt and the sensor wiring harness retaining bracket.
20   Remove the 24X Crankshaft Position sensor mounting bolts. Remove the sensor and withdraw the wiring harness, noting the harness routing for installation.
21   Installation is the reverse of removal.

10 Camshaft Position (CMP) sensor - check and replacement

1   The Camshaft Position sensor is very similar in operation to the Crankshaft Position sensor, but it produces a signal pulse only once every two crankshaft revolutions, corresponding to cylinder number one Top Dead Center. The Camshaft Position sensor, in conjunction with the Crankshaft Position sensor, determines the timing for the fuel injection on each cylinder.

Check

Refer to illustrations 10.2, 10.3a and 10.3b
Note: *Performing the following test will set a diagnostic trouble code and illuminate the SERVICE ENGINE SOON or CHECK ENGINE light. Clear the diagnostic trouble code after performing the tests and making the necessary repairs (see Section 2).*
2   The Camshaft Position sensor is located at the front of the engine block, below the power steering pump **(see Illustration)**. Check the terminals in the connector for corrosion and tightness. Check the wiring harness leading to the sensor for damage. Repair as required.
3   Before checking the Camshaft Position sensor, check the voltage supply and ground circuits from the PCM. Disconnect the electrical connector from the Camshaft Position sensor and connect the positive lead of a voltmeter to the red/white wire terminal and the negative lead to the black wire terminal at the harness connector **(see illustrations)**. Turn the ignition key On - the voltage should read approximately 12.0 volts. If the voltage

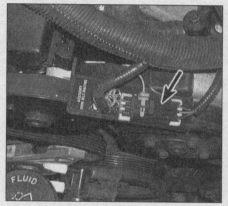

10.3a Camshaft position sensor electrical connector location

is incorrect, check the wiring from the Camshaft Position sensor to the PCM. If the circuits are good, have the PCM checked at a dealer service department or other properly equipped repair facility.
4   To check the Camshaft Position sensor operation, reconnect the connector to the Camshaft Position sensor and using a suitable probe, backprobe the center wire terminal of the Camshaft Position sensor connector (see Chapter 12 for additional information on how to backprobe a connector). Connect the positive lead of a voltmeter to the probe and the negative lead to a good engine ground point. Turn the ignition key On. The meter should indicate approximately 10.0 volts. Rotate the engine slowly with a breaker bar and socket attached to the crankshaft pulley center bolt while watching the meter. The voltage should remain a steady 10.0 volts then quickly drop to zero and back to 10.0 volts as the magnet passes the sensor. If the test results are incorrect, replace the Camshaft Position sensor. **Note:** *Rotate the engine slowly through at least two complete revolutions. Removing the spark plugs from the engine will make the crankshaft much easier to turn.*

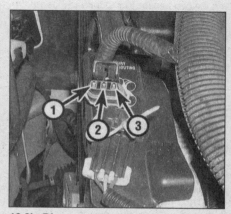

10.3b Disconnect the electrical connector from the Camshaft Position sensor and check the voltage supply and ground circuits at the harness connector

1   Sensor ground
2   Sensor signal
3   12-volt supply

Replacement

5   Remove the drivebelt (see Chapter 1).
6   Without disconnecting the hoses, remove the power steering pump and position it aside (see Chapter 10).
7   Disconnect the electrical connector from the sensor harness, noting the harness routing for installation.
8   Remove the Camshaft Position sensor mounting bolt and withdraw the sensor from the engine block.
9   Installation is the reverse of removal.

11 Oxygen sensor - check and replacement

Note: *All models are equipped with two oxygen sensors; one pre-converter oxygen sensor and one post-converter oxygen sensor.*
1   An oxygen sensor, if effect, measures the oxygen remaining in the exhaust gas after

6

11.6a The pre-converter oxygen sensor is located in the exhaust manifold

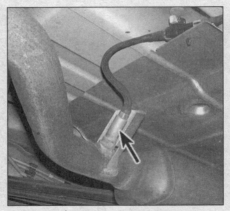

11.6b The post-converter oxygen sensor is located in the exhaust pipe after the catalytic converter

11.6c Backprobe the oxygen sensor signal wire at the electrical connector for testing

the combustion process. The leftover oxygen in the exhaust reacts with the elements inside the oxygen sensor to produce a voltage output that varies from 0.1 volt (high oxygen, lean mixture) to 0.9 volt (low oxygen, rich mixture). The pre-converter oxygen sensor is mounted in the exhaust system before the catalytic converter. The PCM monitors the varying voltage signal from the pre-converter oxygen sensor continuously to determine the required fuel injector pulse width, controlling the engine air/fuel ratio. A mixture ratio of 14.7 parts air to 1 part fuel is the ideal ratio for gasoline fuel to minimize exhaust emissions, as well as the best combination of fuel economy and engine performance. Based on oxygen sensor signals, the PCM tries to maintain this air/fuel ratio of 14.7:1 at all times.

2   The post-converter oxygen sensor (mounted in the exhaust system after the catalytic converter) has no effect on PCM control of the air/fuel ratio. However, the post-converter sensor is identical to the pre-converter sensor and operates in the same way. The PCM uses the post-converter signal to monitor the efficiency of the catalytic converter. A post-converter oxygen sensor will produce a slower fluctuating voltage signal that reflects the lower oxygen content in the post-catalyst exhaust.

3   An oxygen sensor produces no voltage when it is below its normal operating temperature of about 600-degrees F. During this warm-up period, the PCM operates in an open-loop fuel control mode. It does not use the oxygen sensor signal as a feedback indication of residual oxygen in the exhaust. Instead, the PCM controls fuel metering based on the inputs of other sensors and its own programs. All oxygen sensors are equipped with a heating element, powered by fused ignition voltage, to heat the oxygen sensor to operating range as quickly as possible.

4   Proper operation of an oxygen sensor depends on four conditions:

a) *Electrical - The low voltages generated by the sensor require good, clean connections which should be checked whenever a sensor problem is suspected or indicated.*

b) *Outside air supply - The sensor needs air circulation to the internal portion of the sensor. Whenever the sensor is installed, make sure the air passages are not restricted.*

c) *Proper operating temperature - The PCM will not react to the sensor signal until the sensor reaches approximately 600-degrees F. This factor must be considered when evaluating the performance of the sensor.*

d) *Unleaded fuel - Unleaded fuel is essential for proper operation of the sensor.*

5   The PCM can detect several different oxygen sensor problems and set diagnostic trouble codes to indicate the specific fault (see Section 2). When an oxygen sensor fault occurs, the PCM will disregard the oxygen sensor signal voltage and revert to open-loop fuel control as described previously.

Check

Refer to illustrations 11.6a, 11.6b, 11.6c, 11.8a and 11.8b

Caution: *The oxygen sensor is very sensitive to excessive circuit loads and circuit damage of any kind. For safest testing, disconnect the oxygen sensor connector, install jumper wires between the two connectors and connect your voltmeter to the jumper wires. If jumper wires aren't available, carefully backprobe the wires in the connector shell with suitable probes (such as T-pins). Do not puncture the oxygen sensor wires or try to backprobe the sensor itself. Use only a digital voltmeter to test an oxygen sensor.*

Note: *Performing the following test will set a diagnostic trouble code and illuminate the SERVICE ENGINE SOON or CHECK ENGINE light. Clear the diagnostic trouble code after performing the tests and making the necessary repairs (see Section 2).*

6   Connect your voltmeter positive (+) lead to the purple or purple/white wire and connect the negative (-) lead to the tan or tan/white wire at the oxygen sensor connector **(see illustrations)**. Turn the ignition ON but do not start the engine. The meter should read approximately 400 to 450 millivolts (0.40

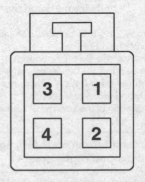

11.8a Pre-converter oxygen sensor connector terminal identification (harness-side)

1   Sensor ground
2   Sensor signal
3   Heater ground
4   Heater 12-volt supply

to 0.45 volt). If it doesn't, trace and repair the circuit from the sensor to the PCM. **Note:** *Refer to the wiring diagrams at the end of Chapter for additional information on the oxygen sensor circuits.*

7   Start the engine and let it warm up to normal operating temperature; again check the oxygen sensor signal voltage.

a) *Voltage from an pre-converter sensor should range from 100 to 900 millivolts (0.1 to 0.9 volt) and switch actively between high and low readings.*

b) *Voltage from a post-converter sensor should also read between 100 to 900 millivolts (0.1 to 0.9 volt) but it should not switch actively. The post-converter oxygen sensor voltage may stay toward the center of its range (about 400 millivolts) or stay for relatively longer periods of time at the upper or lower limits of the range.*

8   Check the battery voltage supply and ground circuits to the oxygen sensor heater. Disconnect the electrical connector and connect the voltmeter negative (-) lead to the black wire terminal and the positive (+) lead

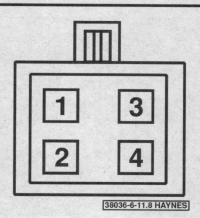

11.8b Post-converter oxygen sensor connector terminal identification (harness-side)

1   *Sensor ground*
2   *Sensor signal*
3   *Heater ground*
4   *Heater 12-volt supply*

11.13 A special slotted socket, allowing clearance for the wiring harness, may be required for oxygen sensor removal (the tool is available at most auto parts stores)

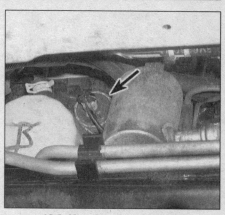

12.2 Knock sensor location

to the pink wire terminal of the sensor connector **(see illustrations)**. Turn the ignition ON, the meter should read approximately 12 volts. If battery voltage is not present, check the power and ground circuits to the sensor (don't forget to check the fuses first).

9   Allow the oxygen sensor to cool and check the resistance of the oxygen sensor heater. With the connector disconnected. Connect an ohmmeter to the two oxygen sensor heater terminals of the connector (oxygen sensor side). The oxygen sensor pigtail is generally not color coded, but the heater wires are usually the white wires. The oxygen sensor heater resistance should be 3.0 to 10.0 ohms. If an open circuit or excessive resistance is indicated, replace the oxygen sensor. **Note:** *If the tests indicate that a sensor is good, and not the cause of a driveability problem or diagnostic trouble code, check the wiring harness and connectors between the sensor and the PCM for an open or short circuit. If no problems are found, have the vehicle checked by a dealer service department or other qualified repair shop.*

Replacement

Refer to illustration 11.13

10   Observe these guidelines when replacing an oxygen sensor.
   a)   *The sensor has a permanently attached pigtail and electrical connector which should not be removed from the sensor. Damage or removal of the pigtail or electrical connector can harm operation of the sensor.*
   b)   *Keep grease, dirt and other contaminants away from the electrical connector and the louvered end of the sensor.*
   c)   *Do not use cleaning solvents of any kind on the oxygen sensor.*
   d)   *Do not drop or roughly handle the sensor.*

11   Raise the vehicle and place it securely on jackstands.

12   Disconnect the electrical connector from the sensor.
13   Using a suitable wrench or specialized oxygen sensor socket, unscrew the sensor from the exhaust manifold or pipe **(see illustration)**.
14   Anti-seize compound must be used on the threads of the sensor to aid future removal. The threads of most new sensors will be coated with this compound. If not, be sure to apply anti-seize compound before installing the sensor.
15   Install the sensor and tighten it securely.
16   Reconnect the electrical connector to the sensor and lower the vehicle.

12   Knock sensor and module - check and replacement

1   The knock sensor detects abnormal vibration (spark knock or pinging) in the engine. The knock control system is designed to reduce spark knock during periods of heavy detonation. This allows the engine to use maximum spark advance to improve driveability. Knock sensors produce AC output voltage which increases with the severity of the knock. The signal is fed into the PCM and the timing is retarded to compensate for the severe detonation. All models are equipped with a replaceable knock sensor module in the PCM.

Check

Refer to illustration 12.2

2   The knock sensor is located on the side of the engine block above the oil filter **(see illustration)**.
3   Disconnect the electrical connector from the knock sensor. The knock sensor contains an internal 100 K-ohm resistor. Using an ohmmeter, measure the resistance between the terminal on the knock sensor and the engine block. The resistance should be approximately 90 to 110 K-ohms - if the

resistance is not as specified, replace the knock sensor.
4   To check the sensor operation, reconnect the connector to the sensor. Backprobe the wire terminal at the electrical connector using a suitable probe (see Chapter 12 for additional information on how to backprobe a connector). Connect the positive lead of a voltmeter to the probe and the negative lead to a good engine ground point. Set the voltmeter on the AC volts scale. Start the engine and check for an AC voltage signal from the knock sensor. The AC voltage should increase as the engine speed increases. If a voltage signal is not present, replace the knock sensor.

Replacement

5   Disconnect the cable from the negative battery terminal. **Caution:** *On models equipped with the Theftlock audio system, be sure you have the correct activation code before disconnecting the battery (see the front of this manual).*

Knock sensor

Warning: *The engine must be completely cool before beginning this procedure.*
6   Drain the cooling system (see Chapter 1).
7   Raise the vehicle and support it securely on jackstands.
8   Remove the knock sensor heat shield.
9   Disconnect the electrical connector and remove the knock sensor from the engine block.
10   Installation is the reverse of removal.

Knock sensor module

Refer to illustrations 12.12 and 12.13
Note: *The knock sensor module may be replaced in the original PCM. If a new PCM is being installed, it must be programmed at a dealer service department (see Section 3).*
11   Remove the PCM (see Section 3).
12   Remove the knock sensor module cover **(see illustration)**.

12.12 Remove the screws and the cover to access the knock sensor module

12.13 Pinch the tabs together and pull the knock sensor module straight up

13.2 Vehicle speed sensor location

13   Carefully pinch the retaining tabs and pull the knock sensor straight up **(see illustration)**.

14   To install the knock sensor module, align the tabs on the module with the notches on the socket. Press down on the ends of the knock sensor module until the module is seated in the socket and the retaining tabs click into place.

15   Install the knock sensor module cover.

16   Install the PCM.

13   Vehicle Speed Sensor (VSS) - check and replacement

1   The Vehicle Speed Sensor (VSS) is a permanent magnet generator mounted on the transaxle. The sensor is triggered by a toothed rotor on the transaxle output shaft. As the output shaft rotates, the sensor produces an AC voltage, the frequency of which is proportional to vehicle speed. The PCM uses the sensor input signal for several different engine and transmission control functions. The VSS signal also drives the speedometer on the instrument panel. A defective VSS can cause various driveability and transaxle problems.

Check

Refer to illustration 13.2

2   Raise the vehicle and support it securely on jackstands. Locate the vehicle speed sensor **(see illustration)**. Check the terminals in the connector for corrosion and tightness. Check the wiring harness leading to the sensor for damage. Repair as required.

3   To check the VSS operation, backprobe the two wire terminals of the VSS connector using suitable probes (see Chapter 12 for additional information on how to backprobe a connector). Connect a voltmeter to the probes and set the meter on the AC volts scale. Turn the ignition key On. Rotate the right front tire by hand while watching the voltmeter. The sensor should produce a minimum of 0.5 volts and the voltage should increase as the transaxle output shaft rotates faster.

4   Turn the ignition key Off and disconnect

14.2 IAC valve location

the electrical connector from the sensor. Using an ohmmeter, measure the resistance across the two terminals of the sensor. The sensor resistance should be approximately 900 to 2200 ohms at 68-degrees F. If the test results are incorrect, replace the vehicle speed sensor.

Replacement

5   Raise the vehicle and support it securely on jackstands.

6   Disconnect the electrical connector from the VSS.

7   Remove mounting bolt and withdraw the VSS from the transaxle case.

8   Replace the sensor O-ring.

9   Installation is the reverse of removal.

14   Idle Air Control (IAC) valve - check and replacement

1   The idle speed is controlled by the Idle Air Control (IAC) valve. The IAC valve regulates the air bypassing the throttle plate by moving the pintle in or out of the air passage. The IAC valve is controlled by the PCM, adjusting the idle speed depending upon the running conditions of the engine (air conditioning system, power steering, cold and warm running etc.). The engine idle speed is not adjustable on these models.

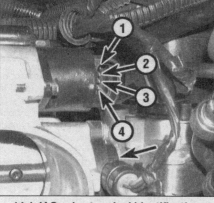

14.4 IAC valve terminal identification

1 and 2   IAC coil no. 1
3 and 4   IAC coil no. 2

Check

Refer to illustrations 14.2 and 14.4

Note: *Performing the following test will set a diagnostic trouble code and illuminate the SERVICE ENGINE SOON or CHECK ENGINE light. Clear the diagnostic trouble code after performing the tests and making the necessary repairs (see Section 2).*

2   The Idle Air Control (IAC) valve is located on the throttle body **(see illustration)**. A scan tool is required for complete testing of the IAC valve and circuits. However, several tests can be performed on the IAC system to verify operation but they are limited and are useful only in the case of definite IAC valve failure.

3   When the engine is started cold, the IAC valve should vary the idle as the engine begins to warm-up. Allow the engine to warm-up, then place a load on the engine by placing the transmission in gear, turning the air conditioning on and operating the power steering. The idle should remain steady or increase slightly. If the engine stumbles or stalls, or if there are obvious signs that the IAC valve is not working, stop the engine and continue testing.

4   Disconnect the electrical connector from the IAC valve. Using an ohmmeter, measure the resistance across terminals 1 and 2 of the IAC valve, then measure the resistance

14.7 Remove the screws (arrows) and withdraw the IAC valve from the throttle body

15.2 PCV valve location

14.9 Before installing a new IAC valve, measure the distance from the tip of the pintle to the mounting flange - press the pintle in until the distance is less than 1-1/8 inch

Replacement

Refer to illustrations 14.7 and 14.9

6   Remove the air intake duct.

7   Disconnect the electrical connector from the IAC valve. Remove the two mounting screws from the valve and withdraw it from the throttle body **(see illustration)**.

8   Inspect the IAC valve pintle and the air passage and valve seat in the throttle body for heavy carbon deposits. Clean the IAC valve with aerosol carburetor cleaner, a shop towel and a soft brush, if necessary. Do not submerge the IAC valve in any liquid cleaner. If the air passage requires further cleaning, remove the throttle body and clean it thoroughly.

9   If installing a new IAC valve, measure the distance from the tip of the IAC valve pintle to the mounting flange **(see illustration)**. If the distance is greater than 1-1/8 inch, press the pintle in by hand, as necessary. **Caution:** *Do not attempt to press the pintle in on a*

across terminals 3 and 4 **(see illustration)** - the resistance should be about the same on both sets (approximately 40 to 80 ohms). If one or both checks indicate an open circuit, replace the IAC valve.

5   If the IAC valve is good, have the PCM diagnosed by a dealer service department or other qualified repair shop.

used IAC valve. The force required to move a pintle shaft with carbon build-up may damage the valve.

10   Install a new O-ring and lubricate it with clean engine oil.

11   Install the IAC valve and tighten the screws securely. Connect the electrical connector.

12   Cycle the ignition key On for ten seconds, then Off for ten seconds to reset the valve. Start the engine, allow it to idle for five minutes, turn the engine off for thirty seconds, then start the engine again and check the idle operation.

15   Crankcase ventilation system

Refer to illustrations 15.2 and 15.3

1   When the engine is running, a certain amount of the gasses produced during combustion escape past the piston rings into the crankcase as blow-by gasses. The crankcase ventilation system is designed to reduce the resulting hydrocarbon emissions (HC) by routing the gasses and vapors from the crankcase into the intake manifold and combustion chambers, where they are consumed during engine operation.

2   All models use a Positive Crankcase Ventilation (PCV) system. The main component of the Positive Crankcase Ventilation (PCV) system is the PCV valve **(see illustration)**. Fresh air flows from the air intake duct through a vent tube into the engine. Crankcase vapors are drawn from the crankcase by the PCV valve.

3   To maintain idle quality and good driveability, the PCV valve restricts the flow when the intake manifold vacuum is high. When intake manifold vacuum is lower, maximum vapor flow is allowed through the valve **(see illustration)**.

4   Checking and replacement of the PCV valve is covered in Chapter 1.

6

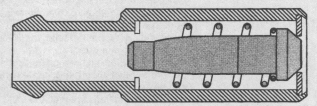

Engine Off or Engine Backfire—No Vapor Flow

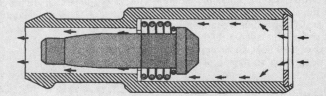

High Intake Manifold Vacuum—Minimal Vapor Flow

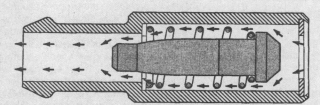

Moderate Intake Manifold Vacuum—Maximum Vapor Flow

15.3 Typical PCV valve operation

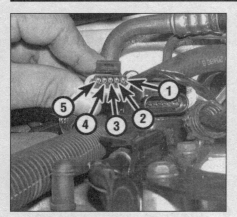

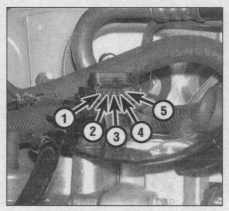

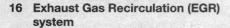

16.4 EGR valve harness connector terminal identification

1   EGR valve control (1997); EGR valve feed (1998 and later)
2   Pintle position sensor ground (1997); 5-volt supply (1998 and later)
3   Pintle position sensor signal
4   Pintle position sensor 5-volt supply (1997); sensor ground (1998 and later)
5   EGR valve feed (1997); EGR valve control (1998 and later)

16   Exhaust Gas Recirculation (EGR) system

1   The Exhaust Gas Recirculation (EGR) system is used to lower NOx (oxides of nitrogen) emission levels caused by high combustion temperatures. The EGR valve recirculates a small amount of exhaust gases into the intake manifold. The additional mixture lowers the temperature of combustion thereby reducing the formation of NOx compounds.
2   The EGR system consists of an electronic EGR valve and the PCM. The PCM controls the EGR flow rate by energizing the EGR valve solenoid coil, opening or closing the EGR passage in small increments. The PCM monitors the EGR valve pintle position with an EGR position sensor built into the EGR valve. This system allows for precise control of EGR flow, achieving optimum EGR flow depending on engine operating conditions.

Check

Refer to illustrations 16.4 and 16.5
3   A scan tool is required for complete testing of the EGR valve, control system and circuits. However, there are several tests the home mechanic can perform on the system to verify operation but they are limited and are useful only in the case of definite system failure.
4   Check the voltage supply and ground circuits to the EGR valve position sensor. Disconnect the electrical connector from the EGR valve. Connect the positive lead of a voltmeter to terminal no. 4 (1997) or no. 2 (1998 and later) of the EGR valve electrical

16.5 EGR valve terminal identification

connector (harness side) **(see illustration)**. Connect the negative lead to terminal no. 2 (1997) or no. 4 (1998 and later). Turn the ignition key On - approximately 5.0 volts should be indicated on the meter. If the 5.0 volt supply voltage is not present, check the circuits from the PCM to the EGR valve. If the circuits are good, have the PCM diagnosed by a dealer service department or other qualified repair shop.
5   To check the EGR valve, use an ohmmeter to check the continuity of the EGR valve position sensor and the EGR solenoid coil. Check for continuity across terminals 2 and 4 (EGR sensor) and across terminals 1 and 5 (EGR solenoid coil) **(see illustration)**. If either check reveals an open circuit, replace the EGR valve.

Replacement

EGR valve

Refer to illustration 16.8
6   Disconnect the electrical connector from the EGR valve.
7   Remove the EGR valve mounting bolts **(see illustration)**. Remove the EGR valve and gaskets. Discard the gaskets.
8   Using a gasket scraper, clean the EGR valve gasket surfaces.
9   Installation is the reverse of removal.

EGR pipe

10   Remove the EGR valve.
11   Loosen the EGR pipe fitting at the exhaust manifold and remove the pipe.
12   Installation is the reverse of removal.

17   Evaporative emissions control system

1   The fuel evaporative emissions control (EVAP) system absorbs fuel vapors from the fuel tank and, during engine operation, releases them into the engine intake system where they mix with the incoming air/fuel mixture. The main components of the evaporative emissions system are the canister (filled with activated charcoal to absorb fuel

16.8 Remove the EGR valve mounting bolts (arrows)

vapors), the purge valve, the vent valve, the fuel tank pressure sensor, the fuel tank and the vapor and purge lines.
2   After passing through a check valve, fuel tank vapor is carried through the vapor hose to the charcoal canister. The activated charcoal in the canister absorbs and stores the vapors. When a programmed set of conditions are met (engine running, warmed to a pre-set temperature, etc.), the PCM opens the purge valve and the vent valve. Fuel vapors from the canister are then drawn through the purge hose by intake manifold vacuum into the intake manifold and combustion chamber where they are consumed during normal engine operation.
3   The PCM regulates the rate of vapor flow from the canister to the intake manifold by controlling the duty cycle of the EVAP purge valve control solenoid. During cold running conditions and hot start time delay, the PCM does not energize the solenoid. After the engine has warmed up to the correct operating temperature, the PCM purges the vapors into the intake manifold according to the running conditions of the engine. The PCM will cycle (ON then OFF) the purge valve control solenoid about 5 to 10 times per second. The flow rate will be controlled by the pulse width, or length of time, the solenoid is allowed to be energized.
4   On 1998 and later models, the system performs a self-diagnostic check when the engine is started cold. When the programmed conditions are met, the PCM opens the EVAP canister purge valve, leaving the vent valve closed. This action allows engine vacuum to draw a vacuum on the entire EVAP system. Once the proper vacuum level is reached, the PCM closes the purge valve, sealing the system. The PCM then monitors the fuel tank pressure sensor voltage and sets a diagnostic code if a leak is detected. **Note:** *1997 models are not equipped with a vent valve or a fuel tank pressure sensor. The PCM uses a vacuum switch mounted near the purge valve to monitor the operation of the system.*
5   The fuel tank pressure sensor operation is similar to the MAP sensor. The PCM sup-

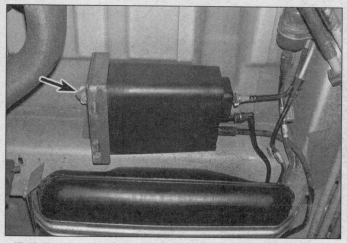

17.12 Remove the EVAP canister bracket mounting bolt (arrow)

17.14 EVAP purge valve/control solenoid location

plies a 5-volt reference voltage and ground circuit to the sensor. The sensor returns a signal voltage to the PCM which varies according to the air pressure inside the fuel tank. When the air pressure inside the tank is equal to the outside air pressure (as with the fuel filler cap removed), the sensor output voltage is approximately 1.5 volts. With 14 in-Hg vacuum inside the tank the sensor output voltage is 4.5 volts.

Check

Note: *The evaporative control system, like all emission control systems, is protected by a Federally-mandated warranty (5 years or 50,000 miles at the time this manual was written). The EVAP system probably won't fail during the service life of the vehicle; however, if it does, the hoses or charcoal canister are usually to blame.*

6   Always check the hoses first. A disconnected, damaged or missing hose is the most likely cause of a malfunctioning EVAP system. Refer to the Vacuum Hose Routing Diagram (attached to the radiator support) to determine whether the hoses are correctly routed and attached. Repair any damaged

17.26 Pry the retaining clips out (arrows) and withdraw the fuel tank pressure sensor from the fuel pump module

hoses or replace any missing hoses as necessary.

7   Check the related fuses and wiring to the purge and vent valves. Refer to the wiring diagrams at the end of Chapter 12, if necessary. The purge and vent valves are normally closed - no vapors will pass through the ports. When the PCM energizes the solenoid (by completing the circuit to ground), the valve opens and vapors flow through.

8   A scan tool is required to thoroughly check the system. If the above checks fail to identify the problem area, have the system diagnosed by a dealer service department or other qualified repair shop.

Component replacement

Refer to illustrations 17.12, 17.14 and 17.26

EVAP canister

9   The EVAP canister is attached to a bracket near the fuel tank.

10   Raise the vehicle and support it securely on jackstands.

11   Label and disconnect the hoses from the canister. **Note:** *The EVAP canister hoses are equipped with quick-connect fittings. Before disconnecting a fitting, clean around the fitting and twist the fitting back-and-forth to loosen the seal. To disconnect a fitting, squeeze the retainer tabs together and pull the fitting off the pipe.*

12   Remove the mounting bolt and remove the canister **(see illustration)**.

13   Installation is the reverse of removal.

Purge valve

14   The purge valve is mounted to a bracket on the cylinder head directly below the ignition coils **(see illustration)**. Rotate the engine forward for access (see Chapter 2B).

15   Disconnect the electrical connector. Label and disconnect the hoses from the purge valve.

16   Depress the bracket locking tab and remove the purge valve.

17   Installation is the reverse of removal.

Vent valve (1998 and later models)

18   The vent valve is mounted on a bracket near the EVAP canister.

19   Raise the vehicle and support it securely on jackstands.

20   Disconnect the electrical connector and remove the hose from the vent valve.

21   Release the retainers and remove the vent valve from the bracket.

22   Installation is the reverse of removal.

Fuel tank pressure sensor (1998 and later models)

23   The fuel tank pressure sensor is located on the fuel pump module.

24   Remove the fuel tank (see Chapter 4).

25   Disconnect the electrical connector from the fuel tank pressure sensor.

26   Release the retaining clip and remove the sensor from the top of the fuel pump module **(see illustration)**.

27   Installation is the reverse of removal.

18 Secondary air injection system

1   2000 and later models are equipped with a secondary air injection (AIR) system. The secondary air injection system is used to reduce tailpipe emissions on initial engine start-up. The system uses an electric motor/pump assembly, relay, check valves and tubing to inject fresh air directly into the exhaust manifolds. The fresh air (oxygen) reacts with the exhaust gas in the catalytic converter to reduce HC and CO levels during open loop operation. The air pump is controlled by the PCM through the AIR relay. During initial start-up, the PCM energizes the AIR relay, the relay supplies battery voltage to the air pump and air flows through the tubing into the exhaust manifolds. The PCM will operate the air pump until closed loop operation is reached. During normal operation, the check valves prevent exhaust backflow into the system.

6

Check

2   Check the air pump hoses. Repair any damaged hoses or replace any missing hoses as necessary.
3   Check the related fuses, the relay and the wiring to the air pump. Refer to Chapter 12 for the relay check and refer to the wiring diagrams at the end of Chapter 12, if necessary. When the PCM energizes the relay (by completing the circuit to ground), the air pump operates and air flows through the tubing into the exhaust manifolds.
4   A scan tool is required to thoroughly check the system. If the above checks fail to identify the problem area, have the system diagnosed by a dealer service department or other qualified repair shop.

Component replacement

Air pump

Note: *The air pump is mounted on the left frame rail, ahead of the front tire.*
5   Remove the splash shield.
6   Disconnect the electrical connector from the air pump motor. Detach the hoses from the air pump.
7   Detach the air pump bracket from the frame and remove the air pump and bracket assembly.
8   Installation is the reverse of removal.

Air pump relay

Note: *The air pump relay is located at the right front of the engine compartment, near the right horn.*
9   Disconnect the electrical connector from the relay.
10   Release the retaining tab and remove the relay from the bracket.
11   Installation is the reverse of removal.

Check valve and pipe

Warning: *The engine must be completely cool before beginning this procedure or serious burns may result.*
12   Rotate the engine forward to access the rear check valve and pipe (see Chapter 2B).
13   Loosen the clamp and remove the air hose from the check valve. Disconnect the vacuum bleed hose.
14   Remove the nut from the air pipe bracket.
15   Disconnect the fitting from the exhaust manifold and remove the check valve and pipe assembly.
16   Remove the bolts and separate the check valve from the pipe, if necessary.
17   Installation is the reverse of removal.

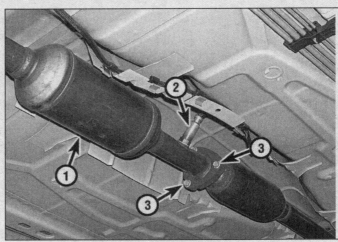

19.7 Catalytic converter and related components

1   *Catalytic converter*
2   *Post-converter oxygen sensor*
3   *Flange bolts*

19   Catalytic converter

Note: *Because of a Federally mandated warranty which covers emissions-related components such as the catalytic converter, check with a dealer service department before replacing the converter at your own expense.*
1   The catalytic converter is an emission control device added to the exhaust system to reduce pollutants from the exhaust gas stream. A three-way (reduction) catalyst design is used. The catalytic coating on the three-way catalyst contains palladium, platinum and rhodium, which lowers the levels of oxides of nitrogen (NOx) as well as hydrocarbons (HC) and carbon monoxide (CO).
2   The test equipment for a catalytic converter is expensive and highly sophisticated. If you suspect that the converter on your vehicle is malfunctioning, take it to a dealer or authorized emissions inspection facility for diagnosis and repair.

Check

3   Whenever the vehicle is raised for servicing of underbody components, check the converter for leaks, corrosion, dents and other damage. Check the flange bolts that attach the front and rear ends of the converter to the exhaust system. If damage is discovered, the converter should be replaced.
4   A catalytic converter may become plugged. The easiest way to check for a restricted converter is to use a vacuum gauge to diagnose the effect of a blocked exhaust on intake vacuum.

a)   *Connect a vacuum gauge to an intake manifold vacuum source.*
b)   *Warm the engine to operating temperature, place the transmission in Park and apply the parking brake.*
c)   *Note and record the vacuum reading at idle.*
d)   *Open the throttle until the engine speed is about 2000 rpm.*
e)   *Release the throttle quickly and record the vacuum reading.*
f)   *Perform the test three more times, recording the reading after each test.*
g)   *If the reading after the fourth test is more than one in-Hg lower than the reading recorded at idle, the catalytic converter, muffler or exhaust pipes may be plugged or restricted.*

Replacement

Refer to illustration 19.7
Note: *Refer to the exhaust system servicing section in Chapter 4 for additional information.*
5   Raise the vehicle and support it securely on jackstands.
6   Disconnect the electrical connector from the post-converter oxygen sensor.
7   Remove the catalytic converter-to-exhaust pipe flange bolts and separate the exhaust pipe from the catalytic converter **(see illustration)**. Support the exhaust pipe.
8   Remove the bolts and detach the catalytic converter header pipe from the exhaust manifold (see Chapter 2A). Remove the catalytic converter and pipe assembly.
9   Clean the carbon deposits from the mounting flanges and install new gaskets.
10   Installation is the reverse of removal.

Chapter 7
Automatic transaxle

Contents

Specifications

General

Fluid type and capacity .... See Chapter 1

Torque specifications
Ft-lbs (unless otherwise indicated)

PNP switch-to-case bolts	18
Manual shift lever-to-shift shaft nut	15
Shift cable bracket bolts (at transaxle)	18
Subframe mounting bolts	133
Transaxle-to-engine bolts	55
Torque converter-to-driveplate bolts	46
Torque converter cover bolts	60 in-lbs
Vacuum modulator clamp bolt	20

1 General information

All vehicles covered by this manual are equipped with a four-speed Hydra-Matic automatic transaxle. Two models of Hydra-Matic automatic transaxles are used on these vehicles: the 4T60E (1997 and 1998 models) and the 4T65E (1999 and later models) electronic four-speeds.

Due to the complexity of the clutches and the hydraulic control system, and because of the special tools and expertise required to perform an automatic transaxle overhaul, it should not be undertaken by the home mechanic. Therefore, the procedures in this Chapter are limited to general diagnosis, routine maintenance, adjustment and transaxle removal and installation.

If the transaxle requires major repair work, it should be left to a dealer service department or an automotive or transmission repair shop. You can, however, remove and install the transaxle yourself and save the expense, even if the repair work is done by a transmission shop (but be sure a proper diagnosis has been made before removing the transaxle).

Replacement and adjustment procedures the home mechanic can perform include those involving the throttle valve (TV) cable and the shift linkage.

Caution: *On models equipped with a Theft-lock audio system, be sure the lockout feature is turned off before performing any procedure which requires disconnecting the battery.*

2 Diagnosis - general

Note: *Automatic transmission malfunctions may be caused by five general conditions: poor engine performance, improper adjustments, hydraulic malfunctions, mechanical malfunctions or malfunctions in the computer or its signal network. Diagnosis of these problems should always begin with a check of the easily repaired items: fluid level and condition (see Chapter 1) and shift linkage adjustment. Next, perform a road test to determine if the problem has been corrected or if more diagnosis is necessary. If the problem persists after the preliminary tests and corrections are completed, additional diagnosis should be done by a dealer service department or transmission repair shop. Refer to the Troubleshooting sec-*

tion at the front of this manual for information on symptoms of transmission problems.

Preliminary checks

1   Drive the vehicle to warm the transaxle to normal operating temperature.
2   Check the fluid level as described in Chapter 1:
   a) *If the fluid level is unusually low, add enough fluid to bring the level within the designated area of the dipstick, then check for external leaks (see below).*
   b) *If the fluid level is abnormally high, drain off the excess, then check the drained fluid for contamination by coolant. The presence of engine coolant in the automatic transmission fluid indicates that a failure has occurred in the internal radiator walls that separate the coolant from the transmission fluid (see Chapter 3).*
   c) *If the fluid is foaming, drain it and refill the transaxle, then check for coolant in the fluid or a high fluid level.*
3   Check the engine idle speed. **Note:** *If the engine is malfunctioning, do not proceed with the preliminary checks until it has been repaired and runs normally.*
4   Check the shift cable (see Section 3). Make sure it's properly adjusted and operates smoothly.

Fluid leak diagnosis

5   Most fluid leaks are easy to locate visually. Repair usually consists of replacing a seal or gasket. If a leak is difficult to find, the following procedure may help.
6   Identify the fluid. Make sure it's transmission fluid and not engine oil or brake fluid (automatic transmission fluid is a deep red color).
7   Try to pinpoint the source of the leak. Drive the vehicle several miles, then park it over a large sheet of cardboard. After a minute or two, you should be able to locate the leak by determining the source of the fluid dripping onto the cardboard.
8   Make a careful visual inspection of the suspected component and the area immediately around it. Pay particular attention to gasket mating surfaces. A mirror is often helpful for finding leaks in areas that are hard to see.
9   If the leak still cannot be found, clean the suspected area thoroughly with a degreaser or solvent, then dry it.
10   Drive the vehicle for several miles at normal operating temperature and varying speeds. After driving the vehicle, visually inspect the suspected component again.
11   Once the leak has been located, the cause must be determined before it can be properly repaired. If a gasket is replaced but the sealing flange is bent, the new gasket will not stop the leak. The bent flange must be straightened.
12   Before attempting to repair a leak, check to make sure that the following conditions are corrected or they may cause another leak. **Note:** *Some of the following conditions cannot be fixed without highly*

specialized tools and expertise. Such problems must be referred to a transmission repair shop or a dealer service department.

Gasket leaks

13   Check the pan periodically. Make sure the bolts are tight, no bolts are missing, the gasket is in good condition and the pan is flat (dents in the pan may indicate damage to the valve body inside).
14   If the pan gasket is leaking, the fluid level or the fluid pressure may be too high, the vent may be plugged, the pan bolts may be too tight, the pan sealing flange may be warped, the sealing surface of the transaxle housing may be damaged, the gasket may be damaged or the transaxle casting may be cracked or porous. If sealant instead of gasket material has been used to form a seal between the pan and the transaxle housing, it may be the wrong type of sealant.

Seal leaks

15   If a transaxle seal is leaking, the fluid level or pressure may be too high, the vent may be plugged, the seal bore may be damaged, the seal itself may be damaged or improperly installed, the surface of the shaft protruding through the seal may be damaged or a loose bearing may be causing excessive shaft movement.
16   Make sure the dipstick tube seal is in good condition and the tube is properly seated. Periodically check the area around the speedometer gear or sensor for leakage. If transmission fluid is evident, check the O-ring for damage.

Case leaks

17   If the case itself appears to be leaking, the casting is porous and will have to be repaired or replaced.
18   Make sure the oil cooler hose fittings are tight and in good condition.

Fluid comes out vent pipe or fill tube

19   If this condition occurs, the transaxle is overfilled, there is coolant in the fluid, the case is porous, the dipstick is incorrect, the vent is plugged or the drain-back holes are plugged.

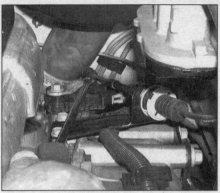

3.3 Pry the shift cable end off the transaxle shift lever

3   Shift cable - removal, installation and adjustment

Warning: *The models covered by this manual are equipped with airbags. Always disable the airbag system before working in the vicinity of any airbag system component to avoid the possibility of accidental deployment of the airbag(s), which could cause personal injury (see Chapter 12).*

Removal and installation

Refer to illustrations 3.3, 3.4a, 3.4b and 3.6
1   Disconnect the cable from the negative battery terminal. **Caution:** *On models equipped with a Theftlock audio system, be sure you have the correct activation code before performing any procedure which requires disconnecting the battery.*
2   Remove the air filter housing cover and the air intake duct that runs to the throttle body.
3   Disconnect the shift cable from the shift lever on the transaxle **(see illustration)**.
4   To detach the shift cable from the transaxle bracket, remove the U-clip retainer (if used), then squeeze the tangs on the cable adjuster and pull the cable through the bracket **(see illustrations)**.
5   Remove the trim panel from under the

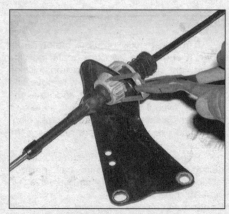

3.4a Remove this metal clip (cable and bracket removed for clarity). . .

3.4b . . . then squeeze the tangs on the adjuster and pass the cable and casing through the bracket

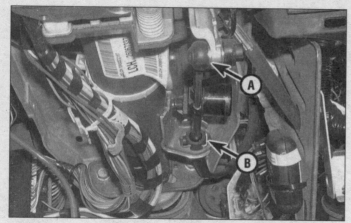

3.6 Pry the cable end from its post at the shift control lever (A), then remove the clip (B) and separate the cable casing from the bracket

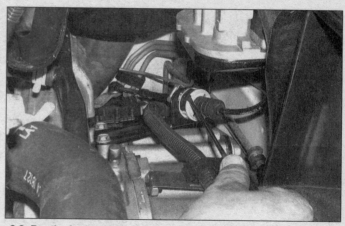

3.9 Pry the lock tab on the cable adjuster up to free the adjuster

steering column. Also remove the lower steering column cover (see Chapter 11).

6   Disconnect the cable end from the shift control lever, then remove the clip and pry the cable casing from the U-shaped mount on the steering column **(see illustration)**.

7   Pull the cable through the hole in the firewall to the engine side. Installation is the reverse of removal, but don't connect the cable to the shift lever on the transaxle until performing the adjustment procedure. Make sure the grommet is properly seated in the firewall.

Adjustment

Refer to illustration 3.9

8   Detach the cable end from the transaxle shift lever if it is connected **(see illustration 3.3)**.

9   Pry up the lock tab on the shift cable **(see illustration)**.

10   Turn the shift lever on the transaxle counterclockwise all the way, then rotate it back two clicks to set it in the Neutral position. Also place the shift control lever inside the vehicle to the Neutral position.

11   Pull the cable end towards the pin on the transaxle shift lever, then connect the

cable end to the pin. **Note:** *Don't pull the cable end beyond the pin then push it back, as this will result in improper adjustment.*

12   Depress the lock tab completely, then start the engine and make sure all gear positions are operating and correspond with the gear position indicator on the instrument panel.

4   Shift interlock system - description, check and component replacement

Warning: *The models covered by this manual are equipped with airbags. Always disable the airbag system before working in the vicinity of any airbag system component to avoid the possibility of accidental deployment of the airbag(s), which could cause personal injury (see Chapter 12).*

Description

1   The Park/Lock system prevents the shift lever from being moved out of Park unless the brake pedal is depressed simultaneously. It also prevents the ignition key from being removed from the ignition switch unless the

shift lever is in the Park position. When the car is started, a solenoid is energized, locking the shift lever in Park; when the brake pedal is depressed, the solenoid is de-energized, unlocking the shift lever so that it can be moved into some other gear.

Solenoid check

2   Remove the trim panel from under the steering column. Also remove the steering column covers (see Chapter 11).

3   Unplug the electrical connector from the shift lock solenoid. **Note:** *The connector is secured by a plastic "lock" that must first be removed.* Using a pair of jumper wires, momentarily apply battery voltage and ground to the solenoid terminals and verify that there's an audible "click." **Caution:** *Don't apply battery voltage any longer than necessary to perform this check.*

4   If the shift lock solenoid doesn't click when energized, replace it.

Component replacement

Solenoid/actuator assembly

Refer to illustrations 4.6 and 4.8

5   Remove the trim panel from under the steering column. Also remove the steering column covers (see Chapter 11).

6   Pry off each end of the actuator assembly from its mounting pins and remove it from the steering column **(see illustration)**.

7   Unplug the electrical connector from the solenoid.

8   To adjust the actuator, push on the adjuster block to disengage it from the teeth on the adjuster, then move the adjuster block away from the solenoid all the way and release the adjuster block **(see illustration)**.

9   Installation is the reverse of removal.

Park lock cable

Refer to illustrations 4.14, 4.15, 4.16 and 4.18

Removal

10   Remove the trim panel from under the steering column. Also remove the steering column covers (see Chapter 11).

7

4.6 The shift lock solenoid/actuator is located on the right side of the steering column

4.8 To adjust the actuator, depress the adjuster block and slide it away from the solenoid

4.14 Depress the tab with a narrow screwdriver and detach the park lock cable from the lock cylinder housing

4.15 Remove the Torx screws and detach the shift control assembly from the steering column

11 Place the shift lever in the Park position. Turn the ignition key to the Off/Lock position.

12 Detach the shift lock solenoid/actuator assembly from shift control lever.

13 Detach the shift cable from the shift control lever.

14 Depress the tab and detach the upper end of the cable from the key lock cylinder housing **(see illustration)**.

15 Remove the three Torx screws and remove the shift control assembly from the steering column **(see illustration)**.

16 Disassemble the shift control assembly and detach the cable **(see illustration)**.

Installation and adjustment

17 Installation is the reverse of the removal procedure. Make sure the ignition key is in the Off/Lock position and the shift lever is in the Park position before installing the cable.

18 Disengage the cable adjuster ring **(see illustration)**, then pull on the cable to remove all slack. Make sure the park lock latch comes into contact with the shift lever, then lock the cable adjuster ring back into place.

19 Check the operation of the park lock cable and make sure the ignition key can't be

removed without the shift lever in Park.

20 The remainder of the installation is the reverse of removal.

---

5 Park/Neutral Position (PNP) switch/back-up light switch - check and replacement

Check

1 Make sure the shift cable is properly adjusted (see Section 3). Remove the air intake duct.

2 Turn the ignition key to the On position and place the shift lever in Reverse. Check to see if the back-up lights come on. If they don't, check the fuses. If the fuses are good, loosen the switch mounting bolts **(see illustration 5.7)** and rotate the switch slightly one direction or the other, while an assistant watches the back-up lights. If the lights come on, tighten the switch mounting bolts with the switch in that position.

3 If the lights still don't come on, check the back-up light circuit (refer to the wiring

diagrams at the back of this manual). If the circuit checks out OK, replace the PNP switch.

4 If you adjusted the switch and the back-up lights now work, check to see that the engine will start when the shift lever is in Park and Neutral only. If the engine cranks over with the shifter in any other position, replace the PNP switch.

Replacement

Refer to illustrations 5.7, 5.12a and 5.12b

5 Turn the ignition Off and disconnect the cable from the negative terminal of the battery. **Caution:** *On models equipped with the Theftlock audio system, be sure you have the correct activation code before performing any procedure which requires disconnecting the battery.*

6 Apply the parking brake and put the shift lever in Neutral. Remove the air filter housing cover and the air intake duct that runs to the throttle body.

7 Locate the Park/Neutral Position (PNP) switch **(see illustration)**, which is mounted on the transaxle at the manual lever.

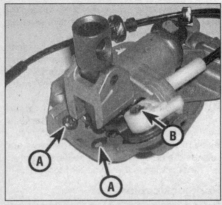

4.16 Remove these two screws (A) and separate the plate holding the park lock cable from the shift control assembly, then remove the small snap-ring (B) and detach the cable end from the post

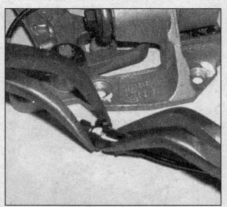

4.18 Disengage the adjuster ring on the park lock cable (cable and shift control assembly removed for clarity)

5.7 The PNP switch is mounted on the left (driver's) side of the transaxle

5.12a To adjust the old PNP switch, pry out the old set pin . . .

5.12b . . . insert a 3/32-inch gauge pin or drill bit into the service adjustment hole and rotate the switch until the pin drops down

8   Disconnect the shift cable from the manual lever.
9   Unplug the electrical connectors from the PNP switch **(see illustration 5.7)**.
10   Remove the manual lever retaining nut and remove the manual lever. **Note:** *Be careful not to move the manual lever shaft from the Neutral position while doing this.*
11   Remove the switch retaining bolts and lift the switch straight up.
12   If you're installing the old switch, pry out the old set pin **(see illustration)**, insert a 3/32-inch gauge pin or drill bit into the service adjustment hole **(see illustration)** and rotate the switch until the pin drops down. Remove the gauge pin or drill bit. **Note:** *If you're installing a new switch you don't need to perform this Step; the switch comes equipped with a set pin that holds the switch in the Neutral position until it has been installed and the shift lever has been moved through its range, at which point the set pin will shear off.*
13   Align the flats of the shift shaft with the flats of the Park/Neutral Position switch and install the switch.
14   Install the switch mounting bolts and tighten them to the torque listed in this Chapter's Specifications.
15   Install the manual lever, tightening the

nut securely.
16   Attach the shift cable and reconnect the electrical connectors.
17   Verify that the engine will start only in Park or Neutral. If it starts in any other gear, readjust the switch (turn it slightly one way or the other and see if the engine now only starts in Park or Neutral; it isn't necessary to remove the switch and adjust it with a gauge pin).
18   The remainder of installation is the reverse of removal.

6   Driveaxle oil seals - replacement

Refer to illustration 6.3
1   Raise the vehicle and support it securely on jackstands.
2   Remove the driveaxle(s) (see Chapter 8).
3   If you're removing the right (passenger's) side seal, use a hammer and chisel to pry up the outer lip of the seal to dislodge it so it can be pried out of the housing **(see illustration)**. If you're removing the left-side seal, pry the seal out using a large screwdriver or a seal removal tool.
4   Compare the new seal to the old one to make sure they're the same.

5   Coat the lips of the new seal with transmission fluid.
6   Place the new seal in position and tap it into the bore with a hammer and seal driver or a large socket that's the same diameter as the outside edge of the seal.
7   Reinstall the various components in the reverse order of removal.

7   Vacuum modulator (4T60-E transaxles) - check and replacement

Check

Refer to illustration 7.2
1   The vacuum modulator is connected to engine manifold vacuum to rapidly respond to changes in engine loading, and has an important effect on shift quality. If your vehicle exhibits shifting problems such as slipping or shifts that are either too soft or too harsh, check the vacuum supply to the modulator. With the engine running, connect a vacuum gauge to the modulator's vacuum line (at the modulator). Anything less than normal engine vacuum of 13 to 17 inches (idling hot in Drive with the brakes applied) could cause shifting problems. If vacuum is too low, find the engine problem, hose kink or hose leak that is causing the low vacuum signal.
2   Connect a hand-held vacuum pump to the vacuum connection on the modulator (removed from vehicle) and apply 15 to 20 inches of vacuum while watching the plunger **(see illustration)**. If the plunger isn't drawn in as vacuum is applied, the modulator should be replaced. The modulator should be able to hold this vacuum for at least half a minute.
3   When the modulator is withdrawn from the transaxle, turn it so the vacuum port is pointing down. If any oil, water or other fluid drips out, the modulator should be replaced. **Note:** *A vehicle with a modulator whose diaphragm has a leak may exhibit excessive smoking at the tailpipe, due to transaxle fluid being drawn into the engine and burned.*
4   The body of the modulator can be checked for leaks by coating the outside with soapy water and blowing (by mouth, no more

7

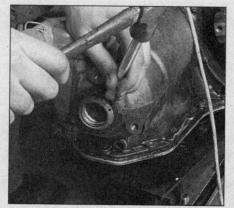

6.3 Dislodge the right-side driveaxle oil seal by working around the outer edge with a hammer and chisel

7.2 Vacuum modulator details

1   *Vacuum port*
2   *Plunger*

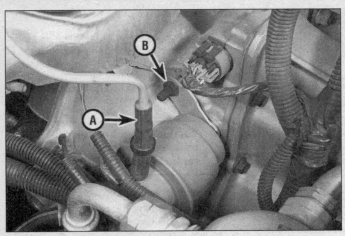

7.6 Disconnect the vacuum line (A) and remove the mounting bolt (B)

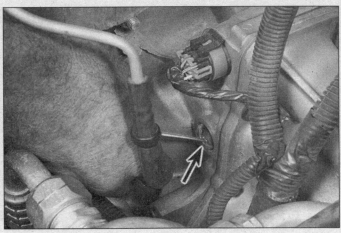

7.7 Remove the O-ring (arrow) from the transaxle case

than 6 psi) into the vacuum port, using a short length of vacuum hose. Bubbles on the outside of the modulator or along the seam indicate a leak.

Replacement

Refer to illustrations 7.6, 7.7 and 7.8

5   The modulator is located on the front (radiator) side of the transaxle, below the exhaust crossover pipe. Remove the air filter housing cover and the air intake duct that runs to the throttle body.

6   Pull up the sheath and disconnect the vacuum line, remove the mounting bolt or stud, then withdraw the modulator **(see illustration).**

7   Remove the O-ring from the modulator cavity, using a small screwdriver or hook **(see illustration).**

8   Use a small magnet to remove the modulator valve from the transaxle **(see illustration).** Inspect the valve for signs of abnormal wear or scoring.

9   Installation is the reverse of the removal procedure. Always use a new O-ring and make sure the modulator valve is installed the same way it came out.

8   Automatic transaxle - removal and installation

Refer to illustrations 8.11 and 8.17
Warning: *This is a difficult procedure for the home mechanic, requiring the use of several specialized tools, including a transmission jack and an engine support fixture. Such tools can be rented, but the job is still difficult to do without a hydraulic lift. Safely raising the vehicle enough for the transaxle and subframe to be pulled out from underneath is a problem without a hoist.*

Removal

1   Disconnect the cable from the negative terminal of the battery. **Caution:** *On models equipped with a Theftlock audio system, be sure you have the correct activation code before performing any procedure which requires disconnecting the battery.*

2   Remove the air filter housing cover and the air intake duct that runs to the throttle body.

3   Remove the bolt securing the transaxle

dipstick tube to the intake manifold.

4   Remove the transaxle-to-engine bolts that are accessible from above; they're beneath the exhaust crossover pipe.

5   Disconnect the shift cable and cable bracket from the transaxle (see Section 3).

6   If you're working on a 1997 or 1998 model, disconnect the vacuum hose from the vacuum modulator (see Section 7).

7   Disconnect any electrical connectors or wiring harnesses from the transaxle that are visible from above.

8   Support the engine using an engine support fixture (available at most equipment rental yards) to retain the engine in the body.

9   Loosen the wheel lug nuts, raise the front of the vehicle and support it securely on jackstands. Remove the wheel. Raise the vehicle and support it securely on jackstands.

10   Drain the transaxle fluid (Chapter 1). Remove the torque converter cover.

11   Mark the torque converter-to-driveplate relationship so they can be installed in the same relative position **(see illustration).**

12   Remove the torque converter-to-driveplate bolts. Turn the crankshaft pulley bolt for access to each bolt.

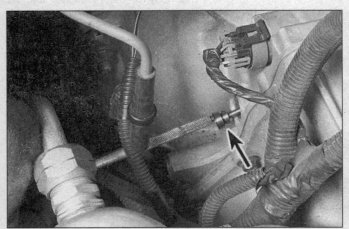

7.8 A magnet can be used to reach in and extract the modulator valve (arrow)

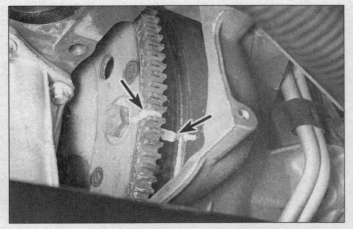

8.11 Make alignment marks (arrows) on the flywheel and torque converter so they can be reinstalled in the same relative positions

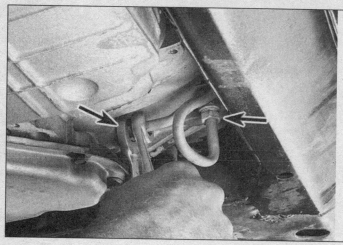

8.17 Use a flare nut wrench on the tube nut and an open end wrench on the fitting adapter when detaching the transaxle cooler lines (arrows) from the transaxle

13   Remove the starter motor (see Chapter 5).

14   Remove the driveaxles (see Chapter 8).

15   Disconnect all electrical connectors and wiring harnesses from the transaxle that are visible from below.

16   Refer to Chapter 10 and disconnect the tie-rod ends, then unbolt the steering rack and hold it to the body with heavy wire, away from the chassis.

17   Disconnect the transaxle cooler lines **(see illustration)**. Plug the lines and fittings.

18   Refer to Chapter 2A and disconnect the engine mount nuts at the chassis, then support the subframe assembly with at least two floor jacks and remove the bolts holding the subframe to the vehicle. **Warning:** *Never put any part of your body under the front subframe while it is unbolted from the vehicle.* **Caution:** *The manufacturer recommends replacing these bolts with new ones whenever they are removed.* Slowly lower the subframe, making sure nothing is connected to it, and remove it from under the vehicle.

19   Support the transaxle with a jack - preferably a special jack made for this purpose. Safety chains will help steady the transaxle on the jack.

20   Remove the brace between the engine and transaxle (attached to the oil pan on the right side) and the bolts securing the transaxle to the flywheel end of the engine.

21   Remove the dipstick tube.

22   Remove the remaining transaxle-to-engine bolts.

23   Move the transaxle away from the engine to disengage it from the engine block dowel pins and make sure the torque converter is detached from the driveplate. Secure the torque converter to the transaxle so it will not fall out during removal. Lower the transaxle from the vehicle.

Installation

24   Prior to installation, make sure the torque converter is fully engaged in the transmission. To do this, rotate the converter while pushing it toward the transaxle. If it wasn't already fully in place, you'll feel it "clunk" into position as it engages with the input shaft and front pump. It may even "clunk" more than once. Lubricate the torque converter hub with multi-purpose grease.

25   Raise the transaxle evenly into position. Be sure to keep it level so the torque converter does not slide out.

26   Turn the torque converter to line up the bolt holes with the holes in the driveplate. The white paint mark on the torque converter

and the driveplate made in Step 5 must line up.

27   Move the transaxle forward carefully until the dowel pins on the engine mate with the transaxle case.

28   Install the lower transaxle-to-engine bolts, tightening them to the torque listed in this Chapter's Specifications.

29   Raise the subframe into position and secure it with new bolts, tightening them to the torque listed in this Chapter's Specifications. Install the engine mount nuts, tightening them to the torque listed in the Chapter 2A Specifications.

30   Install the torque converter-to-driveplate bolts. **Note:** *Install all of the bolts before tightening any of them.* Tighten the bolts to the torque listed in this Chapter's Specifications. Install the torque converter cover.

31   Install the suspension and chassis components which were removed. Tighten the bolts and nuts to the torque values listed in the Chapter 10 Specifications.

32   Remove the jack supporting the transaxle.

33   Install the dipstick tube.

34   Reconnect the transaxle cooler lines, tightening the fittings securely.

35   Install the starter motor (Chapter 5).

36   Connect all wiring harness clips and electrical connectors accessible from below.

37   Install the driveaxles (Chapter 8).

38   Lower the vehicle.

39   Install the upper transaxle-to-engine bolts, tightening them to the torque listed in this Chapter's Specifications.

40   Connect the shift cable bracket and adjust the shift cable (see Section 3).

41   Install the dipstick tube bracket bolt, tightening it securely.

42   Plug in the transaxle electrical connectors.

43   Connect the vacuum line to the vacuum modulator (1997 and 1998 models only).

44   Install the air intake duct/air filter housing cover.

45   Fill the transaxle with the recommended type and amount of fluid (see Chapter 1), run the engine and check for fluid leaks.

7

Notes

Chapter 8   Driveaxles

Contents

Specifications

Inner CV joint boot length (see illustration 3.3s) .... 4-29/32 inches

Torque specifications

Ft-lbs (unless otherwise indicated)

Driveaxle/hub nut
    1997 151
    1998 and later 118
Wheel lug nuts .... See Chapter 1

---

1   Driveaxles - general information and inspection

1   Power is transmitted from the transaxle to the wheels through a pair of driveaxles. The inner ends of the driveaxles are splined into the differential side gears. The outer ends of the driveaxles are splined into the axle hubs and locked in place by a large nut.

2   The inner ends of the driveaxles are equipped with sliding constant velocity joints, which are capable of both angular and axial motion. These joint assemblies consist of a tripot bearing and a joint housing (outer race) in which the joint is free to slide in and out as the driveaxle moves up and down with the wheel. The inner joints can be disassembled, cleaned, inspected and repacked, but they cannot be overhauled. If any parts are damaged, an inner joint must be replaced as a unit.

3   The outer CV joints are of the cross-groove, or "ball-and-cage" type. The outer joints are capable of angular but not axial movement. The outer joints can be disassembled, cleaned, inspected and repacked, but they cannot be overhauled. If any parts are damaged, an outer joint must be replaced as a unit.

4   The boots should be inspected periodically for damage and leaking lubricant. Torn CV joint boots must be replaced immediately or the joints can be damaged. Boot replacement involves removal of the driveaxle (see Section 2). **Note:** *Some auto parts stores carry "split" type replacement boots, which can be installed without removing the driveaxle from the vehicle. This is a convenient alternative; however, the driveaxle should be removed and the CV joint disassembled and cleaned to ensure the joint is free from contaminants such as moisture and dirt which will accelerate CV joint wear.* The most common symptom of worn or damaged CV joints, besides lubricant leaks, is a clicking noise in turns, a clunk when accelerating after coasting and vibration at highway speeds. To check for wear in the CV joints and driveaxle shafts, grasp each axle (one at a time) and rotate it in both directions while holding the CV joint housings, feeling for play indicating worn splines or sloppy CV joints. Also check the driveaxle shafts for cracks, dents and distortion.

8

2.2 Loosen the driveaxle/hub nut with a long breaker bar; prevent the hub from turning by inserting a large screwdriver or prybar through the hole in the caliper and into the cooling vanes of the brake disc

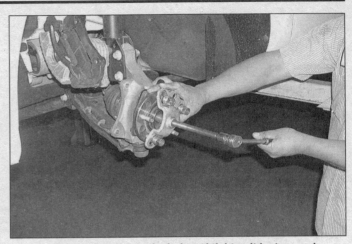

2.4 Attach a puller to the hub and tighten it just enough to break the hub splines loose

2   Driveaxle - removal and installation

Removal

Refer to illustrations 2.2, 2.4, 2.6 and 2.7

1   Set the parking brake. Loosen the front wheel lug nuts, raise the vehicle and support it securely on jackstands. Remove the wheel.
2   Remove the driveaxle/hub nut. To prevent the disc/hub from turning, insert a long punch through the hole in the caliper and into the brake disc cooling vanes **(see illustration)**.
3   Remove the brake caliper and suspend it with a piece of wire from the strut coil spring (see Chapter 9).
4   Attach a puller to the hub flange and tighten it just to the point where the driveaxle moves in the hub **(see illustration)**. **Note:** *If you are using a jaw-type puller it will be necessary to remove the caliper mounting bracket and the brake disc.* **Caution:** *Don't*

attempt to push the end of the driveaxle through the hub yet. Applying force to the end of the driveaxle, beyond just breaking it loose from the hub, can damage the driveaxle or transaxle.
5   Separate the strut from the steering knuckle (see Chapter 10).
6   Tighten the puller to push the end of the driveaxle through the hub, then pull out on the steering knuckle and detach the driveaxle from the hub **(see illustration)**. Don't let the driveaxle hang by the inner CV joint after the outer end has been detached from the steering knuckle, as the inner joint could become damaged. Support the outer end of the driveaxle with a piece of wire, if necessary.
7   Place a drain pan underneath the transaxle to catch any lubricant that may spill out when the driveaxle is removed. Carefully pry the inner CV joint out of the transaxle **(see illustration)**.
8   Refer to Chapter 7 for the driveaxle oil seal replacement procedure, if necessary.

Installation

Refer to illustration 2.9

9   Installation is the reverse of the removal procedure, but with the following additional points:

a) *Replace the retaining ring on the inner end of the left driveaxle* **(see illustration)** *or on the transaxle stub shaft (right side).*
b) *Seat the inner CV joint in the differential side gear by positioning the end of a large screwdriver in the groove in the CV joint housing and tapping it into position with a hammer. Once this has been done, pull out on the joint housing to make sure the retaining ring has seated.*
c) *Tighten the strut-to-knuckle bolts/nuts to the torque listed in the Chapter 10 Specifications.*
d) *Install a* **new** *driveaxle/hub nut, but don't tighten it completely until the vehicle has been lowered.*
e) *If removed, install the caliper mounting*

2.6 Pull the steering knuckle out and slide the end of the driveaxle out of the hub

2.7 To separate the inner end of the driveaxle from the transaxle, pry on the CV joint housing like this with a large screwdriver or prybar - you may need to give the prybar a sharp rap with a brass hammer

bracket and tighten the bolts to the torque listed in the Chapter 9 Specifications.

f) Install the brake caliper and tighten the mounting bolts to the torque listed in the Chapter 9 Specifications.

g) Install the wheel and lug nuts, lower the vehicle and tighten the lug nuts to the torque listed in the Chapter 1 Specifications. Now tighten the driveaxle/hub nut to the torque listed in this Chapter's Specifications.

h) Check the transaxle lubricant and add some, if necessary, to bring it to the proper level (see Chapter 1).

3   Driveaxle boot - replacement

Note: *If the CV joint boots must be replaced, explore all options before beginning the job. Complete rebuilt driveaxles are available on an exchange basis, which eliminates much time and work. Whichever route you choose to take, check on the cost and availability of parts before disassembling the vehicle.*

1   Remove the driveaxle (see Section 2).
2   Place the driveaxle in a vise lined with

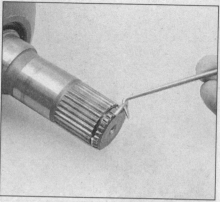

2.9 Replace the driveaxle retaining ring on the left inner CV joint stub shaft (on the right side the ring is on the stub shaft in the transaxle)

rags to avoid damage to the axleshaft. Check the CV joint for excessive play in the radial direction, which indicates worn parts. Check for smooth operation throughout the full range of motion for each CV joint. If a boot is torn, disassemble the joint, clean the components and inspect for damage due to loss of

3.3a Cut off the boot retaining clamps, using wire cutters or a chisel and hammer

lubrication and possible contamination by foreign matter.

Inner CV joint

Refer to illustrations 3.3a through 3.3t

3   To replace the inner boot, refer to the accompanying illustrations **(see illustrations 3.3a through 3.3t).**

3.3b Slide the housing off the spider assembly

3.3c Slide the boot towards the center of the driveaxle

3.3d Spread the ends of the stop ring apart and slide it towards the center of the shaft

3.3e Slide the spider assembly back to expose the retaining ring and pry off the ring

3.3f Carefully tap the spider off the axleshaft with a brass punch (but don't hit it so hard that it flies off, or you'll be picking up needle bearings!)

8

3.3g When you slide the spider off the driveaxle, hold the bearings in place with your hand; even better, use tape or a cloth wrapped around the spider bearing assembly to retain them

3.3h Slide the boot and the stop ring off the axleshaft

3.3i Clean all of the old grease out of the housing and spider assembly, then remove each bearing, one at time

3.3j Carefully disassemble each section of the spider assembly, clean the needle bearings with solvent and inspect the rollers, spider cross, bearings and housing for scoring, pitting and other signs of abnormal wear

3.3k Apply a coat of CV joint grease to the inner bearing surfaces to hold the needle bearings in place and slide the bearing over them

3.3l Wrap the axleshaft splines with tape to avoid damaging the boot, then slide the small clamp and boot onto the axleshaft

3.3m Slide the spider stop ring onto the axleshaft, past the groove in which it seats

3.3n Install the spider bearing with the recess in the counterbore facing the end of the driveaxle

3.3o Install the spider retaining ring, then slide the spider assembly against it and install the stop ring in its groove

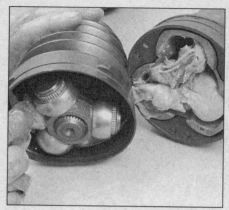

3.3p Pack the housing with half of the grease furnished with the new boot and place the remainder in the boot

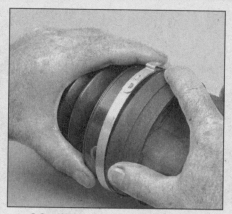

3.3q With the retaining clamps in place (but not tightened), install the tripot housing

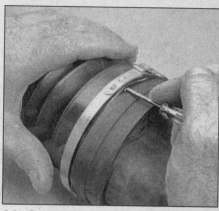

3.3r Seat the boot in the housing and axle seal grooves - a small screwdriver can make the job easier (make sure the boot isn't dimpled, stretched or out of shape)

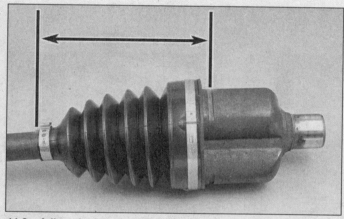

11.3s Adjust the length of the joint so the distance from the small end of the boot to the groove in the housing is the same as the dimension listed in this Chapter's Specifications

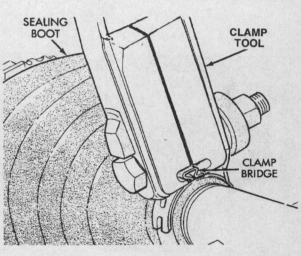

SEALING BOOT

CLAMP TOOL

CLAMP BRIDGE

3.3t With the joint at the proper length, equalize the pressure in the boot by inserting a small screwdriver between the boot and the housing, then secure the boot clamps with a clamp crimping tool (available at auto parts stores)

Outer CV joint

Refer to illustrations 3.4a through 3.4r

4   Refer to the accompanying illustrations and perform the outer CV joint boot replacement procedure **(see illustrations 3.4a through 3.4r).**

3.4a Cut off the boot retaining clamps, using wire cutters or a chisel and hammer

3.4b Spread apart the ends of the internal snap-ring, then slide the CV joint off the shaft

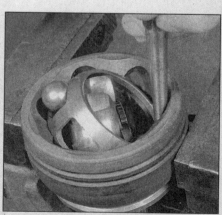

3.4c Press down on the inner race far enough to allow a ball bearing to be removed - if it's difficult to tilt, gently tap the cage and inner race with a brass punch and hammer

8

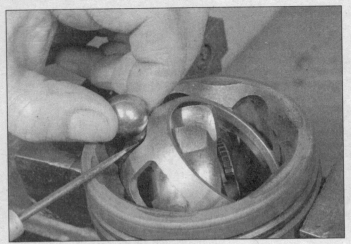

3.4d Pry the balls out of the cage, one at a time

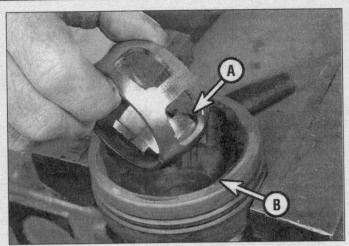

3.4e Tilt the inner race and cage 90-degrees, then align the windows in the cage (A) with the lands of the housing (B) and rotate the inner race up and out of the outer race

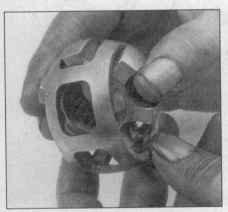

3.4f Align the inner race lands with the cage window and rotate the inner race out of the cage

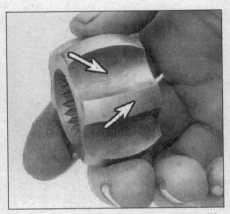

3.4g After cleaning the components with solvent, check the inner race lands and grooves for pitting and score marks

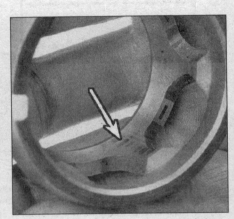

3.4h Check the cage for cracks, pitting and score marks - shiny spots are normal and don't affect operation

3.4i With the race and cage tilted at 90-degrees, lower the assembly into the housing

3.4j Rotate the assembly by gently tapping with a hammer and brass punch . . .

3.4k . . . then press the balls into the cage windows, repeating until all of the balls are installed

3.4l Use needle-nose pliers to lower a new snap-ring into the groove . . .

3.4m . . . then seat it into the groove with snap-ring pliers

3.4n Apply grease through the splined hole, then insert a wooden dowel (with a diameter slightly less than that of the axle) through the splined hole and push down - the dowel will force the grease into the joint - repeat until the bearing is completely packed

3.4o Install the small clamp and the boot on the driveaxle and apply grease to the inside of the axle boot . . .

3.4p . . . until the level is up to the end of axle

8

3.4q Position the CV joint assembly on the driveaxle, aligning the splines, then use a soft-face hammer to drive the joint onto the driveaxle until the snap-ring is seated in the groove

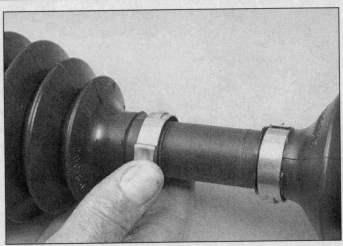

3.4r Seat the inner end of the boot in the groove and install the retaining clamp, then do the same on the other end of the boot - tighten boot clamps with the special tool (see illustration 3.3t)

Chapter 9   Brakes

Contents

Specifications

General

Brake fluid type	See Chapter 1

Disc brakes

Minimum pad thickness	See Chapter 1
Brake disc minimum thickness	Cast into disc
Maximum disc runout	0.003 inch
Maximum disc thickness variation	0.001 inch

Rear drum brakes

Shoe friction material minimum thickness	See Chapter 1
Maximum inside diameter	Cast into drum
Maximum out-of-round	0.006 inch

Brake pedal travel (maximum)

	2-29/32 inches

Torque specifications

	Ft-lbs (unless otherwise indicated)
Brake booster mounting nuts	18
Brake caliper	
Caliper mounting bolts	
Front	63
Rear	33
Caliper mounting bracket bolts	
Front	137
Rear	92
Brake hose-to-caliper banjo bolt	
Front	40
Rear	32
Master cylinder-to-brake booster retaining nuts	20
Wheel cylinder retaining bolts	110 in-lbs
Wheel lug nuts	See Chapter 1

9

2.3 The ABS hydraulic control unit/motor pack on 1999 and earlier models is mounted to the master cylinder

2.4 The Electronic Brake Control Module (EBCM) on 1999 and earlier models is located under the left end of the instrument panel

1   General information

The vehicles covered by this manual are equipped with hydraulically operated front and rear brake systems. The front brakes are disc type and the rear brakes are disc or drum type. Both the front and rear brakes are self adjusting. The disc brakes automatically compensate for pad wear, while the drum brakes incorporate an adjustment mechanism which is activated whenever the brakes are applied.

Hydraulic system

The hydraulic system consists of two separate circuits. The master cylinder has separate reservoirs for the two circuits, and, in the event of a leak or failure in one hydraulic circuit, the other circuit will remain operative. A pair of proportioning valves limit pressure to the rear brakes above a certain input pressure point to prevent rear-wheel lock-up.

Power brake booster

The power brake booster, utilizing engine manifold vacuum and atmospheric pressure to provide assistance to the hydraulically operated brakes, is mounted on the firewall in the engine compartment.

Parking brake

The parking brake operates the rear brakes only, through cable actuation. It's activated by a pedal mounted under the left end of the instrument panel.

Service

After completing any operation involving disassembly of any part of the brake system, always test drive the vehicle to check for proper braking performance before resuming normal driving. When testing the brakes, perform the tests on a clean, dry, flat surface. Conditions other than these can lead to inaccurate test results.

Test the brakes at various speeds with both light and heavy pedal pressure. The vehicle should stop evenly without pulling to one side or the other.

Tires, vehicle load and wheel alignment are factors which also affect braking performance. **Caution:** *On models equipped with the "Theftlock" audio system, be sure you have the correct activation code before performing any procedure which requires disconnecting the battery (see the front of this manual).*

2   Anti-lock Brake System (ABS) - general information

Refer to illustrations 2.3 and 2.4

Anti-lock Brake Systems (ABS) maintain vehicle maneuverability, directional stability, and optimum deceleration under severe braking conditions on most road surfaces. It does so by monitoring the rotational speed of the wheels and controlling the brake line pressure to the wheels during braking. This prevents the wheels from locking up on slippery roads or during hard braking.

Two different ABS systems have been used on the models covered by this manual; Delco ABS VI (1997 through 1999 models) and DBC 7 (2000 models). Each system uses similar wheel speed sensors. The difference lies mainly in the hydraulic modulator; on models with the ABS VI system, the modulator/motor pack assembly is fastened directly to the brake master cylinder - on models with the DBC 7 system, the modulator is bolted to the left (driver's side) strut tower.

Hydraulic modulator

The hydraulic modulator (or on 1999 and earlier models, the hydraulic modulator/motor pack assembly), controls hydraulic pressure to the front calipers and rear wheel cylinders or calipers by modulat-ing hydraulic pressure to prevent wheel lock-up **(see illustration)**. Basically, this unit holds steady or bleeds off pressure in a brake line, as necessary, when the Electronic Brake Control Module (EBCM) detects an abnormal deceleration in the speed of a wheel. When the speed of the wheel is restored to normal, the modulator once again allows full pressure to the brake. This cycle is repeated as many times as necessary, which results in a pulsing of the brake pedal. **Note:** *The modulator can't increase brake line pressure above that which is generated by the master cylinder, and it can't apply the brakes by itself. An exception to this would be if the vehicle is also equipped with the Traction Control System (TCS), which <u>can</u> apply the brake(s) on the drive wheels independently of driver input (but this only happens during acceleration).*

Electronic Brake Control Module (EBCM)

The Electronic Brake Control Module (EBCM) is located under the left end of the instrument panel (1997 through 1999 models) **(see illustration)** or on the hydraulic modulator (2000 models). The EBCM monitors the ABS system and controls the anti-lock valve solenoids. It accepts and processes information received from the brake switch and wheel speed sensors to control the hydraulic line pressure and avoid wheel lock up. It also monitors the system and stores fault codes which indicate specific problems.

Wheel speed sensors

Each wheel is equipped with a speed sensor, which is self-contained in each wheel bearing. The sensors are neither adjustable nor rebuildable. If a sensor malfunctions, the hub/wheel bearing assembly must be replaced (see Chapter 10).

A wheel speed sensor measures wheel speed by monitoring the rotation of a toothed ring. As the teeth of the ring move through the magnetic field of the sensor, an AC volt-

3.5a Before disassembling the brake, wash it thoroughly with brake system cleaner and allow it to dry - position a drain pan under the brake to catch the residue - DO NOT use compressed air to blow off brake dust!

3.5b To make room for the new pads, use a C-clamp to depress the piston into the caliper before removing the caliper and pads - do this a little at a time, keeping an eye on the fluid level in the master cylinder to make sure it doesn't overflow

age signal is generated. This signal frequency increases or decreases in proportion to the speed of the wheel. The EBCM monitors these signals for changes in wheel speed; if it detects the sudden deceleration of a wheel, i.e. wheel lockup, the EBCM activates the ABS system.

Warning lights

The ABS system has self-diagnostic capabilities. Each time the vehicle is started, the EBCM runs a self-test. There are two warning lights on the instrument panel, a red BRAKE light and an amber ABS light, each with their own functions. During starting, these lights should come on briefly then go out. If the red BRAKE light stays on, it indicates a problem with the main braking system, such as low fluid level detected or the parking brake is still on. If the light stays on after the parking brake is released, check the brake fluid level in the master cylinder reservoir (see Chapter 1).

The amber ABS light indicates a problem with the ABS system, not the main or basic brake system. If the light stays on, it indicates that there is a problem with the ABS system, but the main system is still working. Take the vehicle to a dealer service department or other qualified repair shop for diagnosis and repair.

Checks

Although a special electronic tester is necessary to properly diagnose the system, the home mechanic can perform a few preliminary checks before taking the vehicle to a dealer service department or other repair shop which is equipped with this tester:

a) *Check the fuses.*
b) *Check the electrical connectors at the EBCM and the hydraulic modulator/motor pack.*
c) *Follow the wiring harness to the speed sensors and brake light switch and make sure all connections are secure and the wiring isn't damaged.*
d) *Make sure the brake lines, calipers and wheel cylinders are in good condition.*

If the above preliminary checks don't rectify the problem, the vehicle should be diagnosed by a dealer service department or other qualified repair shop.

3   Disc brake pads - replacement

Refer to illustrations 3.5a through 3.5l
Warning: *Disc brake pads must be replaced on both front or both rear wheels at the same time - never replace the pads on only one wheel. Also, the dust created by the brake system is harmful to your health. Never blow it out with compressed air and don't inhale any of it. An approved filtering mask should be worn when working on the brakes. Do not, under any circumstances, use petroleum-based solvents to clean brake parts. Use brake system cleaner only!*
Note: *This procedure applies to the front and, on models so equipped, rear brake pads.*

1   Remove the cap from the brake fluid reservoir. Remove about two-thirds of the fluid from the reservoir. **Caution:** *Brake fluid will damage paint. If any fluid is spilled, wash it off immediately with plenty of clean, cold water.*
2   Loosen the front or rear wheel lug nuts, raise the front or rear of the vehicle and support it securely on jackstands. Block the wheels at the opposite end.
3   Remove the wheels. Work on one brake assembly at a time, using the assembled brake for reference if necessary.
4   Inspect the brake disc carefully as outlined in Section 5. If machining is necessary, follow the information in that Section to remove the disc.
5   Follow the accompanying photo sequence for the actual pad replacement procedure **(see illustrations 3.5a through 3.5l)**. Be sure to stay in order and read the caption under each illustration.

9

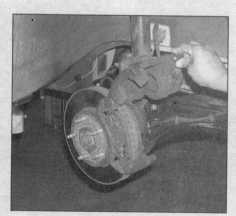

3.5c If you're replacing the front pads, remove the caliper lower mounting bolt - if you're replacing the rear pads, remove the upper bolt

3.5d Pivot the caliper out of its bracket and support it in this position for access to the brake pads

3.5e   Remove the inner brake pad

3.5f   Remove the outer brake pad

3.5g   Remove the upper and lower pad retainers from the caliper mounting bracket - check them for cracks or other signs of damage

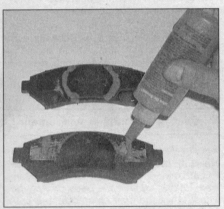

3.5h   Apply anti-squeal compound to the back of both pads (let the compound "set up" a few minutes before installing them)

3.5i   Install the upper and lower pad retainers

3.5j   Clean the caliper bolt and inspect it for scoring and corrosion; coat the shank of the bolt (but not the threads) with high-temperature grease

3.5k   Install the inner brake pad

3.5l   Install the outer brake pad (if you're replacing the front pads, the wear indicator must be positioned at the top; if you're replacing the rear pads, it must be positioned at the bottom). Swing the caliper over the pads and install the mounting bolt, tightening it to the torque listed in this Chapter's Specifications.
Note: *If the caliper won't fit over the pads, use a C-clamp to push the piston into the caliper a little further*

6   When reinstalling the caliper, be sure to tighten the mounting bolts to the torque listed in this Chapter's Specifications. Tighten the wheel lug nuts to the torque listed in the Chapter 1 Specifications.

7   After the job has been completed, firmly depress the brake pedal a few times to bring the pads into contact with the disc. Check the level of the brake fluid, adding some if necessary (see Chapter 1). Check the operation of the brakes carefully before placing the vehicle into normal service.

4   Disc brake caliper - removal and installation

Refer to illustrations 4.2a and 4.2b

Warning: *The dust created by the brake system is harmful to your health. Never blow it out with compressed air and don't inhale any of it. An approved filtering mask should be worn when working on the brakes. Do not, under any circumstances, use petroleum-based solvents to clean brake parts. Use brake system cleaner only!*

Removal

1   Loosen the front or rear wheel lug nuts, raise the front or rear of the vehicle and place it securely on jackstands. Block the wheels at the opposite end. Remove the front or rear wheel.

2   Remove the banjo bolt and disconnect the brake hose from the caliper **(see illustration)**. Discard the old sealing washers **(see illustration)**. Plug the brake hose immediately to keep contaminants and air out of the brake system and to prevent losing any more brake fluid than is necessary. **Note:** *If you are simply removing the caliper for access to other components, leave the brake hose connected and suspend the caliper with a length of wire - don't let it hang by the hose).*

3   Remove the caliper mounting bolts and detach the caliper from the mounting bracket.

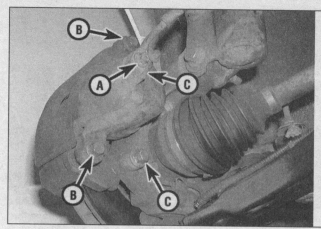

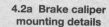

4.2a Brake caliper mounting details

A   *Brake hose banjo fitting bolt*
B   *Caliper mounting bolts*
C   *Caliper mount-to-steering knuckle bolts (don't remove these unless the brake disc must be removed)*

Installation

4   Installation is the reverse of removal. Don't forget to use new sealing washers on each side of the brake hose banjo fitting and be sure to tighten the banjo fitting bolt and the caliper mounting bolts to the torque listed in this Chapter's Specifications.

5   Bleed the brake system (see Section 11). **Note:** *If the brake hose was not disconnected, bleeding won't be required.* Make sure there are no leaks from the hose connections. Test the brakes carefully before returning the vehicle to normal service.

5   Brake disc - inspection, removal and installation

Inspection

Refer to illustrations 5.2, 5.3, 5.4a, 5.4b and 5.5

1   Loosen the wheel lug nuts, raise the vehicle and support it securely on jackstands. Remove the wheel and install the lug nuts to hold the disc in place. **Note:** *If the lug nuts don't contact the disc when screwed on all the way, install washers under them.*

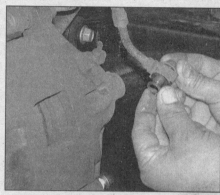

4.2b There is a sealing washer on either side of the brake hose banjo fitting; be sure to replace these with new ones when reconnecting the hose

2   Remove the brake caliper. It isn't necessary to disconnect the brake hose. After removing the caliper bolts, suspend the caliper out of the way with a piece of wire **(see illustration)**.

3   Visually inspect the disc surface for score marks and other damage **(see illustration)**. Light scratches and shallow grooves

5.2 Hang the caliper out of the way with a piece of wire - don't let it hang by the brake hose!

5.3 The brake pads on this vehicle were obviously neglected, as they wore down completely and cut deep grooves into the disc - wear this severe means the disc must be replaced

9

5.4a To check disc runout, mount a dial indicator as shown and rotate the disc

5.4b Using a swirling motion, remove the glaze from the disc with sandpaper or emery cloth

5.5 Use a micrometer to measure disc thickness

are normal after use and may not always be detrimental to brake operation, but deep scoring requires disc removal and refinishing by an automotive machine shop. Be sure to check both sides of the disc. If pulsating has been noticed during application of the brakes, suspect disc runout.

4   To check disc runout, place a dial indicator at a point about 1/2-inch from the outer edge of the disc **(see illustration)**. Set the indicator to zero and turn the disc. The indicator reading should not exceed the specified allowable runout limit. If it does, the disc should be refinished by an automotive machine shop. **Note:** *When replacing the brake pads, it's a good idea to resurface the discs regardless of the dial indicator reading, as this will impart a smooth finish and ensure a perfectly flat surface, eliminating any brake pedal pulsation or other undesirable symptoms related to questionable discs. At the very least, if you elect not to have the discs resurfaced, remove the glaze from the surface with emery cloth or sandpaper, using a swirling motion* **(see illustration)**.

5   It's absolutely critical that the disc not be machined to a thickness under the specified minimum thickness. The minimum wear

(or discard) thickness is cast into the disc. The disc thickness can be checked with a micrometer **(see illustration)**.

Removal

6   Remove the two caliper mounting bracket bolts and detach the mounting bracket **(see illustration 4.2a)**.

7   Remove the lug nuts which you installed to hold the disc in place and slide the disc off the hub.

Installation

8   Place the disc in position over the threaded studs.

9   Install the mounting bracket and tighten the bolts to the torque listed in this Chapter's Specifications. Install the brake pads.

10   Install the caliper onto the mounting bracket, tightening the bolts to the torque listed in this Chapter's Specifications.

11   Install the wheel and lug nuts. Lower the vehicle and tighten the lug nuts to the torque listed in the Chapter 1 Specifications. Depress the brake pedal a few times to bring the brake pads into contact with the disc. Bleeding won't be necessary unless the

brake hose was disconnected from the caliper. Check the operation of the brakes carefully before driving the vehicle.

---

6   Drum brake shoes - replacement

Refer to illustrations 6.2a, 6.2b, 6.3, 6.4a through 6.4o, 6.5a and 6.5b

Warning: *Drum brake shoes must be replaced on both wheels at the same time - never replace the shoes on only one wheel. Also, the dust created by the brake system is harmful to your health. Never blow it out with compressed air and don't inhale any of it. An approved filtering mask should be worn when working on the brakes. Do not, under any circumstances, use petroleum-based solvents to clean brake parts. Use brake system cleaner only!*

1   Loosen the wheel lug nuts, raise the rear of the vehicle and support it securely on jackstands. Block the front wheels to keep the vehicle from rolling. Remove the wheels.

2   Release the parking brake and remove the brake drums **(see illustration)**. If the shoes have worn into the drum, preventing

6.2a If the drum is retained by pressed-metal washers, cut them off and discard them (there is no need to reinstall them)

6.2b If the shoes have worn into the drum, preventing its removal, remove the plug from the backing plate and push the parking brake lever off its stop (this will retract the brake shoes slightly)

6.3 Before removing any internal drum brake components, wash them off with brake system cleaner and allow them to dry - position a drain pan under the brake to catch the residue - **DO NOT USE COMPRESSED AIR TO BLOW THE DUST FROM THE PARTS**

6.4a Drum brake components (left side shown)

1	Leading shoe	5	Adjuster actuator
2	Parking brake lever	6	Adjuster screw assembly
3	Actuator spring	7	Trailing shoe
4	Wheel cylinder	8	Retractor spring

drum removal, remove the access plug from the backing plate, insert a small screwdriver through the hole and pry the parking brake lever from its stop **(see illustration)**.

3   Before disassembling anything, clean off the brake assembly with brake system cleaner **(see illustration)**.

4   Follow the accompanying illustrations for the actual shoe replacement procedure **(see illustrations 6.4a through 6.4o)**. Be sure to stay in order and read the caption under each illustration. **Note:** *All four rear brake shoes must be replaced at the same time, but to avoid mixing up parts, work on only one brake assembly at a time.*

6.4b Detach the spring from the adjuster actuator

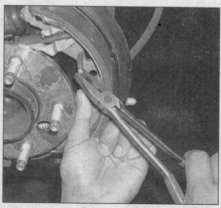

6.4c Pull the retractor spring out of its hole in the trailing shoe . . .

6.4d . . . and also from the leading shoe

6.4e Remove the trailing shoe and adjuster actuator, then the adjuster screw assembly (arrow)

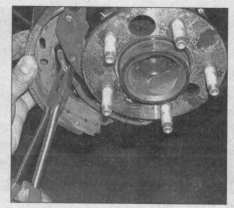

6.4f Pull the retractor spring out of the way, then remove the leading shoe and parking brake lever

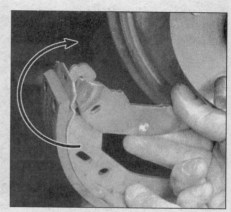

6.4g Unhook the parking brake lever from the leading shoe

9

6.4h Clean the backing plate, then lubricate the shoe contact areas with a thin film of high-temperature grease

6.4i Connect the parking brake lever to the leading shoe, position the shoe on the backing plate and install the end of the retractor spring in its hole

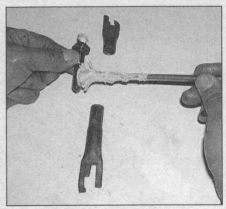

6.4j Clean the adjuster screw assembly, then lubricate the threads and socket end with high-temperature grease

6.4k Install the adjuster screw assembly, making sure it engages properly with the leading shoe and the parking brake lever

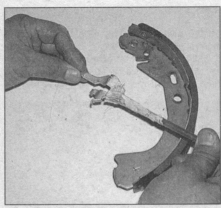

6.4l Lightly lubricate the adjuster actuator . . .

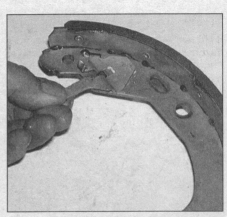

6.4m . . . and install it on the trailing shoe

6.4n Position the trailing shoe on the backing plate, making sure it (and the adjuster actuator) engage properly with the adjuster screw assembly, then insert the retractor spring into its hole in the shoe

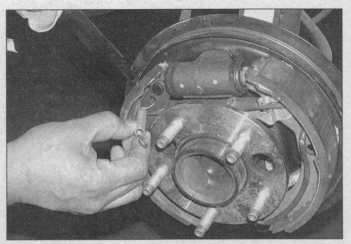

6.4o Insert the actuator spring into its hole in the leading shoe, then stretch it across and connect it to the adjuster actuator

6.5a The maximum permissible diameter is cast into the drum (typical)

6.5b Remove the glaze from the drum surface with sandpaper or emery cloth

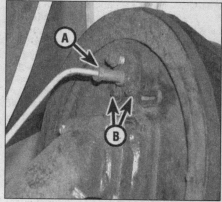

7.4 Unscrew the brake line fitting (A) using a flare-nut wrench to avoid rounding off the corners, then remove the wheel cylinder mounting bolts (B)

5   Before reinstalling the drum it should be checked for cracks, score marks, deep scratches and hard spots, which will appear as small, discolored areas. If the hard spots cannot be removed with emery cloth or if any of the other conditions listed above exist, the drum must be taken to an automotive machine shop to have it resurfaced. **Note:** *Professionals recommend resurfacing the drums whenever a brake job is done. Resurfacing will eliminate the possibility of out-of-round or tapered drums. If the drums are worn so much that they can't be resurfaced without exceeding the maximum allowable diameter (stamped into the drum)* **(see illustration)**, *then new ones will be required. At the very least, if you elect not to have the drums resurfaced, remove the glazing from the surface with emery cloth or sandpaper using a swirling motion* **(see illustration)**.
6   When installing the drum, adjust the brake shoes by turning the star wheel on the adjuster screw until the drum just slips over the shoes. When turning the drum, the shoes should not rub; if they do, remove the drum and back off the star wheel a little bit so they don't. This adjustment is just to get the shoes close to the drum; the brake shoes will self-adjust after you depress the pedal a few times).

7   Wheel cylinder - removal and installation

Refer to illustration 7.4

Removal

1   Raise the rear of the vehicle and support it securely on jackstands. Block the front wheels to keep the vehicle from rolling.
2   Remove the brake shoe assembly (see Section 6).
3   Remove all dirt and foreign material from around the wheel cylinder.
4   Using a flare-nut wrench, unscrew the brake line fitting from the wheel cylinder **(see illustration)**. Don't pull the line away from the wheel cylinder (it could get bent).

5   Remove the wheel cylinder mounting bolts and detach the wheel cylinder from the brake backing plate.

Installation

6   Place the wheel cylinder in position and connect the brake line fitting, being careful not to cross-thread it. Install the mounting bolts, tightening them to the torque listed in this Chapter's Specifications, then tighten the brake line fitting securely.
7   Install the brake shoes (see Section 6).
8   Bleed the brakes (see Section 11).
9   Check the operation of the brakes carefully before driving the vehicle in traffic.

8   Master cylinder - removal and installation

Warning: *On 1999 and earlier models the master cylinder and ABS hydraulic unit/motor pack can be detached from the power brake booster as a single assembly, but the master cylinder itself must not be detached from the hydraulic unit/motor pack. If the master cylinder must be unbolted from the hydraulic unit/motor pack, it must be done at a dealer service department, after the dealer has used a scan tool to relieve tension on the gears*

inside the ABS unit. This procedure can only be performed with the master cylinder/hydraulic unit/motor pack assembly operational. If the master cylinder must be replaced (unbolted from the hydraulic unit/motor pack), have it done by a dealer service department or other qualified repair shop.

Removal

Refer to illustration 8.3
1   Disconnect the cable from the negative battery terminal. **Caution:** *On models equipped with the Theftlock audio system, make sure you have the correct activation code before disconnecting the battery (see the front of this manual).*
2   Unplug the electrical connectors from the Mass Airflow (MAF) sensor and the Intake Air Temperature (IAT) sensor. Detach the air intake duct from the throttle body, then unclip the air filter housing cover and remove the cover and intake duct.
3   Unplug the electrical connector for the fluid level warning switch and, on 1999 and earlier models, the ABS solenoids and motor pack **(see illustration)**.
4   Remove as much fluid as possible from

8.3 Master cylinder mounting details - 1999 and earlier models

1   *Electrical connector for fluid level sensor*
2   *Electrical connectors for the ABS solenoids*
3   *Brake line fittings (two of four shown)*
4   *Mounting nuts*

9

the reservoir with a syringe or suction gun.

5   Place rags under the fittings and pre-pare caps or plastic bags to cover the ends of the lines once they're disconnected. **Caution:** *Brake fluid will damage paint. Cover all painted surfaces and be careful not to spill fluid during this procedure.* Loosen the fit-tings at the ends of the brake lines where they enter the master cylinder or hydraulic unit. To prevent rounding off the flats, use a flare-nut wrench, which wraps around the fit-ting hex.

6   Pull the brake lines away from the mas-ter cylinder or hydraulic unit and plug the ends to prevent contamination.

7   Remove the nuts attaching the master cylinder to the power booster **(see illustra-tion 8.3)**. Pull the master cylinder off the studs to remove it. Again, be careful not to spill the fluid as this is done. Remove and discard the old gasket between the master cylinder and the power brake booster.

Installation

Refer to illustration 8.9

8   Bench bleed the master cylinder before installing it. Mount the master cylinder in a vise, with the jaws of the vise clamping on the mounting flange.

9   Attach a bleeder tube to each outlet port of the master cylinder **(see illustration)**.

10   Fill the reservoir with brake fluid of the recommended type (see Chapter 1).

11   Slowly push the pistons into the master cylinder (a large Phillips screwdriver can be used for this) - air will be expelled from the pressure chambers and into the reservoir. Because the tubes are submerged in fluid, air can't be drawn back into the master cylinder when you release the pistons.

12   Repeat the procedure until no more air bubbles are present.

13   Remove the bleed tubes, one at a time, and install plugs in the open ports to prevent fluid leakage and air from entering. Install the reservoir cap.

14   Install the master cylinder over the studs on the power brake booster and tighten the attaching nuts only finger tight at this time. Don't forget to use a new gasket.

15   Thread the brake line fittings into the master cylinder. Since the master cylinder is still a bit loose, it can be moved slightly so the fittings thread in easily. Don't strip the threads as the fittings are tightened.

16   Tighten the mounting nuts to the torque listed in this Chapter's Specifications. Tighten the brake line fittings securely.

17   Fill the master cylinder reservoir with fluid, then bleed the entire brake system (see Section 11). **Warning:** *If you do not have a firm brake pedal at the end of the bleeding procedure, or have any doubts as to the effectiveness of the brake system, DO NOT drive the vehicle. Have it towed to a dealer service department or other qualified repair shop for diagnosis.*

18   Check the operation of the brake sys-tem carefully before driving the vehicle.

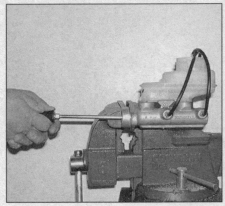

8.9 The best way to bleed air from the master cylinder before installing it on the vehicle is with bleeder tubes that direct brake fluid into the reservoir during bleeding

9   Master cylinder reservoir/O-rings - replacement

Note: *The brake fluid reservoir can be replaced separately from the master cylinder body if it becomes damaged. If there is leak-age between the reservoir and the master cylinder body, the O-rings on the reservoir can be replaced.*

1   Remove the master cylinder (see Sec-tion 8).

2   Using a hammer and a small punch, drive out the roll pins that retain the reservoir to the master cylinder.

3   Pull the reservoir out of the master cylin-der body.

4   If you are simply replacing the O-rings, carefully pry the old O-rings off and install new ones.

5   Lubricate the reservoir O-rings with clean brake fluid, then press the reservoir into place on the master cylinder body and secure it with new roll pins.

6   Refill the reservoir with the recom-mended brake fluid (see Chapter 1) and check for leaks.

7   Reinstall the master cylinder (see Sec-tion 8).

9   Bleed the brake system (see Section 11).

10   Brake hoses and lines - inspection and replacement

Inspection

1   About every six months, with the vehicle raised and supported securely on jackstands, the rubber hoses which connect the steel brake lines with the front and rear brake assemblies should be inspected for cracks, chafing of the outer cover, leaks, blisters and other damage. These are important and vul-nerable parts of the brake system and inspection should be complete. A light and mirror will be helpful for a thorough check. If

10.3 Using a flare-nut wrench, unscrew the threaded fitting on the brake line (1), then pry the U-clip (2) off the end of the hose and separate the hose from the bracket

a hose exhibits any of the above conditions, replace it with a new one.

Replacement

Flexible brake hose

Refer to illustration 10.3

2   Loosen the wheel lug nuts, raise the vehicle and support it securely on jackstands. Remove the wheel.

3   At the bracket, unscrew the brake line fitting from the hose **(see illustration)**. Use a flare-nut wrench to prevent rounding off the corners. If the bracket begins to bend, hold the hose fitting with an open-end wrench.

4   Remove the U-clip from the female fit-ting at the bracket with a pair of pliers, then pass the hose through the bracket.

5   At the caliper end of the hose, remove the banjo bolt, then separate the hose from the caliper. Note that there are two sealing washers on either side of the banjo fitting - they should be replaced with new ones dur-ing installation.

6   To install the hose, connect the fitting to the caliper with the banjo bolt and new seal-ing washers.

7   Route the hose into the frame bracket, making sure it isn't twisted, then connect the brake line fitting, starting the threads by hand. Install the U-clip, then tighten the fitting securely.

8   Bleed the caliper (see Section 11).

9   Install the wheel and lug nuts, lower the vehicle and tighten the lug nuts to the torque listed in the Chapter 1 Specifications.

Metal brake lines

10   When replacing brake lines, be sure to use the correct parts. Don't use copper tub-ing for any brake system components. Pur-chase steel brake lines from a dealer or auto parts store.

11   Prefabricated brake line, with the tube ends already flared and fittings installed, is available at auto parts stores and dealer parts departments. These lines must be bent to the

11.9 When bleeding the ABS hydraulic modulator, start with the rear bleeder (A), then the front bleeder (B) - 1997 through 1999 models only

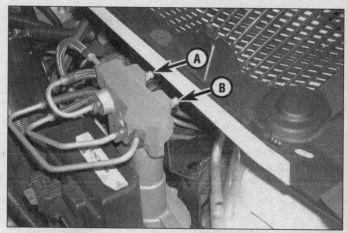

11.14 When bleeding the Traction Control System modulator, bleed the right side first (A), then the left side (B)

proper shapes using a tubing bender.

12   When installing the new line, make sure it's securely supported in the brackets and has plenty of clearance between moving or hot components.

13   After installation, check the master cylinder fluid level and add fluid as necessary. Bleed the brake system (see Section 11) and test the brakes carefully before driving the vehicle in traffic.

11   Brake hydraulic system - bleeding

Warning: *Wear eye protection when bleeding the brake system. If the fluid comes in contact with your eyes, immediately rinse them with water and seek medical attention.*
Note: *Bleeding the hydraulic system is necessary to remove any air that manages to find its way into the system when it's been opened during removal and installation of a hose, line, caliper or master cylinder.*

1   You'll have to bleed the system at all four brakes if air has entered it due to low fluid level, or if the brake lines have been disconnected at the master cylinder.

2   If a brake line was disconnected only at a wheel, then only that caliper or wheel cylinder must be bled.

3   If a brake line is disconnected at a fitting located between the master cylinder and any of the brakes, the entire system must be bled.

4   Remove any residual vacuum from the brake power booster by applying the brake several times with the engine off.

5   Remove the master cylinder reservoir cap and fill the reservoir with brake fluid. Reinstall the cap. **Note:** *Check the fluid level often during the bleeding operation and add fluid as necessary to prevent the fluid level from falling low enough to allow air bubbles into the master cylinder.*

6   Have an assistant on hand, as well as a supply of new brake fluid, a clear plastic con-

tainer partially filled with clean brake fluid, a length of clear tubing to fit over the bleeder valves and a wrench to open and close the bleeder valves.

7   If it is necessary to bleed the entire system, begin the bleeding procedure with the next Step. If it is only necessary to bleed one caliper or wheel cylinder, skip to Step 23.

8   Before bleeding the entire system, sit in the driver's seat and:

a) *Take your foot off the brake pedal.*
b) *Start the engine and let it run for a minimum of 10 seconds. Watch the amber ABS light on the dash.*
c) *If the light comes on and does not turn off after 10 seconds, have the vehicle towed to a dealer service department or other qualified repair shop. A scan tool will have to be used to diagnose the ABS system.*
d) *If the ABS light goes off after three seconds or so, turn off the ignition.*
e) *Repeat paragraphs a) through d) one more time, then proceed with the bleeding operation.*

1999 and earlier models

Refer to illustrations 11.9 and 11.14

9   Fill the master cylinder fluid reservoir with the recommended fluid, then prime the ABS hydraulic modulator. Connect the bleeder hose to the rear bleeder valve on the modulator **(see illustration)** and place the other end into a container partially filled with clean brake fluid. Make sure the end of the hose is submerged.

10   Open the bleeder valve slowly (approximately 1/2 to 3/4 turn), then have an assistant depress the brake pedal to approximately 3/4 of its full stroke, allowing fluid and air to flow out, then close the bleeder valve.

11   Repeat Step 10 until no air bubbles are present in the fluid. Tighten the bleeder valve securely.

12   Move the bleeder hose to the front bleeder valve **(see illustration 11.9)** and perform Steps 10 and 11.

13   Recheck the fluid level in the master cylinder reservoir, adding fluid as necessary.

14   If the vehicle is equipped with a Traction Control System (TCS), the TCS modulator must now be primed. Connect the bleeder hose to the right bleeder valve on the modulator **(see illustration)** and place the other end into a container partially filled with clean brake fluid. Make sure the end of the hose is submerged.

15   Open the bleeder valve slowly (approximately 1/2 to 3/4 turn) and have an assistant depress the brake pedal to approximately 3/4 of its full stroke, allowing fluid and air to flow out, then close the bleeder valve.

16   Repeat Step 15 until no air bubbles are present in the fluid. Tighten the bleeder valve securely.

17   Move the bleeder hose to the left bleeder valve **(see illustration 11.14)** and perform Steps 15 and 16.

18   Recheck the fluid level in the master cylinder reservoir, adding fluid as necessary. Proceed to bleed the remainder of the system (beginning with Step 23).

2000 and later models

19   Fill the master cylinder fluid reservoir with the recommended fluid, place plenty of rags under the ABS hydraulic modulator, then prime the modulator. Beginning with the first brake line fitting on the left (driver's) side of the modulator, slowly loosen the fitting using a flare-nut wrench and have an assistant depress the brake pedal to approximately 3/4 of its full stroke, allowing fluid and air to flow out, then tighten the fitting.

20   Repeat Step 19 until no air bubbles are present in the fluid. Tighten the fitting securely.

21   Repeat Steps 19 and 20 on the remainder of the fittings on the modulator, in order from left to right.

22   Recheck the fluid level in the master cylinder reservoir, adding fluid as necessary. Proceed to bleed the remainder of the system (beginning with Step 23).

9

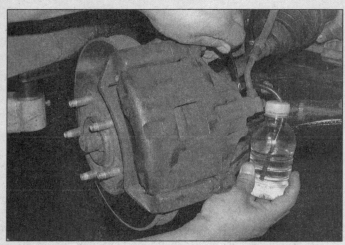

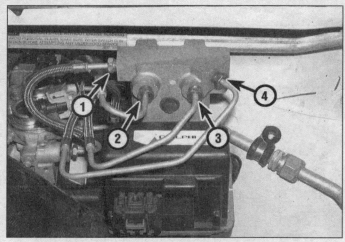

11.26 When bleeding the brakes, a hose is connected to the bleeder valve at the caliper or wheel cylinder and then submerged in brake fluid - air will be seen as bubbles in the tube and container (all air must be expelled before moving to the next wheel)

11.38 After bleeding the TCS modulator, repeat the bleeding procedure to each fitting in the order shown (1997 through 1999 models with TCS only)

All models

Refer to illustration 11.26

23   Check the fluid level in the master cylinder reservoir, adding fluid as necessary. Raise the vehicle and support it securely on jackstands.

24   Bleed the brakes at the wheels in the following sequence:

> Right rear
> Left front
> Left rear
> Right front

25   Beginning at the first wheel in the bleeding sequence, loosen the bleeder valve slightly, then tighten it to a point where it's snug but can still be loosened quickly and easily.

26   Place one end of the tubing over the bleeder valve and submerge the other end in brake fluid in the container **(see illustration)**.

27   Have the assistant depress the brake pedal slowly, holding it in the depressed position.

28   While the pedal is held down, open the bleeder valve just enough to allow a flow of fluid to leave the valve. Watch for air bubbles to exit the submerged end of the tube. When the fluid flow slows after a couple of seconds, close the valve and have your assistant release the pedal.

29   Repeat Steps 27 and 28 until no more air is seen leaving the tube, then tighten the bleeder valve.

30   Perform Steps 26 through 29 at the remaining wheels, following the bleeding sequence. Be sure to check the fluid in the master cylinder reservoir frequently.

31   Refill the master cylinder with fluid at the end of the operation. **Warning:** *Never use old brake fluid. It contains moisture which can cause the fluid to boil, rendering the brake system inoperative.*

32   If you're working on a 1997 through 1999 model, proceed to the next Step. If

you're working on a 2000 or later model, proceed to Step 42.

1999 and earlier models

Refer to illustration 11.38

33   Bleed the ABS hydraulic module once again (see Steps 9 through 13).

34   Place plenty of rags under the ABS hydraulic modulator, then bleed the modulator at the brake line fittings threaded into it. Beginning with the brake line fitting closest to the front of the vehicle, slowly loosen the fitting using a flare-nut wrench and have an assistant depress the brake pedal to approximately 3/4 of its full stroke, allowing fluid and air to flow out, then tighten the fitting.

35   Repeat Step 34 until no air bubbles are present in the fluid. Tighten the fitting securely.

36   Repeat Steps 34 and 35 to the remainder of the fittings on the modulator, in order from front to rear. Recheck the fluid level in the master cylinder reservoir, adding fluid as necessary.

37   If the vehicle is not equipped with a Traction Control System, proceed to Step 42. If the vehicle is equipped with a Traction Control System (TCS), bleed the TCS modulator by following Steps 14 through 17.

38   Fill the master cylinder fluid reservoir with the recommended fluid and place plenty of rags under the TCS modulator. Beginning with the brake line fitting on the right (passenger's) side of the modulator **(see illustration)**, slowly loosen the fitting using a flare-nut wrench and have an assistant depress the brake pedal to approximately 3/4 of its full stroke, allowing fluid and air to flow out, then tighten the fitting.

39   Repeat Step 38 until no air bubbles are present in the fluid. Tighten the fitting securely.

40   Repeat Steps 38 and 39 on the remainder of the fittings on the modulator, in order from right to left.

41   Recheck the fluid level in the master cylinder reservoir, adding fluid as necessary.

All models

42   Check the operation of the brakes. Turn the ignition key to the On position, then Off (don't start the engine). The pedal should feel solid when depressed, with no sponginess. Now start the engine and recheck the pedal travel and feel.

43   If the pedal travel or feel is not satisfactory, take your foot off the brake pedal and start the engine. Let the engine run for a minimum of 10 seconds, then turn it off (don't depress the pedal during this time). Repeat this Step 5 times, which should dislodge any air trapped in the ABS hydraulic modulator, then repeat the entire bleeding procedure.

44   Road test the vehicle in a safe area before returning it to normal service. **Warning:** *Do not operate the vehicle if the brake pedal does not have a firm feel to it, or if the ABS warning light remains on, or if you're in doubt about the effectiveness of the brake system.*

---

12   Power brake booster - check, removal and installation

Refer to illustrations 12.15 and 12.16

Operating check

1   Depress the pedal and start the engine. If the pedal goes down slightly, operation is normal.

2   Depress the brake pedal several times with the engine running and make sure that there is no change in the pedal reserve distance.

Airtightness check

3   Start the engine and turn it off after one or two minutes. Depress the brake pedal sev-

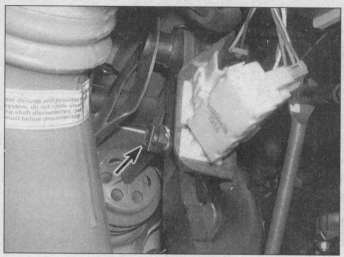

12.15 Pry off the clip retaining the booster pushrod to the pin on the brake pedal

12.16 Unscrew the booster mounting nuts (three of four shown)

eral times slowly. If the pedal goes down farther the first time but gradually rises after the second or third depression, the booster is airtight.

4   Depress the brake pedal while the engine is running, then stop the engine with the pedal depressed. If there is no change in the pedal reserve travel after holding the pedal for 30 seconds, the booster is airtight.

Removal

5   Relieve the fuel system pressure (see Chapter 4).

6   Disconnect the cable from the negative terminal of the battery, then refer to Chapter 12 and disable the airbag system. **Caution:** *On models equipped with the "Theftlock" audio system, be sure you have the correct activation code before performing any procedure which requires disconnecting the battery (see the front of this manual).*

7   Remove the air filter housing (see Chapter 4).

8   Remove the fasteners securing the coolant bypass pipe to the rear of the engine (the pipe will have to be moved slightly to allow booster removal).

9   Remove the master cylinder (see Section 8).

10   Detach the vacuum hose from the booster.

11   Unbolt the throttle cable bracket from the throttle body (see Chapter 4).

12   Unbolt the transaxle dipstick tube from the engine.

13   Detach the fuel feed and return lines from the fuel rail. Also detach the vapor return line from its pipe (see Chapter 4).

14   Remove the left-side under-dash panel.

15   Remove the pushrod retaining clip **(see illustration)** and slip the pushrod off the pin.

16   Remove the four nuts holding the brake booster to the firewall **(see illustration)**.

17   Slide the booster straight out from the firewall until the studs clear the holes and

maneuver the booster and gasket from the engine compartment.

Installation

18   Installation is the reverse of removal. Be sure to tighten the booster mounting nuts and the master cylinder mounting nuts to the torque values listed in this Chapter's Specifications.

13   Brake pedal travel - check

1   The brake pedal is not adjustable, but the travel should be checked if the pedal seems low. You'll need a tape measure, yardstick or ruler for this procedure.

2   Depress the pedal a few times to deplete the vacuum reserve in the power brake booster.

3   Measure the position of the pedal at rest. You can either measure from the floor to the pedal or from the pedal to the steering wheel. Record your reading.

4   Now, depress the pedal (exerting approximately 100 lbs. of force) and measure how far the pedal has traveled. Compare your findings with the measurement listed in this Chapter's Specifications.

5   If the pedal travel is excessive, check for air in the system (bleed the brakes - see Section 11). If that doesn't cure the problem, remove the rear brake shoes and make sure the adjuster screw assemblies are operating properly (see Section 6). Also check the condition of the brake shoes, replacing them if they're worn excessively.

14   Parking brake - adjustment

Refer to illustration 14.5

1   Raise the rear of the vehicle and support it securely on jackstands. Block the front

14.5 The parking brake cable equalizer/adjuster nut is located at the rear axle beam

wheels to prevent the vehicle from rolling.

2   Place the shift lever in Neutral.

3   Apply the parking brake pedal three clicks.

4   Attempt to turn each rear wheel - if both wheels are difficult to turn, the parking brake is sufficiently adjusted. Release the parking brake to make sure the wheels rotate freely.

5   If either wheel can be turned easily, make sure the brake shoes (rear drum brake models) or parking brake shoes (rear disc brake models) are properly adjusted. Then, tighten the adjusting nut on the parking brake cable equalizer until both rear wheels are difficult to turn (or can't be turned) **(see illustration)**.

6   Release the parking brake and make sure both rear wheels rotate freely.

7   On models with rear disc brakes, make sure the parking brake levers on the brake backing plates return to their stops. If they don't, adjust the parking brake shoes so they do.

8   Lower the vehicle and check the operation of the parking brake.

9

15   Parking brake cables - replacement

Front cable

1   Release the parking brake. Remove the left-side under-dash panel.
2   Remove the left-side sill plate and peel back the carpet.
3   Raise the vehicle and support it securely on jackstands.
4   Loosen the parking brake cable adjusting nut at the equalizer, then detach the left rear cable from the equalizer.
5   Detach the end of the front cable from the cable connector and detach the cable from the equalizer.
6   Unbolt the cable brackets from the floorpan.
7   Detach the cable end from the parking brake pedal.
8   Compress the tangs on the cable casing and detach the casing from the parking brake pedal bracket.
9   Push the cable grommet through the hole in floorpan and remove the cable.
10   Installation is the reverse of removal. Make sure the grommet seats properly in the floorpan.
11   Adjust the parking brake (see Section 14).

Rear cable(s)

12   Release the parking brake.
13   Loosen the rear wheel lug nuts, raise the rear of the vehicle and support it securely on jackstands. Block the front wheels to prevent the vehicle from rolling. **Note:** *If you're working on a model with rear disc brakes, it isn't necessary to remove the wheel(s).*
14   Loosen the parking brake cable adjuster nut and disconnect the front parking brake cable from the equalizer at the rear of the vehicle.
15   Depress the tangs on the cable retainer and detach the cable from the bracket.

Disc brake models

16   Detach the cable from the bracket, unhook the cable end from the actuator on the backing plate and remove the cable.

Drum brake models

17   If you're working on a model with drum brakes, remove the brake shoes (see Section 6).
18   Pull back the spring and detach the cable end from the parking brake lever.
19   Depress the tangs of the cable retainer, then pass the cable through the backing plate.

All models

20   Installation is the reverse of the removal procedure. Adjust the parking brake (see Section 14).
21   Tighten the wheel lug nuts to the torque listed in the Chapter 1 Specifications.

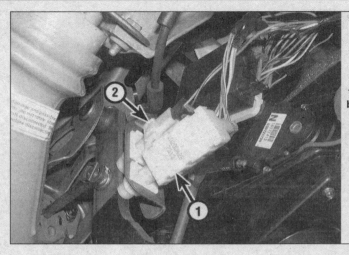

17.1 Location of the brake light switch (1) and the cruise control switch (2)

16   Parking brake shoes - replacement

Note: *This procedure only applies to models with rear disc brakes.*

1   Loosen the rear wheel lug nuts, raise the rear of the vehicle and support it securely on jackstands. Remove the wheels.
2   Remove the brake caliper (see Section 4) and the brake disc (see Section 5).
3   Disconnect the parking brake cable from the bracket and the actuator lever.
4   Unbolt the parking brake cable bracket.
5   Remove the rear hub and bearing assembly (see Chapter 10).
6   Remove the parking brake actuator and the parking brake shoe.
7   When installing the new shoe and lining assembly, turn the adjuster screw until the shoe lining just drags on the braking surface inside the disc. Then remove the disc and back-off the adjuster screw until the shoe lining doesn't drag when the disc is installed and turned.
8   Installation is otherwise the reverse of the removal procedure. Be sure to tighten the hub and bearing assembly bolts to the torque listed in the Chapter 10 Specifications, the caliper mounting bolts and mounting bracket bolts to the torque listed in the Chapter 9 Specifications, and the wheel lug nuts to the torque listed in the Chapter 1 Specifications.

17   Brake light switch - check, adjustment and replacement

Refer to illustration 17.1

Check

1   The brake light switch is located on a bracket near the top of the brake pedal **(see illustration).** The switch activates the brake lights at the rear of the vehicle when the pedal is depressed.
2   If the brake lights are inoperative, check the fuse first (see Chapter 12).
3   If the fuse is good, try adjusting the switch (see Steps 9 through 11).
4   If the brake lights still don't work, check for voltage to the switch on the feed wire (refer to the wiring diagrams at the end of this manual for the proper color wire to check). If no voltage is present, repair the wire between the switch and the fuse box.
5   If voltage is present, depress the brake pedal and check for voltage at the output wire terminal (again, refer to the wiring diagrams). If no voltage is present, replace the switch.
6   If voltage is present, check for power on the brake light wires at the tail light housings (with the brake pedal depressed). If voltage is not present, repair the circuit between the switch and the brake lights.
7   If voltage is present, check for a bad ground; using a jumper wire connected to a good ground, probe the ground wire terminal at the tail light connector. If the brake lights go on, repair the ground circuit (follow the ground wire from the tail light housing).
8   Keep in mind that the brake light bulbs *could* be burned out, but the likelihood of all the bulbs being burned out is very slim.

Adjustment

9   Remove left-side under-dash panel.
10   With the brake pedal depressed, push the switch into the clip. Note that audible clicks will be heard as this is done.
11   Pull the brake pedal all the way to the rear, against the pedal stop until the clicking sounds can no longer be heard. This action will automatically move the switch the proper amount and no further adjustment will be required.

Replacement

12   Remove left-side under-dash panel, if not already done.
13   Unplug the electrical connectors from the switch.
14   Pull the switch straight back and out of its clip.
15   To install the new switch, reverse the removal procedure, then adjust the switch as described in Steps 10 and 11.

Chapter 10
Suspension and steering systems

Contents

Specifications

Torque specifications

Front suspension

	Ft-lbs (unless otherwise indicated)
Balljoint-to-steering knuckle nut	40
Balljoint (replacement)-to-control arm nuts/bolts	50
Control arm	
Rear pivot bolt/nut	83
Front vertical bushing bolt	83
Hub and bearing assembly-to-steering knuckle bolts	96
Stabilizer bar	
Link nuts	17
Bushing clamp bolts	35
Strut assembly	
Strut-to-steering knuckle nuts	90
Strut-to-body nuts	30
Strut damper shaft nut	63

Rear suspension

Hub and bearing assembly retaining bolts	63
Shock absorber bolts/nuts	63
Trailing arm-to-body bolt	162
Track bar bolts/nuts	92

Steering

Airbag module-to-steering wheel bolts (1997 Venture and Silhouette)	168 in-lbs
Intermediate shaft pinch bolts	35
Power steering pump mounting bolts	25
Steering column mounting bolts/nuts	18
Steering gear mounting bolts	59
Steering wheel nut	30
Subframe mounting bolts	133
Tie-rod end-to-steering knuckle nuts	22, plus an additional 120-degrees rotation (two flats of the nut)
Wheel lug nuts	See Chapter 1

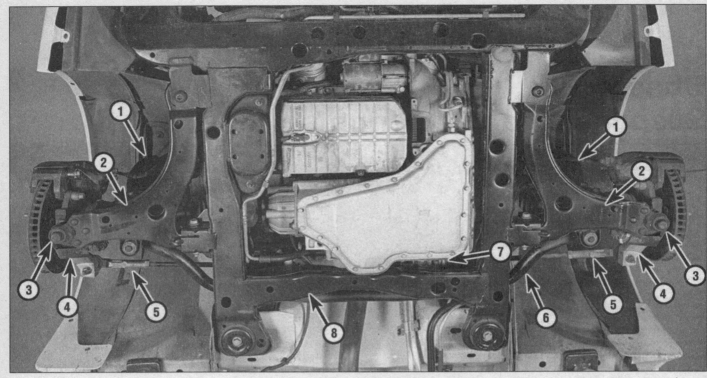

1.1 Front suspension and steering components

1	Strut/coil spring assembly	4	Steering knuckle	7	Steering gear
2	Control arm	5	Tie-rod end	8	Subframe
3	Balljoint	6	Stabilizer bar		

1.2 Rear suspension components

1	Shock absorber	2	Coil spring	3	Rear axle beam	4	Track bar

2.2 To mark the relationship of the strut to the steering knuckle, paint or scribe around the strut-to-knuckle bolt heads

2.3 To remove the strut-to-knuckle bolts, drive them out with a hammer and brass punch

1   General information

Refer to illustrations 1.1 and 1.2

The front suspension is a MacPherson strut design **(see illustration)**. The upper ends of the struts are attached to the body; the lower ends of the struts are bolted to the steering knuckles. The lower ends of the steering knuckles are attached to the control arms by balljoints. The inner ends of the control arms are attached to the subframe. A stabilizer bar reduces body lean during cornering. The stabilizer bar is attached to the subframe by a pair of bushing clamps and to the control arms by link bolts.

The rear suspension features a beam-type axle with coil springs and shock absorbers. The axle beam is connected to the floorpan by integral trailing arms. A track bar locates the axle beam laterally **(see illustration)**.

The rack-and-pinion steering gear, which is located behind the engine/transaxle assembly, is bolted to the suspension subframe. The steering gear turns the steering knuckles via a pair of tie-rod assemblies, each of which consists of an inner tie-rod and a tie-rod end. The inner tie-rods are attached to the steering gear; the outer tie-rods, or tie-rod ends, are attached to the steering knuckles. All models are equipped with power steering.
Warning: *Whenever any of the suspension or steering fasteners are loosened or removed, they must be inspected and, if necessary, replaced with new ones of the same part number or of original equipment quality and design. Torque specifications must be followed for proper reassembly and component retention. Never attempt to heat or straighten any suspension or steering components. Instead, replace any bent or damaged part with a new one.*
Note: *On models equipped with the Theftlock audio system, be sure you have the correct activation code before performing any procedure which requires disconnecting the battery.*

2   Strut/coil spring assembly (front) - removal, inspection and installation

Removal

Refer to illustrations 2.2, 2.3 and 2.5

1   Loosen the wheel lug nuts, raise the front of the vehicle and support it securely on jackstands. Apply the parking brake and block the rear wheels to keep the vehicle from rolling off the jackstands. Remove the wheel.
2   Mark the strut-to-steering knuckle relationship by making a line around the strut-to-steering knuckle bolt heads **(see illustration)**.
3   Remove the nuts from the strut-to-knuckle bolts and knock the bolts out with a brass punch and a hammer **(see illustration)**.
4   Separate the strut from the steering knuckle. Be careful not to overextend the inner CV joint or stretch the brake hose. If necessary, support the control arm with a jack.
5   Have an assistant support the strut and spring, then remove the strut upper mounting nuts **(see illustration)**. **Note:** *If you are removing the right-side strut, you may want to remove the windshield wiper linkage (it will allow better access to the nuts) (see Chapter 12).* Remove the strut and spring assembly.

Inspection

6   Check the strut body for leaking fluid, dents, cracks and other obvious damage which would warrant repair or replacement.
7   Check the coil spring for chips and cracks in the spring coating (this will cause premature spring failure due to corrosion). Inspect the spring seat for hardening, cracks and general deterioration.
8   If wear or damage is evident, replace the strut and/or coil spring as necessary (see Section 3).

Installation

9   Guide the strut assembly up into the fenderwell and insert the upper mounting studs through the holes in the shock tower. Once the studs protrude from the shock tower, install the nuts so the strut won't fall back through. This may require an assistant, since the strut is quite heavy and awkward.
10   Slide the steering knuckle into the strut flange and insert the two bolts. Install the nuts, align the marks you made prior to disassembly and tighten the nuts to the torque listed in this Chapter's Specifications.
11   Install the wheel, lower the vehicle and tighten the wheel lug nuts to the torque listed in the Chapter 1 Specifications.
12   Tighten the upper mounting nuts and bolt to the torque listed in this Chapter's Specifications.
13   Drive the vehicle to a dealer service department or an alignment shop to have the front wheel alignment checked and, if necessary, adjusted (this is only necessary if the strut has been modified for camber adjustment).

10

2.5 Remove the strut upper mounting nuts while supporting the strut assembly (DO NOT remove the large center nut)

3.3a Mark the relationship of the coil spring to the upper spring seat and insulator and to the strut mount . . .

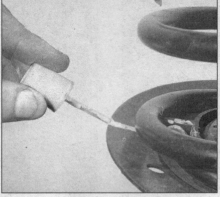

3.3b . . . and to the lower spring seat

3.4 Following the tool manufacturer's instructions, install the spring compressor on the spring and compress it sufficiently to relieve all pressure from the upper spring seat

3 Strut/coil spring - replacement

1   If the struts or coil springs exhibit the telltale signs of wear (leaking fluid, loss of damping capability, chipped, sagging or cracked coil springs) explore all options before beginning any work. The strut assemblies are not serviceable and must be replaced if a problem develops. However, strut assemblies complete with springs may be available on an exchange basis, which eliminates much time and work. Whichever route you choose to take, check on the cost and availability of parts before disassembling your vehicle. **Warning:** *Disassembling a strut is potentially dangerous and utmost attention must be directed to the job, or serious injury may result. Use only a high-quality spring compressor and carefully follow the manufacturer's instructions furnished with the tool. After removing the coil spring from the strut assembly, set it aside in a safe, isolated area.*

Disassembly

Refer to illustrations 3.3a, 3.3b, 3.4, 3.5, 3.6a, 3.6b, 3.7, 3.8 and 3.9

2   Remove the strut and spring assembly (see Section 2). Mount the strut assembly in a vise. Line the vise jaws with wood or rags to prevent damage to the unit and don't tighten the vise excessively.
3   Mark the relationship of the coil spring to the upper insulator and mount and to the lower seat **(see illustrations)**.
4   Following the tool manufacturer's instructions, install the spring compressor (which can be obtained at most auto parts stores or at equipment rental yards) on the spring and compress it sufficiently to relieve all pressure from the upper spring seat **(see illustration)**. This can be verified by wiggling the spring.
5   Loosen the damper shaft nut **(see illustration)**.
6   Remove the washer and strut mount **(see illustrations)**. Inspect the bearing in the strut mount for smooth operation. If it doesn't turn smoothly, replace the strut mount. Check

the rubber portion of the strut mount for cracking and general deterioration. If there is any separation of the rubber, replace it.
7   Remove the upper spring seat and insulator from the damper shaft **(see illustration)**. Check the insulator for cracking and hard-

3.5 Using a wrench on the damper shaft to prevent it from turning, loosen the damper shaft nut

3.6b . . . and the strut mount; inspect the bearing in the mount for smooth operation and the rubber portion of the mount for cracking and general deterioration. If the bearing doesn't turn smoothly, or if there's any separation of the rubber, replace the mount

ness; replace it if necessary.
8   Remove the rubber jounce bumper and dust shield from the damper shaft **(see illustration)**.

3.6a Remove the washer . . .

3.7 Remove the upper spring seat and insulator from the damper shaft; inspect the insulator for cracking and hardness and, if necessary, replace it

3.8 Remove the rubber jounce bumper and dust shield from the damper shaft

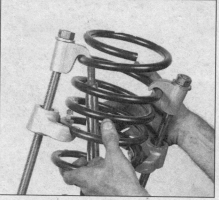

3.9 Carefully lift the compressed spring from the assembly and set it in a safe place; do NOT *place your head near the end of the spring!*

3.12 Place the coil spring onto the lower insulator, with the end of the spring butted against the spring stop on the insulator

3.15a Install the strut mount . . .

3.15b . . . and washer

9   Carefully lift the compressed spring from the assembly **(see illustration)** and set it in a safe place. **Warning:** *Never place your head near the end of the spring!*

10   Check the lower insulator for wear, cracking and hardness and replace it if necessary.

3.16 Hold the damper shaft from turning, then tighten the nut securely (unless you have a special socket with a "window" in it for the back-up wrench, you won't be able to torque the nut until the strut assembly is installed in the vehicle and the vehicle is on the ground)

Reassembly

Refer to illustrations 3.12, 3.15a, 3.15b and 3.16

11   If the lower insulator is being replaced, set it into position with the dropped portion seated in the lowest part of the seat. Extend the damper rod to its full length and install the rubber bumper.

12   Place the coil spring onto the lower insulator, with the end of the spring butted against the spring stop on the insulator **(see illustration)**.

13   Install the dust shield and rubber jounce bumper.

14   Install the upper insulator and spring seat.

15   Install the strut mount and washer **(see illustrations)**. Align the marks made previously.

16   Install the nut and tighten it securely **(see illustration)**.

17   Install the strut/spring assembly (see Section 2).

18   Repeat this entire procedure for the other strut or shock absorber/coil spring assembly.

19   After the vehicle has been lowered to the ground, tighten the damper shaft nuts to the torque listed in this Chapter's Specifications.

4   Steering knuckle and hub - removal and installation

Warning: *Dust created by the brake system is harmful to your health. Never blow it out with compressed air and don't inhale any of it. Do not, under any circumstances, use petroleum-based solvents to clean brake parts. Use brake system cleaner only.*

Removal

1   Loosen the front wheel lug nuts, raise the vehicle and support it securely on jackstands. Remove the wheel.

2   Insert a large screwdriver through the hole in the brake caliper and into the disc cooling vanes, then unscrew the driveaxle/hub nut with a socket and large breaker bar (see Chapter 8, if necessary).

3   Remove the caliper and suspend it out of the way with a piece of wire. Remove the caliper mounting bracket, then lift the disc off the hub (see Chapter 9).

4   Disconnect the electrical connector for the wheel speed sensor **(see illustration 5.5)**.

5   Mark the position of the two strut-to-knuckle bolt heads **(see illustration 2.2)**, then remove the nuts. Don't drive out the bolts at this time.

6   Separate the control arm balljoint from the steering knuckle (see Section 7).

7   Attach a puller to the hub flange and push the driveaxle out of the hub (see Chapter 8). Hang the driveaxle with a piece of wire to prevent damage to the inner CV joint. **Caution:** *Be careful not to pull outward on the driveaxle, as this could separate the inner CV joint components.*

8   Support the knuckle and drive out the two strut-to-knuckle bolts with a hammer and brass punch. Separate the steering knuckle from the strut. If necessary, remove the hub and bearing assembly from the steering knuckle (see Section 5).

10

Installation

9   Position the knuckle in the strut and insert the two splined bolts. Tap the bolts into place and install the nuts, but don't tighten them at this time.

10   Insert the end of the driveaxle into the hub.

11   Connect the control arm balljoint to the steering knuckle and tighten the nut to the torque listed in this Chapter's Specifications. Install a new cotter pin. If necessary, tighten the nut a little more to align the slots in the nut with the hole in the balljoint stud; don't loosen the nut in order to insert the cotter pin.

12   Align the strut-to-knuckle bolt heads with the previously applied marks and tighten the nuts to the torque listed in this Chapter's Specifications.

13   Reconnect the electrical connector for the wheel speed sensor.

14   Install the brake disc, caliper mounting bracket and caliper. Tighten the fasteners to the torque values listed in the Chapter 9 Specifications.

15   Tighten the driveaxle/hub nut to the torque listed in the Chapter 8 Specifications.

16   Install the wheel, lower the vehicle and tighten the lug nuts to the torque listed in the Chapter 1 Specifications.

5   Hub and bearing assembly (front) - removal and installation

Refer to illustrations 5.5, 5.6, 5.7a and 5.7b
Warning: *Dust created by the brake system is harmful to your health. Never blow it out with compressed air and don't inhale any of it. Do not, under any circumstances, use petroleum-based solvents to clean brake parts. Use brake cleaner or denatured alcohol only.*
Note: *The hub and bearing assembly is sealed-for-life. If worn or damaged, it must be replaced as a unit.*

1   Loosen the front wheel lug nuts, raise

5.5 Unplug the electrical connector for the wheel speed sensor, then unclip the connector from its mount

the vehicle and support it securely on jackstands. Remove the wheel.

2   Insert a large screwdriver through the hole in the brake caliper and into the disc cooling vanes, then unscrew the driveaxle/hub nut with a socket and large breaker bar (see Chapter 8, if necessary).

3   Remove the caliper and hang it out of the way with a piece of wire (see Chapter 9).

4   Remove the caliper mounting bracket (see Chapter 9). Pull the disc off the hub.

5   Unplug the electrical connector for the wheel speed sensor **(see illustration)**.

6   Working from the back side of the steering knuckle, remove the hub retaining bolts from the steering knuckle **(see illustration)**. Remove the disc shield.

7   Attach a puller to the hub flange and draw it off the driveaxle **(see illustration)**. The hub assembly should come right out of the steering knuckle, but if it doesn't, tap it from side-to-side to free it. Carefully guide the wiring harness and electrical connector for the wheel speed sensor through the opening between the driveaxle outer CV joint and

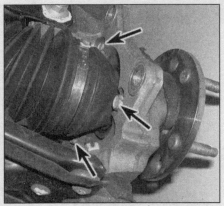

5.6 Remove the hub retaining bolts (arrows); using a swivel socket and a short extension it is possible to remove the bolts without removing the driveaxle (if you don't have a swivel socket or U-joint attachment, you'll have to remove the driveaxle)

the steering knuckle **(see illustration)**. **Caution:** *Be careful not to pull outward on the driveaxle, as this could separate the inner CV joint components.*

8   Clean the mating surfaces on the steering knuckle, bearing flange and knuckle bore.

9   Insert the hub and bearing assembly into the steering knuckle and onto the end of the driveaxle. Position the disc shield and install the three bolts, tightening them to the torque listed in this Chapter's Specifications.

10   Install the brake disc, caliper mounting bracket and caliper (see Chapter 9).

11   Install the driveaxle/hub nut and tighten it to the torque listed in the Chapter 8 Specifications. Prevent the axle from turning by inserting a screwdriver through the caliper and into a disc cooling vane.

12   Install the wheel, lower the vehicle and tighten the lug nuts to the torque listed in the Chapter 1 Specifications.

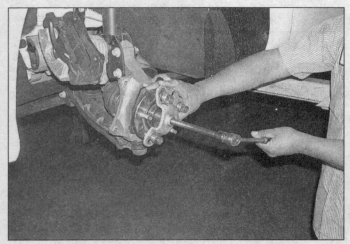

5.7a Use a puller to draw the hub and bearing assembly off the end of the driveaxle

5.7b While removing the hub and bearing assembly, carefully guide the wiring harness and electrical connector for the wheel speed sensor through the opening

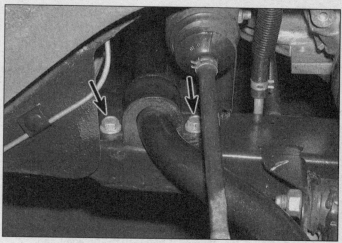

6.2 To disconnect the stabilizer bar from the link bolts that connect it to the control arms, remove the link bolt nut (arrow) from each end; make sure that you note the order in which the bushings, spacers and washers on the link are installed

6.3 To detach the stabilizer bar from the subframe, remove the bushing clamp bolts (arrow) and clamp from each bushing

6 Stabilizer bar and bushings (front) - removal and installation

Refer to illustrations 6.2 and 6.3

Removal

1 Loosen the lug nuts on the left front wheel, raise the front of the vehicle and support it securely on jackstands. Apply the parking brake and remove the wheel.

2 Remove the nuts from the upper ends of the link bolts that connect the stabilizer bar to the control arms **(see illustration)**. Note the order in which the bushings, spacers and washers are installed on the links; they must be installed in exactly the same order in which they are removed.

3 Remove the stabilizer bar bushing clamp bolts and bushing clamps from the upper side of the subframe **(see illustration)**.

4 Guide the stabilizer bar and bushings out through the left side wheel well.

5 Inspect the stabilizer bar bushings for wear and damage and replace them if necessary. To ease installation of the new bushings, spray the inside and outside of the bushings with a silicone-based lubricant (don't use petroleum-based lubricants). Inspect the link bushings, spacers and washers for wear and replace as necessary.

Installation

6 Install the stabilizer bar bushings and clamps, guide the stabilizer bar through the wheel well, over the subframe and into position.

7 Center the stabilizer bar, install the bushing clamp bolts and tighten them to the torque listed in this Chapter's Specifications.

8 Install the spacers, bushings and washers on the links in the same order in which they were removed. Tighten the link nuts to the torque listed in this Chapter's Specifications.

9 Install the wheel and lug nuts. Lower the vehicle and tighten the lug nuts to the torque listed in the Chapter 1 Specifications.

7 Control arm (front) - removal and installation

Refer to illustrations 7.3 and 7.6

Removal

1 Loosen the wheel lug nuts, raise the front of the vehicle and support it securely on jackstands. Apply the parking brake and block the rear wheels to keep the vehicle from rolling off the jackstands. Remove the wheel(s).

2 Disconnect the stabilizer bar link from the control arm being removed (see Section 6).

3 Remove the cotter pin and loosen the balljoint stud-to-steering knuckle nut a few turns **(see illustration)**.

4 Using a balljoint separator, detach the balljoint from the steering knuckle. A "picklefork" -type tool will also work, but keep in mind that a picklefork will damage or destroy the boot, so it should be used only as a last resort.

5 Remove the nut from the ballstud. Using a large prybar positioned between the control arm and steering knuckle, separate the ballstud from the knuckle. **Caution:** *When removing the balljoint from the knuckle, be careful not to overextend the inner CV joint or it may be damaged.*

6 Remove the control arm pivot bolt/nut and the vertical bushing bolt **(see illustration)**. Detach the control arm.

7 The control arm bushings are replaceable, but special tools and expertise are necessary to do the job. Carefully inspect the bushings for hardening, excessive wear and cracks. If they appear to be worn or deteriorated, take the control arm to an automotive machine shop or other repair facility.

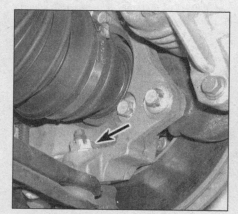

7.3 Remove the cotter pin and loosen - but don't remove - the nut (arrow) from the balljoint stud

7.6 The front end of the control arm is secured to the subframe by a vertical bushing bolt (1); at the rear end it's secured with a pivot bolt and nut (2)

10

8.3a Check for movement between the balljoint and steering knuckle when prying up

8.3b With the prybar positioned between the steering knuckle boss and the balljoint, pry down and check for play in the balljoint - if there's any play, replace the balljoint

Installation

8   Position the control arm in the subframe and install the pivot bolt and the vertical bushing bolt. Do not tighten them completely at this time.

9   Insert the balljoint stud into the steering knuckle boss, install the nut and tighten it to the torque listed in this Chapter's Specifications. If necessary, tighten the nut a little more if the cotter pin hole doesn't line up with an opening on the nut. Install a new cotter pin.

10   Install the stabilizer bar-to-control arm link bolt, bushings, spacers and washers (see Section 6) and tighten the link nut to the torque listed in this Chapter's Specifications.

11   Place a floor jack under the outer end of the control arm and raise it to simulate normal ride height. Now tighten the control arm pivot bolt and the vertical bushing bolt to the torque listed in this Chapter's Specifications. **Caution:** *If the bolts aren't tightened with the weight of the vehicle on the suspension (or the control arm raised to simulate normal ride height), control arm bushing damage may occur.*

12   Install the wheel and lower the vehicle. Tighten the lug nuts to the torque listed in the Chapter 1 Specifications.

8   Balljoints - check and replacement

Check

Refer to illustrations 8.3a and 8.3b

1   Raise the front of the vehicle and support it securely on jackstands. Apply the parking brake and block the rear wheels to keep the vehicle from rolling off the jack-stands.

2   Visually inspect the rubber dust boot for damage, deterioration and leaking grease. If the boot is damaged, deteriorated or leaking, replace the balljoint.

3   Place a large prybar under the balljoint and resting on the wheel, then try to pry the balljoint up while feeling for movement between the balljoint and steering knuckle **(see illustration)**. Now, pry between the control arm and the steering knuckle and try to lever the control arm down while feeling for movement between the balljoint and steering knuckle **(see illustration)**. If any movement is evident in either check, the balljoint is worn.

4   Have an assistant grasp the tire at the top and bottom and move the top of the tire in-and-out. Touch the balljoint stud nut. If any looseness is felt, suspect a worn balljoint stud or a widened hole in the steering knuckle boss. If the latter problem exists, the steering knuckle should be replaced as well as the balljoint.

5   Separate the control arm from the steering knuckle (Section 7). Using your fingers (don't use pliers), try to twist the stud in the socket. If the stud turns, replace the balljoint.

Replacement

6   Loosen the wheel lug nuts, raise the front of the vehicle and support it securely on jackstands. Apply the parking brake and block the rear wheels to keep the vehicle from rolling off the jackstands. Remove the wheel.

7   Separate the control arm from the steering knuckle (see Section 7). Temporarily insert the balljoint stud back into the steering knuckle (loosely). This will ease balljoint removal after Step 9 has been performed, as well as hold the assembly stationary while drilling out the rivets.

8   Using a 1/8-inch drill bit, drill a pilot hole into the center of each balljoint-to-control arm rivet. Be careful not to damage the CV joint boot in the process.

9   Using a 1/2-inch drill bit, drill the *head* off each rivet (don't drill any farther). Work slowly and carefully to avoid deforming the holes in the control arm. Knock the rivet shanks out with a hammer and punch.

10   Loosen (but don't remove) the stabilizer bar-to-control arm link nut. Pull the control arm and balljoint down to remove the balljoint stud from the steering knuckle, then dislodge the balljoint from the control arm.

11   Position the new balljoint on the control arm and install the bolts (supplied in the balljoint kit) from the top of the control arm. Tighten the bolts to the torque listed in this Chapter's Specifications.

12   Insert the balljoint into the steering knuckle, install the castle nut, tighten it to the torque listed in this Chapter's Specifications and install a new cotter pin. It may be necessary to tighten the nut a little more to align the cotter pin hole with an opening in the nut, which is acceptable. Never loosen the nut to allow cotter pin insertion.

13   Tighten the stabilizer bar-to-control arm link nut to the torque listed in this Chapter's Specifications.

14   Install the wheel, lower the vehicle and tighten the lug nuts to the torque listed in the Chapter 1 Specifications.

9   Shock absorber (rear) - removal and installation

Refer to illustrations 9.2, 9.4a and 9.4b

1   Loosen the rear wheel lug nuts, raise the rear of the vehicle and support it securely on jackstands. Block the front wheels to prevent the vehicle from rolling. Remove the wheel.

2   If the vehicle is equipped with Electronic Level Control (ELC), the air lines must be disconnected before the shocks can be removed. The air lines use spring clip connections and are sealed with O-rings. Clean the area around the connection, then rotate the spring clip 90-degrees and detach the connector from the fitting on the shock absorber **(see illustration)**.

3   Support the rear axle beam with a floor jack.

4   Remove the shock absorber lower mounting nut and bolt, followed by the upper mounting bolt and nut **(see illustrations)** then remove the shock absorber.

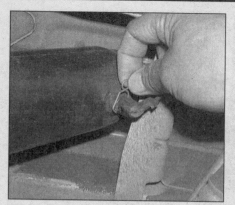

9.2 Rotate the spring clip 90-degrees then pull the air line off the fitting on the shock absorber

9.4a Remove the shock absorber lower mounting nut and bolt . . .

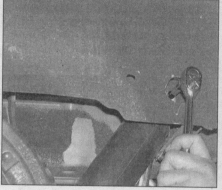

9.4b . . . and the upper mounting bolt, accessed through the hole in the inner fender panel

5   Installation is the reverse of the removal procedure. Tighten the mounting fasteners to the torque listed in this Chapter's Specifications.

6   Install the wheel and lug nuts. Lower the vehicle and tighten the lug nuts to the torque listed in the Chapter 1 Specifications.

10 Coil springs (rear) - removal and installation

Warning: *Always replace the coil springs in pairs - never replace just one of them.*

1   Loosen the wheel lug nuts. Block the front wheels to prevent the vehicle from rolling, then raise the rear of the vehicle and support it securely on jackstands. Remove the wheels. **Note:** *It is not absolutely necessary to remove the wheels, but doing so greatly improves access to the springs.*

2   Support the rear axle beam with a floor jack placed under the center of the beam. Raise the jack slightly to take the spring pressure off the shock absorbers.

3   Remove the shock absorber lower mounting bolts **(see illustration 9.4a)**.

4   If the vehicle is equipped with Electronic Level Control (ELC), detach the height sensor link from the track bar to prevent damage to the height sensor (see Section 12).

5   Detach the track bar from the axle beam (see Section 12).

6   Remove the nut from the parking brake cable bracket above the left side of the axle.

7   Slowly lower the floor jack until the springs are fully extended, then remove the springs and insulators.

8   Check the springs for cracks and chips, replacing the springs as a set if any defects are found. Also check the insulators for damage and deterioration, replacing them as necessary.

9   Installation is the reverse of the removal procedure, but make sure each coil spring is positioned with the paint stripe facing the rear of the vehicle.

10   Raise the rear axle beam to simulate normal ride height, then tighten the shock absorber mounting bolts and the track bar

fasteners to the torque values listed in this Chapter's Specifications. Tighten the wheel lug nuts to the torque listed in the Chapter 1 Specifications.

11 Rear axle assembly - removal and installation

Refer to illustrations 11.13 and 11.15

Removal

1   Loosen the wheel lug nuts. Block the front wheels, then raise the rear of the vehicle and support it securely on jackstands placed underneath the rocker panel flanges (where the vehicle jack engages). Remove both rear wheels.

2   Referring to Chapter 9, Detach the front parking brake cable from the equalizer and the right rear parking brake cable.

3   On models with rear drum brakes, remove the brake drums.

4   Detach the parking brake cables from the parking brake levers and backing plates, or, on models with rear disc brakes, from the actuator levers (see Chapter 9).

5   On models with rear disc brakes, remove the brake calipers, mounting brackets and discs (see Chapter 9).

6   Detach the electrical connectors for the ABS wheel speed sensors - these connectors

are located near the trailing arm pivot bolts.

7   If the axle is to be replaced with a new one, remove the hub and bearing assemblies (see Section 13).

8   If the vehicle is equipped with Electronic Level Control (ELC), detach the height sensor link from the track bar to prevent damage to the height sensor (see Section 12). Unbolt the track bar from the axle.

9   Remove the coil springs (see Section 10).

10   Unscrew the brake line fittings from the brake hoses on the left side of the rear axle. Use a flare-nut wrench, if available, to prevent rounding-off the fittings (see Chapter 9). Plug the hoses to minimize fluid loss and prevent the entry of dirt into the hydraulic system. If the rear axle is to be replaced with a new one, detach the brake lines from the clips on the axle.

11   Unbolt the brake line bracket from the left-side trailing arm.

12   Make a final check that all necessary components have been disconnected and positioned so that they will not hinder the removal procedure, then position the floor jack beneath the center of the rear axle assembly. Raise the jack until it is just supporting the weight of the axle.

13   Remove the nuts from the trailing arm pivot bolts on each side of the vehicle, then remove the bolts **(see illustration)**. Slowly lower the jack, being careful not to let the

11.13 Trailing arm pivot bolt/nut

10

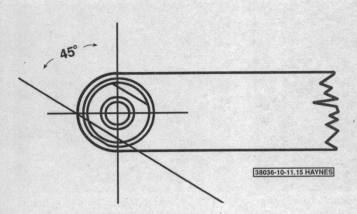

11.15 The trailing arm bushings must be installed with their cutouts at a 45-degree angle

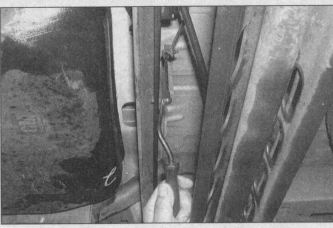

12.2 Carefully pry the height sensor link from the ballstud on the track bar

axle hit the brake pressure regulator valve (models without ABS only).

14   Inspect the axle pivot bushings for signs or damage or deterioration. If replacement is necessary, they can be removed and installed with a drawbolt-type bushing replacement tool (and suitable adapters). If you don't have access to the necessary tools, take the axle to an automotive machine shop to have the old bushings removed and the new ones installed.

15   If the bushings are in need of replacement, make sure the new ones are installed properly **(see illustration)**.

Installation

16   Installation of the rear axle is the reverse of the removal procedure, with the following points:

a) *Ensure that the brake lines, parking brake cables and wiring are correctly routed, and retained by all the necessary retaining clips.*

b) *Don't tighten the rear axle pivot bolts until the weight of the vehicle is on its wheels (or until the rear suspension has been raised to simulate normal ride height). This will prevent the bushings from "winding-up," which could eventually damage them.*

c) *Tighten all fasteners to the proper torque Specifications.*

d) *Bleed the brake system (see Chapter 9).*

12   Track bar - removal and installation

Refer to illustrations 12.2, 12.3a and 12.3b

1   Raise the rear of the vehicle and support it securely on jackstands placed underneath the rocker panel flanges (where the vehicle jack engages). Block the front wheels to prevent the vehicle from rolling.

2   If the vehicle is equipped with Electronic Level Control (ELC), carefully pry the height sensor link from the ballstud on the track bar **(see illustration)**.

3   Remove the bolts from each end of the bar **(see illustrations)**. **Note:** *Unscrew the bolts, not the nuts (the nuts have metal tabs on them to prevent them from rotating.*

4   Remove the bar. Check the bushings in the bar for cracking, hardness or other signs of deterioration. If the bushings are in need of replacement, check with your local auto parts store or dealer parts department regarding the availability of replacement bushings. If the bushings are in need of replacement (and parts are available), take the bar to an auto-

motive machine shop or other qualified repair facility to have the old ones pressed out and new ones pressed in.

5   Installation is the reverse of removal. Before tightening the bolts, either lower the vehicle to the ground or raise the rear axle with a floor jack to simulate normal ride height, then tighten the fasteners to the torque listed in this Chapter's Specifications.

13   Hub and bearing assembly (rear) - removal and installation

Refer to illustration 13.3
Note: *The rear hub and wheel bearing assembly is sealed-for-life and must be replaced as a unit.*

Removal

1   Loosen the wheel lug nuts, raise the rear of the vehicle and support it securely on jackstands. Block the front wheels to keep the vehicle from rolling off the jackstands. Remove the wheel.

2   Remove the brake drum or the brake caliper, caliper mounting bracket and disc (see Chapter 9). Support the caliper with a piece of wire.

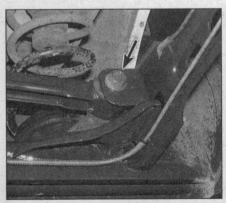

12.3a Remove the track bar-to-axle bolt . . .

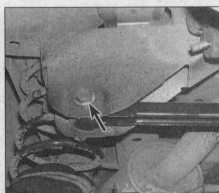

12.3b . . . and the track bar-to-body bolt

13.3 The rear hub and bearing assembly is retained to the axle with four bolts

14.3 Use a small press tool such as this to push the stud out of the flange

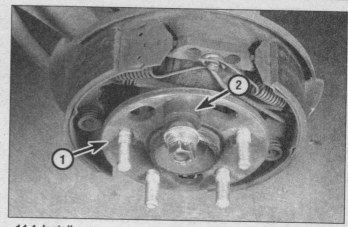

14.4 Install a spacer or washers and a lug nut on the stud, then tighten the nut to draw the stud into place

1   Hub flange   2   Spacer

3   Remove the four hub-to-axle bolts **(see illustration)**.
4   Remove the hub and bearing assembly from the axle and disconnect the wheel speed sensor electrical connector. On models equipped with rear drum brakes, support the brake backing plate with a piece of wire to prevent damage to the brake line.

Installation

5   Reconnect the electrical connector for the wheel speed sensor, position the hub and bearing assembly on the axle and align the holes. Install the bolts. After all four bolts have been installed, tighten them to the torque listed in this Chapter's Specifications.
6   Install the brake drum or the brake caliper and disc, tightening the caliper mounting bracket bolts and the caliper bolts to the torque listed in the Chapter 9 Specifications. Install the wheel. Lower the vehicle and tighten the wheel lug nuts to the torque listed in the Chapter 1 Specifications.

14   Wheel studs - replacement

Refer to illustrations 14.3 and 14.4
Note: *This procedure applies to both the front and rear wheel studs.*
1   Loosen the wheel lug nuts, raise the vehicle and support it securely on jackstands. Remove the wheel.
2   Remove the brake disc or drum (see Chapter 9).
3   Push the stud out of the hub flange with a press tool **(see illustration)**.
4   Insert the new stud into the hub flange from the back side and install some flat washers and a lug nut on the stud **(see illustration)**.
5   Tighten the lug nut until the stud is seated in the flange.
6   Reinstall the disc and caliper or brake drum (see Chapter 9).
7   Install the wheel and lug nuts. Lower the vehicle and tighten the lug nuts to the torque listed in the Chapter 1 Specifications.

15   Steering wheel - removal and installation

Warning: *These models are equipped with airbags. Always disable the airbag system before working in the vicinity of any airbag system components to avoid the possibility of accidental deployment of the airbag, which could cause personal injury*(see Chapter 12).

Removal

Refer to illustrations 15.2a, 15.2b, 15.3a, 15.3b, 15.3c, 15.3d, 15.5, 15.6a and 15.6b
1   Disconnect the cable from the negative terminal of the battery and disable the airbag system (see Chapter 12). **Note:** *On models equipped with the Theftlock audio system, be sure you have the correct activation code before performing any procedure which requires disconnecting the battery (see the front of this manual).*
2   Remove the airbag module from the steering wheel. On 1997 Chevrolet and Oldsmobile models, remove the screws from the backside of the steering wheel **(see illus-**

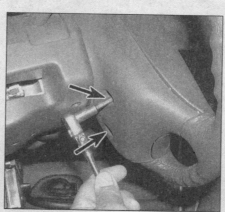

15.2a   On 1997 Chevrolet and Oldsmobile models the airbag module is retained by Torx screws

tration). Note: *Chevrolet models have two screws, Oldsmobile models have four. If you're working on a 1997 Pontiac or any 1998 and later model, the airbag module is retained by four spring clips; insert a screwdriver into the holes in the backside of the steering wheel and disengage the clips from the retaining posts (pull on the airbag module while doing this)* **(see illustration)**.
3   Lift the airbag module carefully away from the steering wheel and unplug the horn wire and the airbag electrical connector **(see illustrations)**. Remove the module. **Warning:** *When carrying the airbag module, keep the*

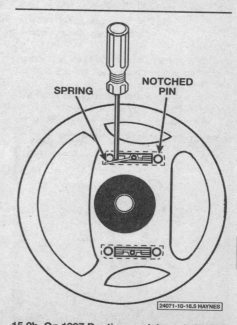

SPRING   NOTCHED PIN

24071-10-16.5 HAYNES

15.2b   On 1997 Pontiac models and all 1998 and later models the airbag is retained by spring clips; insert a screwdriver into the holes in the backside of the steering wheel and pry the clips away from the airbag module retaining pins

10

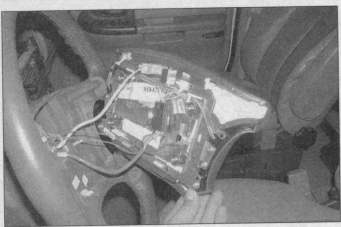

15.3a   Lift the airbag module away from the steering wheel . . .

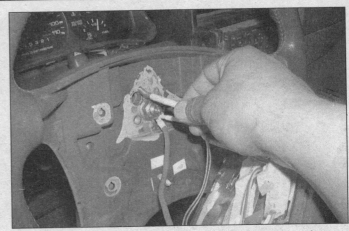

15.3b   . . . twist the connector counterclockwise and detach the horn wire . . .

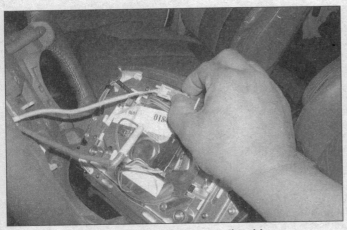

15.3c   . . . squeeze the tabs on the airbag module electrical connector . . .

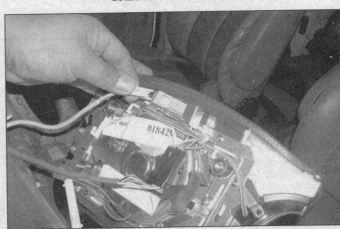

15.3d   . . . and unplug the connector from the module

driver's (trim) side of it away from your body, and when you set it down, have the driver's side facing up.

4   Unplug the cruise control, horn and radio control electrical connectors, as equipped.

5   Remove the steering wheel nut. If no marks are present, mark the relationship of the steering wheel to the shaft **(see illustration)**.

6   Install a puller and turn the center bolt until the wheel is free **(see illustrations)**. **Note:** *On some models the steering wheel* hub does not have tapped holes for the bolts of a steering wheel puller, so a conventional steering wheel puller will not work but a small two-jaw puller will. **Warning:** *Do not hammer on the shaft or the puller in an attempt to loosen the wheel from the shaft.*

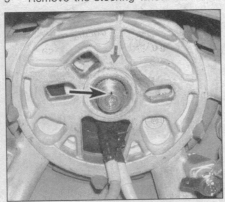

15.5   There should already be alignment marks on the steering wheel and steering shaft; if not, make your own

15.6a   Special puller attachments are available for removing a steering wheel without threaded holes in the hub, but a small jaw-type puller of good quality can be used to remove the steering wheel from the shaft

15.6b   On steering wheels with threaded holes in the hub, a conventional steering wheel puller can be used

15.8 When the clockspring is centered, the arrow on the housing will be aligned with the arrow on the hub

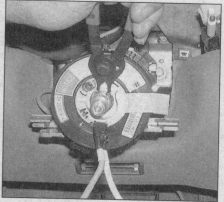

15.9 The clockspring is retained to the steering shaft with a snap-ring

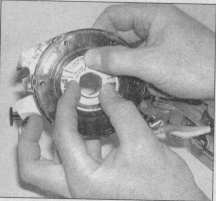

15.10 To center the clockspring, hold it with its underside facing up, depress the spring lock and rotate the hub in the direction of the arrow until it stops, then turn it in the opposite direction the number of turns indicated in the text

7   Lift the steering wheel from the shaft. **Warning:** *Don't allow the steering shaft to turn with the steering wheel removed. If the shaft turns, the airbag clockspring will become uncentered, which may cause the wire inside to break when the vehicle is returned to service.*

Installation

Refer to illustrations 15.8, 15.9 and 15.10

8   Before installing the steering wheel, make sure the airbag clockspring is centered **(see illustration)**.

9   If the airbag system clockspring is not centered, remove the steering column covers (see Chapter 11) and the multi-function switch (see Chapter 12). Unplug the electrical connectors, remove the snap-ring **(see illustration)** and lift the clockspring off the steering column. You may have to cut a plastic wire-tie securing the clockspring harness to the steering column. **Note:** *The clockspring has a locking device to prevent the hub from turning when the steering wheel is off, but it is a good idea to place a piece of tape across the body of the clockspring and the hub, in case the lock is inadvertently depressed.*

10   To center the clockspring, turn the clockspring over, depress the lock lever and turn the hub in the direction of the arrow until it stops (don't apply too much force) **(see illustration)**. Then, turn the hub in the opposite direction approximately 2-1/2 turns, aligning the arrows on the front. Release the lock lever and install the clockspring and snap-ring. Secure the wiring harness with a new wire tie, making sure the harness isn't kinked. Also install the steering column covers.

11   Pull the electrical leads for the airbag module, horn, radio and cruise control switches through the steering wheel and install the wheel on the steering shaft, aligning the marks.

12   Install the steering wheel nut and tighten it to the torque listed in this Chapter's Specifications.

13   Connect the airbag connector to the back of the airbag module and the horn wire

to the horn ring.

14   Position the airbag module on the steering wheel. On 1997 Chevrolet and Oldsmobile models install the bolts, tightening them to the torque listed in this Chapter's Specifications. On all other models, push the airbag module into place until all of the spring clips engage with their respective retaining pins.

15   Refer to Chapter 12 for the procedure to enable the airbag system.

16   Steering column - removal and installation

Refer to illustrations 16.9 and 16.11

Warning: *These models have airbags. Always disable the airbag system before working in the vicinity of any airbag system components to avoid the possibility of accidental deployment of the airbag(s), which could cause personal injury (see Chapter 12).*

Removal

1   Park the vehicle with the front wheels pointing straight ahead.

2   Disconnect the cable from the negative battery terminal and disable the airbag system (see Chapter 12). **Caution:** *On models*

equipped with the Theftlock audio system, be sure you have the correct activation code before performing any procedure which requires disconnecting the battery (see the front of this manual).

3   Remove the steering wheel and airbag system clockspring (see Section 15).

4   Remove the left-side under-dash panel, knee bolster and reinforcement (see Chapter 11).

5   Remove the instrument cluster (see Chapter 12).

6   Follow the airbag clockspring wiring harness along the steering column and cut any wire ties that may be securing it to the column.

7   Pull back the steering column boot and remove the steering shaft-to-intermediate shaft pinch bolt.

8   Remove the shift cable from the ballstud on the lever, then detach the cable casing from the column (see Chapter 7).

9   Remove the steering column lower mounting bolts **(see illustration)**.

10   Insert a large screwdriver into the gap in the intermediate shaft joint and spread it apart slightly to loosen it.

10

16.9 Steering column lower mounting bolts

16.11 Steering column upper mounting nuts

17.2a Before removing the tie-rod end, loosen the jam nut . . .

**17.2b . . . and mark the position of the tie-rod end
on the inner tie-rod**

**17.3 To separate the tie-rod end from the steering knuckle,
loosen - but don't remove - the ballstud nut, then install a balljoint
removal tool (shown) or a small puller to pop the ballstud out of
the knuckle (DO NOT pound on the stud!)**

11   Remove the steering column upper mounting nuts **(see illustration)**.
12   Lower the column then guide it out from under the instrument panel.

Installation

13   Installation is the reverse of the removal procedure, with the following points:

a) *Install all of the steering column fasteners before tightening any of them, then tighten them to the torque listed in this Chapter's Specifications in the following order:*
    1) *Lower mounting bolts*
    2) *Upper mounting nuts*
    3) *Intermediate shaft pinch bolt*
b) *Center and install the airbag system clockspring as described in Section 15.*
c) *Secure the clockspring wiring harness with new wire ties.*
d) *Install the steering wheel as described in Section 15.*
e) *Refer to Chapter 12 for the procedure to enable the airbag system.*

17   Tie-rod ends - removal and installation

Refer to illustrations 17.2a, 17.2b and 17.3

1   Loosen the wheel lug nuts, raise the front of the vehicle and support it securely on jackstands. Remove the wheel.
2   Loosen the tie-rod end jam nut **(see illustration)** and mark the position of the tie-rod end on the threaded portion of the tie-rod **(see illustration)**.
3   Remove the cotter pin and loosen (but do not remove) the castle nut from the tie-rod end balljoint stud, then install a small puller **(see illustration)** and break loose the tie-rod end from the steering knuckle. Remove the nut and detach the tie-rod end.
4   Unscrew the old tie-rod end and install the new one. Make sure the new tie-rod end is aligned with the mark you made on the threads of the tie-rod.
5   Installation is the reverse of removal. Be sure to tighten the tie-rod end balljoint nut to the torque listed in this Chapter's Specifications. Tighten the jam nut securely.
6   Have the wheel alignment checked and, if necessary, adjusted.

18   Steering gear boots - replacement

Refer to illustrations 18.4a and 18.4b

1   If a steering gear boot is torn, dirt and moisture can damage the steering gear. Replace it.
2   Loosen the wheel lug nuts, raise the vehicle and place it securely on jackstands. Remove the front wheels.
3   Disconnect the tie-rod ends from the steering knuckles and remove them from the tie-rods (see Section 17). Also remove the jam nuts.
4   Remove the boot clamps **(see illustrations)** and slide the boots off the tie-rods.
5   Installation is the reverse of removal. Be sure to use new clamps on the boots.

18.4a Squeeze the outer boot clamp with a pair of pliers and slide it down the tie-rod

18.4b Cut off the inner boot clamps (arrow) with diagonal cutters and slide off the old boots

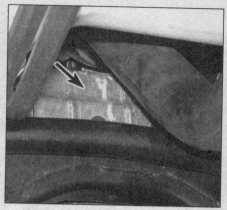

19.4 Unscrew the bolts securing the steering gear heat shield, then remove the shield (arrow)

19 Steering gear - removal and installation

Refer to illustrations 19.4, 19.5, 19.6 and 19.7
Warning: *These models are equipped with airbags. Make sure the steering column shaft is not turned while the steering gear is*

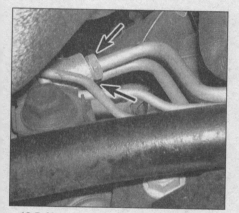

19.5 Unscrew the power steering fluid pressure and return line fittings

removed or you could damage the airbag system. To prevent the shaft from turning, turn the ignition key to the lock position before beginning work or run the seat belt through the steering wheel and clip the seat belt into place.

Removal

1   Park the vehicle with the front wheels pointing straight ahead. Loosen the front wheel lug nuts, raise the front of the vehicle and support it securely on jackstands placed underneath the rocker panel flanges (where the vehicle jack engages).
2   Slide the boot up and remove the intermediate shaft-to-steering gear pinch bolt.
3   Detach the tie-rod ends from the steering knuckles (see Section 17).
4   Remove the bolts and detach the heat shield covering the steering gear **(see illustration)**.
5   Unscrew the power steering pressure and return line fittings from the steering gear **(see illustration)**. Cap the ends to prevent fluid loss and the entry of contaminants.
6   Remove the steering gear mounting bolts **(see illustration)**.
7   Support the rear of the subframe with a

floor jack, then remove the rear subframe mounting bolts **(see illustration)**. Lower the subframe approximately five inches. **Caution:** *Lowering the subframe any more than this could result in damage to engine components near the firewall.*
8   Carefully guide the steering gear through the left (driver's) side wheel opening.

Installation

9   Installation is the reverse of the removal procedure, with the following points:
a) *Replace the subframe mounting bolts (that were removed) with new ones.*
b) *Tighten all fasteners to the torque values listed in this Chapter's Specifications.*
c) *Tighten the power steering pressure and return line fittings securely.*
d) *Add power steering fluid to the pump reservoir to bring it up to the desired level (see Chapter 1).*
e) *Lower the vehicle and tighten the lug nuts to the torque listed in the Chapter 1 Specifications.*
f) *Bleed the power steering system (see Section 21).*
g) *Have the wheel alignment checked and, if necessary, adjusted.*

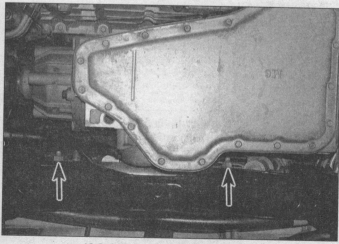

19.6 Steering gear mounting bolts

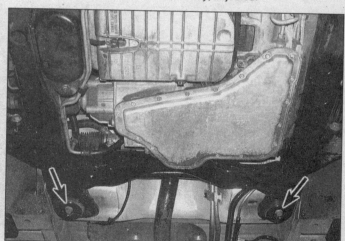

19.7 Subframe rear mounting bolts

10

20.3 Detach the fluid return hose (A) and pressure line (B) from the power steering pump

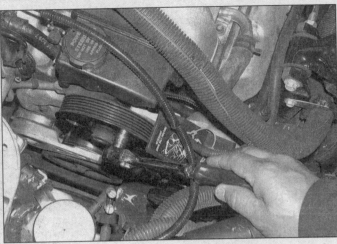

20.4 The power steering pump mounting bolts are accessed through the holes in the pulley

20   Power steering pump - removal and installation

Refer to illustrations 20.3, 20.4, 20.5a and 20.5b

Removal

1   Disconnect the cable from the negative battery terminal. **Caution:** *On models equipped with the Theftlock audio system, be sure the lockout feature is turned off before performing any procedure which requires disconnecting the battery (see the front of this manual).*

2   Remove the drivebelt (see Chapter 1).

3   Using a suction gun or large syringe, remove as much fluid as possible from the power steering pump. Disconnect the pressure line and return hose from the power steering pump **(see illustration)**. Plug the line and hose to prevent fluid spillage and the entry of contaminants.

4   Remove the power steering pump mounting bolts **(see illustration)** and remove the pump.

5   If you're installing a new pump, remove the pulley from the pump with a suitable pulley removal tool and install the pulley on the new pump using a special installation tool **(see illustrations)**. Pulley removal and installation tools are available at most auto parts stores. **Caution:** *Do not use a press to install the pulley.* The pulley should be installed so the face of the pulley is flush with the end of the pump shaft.

9   The remainder of installation is the reverse of the removal procedure. Tighten the pump bolts and the fittings securely.

10   Install the drivebelt (see Chapter 1).

11   Bleed the power steering system (see Section 21).

21   Power steering system - bleeding

1   This is not a routine operation and normally will only be required when the system has been dismantled and reassembled.

2   Fill the reservoir to the correct level with fluid of the recommended type and allow it to remain undisturbed for at least two minutes.

3   Start the engine and run it for two or three seconds only. Check the reservoir and

add more fluid as necessary.

4   Repeat the operations described in the preceding paragraph until the fluid level remains constant.

5   Raise the front of the vehicle until the wheels are clear of the ground.

6   Start the engine and increase the speed to about 1500 rpm. Now turn the steering wheel gently from stop-to-stop. Check the reservoir fluid level.

7   Lower the vehicle to the ground and, with the engine still running, move the vehicle forward sufficiently to obtain full right lock followed by full left lock (but *don't* hold the steering wheel firmly against the stops). Recheck the fluid level. If the fluid in the reservoir is extremely foamy, allow the vehicle to stand for a few minutes with the engine switched off and then repeat the previous operations. At the same time, check the belt tightness and check for a bent or loose pulley. Check also to make sure the power steering hoses are not touching any other part of the vehicle, especially sheet metal or the exhaust manifold.

8   The procedures above will normally remedy an extreme foam condition and/or an objectionably noisy pump (low fluid level and/or air in the power steering fluid are the leading causes of this condition). If, however, either or both conditions persist after a few trials, the power steering system will have to be thoroughly checked. Do not drive the vehicle until the condition(s) have been remedied.

22   Wheels and tires - general information

Refer to illustration 22.1

All vehicles covered by this manual are equipped with metric-sized steel-belted radial tires **(see illustration)**. Use of other size or type of tires may affect the ride and handling of the vehicle. Don't mix different types of tires, such as radials and bias belted

20.5a A typical power steering pump pulley removal tool

20.5b A typical power steering pump pulley installation tool

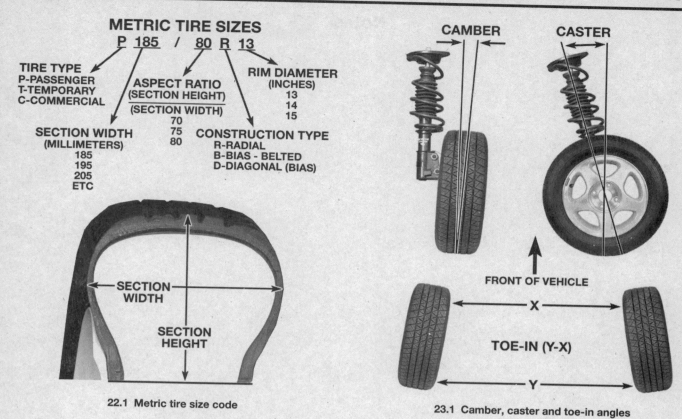

METRIC TIRE SIZES
P 185 / 80 R 13

TIRE TYPE
P-PASSENGER
T-TEMPORARY
C-COMMERCIAL

ASPECT RATIO
(SECTION HEIGHT)
―――――――――
(SECTION WIDTH)
70
75
80

RIM DIAMETER
(INCHES)
13
14
15

SECTION WIDTH
(MILLIMETERS)
185
195
205
ETC

CONSTRUCTION TYPE
R-RADIAL
B-BIAS - BELTED
D-DIAGONAL (BIAS)

SECTION WIDTH

SECTION HEIGHT

22.1 Metric tire size code

CAMBER   CASTER

FRONT OF VEHICLE

X

TOE-IN (Y-X)

Y

23.1 Camber, caster and toe-in angles

on the same vehicle as handling may be seriously affected. It's recommended that tires be replaced in pairs on the same axle, but if only one tire is being replaced, be sure it's the same size, structure and tread design as the other. Because tire pressure has a substantial effect on handling and wear, the pressure on all tires should be checked at least once a month or before any extended trips (see Chapter 1).

Wheels must be replaced if they are bent, dented, leak air, have elongated bolt holes, are heavily rusted, out of vertical symmetry or if the lug nuts won't stay tight. Wheel repairs that use welding or peening are not recommended.

Tire and wheel balance is important to the overall handling, braking and performance of the vehicle. Unbalanced wheels can adversely affect handling and ride characteristics as well as tire life. Whenever a tire is installed on a wheel, the tire and wheel should be balanced by a shop with the proper equipment.

23 Wheel alignment - general information

Refer to illustration 23.1

A wheel alignment refers to the adjustments made to the wheels so they are in proper angular relationship to the suspension and the ground **(see illustration)**. Wheels that are out of proper alignment not only affect steering control, but also increase tire wear. Camber and toe-in are the only angles that can be adjusted on the vehicles covered by this manual, but caster should also be measured to determine if any suspension parts are bent.

Getting the proper wheel alignment is a very exacting process, one in which complicated and expensive machines are necessary to perform the job properly. Because of this, you should have a technician with the proper equipment perform these tasks. We will, however, use this space to give you a basic idea of what is involved with wheel alignment so you can better understand the process

and deal intelligently with the shop that does the work.

Camber is the tilting of the wheels from vertical when viewed from the end of the vehicle. On the vehicles covered in this manual, camber can only be adjusted by elongating the lower strut-to-knuckle hole and moving the steering knuckle within the strut.

Caster is the tilting of the top of the front steering axis from the vertical: a tilt toward the rear is positive caster and a tilt toward the front is negative caster. Caster is not adjustable on these vehicles.

Toe-in is the turning in of the front or rear wheels. The purpose of a toe specification is to ensure parallel rolling of the front or rear wheels. In a vehicle with zero toe-in, the distance between the front edges of the wheels will be the same as the distance between the rear edges of the wheels. The actual amount of toe-in is normally only a fraction of an inch. On the front end, toe-in adjustment is controlled by the position of the tie-rod end on the tie-rod. On the rear end, it isn't adjustable.

10

Notes

Chapter 11   Body

Contents

1   General information

These models feature a "unibody" construction, using a floor pan with left and right frame side rails which support the body components, front and rear suspension systems and other mechanical components. Certain components are particularly vulnerable to accident damage and can be unbolted and repaired or replaced. Among these parts are the body moldings, bumpers, hood and trunk lids and all glass.

Only general body maintenance practices and body panel repair procedures within the scope of the do-it-yourselfer are included in this Chapter.

2   Body - maintenance

1   The condition of your vehicle's body is very important, because the resale value depends a great deal on it. It's much more difficult to repair a neglected or damaged body than it is to repair mechanical components. The hidden areas of the body, such as the wheel wells, the frame and the engine compartment, are equally important, although they don't require as frequent attention as the rest of the body.

2   Once a year, or every 12,000 miles, it's a good idea to have the underside of the body steam cleaned. All traces of dirt and oil will be removed and the area can then be inspected carefully for rust, damaged brake lines, frayed electrical wires, damaged cables and other problems. The front suspension components should be greased after completion of this job.

3   At the same time, clean the engine and the engine compartment with a steam cleaner or water soluble degreaser.

4   The wheel wells should be given close attention, since undercoating can peel away and stones and dirt thrown up by the tires can cause the paint to chip and flake, allowing rust to set in. If rust is found, clean down to the bare metal and apply an anti-rust paint.

5   The body should be washed about once a week. Wet the vehicle thoroughly to soften the dirt, then wash it down with a soft sponge and plenty of clean soapy water. If the surplus dirt is not washed off very carefully, it can wear down the paint.

6   Spots of tar or asphalt thrown up from the road should be removed with a cloth soaked in solvent.

7   Once every six months, wax the body and chrome trim. If a chrome cleaner is used to remove rust from any of the vehicle's plated parts, remember that the cleaner also removes part of the chrome, so use it sparingly.

3   Vinyl trim - maintenance

Don't clean vinyl trim with detergents, caustic soap or petroleum-based cleaners. Plain soap and water works just fine, with a soft brush to clean dirt that may be ingrained. Wash the vinyl as frequently as the rest of the vehicle.

After cleaning, application of a high quality rubber and vinyl protectant will help prevent oxidation and cracks. The protectant can also be applied to weather-stripping, vacuum lines and rubber hoses (which often fail as a result of chemical degradation) and to the tires.

4   Upholstery and carpets - maintenance

1   Every three months remove the carpets or mats and clean the interior of the vehicle (more frequently if necessary). Vacuum the upholstery and carpets to remove loose dirt and dust.

2   Leather upholstery requires special care. Stains should be removed with warm water and a very mild soap solution. Use a clean, damp cloth to remove the soap, then wipe again with a dry cloth. Never use alcohol, gasoline, nail polish remover or thinner to clean leather upholstery.

3   After cleaning, regularly treat leather upholstery with a leather wax. Never use car wax on leather upholstery.

4   In areas where the interior of the vehicle is subject to bright sunlight, cover leather seats with a sheet if the vehicle is to be left out for any length of time.

11

5   Body repair - minor damage

Plastic body panels

The following repair procedures are for minor scratches and gouges. Repair of more serious damage should be left to a dealer service department or qualified auto body shop. Below is a list of the equipment and materials necessary to perform the following repair procedures on plastic body panels. Although a specific brand of material may be mentioned, it should be noted that equivalent products from other manufacturers may be used instead.

> *Wax, grease and silicone removing solvent*
> *Cloth-backed body tape*
> *Sanding discs*
> *Drill motor with three-inch disc holder*
> *Hand sanding block*
> *Rubber squeegees*
> *Sandpaper*
> *Non-porous mixing palette*
> *Wood paddle or putty knife*
> *Curved tooth body file*
> *Flexible parts repair material*

Flexible panels (front and rear bumper fascia)

1   Remove the damaged panel, if necessary or desirable. In most cases, repairs can be carried out with the panel installed.

2   Clean the area(s) to be repaired with a wax, grease and silicone removing solvent applied with a water-dampened cloth.

3   If the damage is structural, that is, if it extends through the panel, clean the backside of the panel area to be repaired as well. Wipe dry.

4   Sand the rear surface about 1-1/2 inches beyond the break.

5   Cut two pieces of fiberglass cloth large enough to overlap the break by about 1-1/2 inches. Cut only to the required length.

6   Mix the adhesive from the repair kit according to the instructions included with the kit, and apply a layer of the mixture approximately 1/8-inch thick on the backside of the panel. Overlap the break by at least 1-1/2 inches.

7   Apply one piece of fiberglass cloth to the adhesive and cover the cloth with additional adhesive. Apply a second piece of fiberglass cloth to the adhesive and immediately cover the cloth with additional adhesive insufficient quantity to fill the weave.

8   Allow the repair to cure for 20 to 30 minutes at 60-degrees to 80-degrees F.

9   If necessary, trim the excess repair material at the edge.

10   Remove all of the paint film over and around the area(s) to be repaired. The repair material should not overlap the painted surface.

11   With a drill motor and a sanding disc (or a rotary file), cut a "V" along the break line approximately 1/2-inch wide. Remove all dust and loose particles from the repair area.

12   Mix and apply the repair material. Apply a light coat first over the damaged area; then continue applying material until it reaches a level slightly higher than the surrounding finish.

13   Cure the mixture for 20 to 30 minutes at 60-degrees to 80-degrees F.

14   Roughly establish the contour of the area being repaired with a body file. If low areas or pits remain, mix and apply additional adhesive.

15   Block sand the damaged area with sandpaper to establish the actual contour of the surrounding surface.

16   If desired, the repaired area can be temporarily protected with several light coats of primer. Because of the special paints and techniques required for flexible body panels, it is recommended that the vehicle be taken to a paint shop for completion of the body repair.

Steel body panels

See photo sequence

Repair of minor scratches

17   If the scratch is superficial and does not penetrate to the metal of the body, repair is very simple. Lightly rub the scratched area with a fine rubbing compound to remove loose paint and built-up wax. Rinse the area with clean water.

18   Apply touch-up paint to the scratch, using a small brush. Continue to apply thin layers of paint until the surface of the paint in the scratch is level with the surrounding paint. Allow the new paint at least two weeks to harden, then blend it into the surrounding paint by rubbing with a very fine rubbing compound. Finally, apply a coat of wax to the scratch area.

19   If the scratch has penetrated the paint and exposed the metal of the body, causing the metal to rust, a different repair technique is required. Remove all loose rust from the bottom of the scratch with a pocket knife, then apply rust inhibiting paint to prevent the formation of rust in the future. Using a rubber or nylon applicator, coat the scratched area with glaze-type filler. If required, the filler can be mixed with thinner to provide a very thin paste, which is ideal for filling narrow scratches. Before the glaze filler in the scratch hardens, wrap a piece of smooth cotton cloth around the tip of a finger. Dip the cloth in thinner and then quickly wipe it along the surface of the scratch. This will ensure that the surface of the filler is slightly hollow. The scratch can now be painted over as described earlier in this section.

Repair of dents

20   When repairing dents, the first job is to pull the dent out until the affected area is as close as possible to its original shape. There is no point in trying to restore the original shape completely as the metal in the damaged area will have stretched on impact and cannot be restored to its original contours. It is better to bring the level of the dent up to a

point which is about 1/8-inch below the level of the surrounding metal. In cases where the dent is very shallow, it is not worth trying to pull it out at all.

21   If the back side of the dent is accessible, it can be hammered out gently from behind using a soft-face hammer. While doing this, hold a block of wood firmly against the opposite side of the metal to absorb the hammer blows and prevent the metal from being stretched.

22   If the dent is in a section of the body which has double layers, or some other factor makes it inaccessible from behind, a different technique is required. Drill several small holes through the metal inside the damaged area, particularly in the deeper sections. Screw long, self-tapping screws into the holes just enough for them to get a good grip in the metal. Now the dent can be pulled out by pulling on the protruding heads of the screws with locking pliers.

23   The next stage of repair is the removal of paint from the damaged area and from an inch or so of the surrounding metal. This is done with a wire brush or sanding disk in a drill motor, although it can be done just as effectively by hand with sandpaper. To complete the preparation for filling, score the surface of the bare metal with a screwdriver or the tang of a file, or drill small holes in the affected area. This will provide a good grip for the filler material. To complete the repair, see the subsection on filling and painting later in this Section.

Repair of rust holes or gashes

24   Remove all paint from the affected area and from an inch or so of the surrounding metal using a sanding disk or wire brush mounted in a drill motor. If these are not available, a few sheets of sandpaper will do the job just as effectively.

25   With the paint removed, you will be able to determine the severity of the corrosion and decide whether to replace the whole panel, if possible, or repair the affected area. New body panels are not as expensive as most people think and it is often quicker to install a new panel than to repair large areas of rust.

26   Remove all trim pieces from the affected area except those which will act as a guide to the original shape of the damaged body such as headlight shells, etc. Using metal snips or a hacksaw blade, remove all loose metal and any other metal that is badly affected by rust. Hammer the edges of the hole in to create a slight depression for the filler material.

27   Wire brush the affected area to remove the powdery rust from the surface of the metal. If the back of the rusted area is accessible, treat it with rust inhibiting paint.

28   Before filling is done, block the hole in some way. This can be done with sheet metal riveted or screwed into place, or by stuffing the hole with wire mesh.

29   Once the hole is blocked off, the affected area can be filled and painted. See the following subsection on filling and painting.

Filling and painting

30   Many types of body fillers are available, but generally speaking, body repair kits which contain filler paste and a tube of resin hardener are best for this type of repair work. A wide, flexible plastic or nylon applicator will be necessary for imparting a smooth and contoured finish to the surface of the filler material. Mix up a small amount of filler on a clean piece of wood or cardboard (use the hardener sparingly). Follow the manufacturer's instructions on the package, otherwise the filler will set incorrectly.

31   Using the applicator, apply the filler paste to the prepared area. Draw the applicator across the surface of the filler to achieve the desired contour and to level the filler surface. As soon as a contour that approximates the original one is achieved, stop working the paste. If you continue, the paste will begin to stick to the applicator. Continue to add thin layers of paste at 20-minute intervals until the level of the filler is just above the surrounding metal.

32   Once the filler has hardened, the excess can be removed with a body file. From then on, progressively finer grades of sandpaper should be used, starting with a 180-grit paper and finishing with 600-grit wet-or-dry paper. Always wrap the sandpaper around a flat rubber or wooden block, otherwise the surface of the filler will not be completely flat. During the sanding of the filler surface, the wet-or-dry paper should be periodically rinsed in water. This will ensure that a very smooth finish is produced in the final stage.

33   At this point, the repair area should be surrounded by a ring of bare metal, which in turn should be encircled by the finely feathered edge of good paint. Rinse the repair area with clean water until all of the dust produced by the sanding operation is gone.

34   Spray the entire area with a light coat of primer. This will reveal any imperfections in the surface of the filler. Repair the imperfections with fresh filler paste or glaze filler and once more smooth the surface with sandpaper. Repeat this spray-and-repair procedure until you are satisfied that the surface of the filler and the feathered edge of the paint are perfect. Rinse the area with clean water and allow it to dry completely.

35   The repair area is now ready for painting. Spray painting must be carried out in a warm, dry, windless and dust free atmosphere. These conditions can be created if you have access to a large indoor work area, but if you are forced to work in the open, you will have to pick the day very carefully. If you are working indoors, dousing the floor in the work area with water will help settle the dust which would otherwise be in the air. If the repair area is confined to one body panel, mask off the surrounding panels. This will help minimize the effects of a slight mismatch in paint color. Trim pieces such as chrome strips, door handles, etc., will also need to be masked off or removed. Use masking tape and several thickness of newspaper for the masking operations.

36   Before spraying, shake the paint can thoroughly, then spray a test area until the spray painting technique is mastered. Cover the repair area with a thick coat of primer. The thickness should be built up using several thin layers of primer rather than one thick one. Using 600-grit wet-or-dry sandpaper, rub down the surface of the primer until it is very smooth. While doing this, the work area should be thoroughly rinsed with water and the wet-or-dry sandpaper periodically rinsed as well. Allow the primer to dry before spraying additional coats.

37   Spray on the top coat, again building up the thickness by using several thin layers of paint. Begin spraying in the center of the repair area and then, using a circular motion, work out until the whole repair area and about two inches of the surrounding original paint is covered. Remove all masking material 10 to 15 minutes after spraying on the final coat of paint. Allow the new paint at least two weeks to harden, then use a very fine rubbing compound to blend the edges of the new paint into the existing paint. Finally, apply a coat of wax.

6   Body repair - major damage

1   Major damage must be repaired by an auto body shop specifically equipped to perform unibody repairs. These shops have the specialized equipment required to do the job properly.

2   If the damage is extensive, the body must be checked for proper alignment or the vehicle's handling characteristics may be adversely affected and other components may wear at an accelerated rate.

3   Due to the fact that all of the major body components (hood, fenders, etc.) are separate and replaceable units, any seriously damaged components should be replaced rather than repaired. Sometimes the components can be found in a wrecking yard that specializes in used vehicle components, often at considerable savings over the cost of new parts.

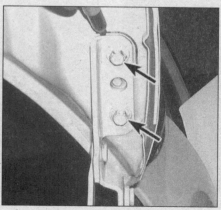

9.2 Before removing the hood, draw a mark around the hinge plate - arrows indicate the hood-to-hinge retaining bolts

7   Hinges and locks - maintenance

Once every 3000 miles, or every three months, the hinges and latch assemblies on the doors, hood and trunk should be given a few drops of light oil or lock lubricant. The door latch strikers should also be lubricated with a thin coat of grease to reduce wear and ensure free movement. Lubricate the door and trunk locks with spray-on graphite lubricant.

8   Windshield and fixed glass - replacement

Replacement of the windshield and fixed glass requires the use of special fast-setting adhesive/caulk materials and some specialized tools. It is recommended that these operations be left to a dealer or a shop specializing in glass work.

9   Hood - removal, installation and adjustment

Note: *The hood is heavy and somewhat awkward to remove and install - at least two people should perform this procedure.*

Removal and installation

Refer to illustration 9.2

1   Use blankets or pads to cover the cowl area of the body and fenders. This will protect the body and paint as the hood is lifted off.

2   Make marks or scribe a line around the hood hinge to ensure proper alignment during installation **(see illustration)**.

3   Disconnect any cables or wires that will interfere with removal.

4   Have an assistant support one side of the hood. Take turns removing the hinge-to-hood retaining bolts.

5   Lift off the hood.

6   Installation is the reverse of removal.

Adjustment

Refer to illustrations 9.10 and 9.11

7   Fore-and-aft and side-to-side adjustment of the hood is done by moving the hinge plate slot after loosening the bolts or nuts.

8   Scribe a line around the entire hinge plate so you can determine the amount of movement **(see illustration 9.2)**.

9   Loosen the bolts or nuts and move the hood into correct alignment. Move it only a little at a time. Tighten the hinge bolts and carefully lower the hood to check the position.

10   If necessary after installation, the entire hood latch assembly can be adjusted up-and-down as well as from side-to-side on the radiator support so the hood closes securely and flush with the fenders. To make the adjustment, first scribe a line or mark around

11

These photos illustrate a method of repairing simple dents. They are intended to supplement *Body repair - minor damage* in this Chapter and should not be used as the sole instructions for body repair on these vehicles.

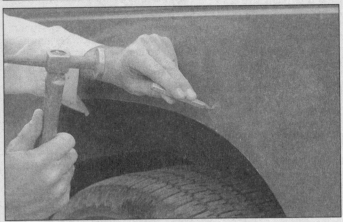

1   If you can't access the backside of the body panel to hammer out the dent, pull it out with a slide-hammer-type dent puller. In the deepest portion of the dent or along the crease line, drill or punch hole(s) at least one inch apart . . .

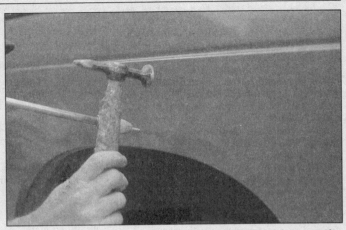

2   . . . then screw the slide-hammer into the hole and operate it. Tap with a hammer near the edge of the dent to help 'pop' the metal back to its original shape. When you're finished, the dent area should be close to its original contour and about 1/8-inch below the surface of the surrounding metal

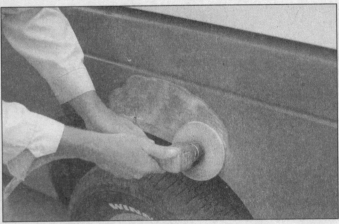

3   Using coarse-grit sandpaper, remove the paint down to the bare metal. Hand sanding works fine, but the disc sander shown here makes the job faster. Use finer (about 320-grit) sandpaper to feather-edge the paint at least one inch around the dent area

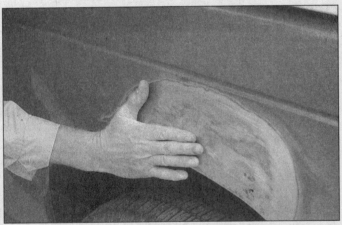

4   When the paint is removed, touch will probably be more helpful than sight for telling if the metal is straight. Hammer down the high spots or raise the low spots as necessary. Clean the repair area with wax/silicone remover

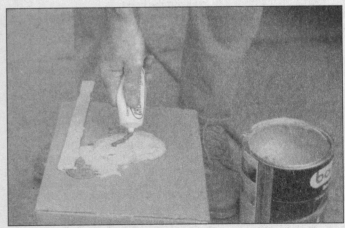

5   Following label instructions, mix up a batch of plastic filler and hardener. The ratio of filler to hardener is critical, and, if you mix it incorrectly, it will either not cure properly or cure too quickly (you won't have time to file and sand it into shape)

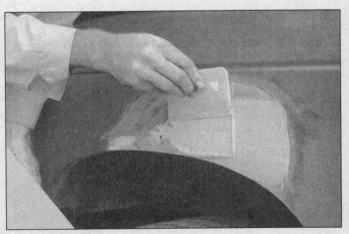

6   Working quickly so the filler doesn't harden, use a plastic applicator to press the body filler firmly into the metal, assuring it bonds completely. Work the filler until it matches the original contour and is slightly above the surrounding metal

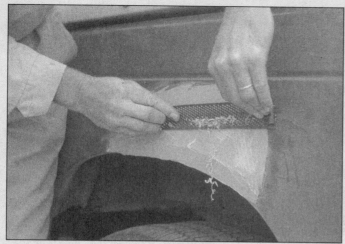

7   Let the filler harden until you can just dent it with your fingernail. Use a body file or Surform tool (shown here) to rough-shape the filler

8   Use coarse-grit sandpaper and a sanding board or block to work the filler down until it's smooth and even. Work down to finer grits of sandpaper - always using a board or block - ending up with 360 or 400 grit

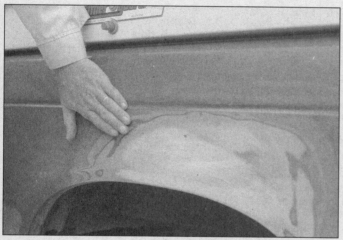

9   You shouldn't be able to feel any ridge at the transition from the filler to the bare metal or from the bare metal to the old paint. As soon as the repair is flat and uniform, remove the dust and mask off the adjacent panels or trim pieces

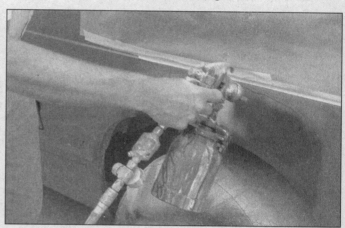

10   Apply several layers of primer to the area. Don't spray the primer on too heavy, so it sags or runs, and make sure each coat is dry before you spray on the next one. A professional-type spray gun is being used here, but aerosol spray primer is available inexpensively from auto parts stores

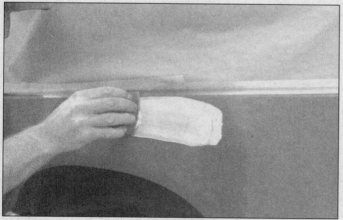

11   The primer will help reveal imperfections or scratches. Fill these with glazing compound. Follow the label instructions and sand it with 360 or 400-grit sandpaper until it's smooth. Repeat the glazing, sanding and respraying until the primer reveals a perfectly smooth surface

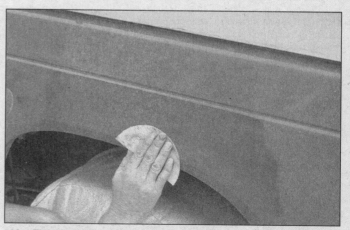

12   Finish sand the primer with very fine sandpaper (400 or 600-grit) to remove the primer overspray. Clean the area with water and allow it to dry. Use a tack rag to remove any dust, then apply the finish coat. Don't attempt to rub out or wax the repair area until the paint has dried completely (at least two weeks)

9.10 Make a line around the latch to use as a reference point - to adjust the hood latch, loosen the retaining bolts (arrows), move the latch and retighten bolts, then close the hood to check the fit

9.11 Adjust the hood closing height by turning the hood bumpers in or out

10.1a To disconnect the cable from the hood latch mechanism, use pliers to disengage the cable housing end from its slot in the latch . . .

the hood latch mounting bolts to provide a reference point, then loosen them and reposition the latch assembly, as necessary **(see illustration)**. Following adjustment, retighten the mounting bolts.

11   Finally, adjust the hood bumpers on the radiator support so the hood, when closed, is flush with the fenders **(see illustration)**.

12   The hood latch assembly, as well as the hinges, should be periodically lubricated with white, lithium-base grease to prevent binding and wear.

10   Hood release latch and cable - removal and installation

Latch

Refer to illustrations 10.1a and 10.1b

1   Disconnect the hood release cable by disengaging the cable from the latch assembly **(see illustrations)**.

2   Scribe a line around the latch to aid alignment when installing, detach the latch retaining bolts from the hood latch support **(see illustration 9.10)** and remove the latch.

3   Installation is reverse of the removal. **Note:** *Adjust the latch so the hood engages securely when closed and the hood bumpers are slightly compressed.*

Cable

Refer to illustration 10.6

4   Disconnect the hood release cable from the latch assembly as described above.

5   Attach a piece of stiff wire to the latch end of the cable, then detach all the cable retaining clips.

6   Working in the passenger's compartment, remove the knee bolster (see Chapter 11). Then remove the two release lever mounting screws and detach the hood release lever **(see illustration)**.

7   Detach the cable grommet from the cowl and pull the cable through the firewall into the passenger compartment. Ensure that the new cable has a grommet attached, then remove the old cable from the wire and replace it with the new cable.

8   Pull the wire back through the firewall.

9   Installation is the reverse of the removal **Note:** *Push on the grommet to seat it in the firewall completely.*

11   Bumpers - removal and installation

Warning: *The models covered by this manual are equipped with a Supplemental Inflatable Restraint (SIR) system, more commonly known as airbags. Always disable the airbag system before working in the vicinity of any airbag system components to avoid the possibility of accidental deployment of the airbags, which could cause personal injury* (see Chapter 12).

Front bumper

Refer to illustrations 11.2, 11.3 and 11.6

1   Loosen the lug nuts on the front wheels, apply the parking brake, raise the vehicle and support it securely on jackstands.

2   Remove the front wheels. Detach the inner fender wells from the left and right side of the vehicle **(see illustration)**.

3   Working under the vehicle, use a trim removal tool to release the push pin fasteners securing the lower edges of the bumper cover **(see illustration)**.

4   Working in the front wheel opening,

10.1b . . . then disengage the cable ferrule from the slot on the arm

10.6 Remove the hood release lever retaining screws (arrows), detach the cable grommet from the cowl and pull it into the passenger compartment

11.2 Inner fenderwell mounting fasteners

11.3 Pry the center pin outward to release the push pin fasteners (arrows) securing the lower edge of the bumper cover

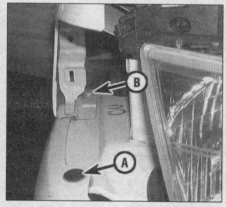

11.6 Remove the side marker lights and detach the push pin fastener (A) and the bolt (B) located in the side marker light opening

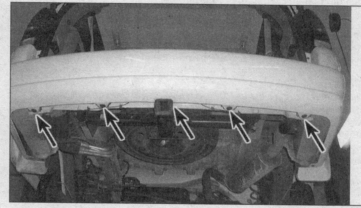

11.11 Lower push pin fastener locations - rear bumper

detach the push pin fastener securing the corners of the bumper cover to the fender.
5   Remove the side marker lights (see Chapter 11).
6   Detach the fasteners located in the side marker light opening **(see illustration)** and pull the bumper cover out and away from the vehicle.

7   Disconnect the electrical connections from the fog lamps if equipped.
8   To remove the bumper, pry out the clips securing the foam isolator, then remove the bumper retaining bolts and pull the bumper assembly out and away from the vehicle.
9   Installation is the reverse of removal.

Rear bumper

Refer to illustrations 11.11, 11.12, 11.13 and 11.14
10   Apply the parking brake, raise the rear of

the vehicle and support it securely on jack-stands.
11   Working under the vehicle, detach the push pin fasteners securing the lower edge of the bumper cover **(see illustration)**.
12   Remove the screws securing the bumper cover in the rear wheel openings **(see illustration)**.
13   Remove the nut(s) securing the upper corners of the bumper cover to the rear quarter panel **(see illustration)**.
14   Open the rear liftgate and remove the

11.12 Remove the screws (arrows) securing the bumper cover to the wheel opening and detach the splash shield (A)

11.13 Remove the nut (arrow) from the rear of the wheel lip

11

11.14 Upper push pin fastener locations - rear bumper

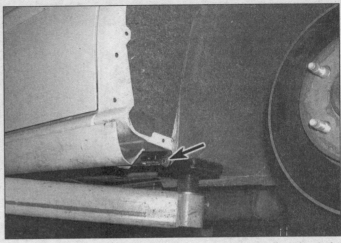

12.4a Remove the fender-to-rocker panel retaining bolt (arrow)

push pin fasteners securing the upper edge of the bumper cover **(see illustration)**. Pull the bumper cover assembly out and away from the vehicle.

15   To remove the bumper, pry out the clips securing the foam isolator, then remove the bumper retaining bolts and pull the bumper assembly out and away from the vehicle.

16   Installation is the reverse of removal.

12 Front fender - removal and installation

Refer to illustrations 12.4a, 12.4b and 12.4c

1   Raise the vehicle, support it securely on jackstands and remove the front wheels.

2   Remove the side marker lights, the inner fenderwell and the front bumper cover (see Section 11).

3   If you're removing the left fender, detach the cruise control module from the top of the fender.

4   Remove the fender mounting bolts **(see illustrations)**.

5   Detach the fender. It's a good idea to have an assistant support the fender while it's being moved away from the vehicle to prevent damage to the surrounding body panels.

6   Installation is the reverse of removal.

13 Liftgate support struts - removal and installation

Refer to illustration 13.3

Note: *The rear liftgate is heavy and somewhat awkward to hold - at least two people should perform this procedure.*

1   Open the liftgate and support it securely.

2   Remove the taillight lens (see Chapter 12).

3   Use a small screwdriver to detach the retaining clips at both ends of the support strut. Then pry or pull sharply to detach it from the vehicle **(see illustration)**.

4   Installation is the reverse of removal.

14 Liftgate - removal, installation and adjustment

Note: *The liftgate is heavy and somewhat awkward to hold - at least two people should perform this procedure.*

Removal and installation

Refer to illustrations 14.2a, 14.2b and 14.4

1   Open the liftgate and support it securely.

2   Remove the upper trim moulding from the lift gate opening and disconnect all wiring harness connectors leading to the liftgate **(see illustrations)**. Working through the opening between the liftgate and the body, detach the rubber conduit from the body. Then pull wiring harness through conduit hole and detach it from the body.

3   While an assistant supports the liftgate, detach both ends of the support struts. Then pry or pull sharply to remove them from the vehicle (see Section 13).

4   Detach the hinge-to-liftgate bolts **(see illustration)** and remove the liftgate from the vehicle.

5   Installation is the reverse of removal.

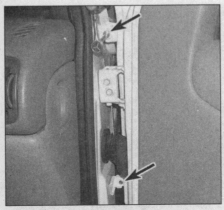

12.4b Open the door to access and remove the fender-to-door pillar bolts (arrows)

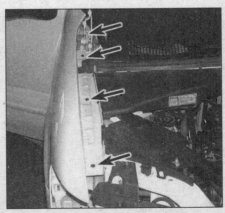

12.4c Detach the remaining bolts (arrows) located in the hood opening

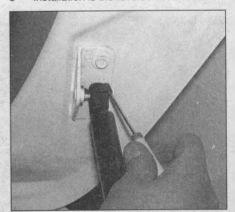

13.3 Use a small screwdriver to pry the clips out of its locking groove, then detach both ends of the strut from the locating studs

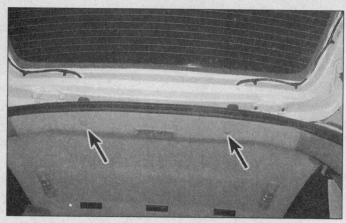

14.2a Detach the upper trim moulding retaining clips (arrows)

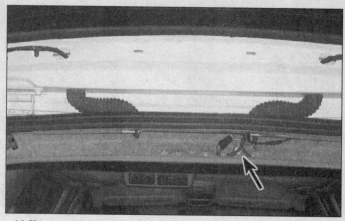

14.2b ... and disconnect all wiring harness connectors (arrow) leading to the liftgate.

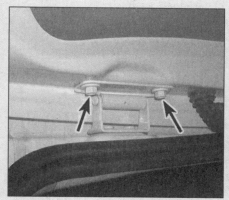

14.4 Scribe a mark around the hinge plate for realignment purposes - then remove the retaining bolts (arrows) on each side of the liftgate

14.7 If the liftgate does not close properly, it will be necessary to remove the tail light housing and loosen the nuts (arrows) to adjust the striker plate

14.8 Adjust the liftgate closing height by turning the liftgate bumpers in or out

Adjustment

Refer to illustrations 14.7, 14.8 and 14.9

6   Adjustments are made by loosening the hinge-to-liftgate bolts and moving the liftgate. Proper alignment is achieved when the edges of the liftgate are parallel with the rear quarter panels and the roof panel.

7   Adjust the latch striker assembly as nec-essary to provide positive engagement with the latch mechanism **(see illustration)**.

8   Finally, adjust the liftgate bumpers on the body so the liftgate when closed, is flush with the rear quarter panels **(see illustration)**.

9   The liftgate wedges can also be adjusted as necessary to prevent squeaks and rattles **(see illustration)**.

15 Liftgate latch, handle and lock cylinder - removal and installation

Refer to illustrations 15.1a, 15.1b, 15.1c, 15.2, 15.3, 15.5, 15.6, 15.7 and 15.11

1   Open the liftgate and remove the liftgate trim panel retaining screws and clips **(see illustrations)**.

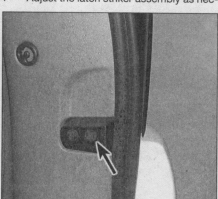

14.9 The liftgate wedge (arrow) is used to prevent squeaks and rattling

15.1a Remove the inside pull handle retaining screws (arrows)

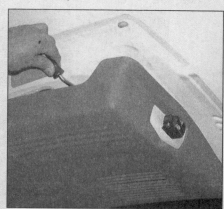

15.1b Using a trim removal tool or a small screwdriver, detach the clips and remove the liftgate trim panel

11

15.1c The liftgate trim panel has twelve retaining clips (arrows) - pry only at the clip locations, being careful not to distort the panel

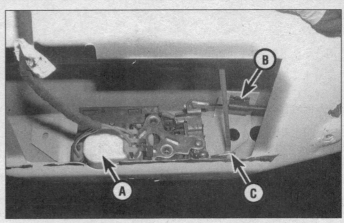

15.2 Disconnect the electrical connector (A), the latch release cable (B) and the lock cylinder rod (C) from the rear of the liftgate latch

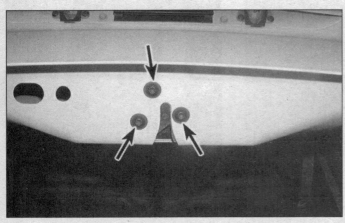

15.3 Liftgate latch retaining screws (arrows)

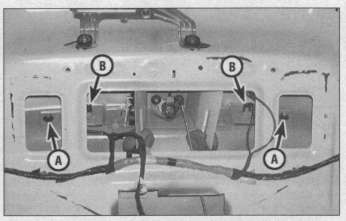

15.5 Remove the liftgate handle cover retaining bolts (A) and the license plate lamp bulbs (B)

Latch

2   Disconnect the actuating rods and cables from the latch and any electrical connections, then remove the latch from the liftgate **(see illustration)**.

3   Remove the latch mounting screws **(see illustration)** from the liftgate.

4   Installation is the reverse of removal.

Handle

5   Working through the access hole in the liftgate, turn the license plate lamp bulb sockets one quarter turn counterclockwise and pull outward to release them from the liftgate. Then detach the handle cover retaining nuts **(see illustration)**.

6   Disconnect the handle release cable

from the rear of the handle **(see illustration)**.

7   Close the liftgate and remove the handle retaining bolts and the license plate lamp lens mounting screws **(see illustration)**.

8   Detach the handle cover and the handle from the liftgate.

9   Installation is the reverse of removal.

15.6 Location of the liftgate handle release cable (arrow)

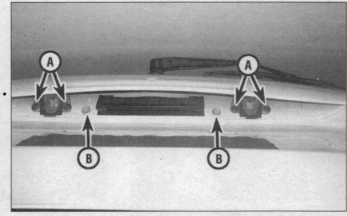

15.7 Remove the lens mounting screws (A) and the liftgate handle retaining bolts (B), then detach the handle cover

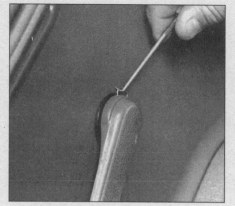

15.11 Disconnect the electrical connector (A) and the lock cylinder retaining nuts (B)

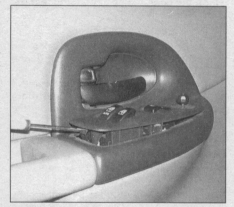

16.3 Using a small screwdriver, pry off the armrest switch control plate and disconnect the electrical connectors from the backside of the switches

Lock cylinder

10   Detach the lock actuating rod from the latch **(see illustration 15.2)**.
11   Disconnect the electrical connector (if equipped) and lock cylinder retaining nuts **(see illustration)**.
12   Refer to steps 5 through 8 and detach the handle trim cover.

16.2a If your vehicle is equipped with manual windows, use a hooked tool like this to remove the window crank retaining clip . . .

13   Pull the lock cylinder out to remove it from the door.
14   Installation is the reverse of removal.

---

16   Door trim panel - removal and installation

---

1   Disconnect the cable from the negative terminal of the battery.

Front door

Refer to illustrations 16.2a, 16.2b, 16.3, 16.4, 16.5 and 16.6
2   On manual window equipped models, remove the window crank, using a hooked tool to remove the retainer clip or work a cloth back-and-forth behind the handle to dislodge the retaining clip **(see illustrations)**. A special tool is available for this purpose, but it's not essential. With the clip removed, pull off the handle.
3   On power window equipped models, pry out the armrest switch control plate and disconnect the electrical connections **(see illustration)**.

16.2b . . . or work a cloth up behind the inside door handle, then move it back-and-forth until the handle retaining clip releases itself from the shaft

4   Pry out the inside handle trim cover **(see illustration)**
5   Detach the retaining bolts at the center of the door trim panel **(see illustration)**.
6   Remove the clips securing the outer edge of the door trim panel **(see illustration)**.
7   Once all of the clips and screws are disengaged, pull the lower edge of the trim panel away from the door, disconnect any electrical connectors and remove the trim panel from the vehicle by gently pulling it up and out.
8   For access to the inner door, peel back the watershield, taking care not to tear it. To install the trim panel, first press the watershield back into place. If necessary, add more sealant to hold it in place.
9   The remainder of the installation is the reverse of removal.

Sliding door

Refer to illustrations 16.11, 16.12 and 16.14
10   Remove the inside door handle from the sliding door **(see illustrations 16.2a and 16.2b)**. With the retaining clip removed, pull off the handle.

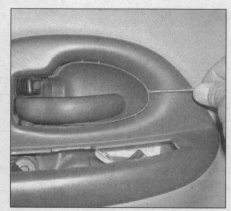

16.4 Pry off the inside handle trim cover

16.5 Remove the retaining bolts securing the center of the door trim panel

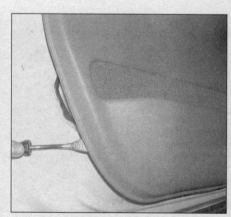

16.6 Using a trim removal tool, detach the clips (arrows) securing the outer edge of the door trim panel

11

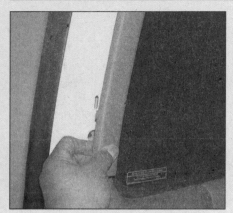

16.11　Carefully pry outward on the upper trim moulding to detach it from the sliding door

16.12　Use a trim panel removal tool to detach the trim panel retaining clips, then pull the sliding door trim panel up and out to remove it

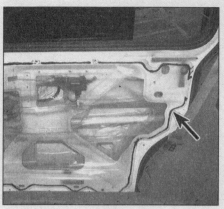

16.14　The watershield is fastened to the door with special adhesive - carefully peel it off the door, taking care not to tear it

11　Detach the clips and remove the upper window moulding **(see illustration)**.

12　Insert a wide putty knife or a special trim panel removal tool between the door trim panel and the head of the retaining clip to disengage the door panel retaining clips **(see illustration)**. **Note:** *Door trim panel retaining clips are approximately six to ten inches apart. Pry at the clip location only. Prying in between clips will result in distorted or damaged door trim panels.*

13　Once all of the clips are disengaged, detach the trim panel and remove the trim panel from the vehicle by gently pulling it up and out.

14　For access to the inner door, peel back the watershield, taking care not to tear it **(see illustration)**. To install the trim panel, first press the watershield back into place. If necessary, add more sealant to hold it in place.

14　Installation is the reverse of removal.

17　Door - removal, installation and adjustment

Note: *The doors are heavy and somewhat awkward to remove and install - at least two people should perform this procedure.*

Removal and installation

Front door

Refer to illustration 17.8

1　Raise the window completely in the door and then disconnect the cable from the negative terminal of the battery. **Caution:** *On models equipped with the Theftlock audio system, be sure you have the correct activation code before disconnecting the battery (see the front of this manual).*

2　Open the door all the way and support it on jacks or blocks covered with rags to prevent damaging the paint.

3　Remove the door trim panel and water deflector as described in (see Section 16).

4　Remove the door speaker (see Chapter 12).

5　Unplug all electrical connections, ground wires and harness retaining clips from the door. **Note:** *It is a good idea to label all connections to aid the reassembly process.*

6　Working through the door speaker hole and the door opening, detach the rubber conduit between the body and the door. Then pull the wiring harness through the conduit hole and remove it from the door.

7　Mark around the door hinges with a pen or a scribe to facilitate realignment during reassembly.

8　Have an assistant hold the door, remove the hinge-to-door bolts **(see illustration)** from the upper and lower hinge and lift the door off.

9　Installation is the reverse of the removal.

Sliding door

Refer to illustrations 17.11, 17.12a and 17.12b

10　Open the sliding door several inches and support it on jacks or blocks covered with rags to prevent damaging the paint.

11　Remove the locating pin from the center roller bracket **(see illustration)**.

12　Mark around the sliding door guide roller brackets with a pen or a scribe to facilitate realignment during reassembly. Remove the bolts securing the sliding door to the upper and lower guide roller brackets **(see illustrations)**.

13　With the help of an assistant, lift the sliding door away from the body and remove it from the vehicle.

14　Installation is the reverse of the removal.

17.8　Before loosening the door retaining bolts (arrows), draw a line around the hinge plates for a reinstallation reference

17.11　Remove the retaining clip (arrow) and tap the locating pin upward to remove it from the center roller bracket

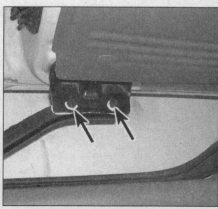

17.12a　Remove the bolts (arrows) from the lower guide roller bracket . . .

17.12b . . . and the upper guide roller bracket - note that these four bolts also provide the in-and-out adjustment on the sliding door - be sure to mark around the sliding door guide roller brackets with a pen or a scribe to facilitate realignment during reassembly

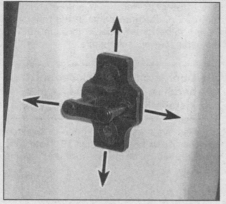

17.18 Adjust the door latch striker by loosening the mounting screws and gently tapping the striker in the desired direction (arrows)

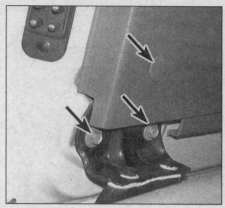

17.19a Lower guide roller up and down adjustment bolts (arrows) - pry out the trim cap to access the upper bolt

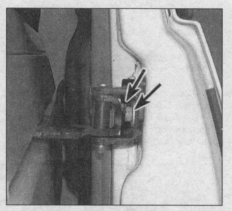

17.19b Center guide roller up-and-down adjustment bolts

17.22 Adjust the sliding door lock striker by loosening the mounting screws and gently tapping the striker in the desired direction (arrows)

Adjustment

Front door
Refer to illustration 17.18

15   Having proper door-to-body alignment is a critical part of a well-functioning door assembly. First check the door hinge pins for excessive play. Fully open the door and lift up and down on the door without lifting the body. If a door has 1/16-inch or more excessive play, the hinges should be replaced.

16   Door to body alignment adjustments are made by loosening the hinge-to-body or hinge-to-door bolts and moving the door. Proper body alignment is achieved when the top of door is aligned parallel with the roof panel and the bottom of the door is aligned parallel with the lower rocker panel. If these goals can't be reached by adjusting the hinge-to-body or hinge-to-door bolts, body alignment shims may have to be purchased and inserted behind the hinges to achieve correct alignment.

17   To adjust the door closed position, first check that the door latch is contacting the center of the latch striker. If not, remove striker and add or subtract shims to achieve correct alignment.

18   Finally, adjust the latch striker as necessary (up-and-down or sideways) to provide positive engagement with the latch mechanism **(see illustration)** and so the door panel is flush with the center pillar.

Sliding door
Refer to illustrations 17.19a, 17.19b and 17.22

19   First adjust the up-and-down position by loosening the lower guide bracket retaining bolts and the center guide bracket bolts and moving the door as necessary **(see illustrations)**. Proper door alignment is achieved when the top of the door is aligned parallel with the roof panel and the bottom of the door is aligned parallel with the lower rocker panel.

20   Next, adjust the in-and-out position of the door by loosening the upper guide roller adjustment bolts and the lower guide roller adjustment bolts **(see illustrations 17.12a and 17.12b)**. Proper door alignment is achieved when the top of the door is flush with the roof panel and the center pillar, and the bottom of the door is flush with the lower rocker panel and the center pillar with the door closed.

21   To adjust the door closed position, first check that the door latch is contacting the center of the rear latch striker. If not, remove the striker and add or subtract shims to achieve correct alignment.

22   Finally, adjust the latch striker as necessary (sideways) to provide positive engagement with the latch mechanism **(see illustration)**. Make sure the door panel is flush with the rear quarter panel.

Power sliding door
Cable tension adjustment
Refer to illustration 17.27

23   Position the sliding door in the fully open position and then disconnect the cable from negative terminal of the battery. **Caution:** *On models equipped with the Theftlock audio system, be sure you have the correct activa-* tion code before disconnecting the battery *(see the front of this manual).*

24   Remove the locating pin from the center roller bracket **(see illustration 17.11)**. Manually close the sliding door and check for proper alignment. If the door does not shut properly adjust it as described in Steps 19 through 22. Make sure the door closes OK manually and engages the latch properly, before proceeding with the cable tension adjustment.

25   Remove the right rear quarter trim panel (see Section 27).

26   Position the center roller bracket approximately one inch from the front of the guide track.

27   Insert a 3/8 inch drill bit through the access window on the motor housing and into the tensioner slot on the sliding door motor. This is neutral position in which the motor must be set at while the cable is being adjusted. **Note:** *The sliding door may have to be repositioned (back and forth) slightly to allow the slot on the motor to be seen through the access window in the motor housing* **(see illustration)**.

11

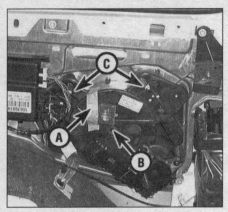

17.27 Power sliding door cable adjustment details

A *Motor housing access window (behind tape)*
B *Cable adjustment nut location*
C *Upper alignment windows*

28 Turn cable adjustment nut counter-clockwise until the tensioner pins align with the indicator marks in the upper alignment windows.

29 Remove the 3/8 drill bit from the motor access window and the tensioner slot on the motor, then perform the reinitialization procedure (see Chapter 12).

30 If the cable tension is correct, reinstall the rear quarter trim panel. If the tension is incorrect, perform Steps 26 through 29 until the cable tension is adequate.

18 Door latch, lock cylinder and handles - removal and installation

1 Remove the door trim panel and water-shield as described in Section 16. **Note:** *This step applies to both the front and sliding doors.*

Front door

Door latch

Refer to illustrations 18.2 and 18.7

2 Remove the screws securing the latch to the door **(see illustration)**.
3 Remove the door window glass (see Section 19).
4 Remove the front door outside handle (see Steps 9 and 10).
5 Remove the door window glass regula-tor module with the door latch attached (see Section 20).
6 Disconnect any electrical connectors (if equipped) from the latch.
7 Depress the plastic retaining tab and detach the latch from the regulator module assembly **(see illustration)**. Rotate the latch

as necessary to detach the inside handle and the inside lock rod from the latch.
8 Installation is the reverse of removal.

Door lock cylinder and outside handle

Refer to illustrations 18.9, 18.10 and 18.11

9 Working through the access holes in the door frame, disconnect the outside door han-dle lock cylinder harness connector **(see illustration 18.7)**. Pry out the plastic plug at the corner of the door frame and remove the outside handle retaining bolts **(see illustra-tion)**.
10 Tilt the handle outward and disconnect the door lock cylinder and handle actuating rods **(see illustration)**. Remove the handle from the door.
11 Using a pair of pliers, pull the lock cylin-der retaining clip from the notch in the handle and remove the lock cylinder from the handle **(see illustration)**.
12 Installation is the reverse of removal.

Inside handle

Refer to illustration 18.13

13 Unsnap the inside handle from the door window glass regulator module **(see illustra-tion)**.
14 Rotate the handle as necessary to detach the actuating rods from the handle.
15 Installation is the reverse of removal.

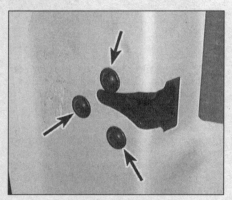

18.2 Front door latch retaining screws (arrows)

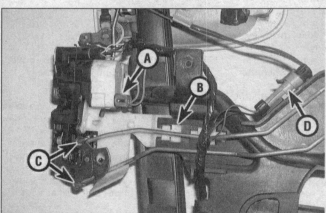

18.7 Detach the power door lock solenoid connector (A), then depress the plastic retaining tab (B) and rotate the latch outward until the lock rods (C) can disengaged from the latch - (D) indicates the outside door handle lock cylinder harness connector

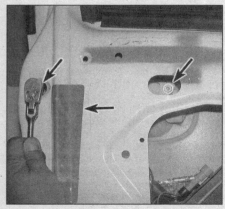

18.9 Outside handle retaining bolts (arrows) - front door

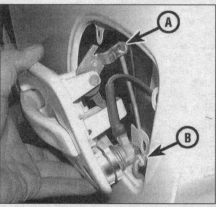

18.10 Front door handle (A) and the door lock cylinder actuating rods (B)

18.11 Detach the retaining clip and remove the lock cylinder

18.13 Use a screwdriver to unsnap the inside handle from the window regulator module

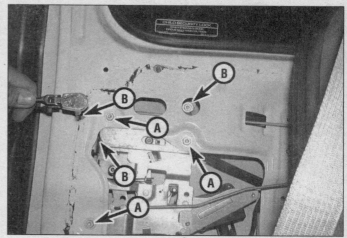

18.20 On sliding doors, it will be necessary to detach the inside handle control mechanism nuts (A) and position it aside to access the lower bolt (B) on the outside door handle

Sliding door

Door latches

16   Remove the screws securing the latch to the door **(see illustration 18.2)**.
17   Working through the large access hole, position the latch as necessary to disengage the actuating rod from the rear of the latch.
18   Disconnect any electrical connectors from the latch and remove the latch assembly from the sliding door.
19   Installation is the reverse of removal.

Door lock cylinder and outside handle

Refer to illustration 18.20

20   Remove the nuts securing the inside handle control mechanism to the door **(see illustration)**. Position the inside handle control mechanism as necessary to access the outside door handle and outside lock cylinder.
21   Working through the large access hole, disengage the latch rod from the door lock cylinder.
22   Disengage the actuating cable from the outside handle.

23   Disconnect the lock cylinder electrical connector if equipped.
24   Remove the outside handle retaining bolts and detach the handle from the door.
25   Using a pair of pliers, slide the lock cylinder retaining clip out of engagement and remove the lock cylinder from the door handle **(see illustration 18.11)**.
26   Installation is the reverse of removal.

19   Door window glass - removal and installation

Refer to illustrations 19.5a and 19.5b
Note: *The procedure described below applies to front doors only.*
1   Remove the door trim panel and the plastic watershield (see Section 16).
2   Lower the window glass all the way down into the door.
3   Carefully pry the inner and outer weather-stripping out of the door window opening.
4   Raise the window just enough to access

both of the window retaining clips through the holes in the door frame.
5   Using a screwdriver, depress the retaining tabs on the window clips, then slide the equalizer arm off the window retaining clips **(see illustrations)**.
6   Place a rag over the glass to help prevent scratching the glass and remove the glass by pulling it up and out.
7   Installation is the reverse of removal.

20   Front door window regulator module - removal and installation

Refer to illustration 20.4
Warning: *The regulator arms are under extreme pressure and can cause serious injury if the motor or counterbalance spring is removed without locking the sector gear or releasing tension on the counterbalance spring. A special tool is required to release the tension on the counterbalance spring which is available through dealer service departments. Do not remove the regulator motor unless this tool is available.*

19.5a Raise the window just enough to access the retaining clips - depress the retaining tabs (arrow) . . .

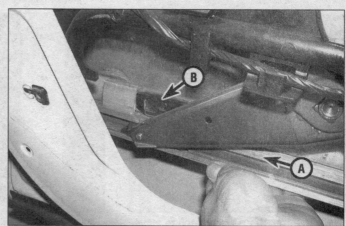

19.5b . . . and slide the equalizer arm (A) off the window retaining clips (B)

11

20.4 Front door window regulator module retaining bolts (arrows)

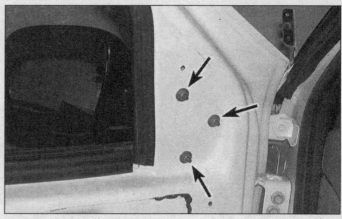

21.3 Outside mirror retaining nuts (arrows)

1   Remove the door trim panel and the plastic watershield (see Section 16).
2   Remove the window glass (see Section 19).
3   Disconnect the electrical connectors from the components on the window regulator module.
4   Remove window regulator module mounting screws **(see illustration)**.
5   Pull the module assembly through the service hole in the door frame to remove it.
6   Installation is the reverse of removal.

21   Mirrors - removal and installation

Outside mirrors

Refer to illustration 21.3
1   Remove the door trim panel and the plastic watershield (see Section 16).
2   Disconnect the electrical connector from the mirror (if equipped).
3   Remove the three mirror retaining nuts and detach the mirror from the vehicle **(see illustration)**.

Inside mirror

4   Loosen the set screw at the base of the mirror.

5   Slip the mirror of its mounting base and remove it from vehicle.
6   Installation is the reverse of removal.

22   Rear quarter window - replacement

Refer to illustrations 22.2 and 22.3
Note: *The rear quarter window glass is fragile and somewhat awkward to remove and install - at least two people should perform this procedure.*
1   Remove the upper rear quarter trim panels (see Section 27).
2   Open the window latch assembly. Remove the retaining bolts securing the latch to the body **(see illustration)**. On power window equipped models, disconnect the electrical connector from the actuator.
3   With an assistant holding the window glass, remove the retaining nuts securing the hinges to the body **(see illustration)**.
4   Remove the rear quarter window glass from the vehicle.
5   To remove the rear quarter window latch from the glass, first tap out the pin securing the latch to the glass retainer, then remove the screw securing the retainer to the glass.
6   Installation is the reverse of removal.

23   Center console - removal and installation

Refer to illustration 23.3
Warning: *The models covered by this manual are equipped with a Supplemental Inflatable Restraint (SIR) system, more commonly known as airbags. Always disable the airbag system before working in the vicinity of any airbag system components to avoid the possibility of accidental deployment of the airbags, which could cause personal injury (see Chapter 12).*
1   Disconnect the cable from the negative terminal of the battery. **Caution:** *On models equipped with the Theftlock audio system, be sure you have the correct activation code before disconnecting the battery (see the front of this manual).*
2   Use a small screwdriver to pry off the CD player trim bezel and remove the CD player if equipped.
3   Lower the console door and remove the screws from the center of the console **(see illustration)**.
4   Pull the console rearward and remove it from the vehicle.
5   Installation is the reverse of removal.

22.2 Rear quarter window latch to glass retaining screw (A) and latch to body bolts (B)

22.3 While an assistant holds the rear quarter window glass remove the hinge retaining nuts (arrows)

23.3 Center console retaining screws (arrows)

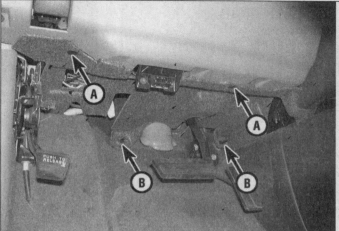

24.4 Pull the bezel outward to disengage the retaining clips

25.2 Lower sound insulator panel mounting details (drivers side shown, passengers side similar)

A   Upper push pin retainers
B   Lower push-on retainers

24 Instrument cluster bezel - removal and installation

Refer to illustration 24.4

Warning: *The models covered by this manual are equipped with a Supplemental Inflatable Restraint (SIR) system, more commonly known as airbags. Always disable the airbag system before working in the vicinity of any airbag system components to avoid the possibility of accidental deployment of the airbags, which could cause personal injury (see Chapter 12).*

1   Disconnect the cable from the negative terminal of the battery. **Caution:** *On models equipped with the Theftlock audio system, be sure you have the correct activation code before disconnecting the battery (see the front of this manual).*

2   Remove the lower left sound insulator panel, the knee bolster and the center trim panel from the instrument panel (see Section 25).

3   Tilt the steering wheel down to the lowest position.

4   Starting at the top, pull the instrument cluster bezel outward while disengaging the

clips on the bezel **(see illustration)**. Remove the bezel from the vehicle.

5   Installation is the reverse of removal.

25 Dashboard trim panels - removal and installation

Warning: *The models covered by this manual are equipped with a Supplemental Inflatable Restraint (SIR) system, more commonly known as airbags. Always disable the airbag system before working in the vicinity of any airbag system components to avoid the possibility of accidental deployment of the airbags, which could cause personal injury (see Chapter 12).*

1   Disconnect the cable from the negative terminal of the battery. **Caution:** *On models equipped with the Theftlock audio system, be sure you have the correct activation code before disconnecting the battery (see the front of this manual).*

Lower sound insulator panels

Refer to illustration 25.2

2   Pry off the lower push-on retainers from

the studs on the floor mat, then pull out the center pin on the upper push pin fasteners **(see illustration)**.

3   Pull downward to release the sound insulator panel, disconnect any courtesy lamps from the panel and remove it from the vehicle.

4   Installation is the reverse of removal.

Knee bolster

Refer to illustration 25.6

5   Remove the driver's side lower sound insulator panel (see Steps 2 and 3).

6   Remove the retaining screws along the lower edge of the knee bolster **(see illustration)**.

7   Pull outward on the lower edge of the knee bolster and detach it from the vehicle.

8   Installation is the reverse of removal.

Center trim panel

Refer to illustrations 25.9 and 25.10

9   Open the ash tray and the DC power outlet cover, then remove the two retaining screws located along the lower edge of the bezel **(see illustration)**.

10   Grasp the bezel securely and detach it

25.6 Remove the screws (arrows) at the lower edge of the knee bolster - pull the bottom edge outward slightly, then downward to remove it

25.9 Pull the ashtray and DC outlet cover outward, then remove the screws (arrows) securing the lower edge of the center trim panel

11

25.10 Carefully pull the center trim panel straight back to release the tabs at the top

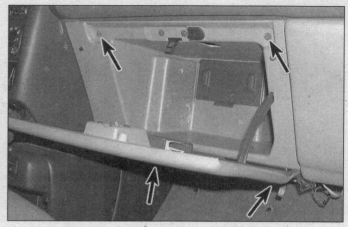

25.14 Glove box mounting screws (arrows)

from the instrument panel by pulling it straight back **(see illustration)**.

11   Disconnect any electrical connections and remove the bezel from the instrument panel.

12   Installation is the reverse of the removal.

Glove box

Refer to illustrations 25.14 and 25.15

13   Remove the passenger's side lower sound insulator panel (see Steps 2 and 3).

14   Open the glove box door and remove the mounting screws **(see illustration)**.

15   Pull the glove box outward to release the remaining retaining clips and disconnect the electrical connector for glove box light **(see illustration)**. Remove the glove box from the instrument panel.

16   Installation is the reverse of removal.

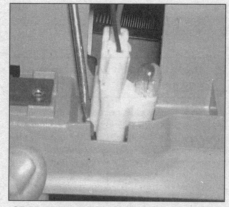

25.15 Use a small screwdriver to release the tab securing the glove box light

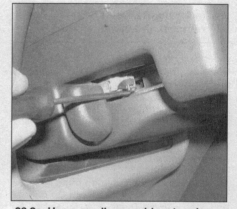

26.3a Use a small screwdriver to release the clip securing the steering column tilt lever

26   Steering column covers - removal and installation

Refer to illustrations 26.3a, 26.3b and 26.4
Warning: *The models covered by this manual are equipped with a Supplemental Inflatable Restraint (SIR) system, more commonly*

known as airbags. Always disable the airbag system before working in the vicinity of any airbag system components to avoid the possibility of accidental deployment of the airbags, which could cause personal injury* (see Chapter 12).

1   Remove the knee bolster (see Section 25).

2   Remove the key lock cylinder (see

Chapter 12).

3   Detach the steering column tilt lever and remove the screws from the lower steering column cover **(see illustrations)**. Separate the lower cover from the steering column.

4   Remove the screws securing the upper cover and detach it from the steering column **(see illustration)**.

5   Installation is the reverse of removal.

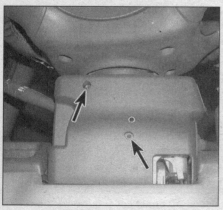

26.3b Remove the screws from the lower cover

26.4 Remove the screws from the upper cover

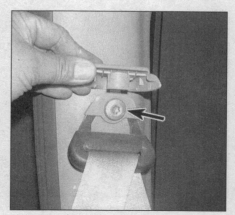

27.2a Pry open the trim covers to access the upper seat belt anchor bolts

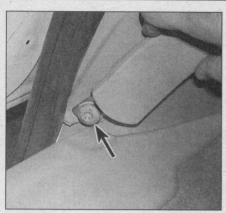

27.2b To access the lower anchor bolt on the middle seat belt, slide the cover upward until the bolt is exposed

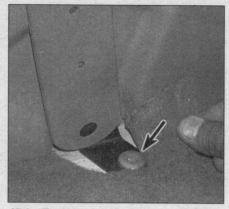

27.2c To access the lower anchor bolt on the rear seat belt, peel back the carpeting

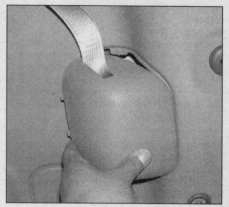

27.2d The rear seat belt retractors are removed after unsnapping the trim cover . . .

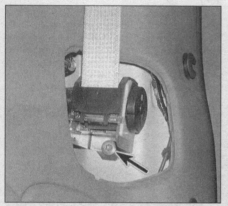

27.2e . . . and detaching the anchor bolt

27 Rear quarter trim panels - removal and installation

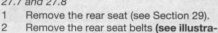

Refer to illustrations 27.2a, 27.2b, 27.2c, 27.2d, 27.2e, 27.3, 27.4, 27.5, 27.6a, 27.6b, 27.7 and 27.8

1   Remove the rear seat (see Section 29).
2   Remove the rear seat belts **(see illustrations)**.

27.3 Pry outward at top of the upper rear quarter trim panels to detach the clips, then pull upward to disengage the locating tabs at the bottom - Do Not pull the panel straight off or the tabs at the bottom will break

3   Remove the upper rear quarter trim panels surrounding the rear quarter window glass **(see illustration)**.
4   Remove the rear sill plate **(see illustration)**.

27.4 Use a trim removal tool to pry off the rear sill plate

5   Remove the screws from the rear cargo net if equipped **(see illustration)**.
6   When removing left side lower trim panel, detach the accessory panel service cover, the accessory panel and disconnect the electrical connectors from the rear of the panel **(see illustrations)**.

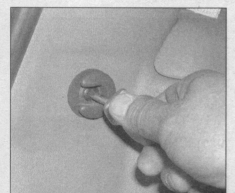

27.5 Remove the cargo net retainers if equipped

27.6a When removing the left side lower quarter trim panel, remove the accessory panel service cover . . .

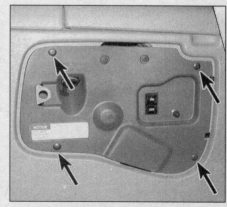

27.6b . . . and the accessory panel mounting screws (arrows) - pull the panel outward and disconnect the electrical connectors from the rear

11

7   Remove the rear cup holder **(see illustration)**.

8   Using a trim removal tool or a small screwdriver, detach the clips and remove the rear quarter trim panel **(see illustration)**.

9   Installation is the reverse of removal.

28   Cowl cover - removal and installation

Refer to illustration 28.2

1   Remove the windshield wiper arms and the antenna mast (see Chapter 12).

2   Remove the retaining screws securing the cowl **(see illustration)**.

3   Detach the cowl and remove it from the vehicle.

4   Installation is the reverse of removal.

29   Seats - removal and installation

Warning: *The models covered by this manual are equipped with a Supplemental Inflatable Restraint (SIR) system, more commonly known as airbags. Always disable the airbag*

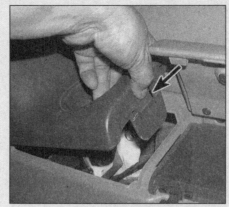

27.7 Depress the retaining tab (arrow) to release the cup holder from the rear trim panel

system before working in the vicinity of any airbag system components to avoid the possibility of accidental deployment of the airbags, which could cause personal injury (see Chapter 12).

Front seat

Refer to illustration 29.2

1   Position the seat all the way forward or all the way to the rear to access the front seat retaining bolts.

2   Remove the retaining bolts **(see illustration)**. If you're removing the passengers seat remove the under seat storage tray first.

3   Tilt the seat upward to access the underneath, then disconnect any electrical connectors and lift the seat from the vehicle.

4   Installation is the reverse of removal.

Rear seats

Refer to illustrations 29.6 and 29.8

5   Fold the rear seat back to the down position.

6   Position the seat all the way forward to access the rear release strap **(see illustration)**.

7   Pull the rear release strap and tilt the seat forward to an up right position.

8   Squeeze the bars at the front of the seat bottom **(see illustration)** to disengage the rear seats from the hooks in the floor and remove it from the vehicle.

9   Installation is the reverse of removal.

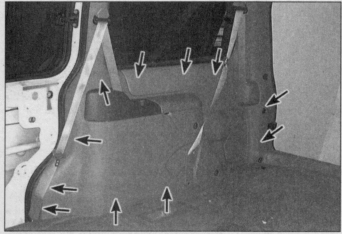

27.8 Detach the trim panel retaining clips (arrows) (right hand panel shown, left side similar)

28.2 Cowl fasteners are located on the leading edge and on the corners

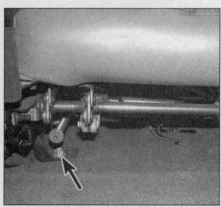

29.2 Front seat retaining bolts (arrow) - there are two at the front and two at the rear

29.6 Pull the release strap (arrow) and tilt the rear of the seat upward

29.8 Squeeze the bars together to release the seat from the hooks in the floor

Chapter 12
Chassis electrical system

Contents

1 General information

The electrical system is a 12-volt, negative ground type. A lead/acid-type battery that is charged by the alternator supplies power for the lights and all electrical accessories.

This Chapter covers the various electrical components not associated with the engine. Information on the battery, alternator, ignition system and starter motor can be found in Chapter 5.

It should be noted that when portions of the electrical system are serviced, the cable should be disconnected from the negative battery terminal to prevent electrical shorts and/or fires.

Caution: *On models equipped with the Theft-lock audio system, be sure the lockout feature is turned off before performing any procedure which requires disconnecting the battery (see the front of this manual).*

2 Electrical troubleshooting - general information

Refer to illustrations 2.5a, 2.5b, 2.6, 2.9 and 2.15

Warning: *The models covered by this manual are equipped with a Supplemental Inflatable Restraint (SIR) system, more commonly known as airbags. Always disable the airbag system before working in the vicinity of any airbag system components to avoid the possibility of accidental deployment of the airbags, which could cause personal injury (see Section 29).*

A typical electrical circuit consists of an electrical component, any switches, relays, motors, fuses, fusible links or circuit breakers related to that component and the wiring and connectors that link the component to both the battery and the chassis. To help you pinpoint an electrical circuit problem, wiring diagrams are included at the end of this Chapter.

Before tackling any troublesome electrical circuit, first study the appropriate wiring diagrams to get a complete understanding of what makes up that individual circuit. Trouble spots, for instance, can often be narrowed down by noting if other components related to the circuit are operating properly. If several components or circuits fail at one time, chances are the problem is in a fuse or ground connection, because several circuits are often routed through the same fuse and ground connections.

Electrical problems usually stem from simple causes, such as loose or corroded connections, a blown fuse, a melted fusible link or a failed relay. Visually inspect the condition of all fuses, wires and connections in a problem circuit before troubleshooting the circuit.

If test equipment and instruments are going to be utilized, use the diagrams to plan ahead of time where you will make the necessary connections in order to accurately pinpoint the trouble spot.

12

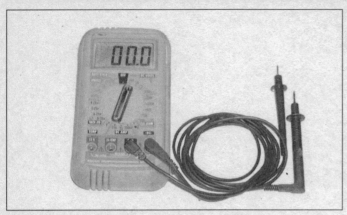

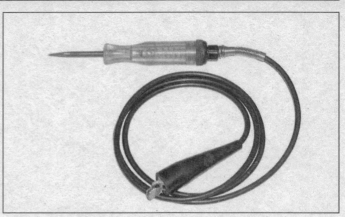

2.5a The most useful tool for electrical troubleshooting is a digital multimeter that can measure voltage, amperage and resistance (ohms)

2.5b A test light can be used to check for the presence of voltage in a circuit

The basic tools needed for electrical troubleshooting include a multimeter, a test light (a 12-volt bulb with a set of test leads can also be used) or a continuity tester (which includes a bulb, battery and set of test leads) **(see illustrations)**. Also useful is a pair of jumper wires, preferably with a circuit breaker incorporated into one, which can be used to apply power and ground to electrical components. Before attempting to locate a problem with test instruments, use the wiring diagram(s) to decide where to make the connections.

Voltage checks

Voltage checks should be performed if a circuit is not functioning properly. Connect one lead of a test light to either the negative battery terminal or a known good ground. Connect the other lead to a connector in the circuit being tested, preferably nearest to the battery or fuse **(see illustration)**. If the bulb of the tester lights, voltage is present, which means that the part of the circuit between the connector and the battery is problem free.

Continue checking the rest of the circuit in the same fashion. When you reach a point at which no voltage is present, the problem lies between that point and the last test point with voltage. Most of the time the problem can be traced to a loose connection. **Note:** *Keep in mind that some circuits receive voltage only when the ignition key is in the Accessory or Run position.*

Finding a short

A short-to-ground in a live circuit causes the fuse protecting the circuit to blow. When the fuse is replaced it will immediately blow again.

One method of finding the location of a short is to remove the fuse protecting the problem circuit and connect a test light in place of the fuse. Disconnect the load or ground from the circuit. Turn the ignition key on, if the circuit is shorted to ground there should be voltage present in the circuit and the test light should light. Move the suspected wiring harness from side-to-side while watching the test light. If the bulb goes

out, there is a short to ground somewhere in that area, probably where the insulation has rubbed through allowing the bare wire to contact the body. The same test can be performed on each component in the circuit, even a switch.

Ground check

Perform a ground test to check whether a component is properly grounded. Disconnect the battery and connect one lead of a continuity tester or multimeter (set to the ohms scale), to a known good ground. Connect the other lead to the wire or ground connection being tested. If the resistance is low (less than 5 ohms), the ground is good. If using a self-powered continuity tester, the bulb will light if the ground is good.

Continuity check

A continuity check is done to determine if there are any breaks in a circuit - if it is passing electricity properly. With the circuit off (no power in the circuit), a self-powered continuity tester or multimeter can be used to

2.6 In use, the test light lead is clipped to a known good ground, the pointed tip is used to probe connectors, wires or electrical sockets - if the bulb lights, the circuit being tested has battery voltage present

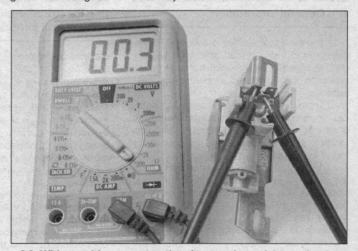

2.9 With a multimeter set to the ohms scale, resistance can be checked across two terminals - when checking for continuity, a low reading indicates continuity, a high reading indicates lack of continuity

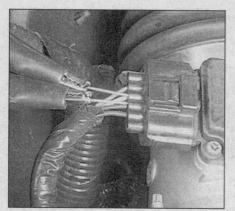

2.15 To backprobe a connector, insert a small, sharp probe (such as a straight-pin) into the back of the connector alongside the desired wire until it contacts the metal terminal inside; connect your meter leads to the probes - this allows you to test a functioning circuit

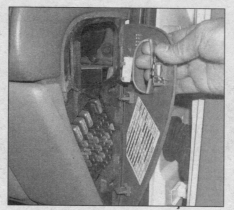

3.1a The interior fuse center, located at the right end of the instrument panel, contains fuses and several circuit breakers - an identification legend is located on the inside of the cover

3.1b The engine compartment fuse panel is located on the left side of the engine compartment and contains fuses and relays - a legend is provided the inside of the cover to identify the fuses and relays

check the circuit. Connect the test leads to both ends of the circuit (or to the "power" end and a good ground), and if the test light comes on the circuit is passing current properly **(see illustration)**. If the resistance is low (less than 5 ohms), there is continuity; if the reading is 10,000 ohms or higher, there is a open somewhere in the circuit. The same procedure can be used to test a switch, by connecting the continuity tester or multimeter to the switch terminals. With the switch turned On, the test light should come on (or low resistance should be indicated on a meter).

Finding an open circuit

When diagnosing for possible open circuits, it is often difficult to locate them by sight because the connectors hide oxidation or terminal misalignment. Merely wiggling a connector on a sensor or in the wiring harness may correct the open circuit condition. Remember this when an open circuit is indicated when troubleshooting a circuit. Intermittent problems may also be caused by oxidized or loose connections.

Electrical troubleshooting is simple if you keep in mind that all electrical circuits are basically electricity running from the battery, through the wires, switches, relays, fuses and fusible links to each electrical component (light bulb, motor, etc.) and to ground, from which it is passed back to the battery. Any electrical problem is an interruption in the flow of electricity to and from the battery.

Connectors

Most electrical connections on these vehicles are made with multi-wire plastic connectors. The mating halves of many connectors are secured with locking clips molded into the plastic connector shells. The mating halves of large connectors, such as some of those under the instrument panel, are held together by a bolt through the center

of the connector.

To separate a connector with locking clips, use a small screwdriver to pry the clips apart carefully, then separate the connector halves. Pull only on the shell, never pull on the wiring harness as you may damage the individual wires and terminals inside the connectors. Look at the connector closely before trying to separate the halves. Often the locking clips are engaged in a way that is not immediately clear. Additionally, many connectors have more than one set of clips.

Each pair of connector terminals has a male half and a female half. When you look at the end view of a connector in a diagram, be sure to understand whether the view shows the harness side or the component side of the connector. Connector halves are mirror images of each other, and a terminal shown on the right side end-view of one half will be on the left side end view of the other half.

Backprobing a connector

It is often necessary to take circuit voltage measurements with a connector connected. Whenever possible, carefully insert a small straight pin (not your meter probe) into the rear of the connector shell to contact the metal terminal inside, then clip your meter lead to the pin. This kind of connection is called "backprobing" **(see illustration)**.

When inserting a test probe into a male terminal, be careful not to distort the terminal opening. Doing so can lead to a poor connection and corrosion at that terminal later. Using the small straight pin instead of a meter probe results in less chance of deforming the terminal connector.

3   Fuses and fusible links - general information

Fuses

Refer to illustrations 3.1a, 3.1b, 3.3a and 3.3b

The electrical circuits of the vehicle are protected by a combination of fuses, circuit breakers and fusible links. The fuse panels are located at the right end of the instrument panel and in the engine compartment **(see illustrations)**.

Each of the fuses is designed to protect a specific circuit, and the various circuits are identified on the inside of the fuse panel cover.

Mini and Maxi fuses are employed in the fuse panels **(see illustration)**. The fuses are different size, but all use the same blade terminal design. The large fuses may be removed with your fingertips, but the small fuses require the use of a fuse puller found in

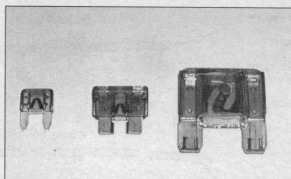

3.3a Several different size fuses may be used in the fuse panels - mini fuse (left), standard fuse (middle) and maxi fuse (right) - all three fuses may be available in the same amperage rating, so make sure you get the correct size fuse and amperage rating when purchasing a replacement

12

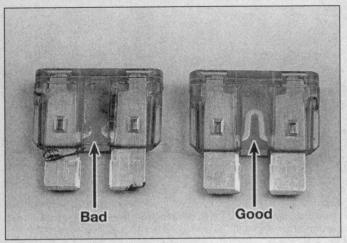

3.3b When a fuse blows, the element between the terminals melts - the fuse on the left is blown, the one on the right is good

3.7 Fusible links (arrow) are attached to the starter motor terminal

the fuse panel. If an electrical component fails, always check the fuse first. The best way to check the fuses is with a test light. Check for power at the exposed terminal tips of each fuse. If power is present at one side of the fuse but not the other, the fuse is blown. A blown fuse can also be identified by visually inspecting it **(see illustration)**.

Be sure to replace blown fuses with the correct type. Fuses of different ratings are physically interchangeable, but only fuses of the proper rating should be used. Replacing a fuse with one of a higher or lower value than specified is not recommended. Each electrical circuit needs a specific amount of protection. The amperage value of each fuse is molded into the fuse body.

If the replacement fuse immediately fails, don't replace it again until the cause of the problem is isolated and corrected. In most cases, this will be a short circuit in the wiring caused by a broken or deteriorated wire.

Fusible links

Refer to illustrations 3.7 and 3.9

Some circuits are protected by fusible links. The links are used in circuits that are not ordinarily fused, such as the alternator circuit.

The fusible links are attached directly to the starter motor, at the solenoid post along with the positive battery cable **(see illustration)**. The link is a short length of heavy insulation spliced into a red wire. If a circuit protected by a fusible link is shorted, the wire inside the heavy insulation melts, opening the circuit and stopping further damage to the wiring harness.

To replace a fusible link, first disconnect the negative battery cable. **Caution:** *On models equipped with the Theftlock audio system, be sure you have the correct activation code before disconnecting the battery (see the front of this manual).*

Although the fusible links appear to be a heavier gauge than the wires they're protect-

ing, the appearance is due to the thick insulation. All fusible links are several wire gauges smaller than the wire they're designed to protect. Fusible links can't be repaired, but a new link of the same size wire can be installed. The procedure is as follows **(see illustration)**:

a) *Cut the damaged fusible link out of the wire just behind the connector.*
b) *Strip the insulation back approximately 1-inch.*
c) *Spread the strands of the exposed wire apart, push them together and twist them in place.*
d) *Use rosin core solder at each end of the new link to obtain a good solder joint.*
e) *Use plenty of electrical tape around the soldered joint. No wires should be exposed.*
f) *Connect the negative battery cable. Test the circuit for proper operation.*

4   Circuit breakers - general information and check

Circuit breakers protect certain circuit, such as the headlights, power windows and power seats. There are several 20-amp and 30-amp circuit breakers located in the interior fuse panel at the end of the dashboard.

Because the circuit breakers reset automatically, an electrical overload in a circuit-breaker-protected system will cause the circuit to fail momentarily, then come back on. If the circuit does not come back on, check it immediately.

For a basic check, pull the circuit breaker up out of its socket on the fuse panel, but just far enough to probe with a voltmeter. The breaker should still contact the sockets.

With the voltmeter negative lead on a

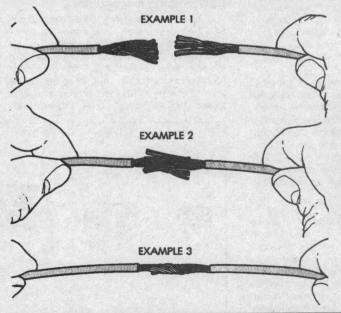

EXAMPLE 1

EXAMPLE 2

EXAMPLE 3

3.9 To repair a fusible link, cut out the damaged section, then join a new section by stripping the wire and twisting it together, as shown here - when securely joined, solder the connections and wrap them with electrical tape

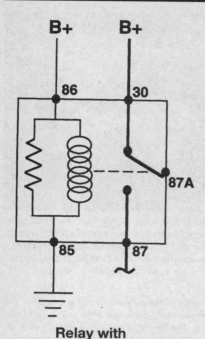

Relay with internal resistor

Relay with internal diode

24053-12-5.2a HAYNES

5.2a Typical ISO relay designs, terminal numbering and circuit connections

good chassis ground, touch each end prong of the circuit breaker with the positive meter probe. There should be battery voltage at each end. If there is battery voltage only at one end, the circuit breaker must be replaced.

5 Relays - general information and testing

General information

1   Several electrical systems in the vehicle, such as the cooling fans, air conditioning compressor, fuel pump and ignition system

5.2b Most relays are marked on the outside to easily identify the control circuit and power circuits - this one is of the four-terminal type

use relays to transmit the electrical signal to the component. Relays use a low-current circuit (the control circuit) to open and close a high-current circuit (the power circuit). If the relay is defective, that component will not operate properly. Most relays are mounted in the engine compartment fuse/relay panel. If a faulty relay is suspected, it can be removed and tested using the procedure below or by a dealer service department or a repair shop. Defective relays must be replaced as a unit.

Testing

Refer to illustrations 5.2a and 5.2b

2   Most of the relays used in these vehicles are often called "ISO" relays, which refers to the International Standards Organization. The terminals of ISO relays are numbered to indicate their usual circuit connections and functions. There are two basic layouts of terminals on the relays used in the covered vehicles **(see illustrations)**.

3   Refer to the wiring diagram for the circuit to determine the proper connections for the relay you're testing. If you can't determine the correct connection from the wiring diagrams, however, you may be able to determine the test connections from the information that follows.

4   Two of the terminals are the relay control circuit and connect to the relay coil. The other relay terminals are the power circuit. When the relay is energized, the coil creates a magnetic field that closes the larger contacts of the power circuit to provide power to the circuit loads.

5   Terminals 85 and 86 are normally the control circuit. If the relay contains a diode, terminal 86 must be connected to battery positive (B+) voltage and terminal 85 to ground. If the relay contains a resistor, terminals 85 and 86 can be connected in either direction with respect to B+ and ground.

6   Terminal 30 is normally connected to the battery voltage (B+) source for the circuit loads. Terminal 87 is connected to the ground side of the circuit, either directly or through a load. If the relay has several alternate terminals for load or ground connections, they usually are numbered 87A, 87B, 87C, and so on.

7   Use an ohmmeter to check continuity through the relay control coil.

a) *Connect the meter according to the polarity shown in* **illustrations 5.2a or 5.2b** *for one check; then reverse the ohmmeter leads and check continuity in the other direction.*

b) *If the relay contains a resistor, resistance should be the specified value with the ohmmeter in either direction.*

c) *If the relay contains a diode, resistance should be the specified coil resistance value with the ohmmeter in the forward polarity direction. With the meter leads reversed, resistance should be lower.*

d) *If the ohmmeter shows infinite resistance in both directions, replace the relay.*

8   Remove the relay from the vehicle and use the ohmmeter to check for continuity between the relay power circuit terminals. There should be no continuity between terminal 30 and 87 with the relay de-energized. On the smaller micro-relays, make sure you have the polarity correct before testing them.

9   Connect a fused jumper wire to terminal 86 and the positive battery terminal. Connect another jumper wire between terminal 85 and ground. When the connections are made, the relay should click.

10   With the jumper wires connected, check for continuity between the power circuit terminals. Now, there should be continuity between terminals 30 and 87.

11   If the relay fails any of the above tests, replace it.

6   Turn signal/hazard flasher - check and replacement

Refer to illustration 6.1

Warning: *The models covered by this manual are equipped with a Supplemental Inflatable Restraint (SIR) system, more commonly known as airbags. Always disable the airbag system before working in the vicinity of any airbag system components to avoid the possibility of accidental deployment of the airbags, which could cause personal injury (see Section 29).*

1   The combination turn signal and hazard flasher unit is mounted under the instrument panel on a steering column extension bracket

12

6.1 The combination turn signal and hazard flasher unit (arrow) is mounted under the instrument panel to the left of the steering column

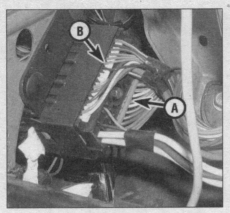

7.3 The turn signal and multi-function switch connectors are plugged into the steering column bulkhead connector

A   *Turn signal switch connector*
B   *Windshield wiper/washer switch connector*

7.10 Detach the wiring harness retainers (arrow) from the turn signal switch wiring harness (the harness from the switch to the steering column bulkhead connector is replaced with the switch)

to the left of the steering column **(see illustration)**. The flasher pulses either the right or left turn signals on and off when the turn signal switch is operated and pulses all the turn signal lights on and off when the hazard switch is switched on.

2   When the flasher unit is functioning properly, an audible click can be heard during its operation. If one of the turn signals flashes much more rapidly than normal, a faulty turn signal bulb is indicated.

3   If a problem in the turn signal/hazard system is indicated, check the turn signal, hazard, brake light and park light fuses first. Also check all the turn signal, park light and brake light bulbs. Replace any defective bulbs and repair the brake light system if necessary.

4   Operate the turn signal switch in both the right turn and left turn positions. If both right and left turn signal lights illuminate but fail to flash, replace the turn signal/hazard flasher. If one side operates normally but not the other, check the turn signal switch and/or related wiring.

5   Turn the hazard switch on. If the hazard lights illuminate but fail to flash, replace the turn signal/hazard flasher. **Note:** *Before replacing the flasher check the brake lights for proper operation and repair if necessary.*

6   To replace the flasher, remove the driver's knee bolster (see Chapter 11).

7   Locate the flasher under the instrument panel and detach it from the steering column bracket.

8   Disconnect the electrical connector and remove the flasher.

9   Installation is the reverse of removal.

---

7   Turn signal and multi-function switch - check and replacement

Warning: *The models covered by this manual are equipped with a Supplemental Inflatable Restraint (SIR) system, more commonly known as airbags. Always disable the airbag system before working in the vicinity of any*

airbag system components to avoid the possibility of accidental deployment of the airbags, which could cause personal injury (see Section 29).

Check

Refer to illustration 7.3

1   Check the T/SIG, HAZ and WRR/WSHR fuses. If a fuse is blown, replace it. If it blows again, locate the electrical short and repair the condition (see Section 2).

2   Remove the driver's knee bolster and lower steering column cover (see Chapter 11).

3   Follow the turn signal and multi-function switch wiring harness down the steering column to locate the electrical connectors **(see illustration)**. The connectors are plugged into a large bulkhead connector.

4   Turn the ignition switch On. Using a test light connected to a good chassis ground point, backprobe the pink and orange wire terminals of the turn signal switch connector. The test light should illuminate, indicating battery power is available to the turn signal switch.

5   Place the turn signal lever in the right turn position, backprobe the dark green and dark blue/white wire terminals, in turn. The test light should flash at each terminal indicating the turn signal switch and flasher are operating properly. Place the turn signal lever in the left turn position and check the light blue/white and yellow terminals in the same manner. If the test light fails to illuminate on any one of the checks, the turn signal switch or wiring harness is defective. If the test light illuminates but fails to flash, check the turn signal/hazard warning flasher (see Section 6).

6   To check the windshield wiper/washer portion of the switch, backprobe the yellow wire terminal of the windshield wiper/washer switch connector **(see illustration 7.3)**. The test light should illuminate, indicating battery power is available to the windshield wiper/washer switch.

7   Place the windshield wiper switch in the High position, backprobe the purple wire terminal. The test light should illuminate indicating the windshield wiper switch is operating properly. Place the wiper switch in the Low position and backprobe the gray wire terminal, again the test light should illuminate. To check the delay function, backprobe the gray wire terminal and turn the switch through the delay functions. The test light should progressively dim as the longer delay functions are selected. To check the windshield washer, backprobe the red wire terminal and turn the washer switch On. If the test light fails to illuminate on any one of the checks, the windshield wiper/washer switch or wiring harness is defective.

Replacement

Refer to illustrations 7.10 and 7.13

8   Disconnect the negative battery cable. **Caution:** *On models equipped with the Theftlock audio system, be sure the lockout feature is turned off before performing any procedure which requires disconnecting the battery (see the front of this manual).*

9   Remove the driver's knee bolster and lower steering column cover (see Chapter 11). Remove the ignition switch lock cylinder and upper steering column cover (see Section 8).

10   Detach the wiring harness retainers from the steering column **(see illustration)**.

11   Loosen the screw in the middle of the steering column bulkhead connector and disconnect the bulkhead connector **(see illustration 7.3)**. Disconnect the turn signal/multi-function switch connectors from the bulkhead connector.

12   Disconnect the electrical connector from the brake/transaxle shift interlock actuator.

13   Remove the turn signal/multi-function switch retaining screws and remove the turn signal/multi-function switch and wiring harness **(see illustration)**.

14   The remainder of installation is the reverse of removal.

7.13 Multi-function switch mounting screws (arrows)

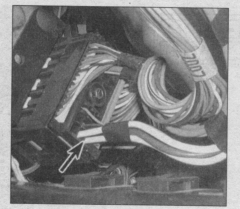

8.4 The ignition switch wiring harness (arrow) is part of the steering column bulkhead connector (the large wires in the center of the bulkhead connector are connected to the ignition switch)

8.12 To remove the lock cylinder, insert a 1/16-inch Allen wrench in the access hole, turn the key to Run, then depress the pin and pull the lock cylinder out of the housing

8   Ignition switch and key lock cylinder - check and replacement

Warning: *The models covered by this manual are equipped with a Supplemental Inflatable Restraint (SIR) system, more commonly known as airbags. Always disable the airbag system before working in the vicinity of any airbag system components to avoid the possibility of accidental deployment of the airbags, which could cause personal injury (see Section 29).*

Ignition switch

Check

Refer to illustration 8.4

1   Check the lock cylinder in each position to make sure it isn't worn or loose and that the key position corresponds to the markings on the housing.

2   Check the IGN MAIN fuses in the underhood fuse/relay box. If a fuse is blown, replace it. If it blows again, locate the electrical short and repair the condition (see Section 2).

3   Remove the driver's knee bolster and lower steering column cover (see Chapter 11).

4   Follow the ignition switch wiring harness down the steering column to locate the electrical connector **(see illustration)**. The large bulkhead connector is part of the ignition switch and wiring harness assembly.

5   Using a test light connected to a good chassis ground point, backprobe the large red wire terminals of the bulkhead connector. The test light should illuminate, indicating battery power is available to the ignition switch.

6   Turn the ignition switch to the Accessory position and backprobe the brown wire terminal of the ignition switch section of the bulkhead connector **(see illustration 8.4)**. The test light should illuminate indicating the ignition switch is operating in the ACC position.

7   Turn the ignition switch to the Run posi-

8.13 Carefully remove the key alarm switch from the housing

tion and backprobe the brown, orange and pink wire terminals of the ignition switch section of the bulkhead connector **(see illustration 8.4)**. The test light should illuminate at each terminal indicating the ignition switch is operating in the Run position.

8   If the engine won't start, place the ignition switch in the Start position and backprobe the pink and yellow wire terminals of the ignition switch section of the bulkhead connector **(see illustration 8.4)**. The test light should illuminate at each terminal indicating the ignition switch is operating in the Start position.

9   If the test light fails to illuminate on any one of the checks, the ignition switch or wiring harness is defective.

Replacement

Refer to illustrations 8.12, 8.13 and 8.16

10   Disconnect the negative battery cable.
Caution: *On models equipped with the Theft-lock audio system, be sure the lockout feature is turned off before performing any procedure which requires disconnecting the battery (see the front of this manual).*

11   Remove the driver's knee bolster and

8.16 Remove the ignition switch mounting screws (arrows)

lower steering column cover (see Chapter 11).

12   While holding the upper steering column cover up, turn the ignition key to the Start position and insert a 1/16-inch Allen wrench in the access hole **(see illustration)**. Press the lock cylinder retaining pin in, release the ignition key to the Run position and pull the lock cylinder out of the housing. Remove the lock cylinder and upper steering column cover.

13   Carefully pry the key alarm switch retaining clip in, rotate the switch 1/4-turn and remove the key alarm switch from the steering column lock housing **(see illustration)**.

14   Detach the wiring harness retainers from the steering column.

15   Loosen the screw in the middle of the steering column bulkhead connector and disconnect the bulkhead connector **(see illustration 8.4)**. Disconnect the turn signal/multifunction switch connectors from the bulkhead connector.

16   Remove the ignition switch retaining screws and remove the ignition switch and wiring harness **(see illustration)**.

17   Installation is the reverse of removal.

12

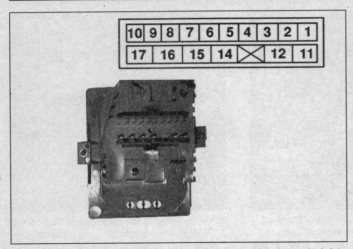

9.2 Headlight switch terminal identification - with the switch in the Headlight position, continuity should be indicated between terminals 12 and 14, and between terminals 15 and 17 - with the switch in the Parking light position, continuity should be indicated between terminals 15 and 17

9.4 Carefully pull the headlight switch from the instrument panel

9   Headlight switch - check and replacement

Warning: *The models covered by this manual are equipped with a Supplemental Inflatable Restraint (SIR) system, more commonly known as airbags. Always disable the airbag system before working in the vicinity of any airbag system components to avoid the possibility of accidental deployment of the airbags, which could cause personal injury (see Section 29).*

Check

Refer to illustration 9.2

1   Refer to Steps below to remove the headlight switch for testing.
2   Using an ohmmeter, check the switch for continuity between the indicated terminals with the switch in each of the indicated positions **(see illustration)**. If the continuity is not as specified, replace the switch.

Replacement

Refer to illustration 9.4

3   Remove the instrument cluster trim bezel (see Chapter 11).
4   Carefully pull the headlight switch from the instrument panel **(see illustration)**. Disconnect the electrical connector.
5   Installation is the reverse of the removal procedure.

10   Instrument panel gauges - check

Note: *Refer to the gauges and warning lights system wiring diagram at the end of this Chapter to familiarize yourself with the circuits before beginning this procedure.*

1   If the gauges and all the warning lights are inoperative, check the system fuses. If

the fuses are good, check the instrument panel power and ground circuits. Remove the instrument cluster and check for battery voltage and continuity to ground at the appropriate terminals of the instrument cluster connector. Refer to the wiring diagrams to determine the terminals for testing. For example; battery voltage should be present at the pink wire terminal with the ignition key On. Continuity to a good chassis ground point should be indicated on the black wire terminal. If the power and ground circuits are good, the instrument cluster is probably defective.
2   If the temperature gauge does not respond or its accuracy is suspected, locate the Engine Coolant Temperature sensor (see Chapter 6). On 1999 and earlier models, disconnect the connector from the sensor and connect the terminal in the harness connector corresponding to the green wire to a good engine ground point with a jumper wire. Turn the ignition key On, the gauge pointer should move to the hot position. **Note:** *Turn the key Off right away; grounding the sending unit for too long could damage the gauge.* If the gauge responds correctly, the sending unit is probably defective. If the gauge does not respond, the wiring harness, gauge or instrument cluster is probably defective. On 2000 and later models, the temperature gauge is controlled by the PCM with input from the Engine Coolant Temperature sensor. Check the Engine Coolant Temperature sensor as described in Chapter 6. If the sensor is good, have the PCM and instrument cluster diagnosed by a dealer service department or other qualified repair facility.
3   The same check can be performed on the fuel gauge, locate the fuel gauge sending unit connector at the fuel tank (see Chapter 4). Disconnect the connector and connect the fuel gauge terminal in the harness connector to a good engine ground point with a jumper wire. Turn the ignition key On, the

gauge pointer should move to the full position. **Note:** *Turn the key Off right away; grounding the sending unit for too long could damage the gauge.* If the gauge responds correctly, the sending unit is probably defective (refer to Chapter 4 for the fuel level sending unit check). If the gauge does not respond, the wiring harness, gauge or instrument cluster is probably defective.
4   If the engine oil pressure warning light comes on with the engine running, refer to Chapter 2B and check the engine oil pressure. If the oil pressure is good, disconnect the electrical connector from the oil pressure switch (see Chapter 2B for the oil pressure switch location) and connect the terminal in the harness connector to a good engine ground point. Turn the ignition key On, the warning light should illuminate, if it doesn't the wiring harness or instrument cluster is defective or the bulb is burned out (refer to Section 17 for bulb replacement). If the bulb illuminates, check for continuity between the terminal on the oil pressure switch and the engine block, there should be continuity with the engine off and no continuity with the engine running. If continuity exists with the engine running, replace the oil pressure switch. Other warning lights may be checked in a similar manner (refer to the wiring diagrams).
5   If the speedometer is inoperative, check the vehicle speed sensor (see Chapter 6).

11   Instrument cluster - removal and installation

Refer to illustrations 11.3a and 11.3b
Warning: *The models covered by this manual are equipped with a Supplemental Inflatable Restraint (SIR) system, more commonly known as airbags. Always disable the airbag*

11.3a Remove the mounting screws (arrows) and pull the instrument cluster away from the dash

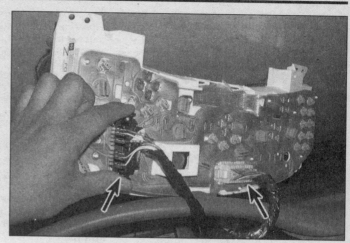

11.3b Disconnect the electrical connectors (arrows) at the back of the cluster

12.3 Remove the radio mounting screws (arrows)

system before working in the vicinity of any airbag system components to avoid the possibility of accidental deployment of the airbags, which could cause personal injury (see Section 29).

1   Disable the airbag system (see Section 29).

2   Remove the instrument cluster bezel (see Chapter 11).

3   Remove the retaining screws and pull the cluster forward enough to disconnect the electrical connectors **(see illustrations)**.

4   Installation is the reverse of the removal procedure.

12   Radio and speakers - removal and installation

Warning: *The models covered by this manual are equipped with a Supplemental Inflatable Restraint (SIR) system, more commonly known as airbags. Always disable the airbag system before working in the vicinity of any airbag system components to avoid the possibility of accidental deployment of the airbags, which could cause personal injury (see Section 29).*

Radio

Refer to illustrations 12.3 and 12.4

1   Disable the airbag system (see Section 29).

2   Remove the center bezel panel from the dash (see Chapter 11).

3   Remove the screws and pull the radio

away from the dash **(see illustration)**.

4   Disconnect the antenna lead and the electrical connectors and remove the radio **(see illustration)**.

5   Installation is the reverse of removal.

Speakers

Front

Refer to illustration 12.7

6   Remove the door trim panel and water deflector (see Chapter 11).

7   Remove the speaker by carefully unsnapping it from the door lock module **(see illustration)**. Disconnect the electrical connector from the speaker.

8   Installation is the reverse of removal.

Rear

Refer to illustration 12.10

9   Remove the liftgate trim panel (see Chapter 11).

10   Disengage the clip at the top of the speaker and remove it from the liftgate **(see illustration)**.

11   Disconnect the electrical connector from the speaker.

12   Installation is the reverse of removal.

12.4 Pull the radio out of the dash and disconnect the electrical connectors and the antenna lead (arrows)

12.7 With the door trim panel removed, unsnap the front speaker from the lock module

12.10 To remove the rear speaker, disengage the clip (arrow)

12

13 Antenna cable - removal and installation

Warning: *The models covered by this manual are equipped with a Supplemental Inflatable Restraint (SIR) system, more commonly known as airbags. Always disable the airbag system before working in the vicinity of any airbag system components to avoid the possibility of accidental deployment of the airbags, which could cause personal injury (see Section 29).*

1   The radio antenna is incorporated into the windshield. The antenna cable is a two-piece cable running from the radio, behind the instrument panel and up the right roof pillar to the center of the windshield.

2   Remove the radio (see Section 12).

3   Remove the insulation panel below the right-side of the instrument panel.

4   Remove the right side-kick panel.

5   Remove the roof pillar trim panels from each side.

6   Remove the sun visors and the overhead console, if equipped. Pull the front of the headliner down slightly and disconnect the cable from the windshield antenna. **Caution:** *Be very careful not to damage the headliner.*

7   Remove the bolt securing the cable to the roof and detach the cable from the clips under the instrument panel.

8   Secure a section of pull wire to the end of the cable and pull the cable and pull wire through the roof pillar.

9   Remove the pull wire from the old cable and attach it to the end of the new cable. Pull the new cable through the roof pillar and remove the pull wire.

10   The remainder of installation is the reverse of removal.

14 Headlight bulb - replacement

Refer to illustration 14.2

Warning: *These models are equipped with halogen gas-filled bulbs, which are under pressure and may shatter if the surface is scratched or the bulb is dropped. Wear eye protection and handle the bulbs carefully, grasping only the base whenever possible.*

15.1 Headlight adjusting screw locations (arrows)

Do not touch the surface of the bulb with your fingers because the oil from your skin could cause it to overheat and fail prematurely. If you do touch the bulb surface, clean it with rubbing alcohol.

Caution: *The headlight housing is filled with nitrogen gas. To prevent the nitrogen gas from escaping, place the headlight housing with the lens down, on a bench before removing the bulb and install the new bulb as quickly as possible.*

1   Remove the headlight housing (see Section 16). Place a shop towel on the bench to protect the lens and place the headlight housing, lens down, on the towel.

2   Rotate the retaining ring counterclockwise until loose and withdraw the bulb assembly from the headlight housing **(see illustration)**.

3   Without touching the glass with your bare fingers, insert the new bulb assembly into the headlight housing and tighten the lock ring.

4   Reinstall the headlight housing (see Section 16) and test the headlight operation.

15 Headlights and fog lights - adjustment

Headlights

Refer to illustrations 15.1 and 15.2

Note: *It is important that the headlights are aimed correctly. If adjusted incorrectly they could blind the driver of an oncoming vehicle and cause a serious accident or seriously*

14.2 Rotate the retaining ring (arrow) counterclockwise until loose and withdraw the headlight bulb assembly from the headlight housing

reduce your ability to see the road. The headlights should be checked for proper aim every 12 months and any time a new headlight is installed or front end body work is performed. It should be emphasized that the following procedure is only an interim step that will provide temporary adjustment until the headlights can be adjusted by a properly equipped shop.

1   The composite headlights are equipped with two adjustment screws, one controlling left-and-right movement and one for up-and-down movement **(see illustration)**.

2   There are several methods of adjusting the headlights. The simplest method requires an open area with a blank wall and a level floor **(see illustration)**.

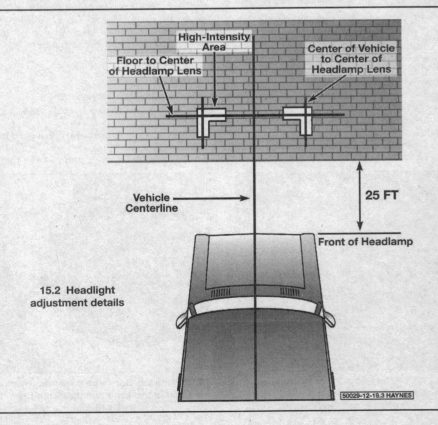

15.2 Headlight adjustment details

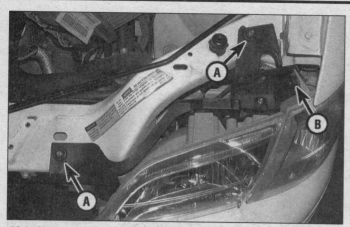

16.3 Remove the headlight housing wingnuts (A); turn signal/side marker/park light housing wingnut (B)

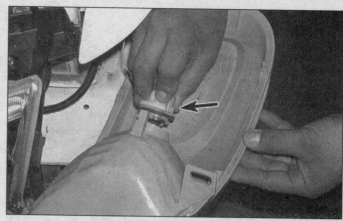

17.2 The bulbs are accessed from the back of the turn signal/side marker/park light housing - squeeze the tab (arrow) to withdraw the bulb holder

3   Position masking tape vertically on the wall in reference to the vehicle centerline and the centerlines of both headlights.

4   Position a horizontal tape line in reference to the centerline of all the headlights. **Note:** *It may be easier to position the tape on the wall with the vehicle parked only a few inches away.*

5   Adjustment should be made with the vehicle parked 25 feet from the wall, sitting level, the gas tank half-full and no unusually heavy load in the vehicle.

6   Starting with the low beam adjustment, position the high intensity zone so it is two inches below the horizontal line and two inches to the side of the vertical headlight line away from oncoming traffic. Twist the adjustment screws until the desired level has been achieved.

7   With the high beams on, the high intensity zone should be vertically centered with the exact center just below the horizontal line. **Note:** *It may not be possible to position the headlight aim exactly for both high and low beams. If a compromise must be made, keep in mind that the low beams are the most used and have the greatest effect on driver safety.*

8   Have the headlights adjusted by a dealer service department at the earliest opportunity.

Fog lights

9   Some models have optional fog lights that can be aimed just like headlights.

10   Tape a horizontal line on the wall that represents the height of the fog lamps, and another tape line four inches below that line **(see illustration 15.2)**. Park the vehicle 25 feet from the wall.

11   Using the adjusting nut on the rear of the fog lamp, adjust the pattern on the wall so that the top of the fog lamp beam meets the lower line on the wall, and that the beam is centered horizontally in front of the fog lamps.

16   Headlight housing - removal and installation

Refer to illustration 16.3

1   Open and support the hood.

2   Remove the front turn signal/side marker/park light housing (see Section 17).

3   Remove the wing nuts from the headlight housing mounting studs **(see illustration)**.

4   Lift the housing up and remove it from the support bracket.

5   Disconnect the electrical connector from the headlight bulb.

6   Installation is the reverse of removal.

17   Bulb replacement

Front turn signal, side marker and parking lights

Refer to illustration 17.2

1   Remove the wing nut from the front turn signal/side marker/park light housing mounting stud and remove the housing from the fender **(see illustration 16.3)**.

2   To remove the bulb holder, depress the tab next to the bulb holder, turn the bulb holder counterclockwise and remove it from the housing **(see illustration)**.

3   Remove the bulb from the holder and insert the new bulb.

4   Reinstall the front turn signal/side marker/park light housing.

Fog light

Refer to illustration 17.6

5   On Pontiac models, disconnect the electrical connector from the fog light, remove the mounting nuts and remove the fog light the front bumper fascia.

6   On Oldsmobile models, remove the screw retaining the fog lamp to the bracket on the front bumper reinforcement beam, pull the fog light out and disconnect the electrical connector **(see illustration)**.

7   Installation is the reverse of removal.

Tail/brake/turn signal and back-up lights

Refer to illustrations 17.9, 17.10 and 17.11

8   Open the liftgate.

9   Remove the taillight housing mounting screws and pull the housing away from the body **(see illustration)**.

17.6 On Oldsmobile models, remove the screw retaining the fog lamp to the bracket on the front bumper reinforcement beam

17.9 Remove the taillight housing mounting screws (arrows)

12

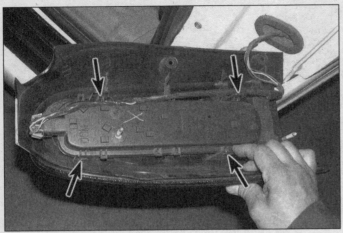

17.10 Release the four clips (arrows) and separate the bulb holder from the taillight housing

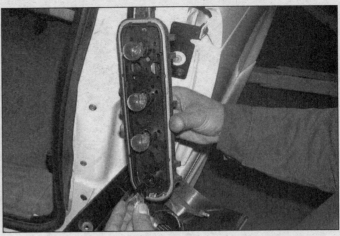

17.11 Pull the taillight bulbs out of the bulb holder

10   Release the four clips to disengage the bulb holder from the taillight housing **(see illustration)**.
11   Carefully pull the bulbs straight out to remove them from the holder **(see illustration)**.
12   Installation is the reverse of removal.

License plate light

Refer to illustration 17.14
13   Remove the two screws and the license plate light lens.
14   Pull the bulb straight out to replace it **(see illustration)**.
15   Install the lens.

High-mounted brake light

Refer to illustrations 17.17
16   The high-mounted brake light must be replaced as a complete assembly.
17   Remove the screws and pull the high-mounted brake light assembly from the body **(see illustration)**. Disconnect the electrical connector and remove the brake light.
18   Installation is the reverse of removal.

Instrument cluster illumination

Refer to illustration 17.20
19   Remove the instrument cluster (see Section 11).
20   Turn the bulb holder 1/4-turn counter-clockwise and remove the bulb holder from the instrument cluster **(see illustration)**.
21   Pull the bulb from the holder and install the new bulb.
22   The remainder of installation is the reverse of removal.

Overhead console reading light

Refer to illustrations 17.23 and 17.24
23   Using a small flat-bladed screwdriver, carefully pry the retaining tabs in to release the switch module and reading light assembly from the overhead console **(see illustration)**.
24   Pry the retaining tabs in and remove the reading light bulb holder from the module **(see illustration)**.
25   Pull the bulb from the holder and install

17.14 Remove the lens and the license plate bulb (arrow)

the new bulb.
26   The remainder of installation is the reverse of removal.

17.17 High-mounted brake light mounting screws (arrows)

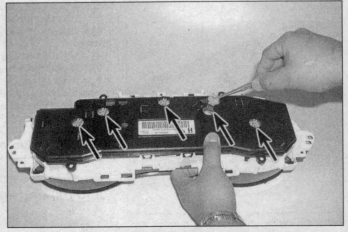

17.20 To remove an instrument cluster bulb (arrows), turn the bulb holder counterclockwise and remove it from the instrument cluster

17.23 Using a small flat-bladed screwdriver, carefully pry the retaining tabs in to release the switch module and reading light assembly from the overhead console

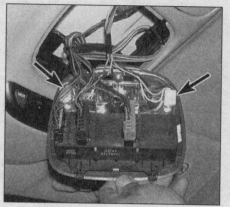

17.24 Remove the reading light bulb holder (arrow) from the module

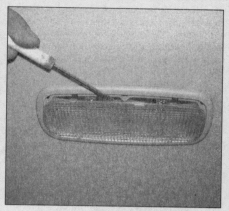

17.27 Using a small flat-bladed screwdriver, carefully pry the lens off the dome light

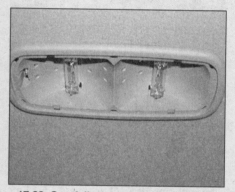

17.28 Carefully pry one end of the bulb from the contacts and remove the bulb

Dome light

Refer to illustrations 17.27 and 17.28

27 Using a small flat-bladed screwdriver, carefully pry the lens off the dome light **(see illustration)**.

28 Carefully pry one end of the bulb from the contacts and remove the bulb **(see illustration)**.

29 Installation is the reverse of removal.

Side rail reading light

Refer to illustrations 17.30 and 17.31

30 Using a small flat-bladed screwdriver, carefully pry the lens off the reading light **(see illustration)**.

31 Pull the bulb straight out of the bulb holder **(see illustration)**.

32 Installation is the reverse of removal.

18 Wiper motor - check and replacement

Check

Refer to illustration 18.2

Note: Refer to the wiring diagrams for wire colors and locations in the following checks. When checking for voltage, probe a grounded 12-volt test light to each terminal at a connector until it lights; this verifies voltage (power) at the terminal. If the following checks fail to locate the problem, have the system diagnosed by a dealer service department or other properly equipped repair facility.

1 If the wipers work slowly, make sure the battery is in good condition and has a strong charge (see Chapter 1). If the battery is in good condition, disconnect the linkage from the wiper motor (see below) and operate the wiper arms by hand. Check for binding linkage and pivots. Lubricate or repair the linkage or pivots as necessary. If the wipers still operate slowly, check for loose or corroded connections, especially the ground connection. If all connections look OK, replace the motor.

2 If the wipers fail to operate when activated, check the fuse. If the fuse is good, disconnect the wiper motor connector, turn the ignition switch On and check for battery voltage at the B+ terminal of the wiper connector **(see illustration)**. Check for continuity to a good chassis ground point at the ground wire terminal of the wiper connector. Turn the wiper switch to the HI position and check for voltage at the wiper motor connector HI terminal. If there's voltage at the connector, the ground circuit is good, the linkage is not binding (see Step 1 above) and the motor does not operate when connected, replace the wiper motor. If there's no voltage to the motor at the HI or LOW terminals of the connector, check the multi-function switch (see Section 7).

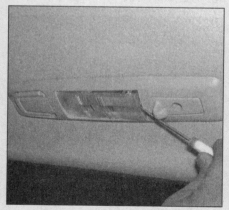

17.30 Using a small flat-bladed screwdriver, carefully pry the lens off the reading light

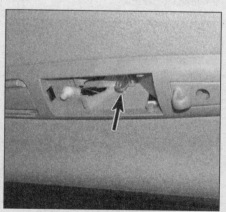

17.31 Pull the bulb (arrow) straight out of the bulb holder

18.2 Windshield wiper motor harness connector terminal identification

A Ground	D On
B B+	E Low/Pulse
C High	

12

3   If the wipers stop at the position they're in when the switch is turned off (fail to park), disconnect the multi-function switch electrical connector (see Section 7). If the wipers now park, replace the multi-function switch. If the wipers still don't park, check the wiring from the wiper motor to the switch for a short circuit. If the circuits are good, replace the wiper motor.

4   If the wipers won't shut off unless the ignition switch is turned Off, disconnect the multi-function switch electrical connector (see Section 7). If the wipers stop, replace the multi-function switch. If the wipers keep running, check the wiring from the wiper motor to the switch for a short circuit. If the circuits are good, replace the wiper motor.

5   If the wipers don't operate when the washer switch is activated, disconnect the wiper motor connector and check for voltage at the wiper On signal terminal **(see illustration 18.2)**. If voltage is present and the wiper motor ground circuit is good, replace the wiper motor. If no voltage is present, check the wiring between the wiper motor and the multi-function switch for continuity. If the circuits are good, replace the multi-function switch (see Section 7).

Replacement

Front

Refer to illustrations 18.9, 18.12 and 18.13

6   Open and support the hood.

7   Remove the windshield washer reservoir mounting screws and position the reservoir aside.

8   Remove the windshield wiper module cover.

9   Loosen the two screws and remove the linkage assembly from the crank arm **(see illustration)**.

10   Remove the crank arm cover. Loosen the crank arm screw several turns. While pulling up on the crank arm, tap the screw with a soft-faced hammer to loosen the crank arm from the wiper motor shaft. Remove the screw and the crank arm.

11   Disconnect the electrical connector from the wiper motor.

12   Remove the wiper motor retaining bolts

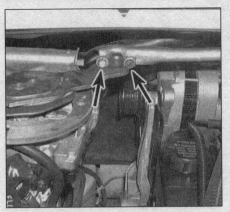

18.9 Loosen (but do not remove) the two screws (arrows) and detach the linkage from the wiper motor crank arm

and remove the motor **(see illustration)**.

13   Installation is the reverse of removal with the following addition. After installing the wiper motor, install the crank arm as follows **(see illustration)**:

a) *Turn the ignition switch to the ACC position.*

b) *Turn the wiper switch to the PULSE position.*

c) *The wiper motor should run momentarily, then stop on delay. When the wiper motor stops, turn the ignition Off.*

d) *Install the crank arm on the wiper motor shaft while maintaining a 5/32 to 5/16-inch (4 to 8 mm) gap between the V-notch in the crank arm and the tab. DO NOT rotate the wiper shaft.*

e) *When the gap is set, tighten the crank arm screw to 150 in-lbs.*

f) *Turn the ignition On and allow the motor to run. When the motor stops on delay, turn the ignition Off and check the gap. If the gap is not correct, repeat the installation.*

Rear

Refer to illustrations 18.14, 18.15 and 18.17

14   Pry open the cap from the wiper arm spindle. Remove the wiper arm nut and wiper arm **(see illustration)**.

18.12 Windshield wiper motor mounting bolts (arrows)

18.13 When installing the crank arm on the wiper motor shaft, maintain a 5/32 to 5/16-inch (4 to 8 mm) gap between the V-notch in the crank arm and the tab

15   Remove the wiper arm spindle nut, grommet and washer **(see illustration)**.

16   Remove the liftgate trim panel (see Chapter 11).

17   Disconnect the electrical connector from the wiper motor, remove the mounting bolts and remove the wiper motor **(see illustration)**.

18   Installation is the reverse of removal.

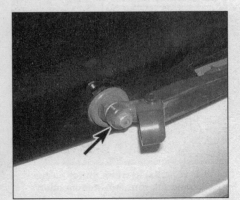

18.14 Pry open the cap from the wiper arm spindle and remove the wiper arm nut (arrow) and wiper arm

18.15 Remove the wiper arm spindle nut (arrow), grommet and washer

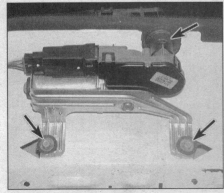

18.17 Rear wiper motor mounting bolts (arrows)

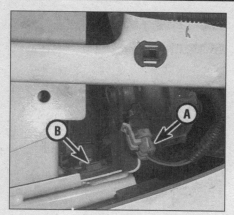

19.1 Horn electrical connector (A) and mounting bolt (B)

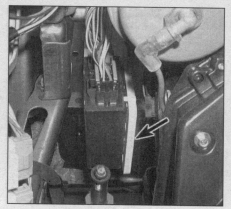

20.2a The Daytime Running Lights module (arrow) is located under the instrument panel to the right of the steering column

20.2b The DRL ambient light sensor is located under the instrument panel pad

19 Horn - check and replacement

Refer to illustration 19.1

Note: *Check the fuse before beginning electrical diagnosis.*

1   Remove the headlight housing (right or left side, depending on which horn you are working on) (see Section 16).

2   Disconnect the electrical connector from the horn **(see illustration)**.

3   Check for battery voltage at the dark green-wire terminal of the connector while an assistant depresses the horn switch. Check for continuity to ground at the black-wire terminal. If battery voltage is present, the ground circuit is good and the horn doesn't sound when connected, replace the horn.

4   If battery voltage is not present at the dark green wire terminal, refer to Section 5 and check the horn relay, which is located in the underhood fuse/relay box. If the relay is good, check the circuit from the horn to the horn relay and from the relay to the switch.

5   To replace the horn, remove the bracket bolt and withdraw the horn through the headlight housing opening.

6   Installation is the reverse of removal.

20 Daytime Running Lights (DRL) - general information

Refer to illustrations 20.2a and 20.2b

The Daytime Running Lights (DRL) system used on all models, operates in two modes; daytime mode and nighttime mode. In the daytime mode only the front turn signal lights are illuminated. In the nighttime mode the headlights, taillights, parking lights, side marker lights and license plate lights are all illuminated, just as if the headlight switch was turned on. The DRL system is activated whenever the ignition switch is turned to the Run position. The only exception is when the ignition switch is turned to the Run position with the parking brake applied. Once the parking brake is released, the lights will turn on and remain on as long as the ignition switch is on, even if the parking brake is later

applied. The headlight switch may be turned on at anytime to override the system.

The DRL system consists of the DRL module and the DRL ambient light sensor **(see illustrations)**. The DRL module contains several solid state relays used to activate the light circuits depending on the conditions. The ambient light sensor is a photodiode element sensitive to changes in light intensity. The DRL module uses this signal to determine day or night mode operation.

21 Rear window defogger - check and repair

1   The rear window defogger consists of a number of horizontal heating elements baked onto the inside surface of the glass. Power is supplied through a mini-relay in the engine compartment fuse/relay box. The heater is controlled by the instrument panel switch, which is part of the heating/air-conditioning controls. Test the switch for continuity (see Chapter 3). **Note:** *On most models, the rear window grid is used as a defogger only, while*

21.5 When measuring the voltage at the rear window defogger grid, wrap a piece of aluminum foil around the negative probe of the voltmeter and press the foil against the wire with your finger

on Alero models, the defogger grid also serves as the antenna for the radio.

2   Small breaks in the element can be repaired without removing the rear window.

Check

Refer to illustrations 21.5, 21.6 and 21.8

3   Turn the ignition switch and defogger switches to the ON position.

4   Using a voltmeter, place the positive probe against the defogger grid positive terminal and the negative probe against the ground terminal. If battery voltage is not indicated, check the fuse, defogger switch, defogger relay and related wiring. If voltage is indicated, but all or part of the defogger doesn't heat, proceed with the following tests.

5   When measuring voltage during the next two tests, wrap a piece of aluminum foil around the tip of the voltmeter positive probe and press the foil against the heating element with your finger **(see illustration)**. Place the negative probe on the defogger grid ground terminal.

6   Check the voltage at the center of each heating element **(see illustration)**. If the voltage is 5 to 6 volts, the element is okay (there

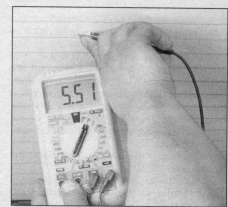

21.6 To determine if a heating element has broken, check the voltage at the center of each element - if the voltage is approximately 6-volts, the element is unbroken

12

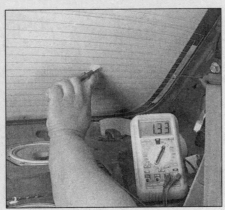

21.8 To find the break, place the voltmeter negative lead against the defogger ground terminal, place the voltmeter positive lead with the foil strip against the heat wire at the positive end and slide it toward the negative terminal end - the point at which the meter deflects is where the wire is broken

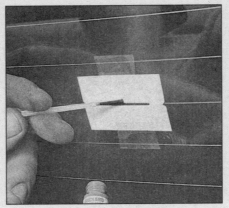

21.14 To use a defogger repair kit, apply masking tape to the inside of the window at the damaged area, then brush on the special conductive coating

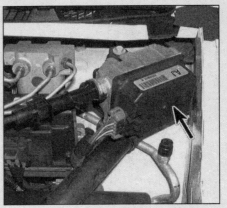

22.1 The cruise control module (arrow) is located in the left rear corner of the engine compartment

is no break). If the voltage is 0 volts, the element is broken between the center of the element and the positive end. If the voltage is 10 to 12 volts the element is broken between the center of the element and the ground side. Check each heating element.

7   If none of the elements are broken, connect the negative probe to a good chassis ground. The voltage reading should stay the same, if it doesn't the ground connection is bad.

8   To find the break, place the voltmeter negative probe against the defogger ground terminal. Place the voltmeter positive probe with the foil strip against the heating element at the positive side and slide it toward the negative side. The point at which the voltmeter deflects from several volts to zero is the point where the heating element is broken **(see illustration)**.

Repair

Refer to illustration 21.14

9   Repair the break in the element using a repair kit specifically for this purpose, such as Dupont paste No. 4817 (or equivalent). The kit includes conductive plastic epoxy.

10   Before repairing a break, turn off the system and allow it to cool for a few minutes.

11   Lightly buff the element area with fine steel wool; then clean it thoroughly with rubbing alcohol.

12   Use masking tape to mask off the area being repaired.

13   Thoroughly mix the epoxy, following the kit instructions.

14   Apply the epoxy material to the slit in the masking tape, overlapping the undamaged area about 3/4-inch on either end **(see illustration)**.

15   Allow the repair to cure for 24 hours before removing the tape and using the system.

22 Cruise control system - description and check

Refer to illustrations 22.1, 22.5 and 22.6

1   The cruise control system consists of the cruise control module, brake switch, control switches and the Powertrain Control Module (PCM). The cruise control system maintains vehicle speed with a servo motor that is connected to the throttle linkage by a cable. The servo motor and control circuits are contained within the cruise control module. The cruise control module is located in the engine compartment attached to the left inner fender **(see illustration)**. Some features of the system require special testers and diagnostic procedures that are beyond the scope of this manual. Listed below are some general procedures that may be used to locate common problems.

2   Check the cruise control fuse in the interior fuse panel (see Section 3). Make sure the brake lights, including the high-mounted brake light, are operating properly. A problem with the brake lights may affect the cruise control system. Make sure the Transaxle Range switch is operating properly (see Chapter 7).

22.5 Adjust the cruise cable by pulling the locking clip out (arrow) to remove slack

3   The cruise control brake release switch (located on a bracket at the brake pedal just above the brake light switch) deactivates the cruise control system when the brake pedal is depressed.

4   To check the brake release switch, disconnect the electrical connector and check the continuity of the switch with an ohmmeter. With the brake pedal at rest, continuity should exist across the switch terminals. With the brake pedal depressed, there should be no continuity. If the switch doesn't operate as described, replace it (see Chapter 9; it's replaced and adjusted just like the brake light switch).

5   Check the control cable between the cruise control module and the throttle linkage. If an excessive amount of slack is noted in the cable at the throttle lever, make sure the throttle linkage is at the full-closed position and release the lock-clip at the cable housing **(see illustration)**. The cable adjuster should automatically remove the slack in the cable. If necessary, push the cable in further by hand, then push the lock-clip back in. Make sure the throttle lever does not move off the fully-closed position.

6   Some tests of the system can be made at the cruise control module connector. Disconnect the electrical connector at the mod-

22.6 Cruise control module harness connector terminal identification

ule and turn the ignition key On (engine not running). Using a voltmeter or test light, check for battery voltage at terminal F on the harness connector **(see illustration)**. If battery voltage isn't present, check the circuit from the module to the fuse panel. If battery voltage is present at terminal F, connect the test light or voltmeter to terminals F and E. If battery voltage isn't present, check terminal E for continuity to ground.

7   To test the cruise control switches, turn the ignition On and place the cruise control switch in the On position. Battery voltage should be present at terminal A (On/Off switch). Press and hold the Set/Coast switch, battery voltage should be present at terminal B. Press and hold the Resume/Accelerate switch, battery voltage should be present at terminal C.

8   The cruise control switches are part of the turn signal and multi-function switch. The terminals are in the same connector as the turn signal switch and can be tested in the same manner at the steering column bulkhead connector (see Section 7). Refer to the wiring diagrams to determine the terminals to test according to wire color. If the switches fail the tests at the steering column connector, replace the turn signal and multi-function switch. If the switches test good at the steering column connector, but failed at the cruise control module connector, there is a problem in the wiring harness between the steering column connector and the cruise control module connector.

9   The cruise control system uses information from the PCM, including the Vehicle Speed Sensor, which is located in the transaxle. To test the speed sensor, see Chapter 6.

10   After making your repairs or adjustments, test-drive the vehicle to determine if the cruise control is now working. If it isn't, take it to a dealer service department or an automotive electrical specialist for further diagnosis.

23   Power window system - description and check

Refer to illustrations 23.7 and 23.8

1   The power window system operates the electric motors mounted in the doors and rear quarter panels which lower and raise the door windows or open and close the quarter windows. The system consists of the control switches, the motors, glass mechanisms and associated wiring.

2   Power door windows are wired so they can be lowered and raised from the master control switch by the driver or by the passenger door switch. The quarter windows are controlled by a switch in the overhead console. Each window has a separate motor that is reversible. The position of the control switch determines the polarity and therefore the direction of operation.

3   The motors are equipped with a sepa-

23.7 Check for battery voltage at the power window motor connector (arrow) while operating the switch

rate circuit breaker in each motor in addition to the fuse or circuit breaker protecting the whole circuit. This prevents one stuck window from disabling the whole system.

4   The power window system will only operate when the ignition switch is ON.

5   These procedures are general in nature, so if you can't find the problem using them, take the vehicle to a dealer service department or other qualified repair facility.

6   If the power windows don't work at all, check the fuse or circuit breaker.

7   If one of the door windows or quarter windows is inoperative, remove the trim panel (see Chapter 11) and check for power at the motor connector with a voltmeter or test light while operating the switch **(see illustration)**. Battery voltage should be present at one terminal of the connector while opening the window and at the other terminal when closing the window. There should be continuity to ground on the opposite terminal. If battery voltage is present, the ground circuit is good and the window motor does not operate when connected, replace the window motor. **Note:** *Be sure to check the window regulator or actuator for binding and damage. If necessary, detach the glass from the mechanism and move the glass up and down by hand while checking for damage. If there's binding or damage, lubricate, repair or replace parts, as necessary.*

8   If voltage isn't reaching the motor, turn the ignition On and backprobe the brown wire terminal of the switch connector **(see illustration)**. If battery voltage isn't present, check the circuit from the fuse panel to the switch. **Note:** *The power window switch connector contains two brown wires, be sure to check both (the other is used for the window down direction, check it as described in Step 9). Also check for continuity to a good chassis ground at the black wire terminal. The system ground connection is located on the right-side pillar between the right front door and the sliding door (you'll have the remove the pillar trim panel to access the ground connection).*

9   Refer to the wiring diagrams to familiar-

23.8 To check the power window switch, backprobe the switch connector wire terminals with a voltmeter or test light while operating the switch

ize yourself with the harness wiring colors relating to the various switch functions. Operate the switch while backprobing the appropriate wire terminal to check the switch operation. For example; battery voltage should be present at the driver's window switch dark blue wire while raising the driver's window. If the switch is good, check the wiring harness for continuity between the switches and motors. **Note:** *The driver's door switch contains an express down function, make sure you press the switch only to the first detent to operate the switch normally and to the second detent to operate the express down function.*

24   Power door lock system - description and check

Refer to illustrations 24.6 and 24.7

1   The power door lock system operates the door lock actuators mounted in each door and the liftgate. The main components of the system include the Body Control Module (BCM), door switches, door lock actuators, door lock cylinder switches and associated wiring. The system is fully controlled by the BCM, diagnosis is limited to simple checks of the wiring connections, switches and actuators for minor faults that can be easily repaired.

2   The door locks are operated by bi-directional actuators located in the doors. The lock switches have two operating positions: Lock and Unlock. These switches signal the BCM, which in turn connects voltage to the door lock actuator. Depending on which function is desired, the BCM reverses polarity to the actuator, allowing the two sides of the circuit to be used alternately as the feed (positive) and ground side. Control switches connected to the key locks in the doors, signal the BCM when one door is locked or unlocked, the BCM will then lock or unlock all the doors.

3   Some vehicles may have keyless entry and anti-theft systems incorporated into the

12

24.6 Check for power at the door lock actuator connector (arrow) with the switch depressed

24.7 Using an ohmmeter, check the door lock switch for continuity - continuity should be indicated between terminals A and E in the Lock position and between terminals D and E in the Unlock position

25.7 Remove the door panel and check for voltage at the power mirror motor connector (arrow)

power door locks. If you are unable to locate the trouble using the following general steps, consult your dealer service department or other qualified repair facility.

4   Always check the circuit protection first, several fuses are used in the circuit. Refer to the wiring diagrams at the end of this Chapter.

5   Operate the door lock switches in both directions (Lock and Unlock) with the engine off. Listen for the sound of the actuator operating in the defective door.

6   If there's no sound, remove the door trim panel (see Chapter 11) and check for voltage at the actuator while operating the switch **(see illustration)**. Battery voltage should be present at one terminal of the connector while unlocking the door and at the other terminal when locking the door. There should be continuity to ground on the opposite terminal. If battery voltage is present, the ground circuit is good and the door lock actuator does not operate when connected, replace the actuator.

7   If no voltage is present, test the switch for continuity at the indicated terminals of the switch while you operate the door lock switch **(see illustration)**. Replace the switch if there's no continuity in either switch position.

8   If the door lock actuator is operating, but not locking or unlocking the door, check the latch mechanism for binding or damage.

25   Power side view mirrors - description and check

Refer to illustration 25.7

1   The power side view mirrors use two electric motors to move the glass; one for up-down adjustments and one for left-right adjustments.

2   The control switch has a selector portion that sends voltage to the left or right side mirror. With the ignition ON but the engine OFF, roll down the windows and operate the mirror control switch through all functions (left-right and up-down) for both the left and right side mirrors.

3   Listen carefully for the sound of the electric motors running in the mirrors.

4   If the motors can be heard but the mirror glass doesn't move, there's probably a problem with the drive mechanism inside the mirror. The mirror will most likely require replacement.

5   If both mirrors are inoperative and no sound comes from the mirrors, check the system fuse.

6   If the fuse is good, remove the door switch assembly from the door panel without disconnecting the electrical connectors. Turn the ignition On and check for voltage at the switch. There should be voltage at the orange wire terminal. If there's no voltage at the switch, check for an open or short in the wiring between the fuse panel and the switch. Also check for continuity to a good chassis ground at the black wire terminal. The system ground connection is located on the right-side pillar between the right front door and the sliding door (you'll have the remove the pillar trim panel to access the ground connection).

7   If one of the mirrors is inoperative, remove the door panel (see Chapter 11) and check for power at the power mirror motor connector **(see illustration)**. Operate the mirror switch in all its positions. There should be voltage at one of the switch-to-mirror wires in each switch position (except the neutral "off" position). For example: if checking the driver's mirror, voltage should be present at the yellow wire in the Up position and at the light green wire in the Down position. Continuity to ground should be indicated on the light green wire in the Up position and on the yellow wire in the Down position.

8   If voltage isn't present in each switch position, check the wiring between the mirror connector and control switch for continuity. If the wiring harness is good, replace the switch.

9   If there's voltage present at the mirror connector, the ground circuit is good, and the mirror doesn't operate when connected, replace the mirror.

26   Power sunroof - description and check

Refer to illustration 26.6

1   The electric sunroof is powered by a single motor at the front of the sunroof assembly, under the headliner. The sunroof motor is controlled by an electronic sunroof control module and the sunroof switch. The sunroof control module is attached to the sunroof assembly near the motor.

2   The control switch sends a ground signal to the sunroof control module when the switch is pressed. With the ignition On but the engine Off, operate the sunroof control switch through the open and close functions.

3   Check the sunroof tracks for obstructions or mechanical problems that may cause binding.

4   If the sunroof glass doesn't move, listen carefully for the sound of the sunroof motor running in the roof. If the motor can be heard, there's probably a problem with the drive mechanism or drive cables.

5   If the sunroof does not operate and no sound comes from the motor, check the SUNROOF fuse in the interior fuse panel.

6   If the fuse is OK, check the switch. Remove the overhead panel multi-function switch and disconnect the electrical connectors. Using an ohmmeter, check for continuity between the sunroof switch terminals H and G while pressing the switch in the Open position, and between F and G while pressing the switch in the Close position **(see illustration)**. If continuity isn't indicated in each position, replace the switch.

7   If the switch is good, use a voltmeter to measure the voltage on the brown and orange wire terminals of the harness connector. Five volts should be indicated on each of the terminals (with the ignition key On), if it isn't there is a problem with the wiring between the sunroof control module and the switch or the control module is defective.

8   Accessing the sunroof control module and motor requires removal of the headliner. If the switch isn't the problem in the sunroof

26.6 Power sunroof switch terminal identification (blue connector)

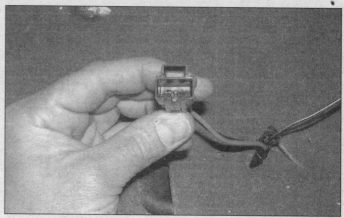

27.7 Check for battery voltage at the orange wire terminal and continuity to ground at the black wire terminal of the power seat main harness connector

circuit, take the vehicle to a dealership service department or other qualified repair facility for further diagnosis and repair.

27 Power seats - description and check

Refer to illustrations 27.7 and 27.8

1   Power seats allow you to adjust the position of the seat with little effort. The optional power seats on these models adjust forward and backward, up and down and tilt forward and backward.

2   The power seat system consists of a motor, a switch on the seat, and the circuit breaker.

3   Look under the seat for any objects which may be preventing the seat from moving.

4   If the seat won't work at all, check the circuit breaker (see Section 4).

5   With the engine off to reduce the noise level, operate the seat controls in all directions and listen for sound coming from the seat motors.

6   If the motors run or click but the seat doesn't move, the seat drive mechanism is

damaged and the motor assembly must be replaced.

7   If the motor doesn't operate or make noise, check for voltage at the orange wire terminal of harness connector **(see illustration)**. If voltage is not present, check the circuit from the fuse panel to the connector. Check for continuity to ground at the black wire terminal. The system ground connection is located on the left-side pillar between the left front door and the sliding door (you'll have the remove the pillar trim panel to access the ground connection).

8   Each motor operates bi-directionally depending on the polarity of the voltage signal from the switch. To check the switch, check for a voltage and ground signal at each motor connector as you operate the switch **(see illustration)**. For example: attempt to move the seat forward with the switch, voltage should be present on the light green wire terminal and continuity to ground should be indicated on the tan wire terminal of the Forward/Back motor connector. Move the seat back, voltage should be present on the tan wire terminal and continuity to ground should be indicated on the light green wire terminal of the Forward/Back motor connector.

9   If voltage isn't present at the motor, check the wiring harness between the motor and the switch. If the wiring is good, replace the switch.

10   If the voltage and ground signal is present at the motor and the motor does not operate, replace the motor.

28 Power sliding door - description and check

Refer to illustrations 28.2 and 28.8

1   The power sliding door system is designed to open or close the sliding door with the push of a button. The power sliding door may be operated from the keyless remote transmitter as well. In addition, anytime the power sliding door lockout switch is On, manual opening and closing of the door is aided with power assist. When the lockout switch is Off the door operates manually.

2   The components of the electrical system include the power sliding door control module, the power sliding door actuator motor, the open/close and lockout switches, the door latch switch and the latch release actuator and switch **(see illustration)**. The control

27.8 Check for voltage at the power seat motor connector as you operate the switch

28.2 The sliding door control module is located behind the right quarter panel trim

28.8 Remove the overhead console multi-function switch panel and check the power sliding door switches for continuity - continuity should be indicated between terminals B and D with the lockout switch On - continuity should be indicated between terminals B and C with the open/close switch depressed

29.1 The airbag control module (arrow) is located on the floor under the front passenger seat (carpeting pulled back)

module also receives input from the Transaxle Range switch and the Vehicle Speed Sensor to sound an alarm if the transaxle is shifted out of Park with the door open.

3   The power sliding door control module has self-diagnostic capabilities. A trouble code may be stored in the control module memory if a fault in door operation is detected. If a problem with the power sliding door system develops and the following checks fail to reveal the problem, take the vehicle to a dealership service department for diagnosis.

4   Check the system fuses and circuit breaker for an open circuit.

5   Before assuming a power sliding door problem lies with the electrical system, check the mechanical operation of the door. Make sure the door is not binding. Check the door tracks for obstructions and the rollers for damage. Check the door for proper fit. Make sure the weatherstrip does not interfere with door operation.

6   Check the power sliding door lock switch plate plungers and springs for damage. Clean the plungers and the striker plate, if necessary.

7   If the door reverses direction while opening or closing, check the actuator motor tension cable adjustment (see Chapter 11).

8   If the system is completely inoperative, remove the overhead console multi-function switch panel and check lockout switch for continuity **(see illustration)**. If the open/close switch does not operate the door, check the open/close switch for continuity.

Reinitialization procedure

9   Anytime power is lost to the power sliding door control module (battery discharged/disconnected or RADIO, PSD, PWR SEAT, B/U fuse blown or removed), the reinitialization procedure must be performed to

ensure proper operation of the power sliding door.

10   Make sure the ignition key is in the Lock position and the sliding door is fully closed, latched and unlocked.

11   Turn the sliding door lockout switch Off.

12   Remove the Radio fuse from the underhood fuse panel. Wait thirty seconds, then reinstall the fuse.

13   Wait ten seconds, then switch the lockout switch On and open the door with the open/close switch.

14   Wait five seconds then close the door with the open/close switch.

15   Cycle the door open and closed two more times, allowing five seconds between each operation.

16   Finally open the door and check to make sure the door is the fully open position. Close the door and check the operation of the door using the manual latches, inside and out.

29   Airbag system - general information

Refer to illustrations 29.1, 29.10, 29.12 and 29.22

1   The vehicle is equipped with a Supplemental Inflatable Restraint system (SIR), more commonly known as airbags. The SIR system is designed to protect the driver and front seat passenger from serious injury in the event of a collision. The system is controlled by a sensing/diagnostic control module, located under the passenger seat, below the carpeting **(see illustration)**. Airbag modules are located in the center of the steering wheel and at the right-side of the instrument panel above the glove box. 1999 and later models are equipped with side impact airbags. Side impact sensors are located in the pillars between the front doors and the sliding doors

and airbag modules are located at the outside edge of the front seat backs. **Warning:** *If your vehicle is ever involved in a flood, or the interior carpeting is soaked for any reason, disconnect the battery and do not start the vehicle until the airbag system can be checked by your dealer. If the SIR system is subjected to flooding, the airbags could go off upon starting the vehicle, even without an accident taking place.*

Airbag modules

2   The airbag modules consist of a housing incorporating the cushion (airbag) and inflator unit. The inflator assembly is mounted on the back of the housing over a hole through which gas is expelled, inflating the bag almost instantaneously when an electrical signal is sent from the system. A specially-wound coil, located under the steering wheel, carries the signal to the driver's airbag module. The coil is a flat, ribbon-like electrically conductive tape wound in a plastic housing and connected to the steering column shaft. The coil transmits the electrical signal regardless of steering wheel position.

Sensing/diagnostic control module

3   The sensing/diagnostic control module contains an on-board microprocessor which monitors the operation of the system, and also contains a crash sensor. The control module checks the system every time the vehicle is started. If the system is operational, the "AIRBAG" light will flash seven times then go off. If there is a fault in the system, the light will remain on, either steadily illuminated or blinking, and the control module will store a fault code indicating the nature of the fault.

Operation

4   For the airbags to deploy, an accelerometer in the diagnostic control module

29.10 Disconnect the driver's airbag connector (arrow)

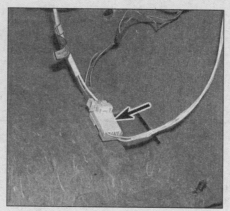

29.12 Disconnect the passenger airbag connector (arrow)

must be activated by a collision of sufficient force. The control module compares the force of the collision to a value stored in its memory. If the control module determines the force is in excess of the value, the circuits to the airbag inflators are closed and the airbags inflate. If the battery is destroyed by the impact, or is too low to power the inflator, a back-up power unit inside the control module provides power.

Self-diagnosis system

5   A self-diagnosis circuit in the control module displays a light on the instrument panel when the ignition switch is turned to the On position. If the system is operating normally, the light should go out after about seven blinks. If the light doesn't come on, or doesn't go out after a short time, or if it comes on while you're driving the vehicle, a malfunction is indicated in the SIR system. Have it inspected and repaired as soon as possible. Do not attempt to troubleshoot or service the SIR system yourself. Even a small mistake could cause the SIR system to malfunction when you need it.

Servicing components near the airbag modules

6   Nevertheless, there are times when you

need to remove the steering wheel, radio or service other components near the airbag modules. At these times, you'll be working around components and wire harnesses for the SIR system. The SIR wiring harnesses are easy to identify: They're all covered with a bright yellow conduit. Do not unplug the connectors for these wires unless absolutely necessary. Do not use electrical test equipment on airbag system wires, connectors or components; it could cause the airbag(s) to deploy. *ALWAYS DISABLE THE SIR SYSTEM BEFORE WORKING NEAR THE SIR SYSTEM COMPONENTS OR RELATED WIRING.*

Disabling the SIR system

Warning: *Any time you are working in the vicinity of airbag wiring or components, DISABLE THE SIR SYSTEM.*
Note: *Before you can disconnect an airbag module connector, you must remove the connector position assurance clip from the connector.*
7   Remove the airbag system (SIR) fuse located in the fuse/relay panel at the right end of the instrument panel.

Driver's airbag

8   Position the steering wheel with the

front wheels pointing straight-ahead, turn the ignition switch to the Lock position and remove the key.
9   Remove the insulation panel below the steering column.
10   Disconnect the yellow airbag connector at the base of the steering column **(see illustration)**.

Passenger's airbag

11   Remove the insulation panel below the glove box.
12   Disconnect the yellow airbag connector under the instrument panel **(see illustration)**.

Side-impact airbags

13   Disconnect the yellow airbag connector under the driver's seat.
14   Disconnect the yellow airbag connector under the passenger seat.

Enabling the system

15   Position the steering wheel with the front wheels pointing straight-ahead, turn the ignition switch to the Lock position and remove the key.
16   Reconnect the airbag connectors and install the connector position assurance clip.
17   Install the airbag system fuse.
18   Turn the ignition key On and make sure the airbag system warning light goes out.
Warning: *Keep your body away from the airbags when turning the key on for the first time after disabling the SIR system.*

Removal and installation
Driver's airbag
19   Refer to Chapter 10, Section 15 for removal and installation of the driver's airbag.

Passenger airbag
20   Disable the airbag system (see the **Warning** above).
21   Remove the glovebox (see Chapter 11).
22   Remove the mounting fasteners and gently remove the airbag unit from the instrument panel **(see illustration)**.
23   Installation is the reverse of the removal procedure. Tighten the mounting nuts to 89 in-lbs.
24   Enable the airbag system.

Side-impact airbags
25   Disable the airbag system (see the **Warning** above).
26   Remove the seat (see Chapter 11).
27   Detach the clips and remove the panel from the back of the seat.
28   Carefully pry the molding from the airbag module and seat frame.
29   Detach the airbag module wiring harness clips from the seat frame and pull the harness out of the seat. Note the routing of the harness for reinstallation.
30   Remove the mounting screw and remove the airbag module from the seat frame.
31   Installation is the reverse of removal.
32   Enable the airbag system.

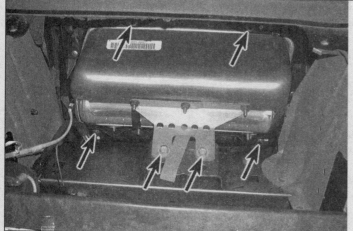

29.22 Passenger airbag module mounting fasteners (arrows)

30   Wiring diagrams - general information

Since it isn't possible to include all wiring diagrams for every year covered by this manual, the following diagrams are those that are typical and most commonly needed.

Prior to troubleshooting any circuits, check the fuse and circuit breakers (if equipped) to make sure they are in good condition. Make sure the battery is properly charged and has clean, tight cable connections (see Chapter 1).

When checking the wiring system, make sure that all electrical connectors are clean, with no broken or loose pins. When unplugging an electrical connector, do not pull on the wires, only on the connector housings themselves.

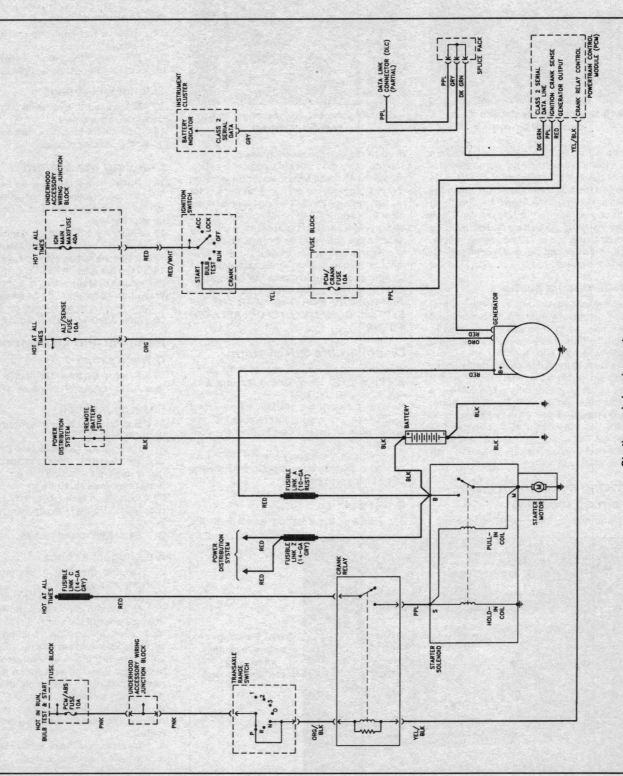

Starting and charging system

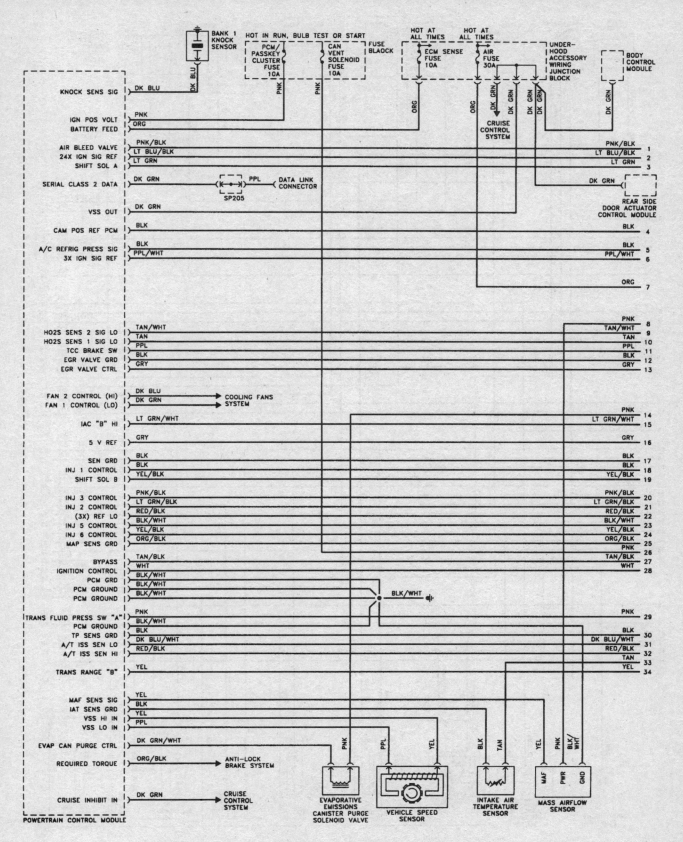

Engine control system (1 of 4)

12

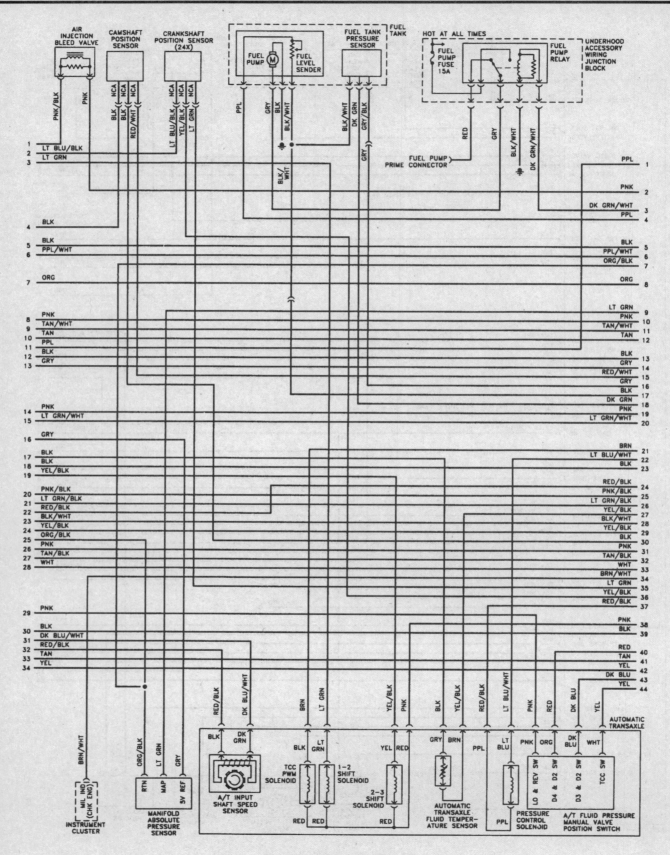

Engine control system (2 of 4)

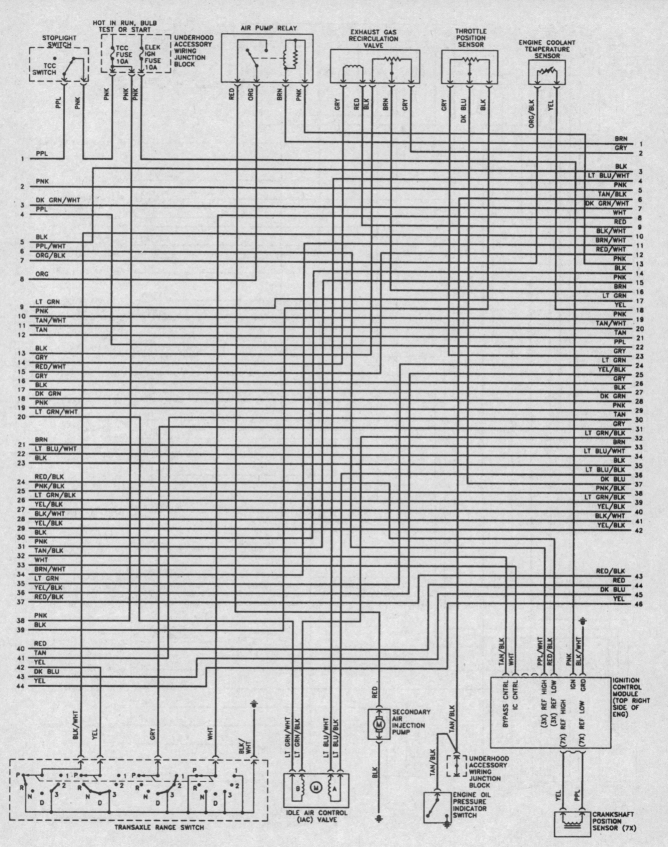

Engine control system (3 of 4)

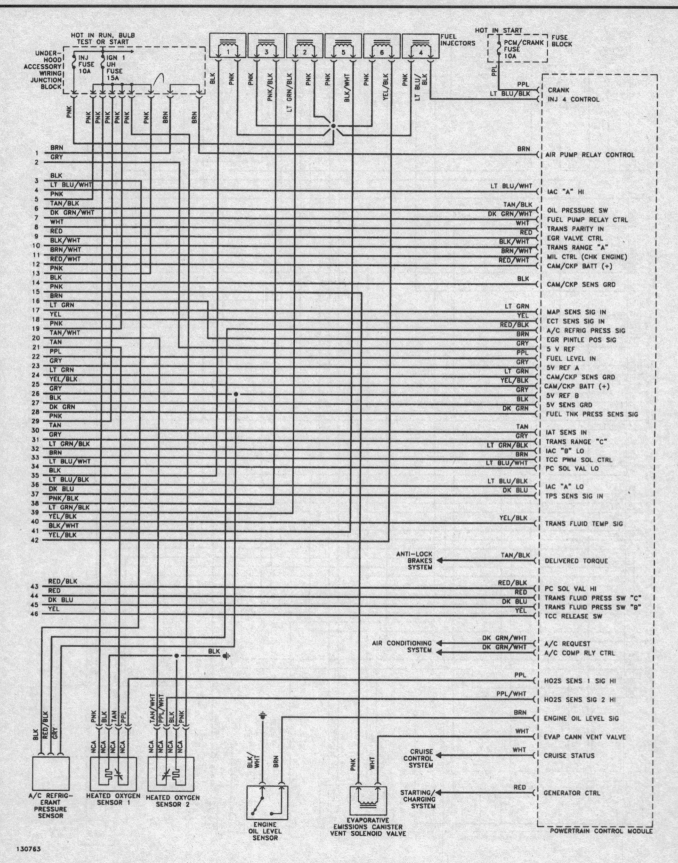

Engine control system (4 of 4)

130763

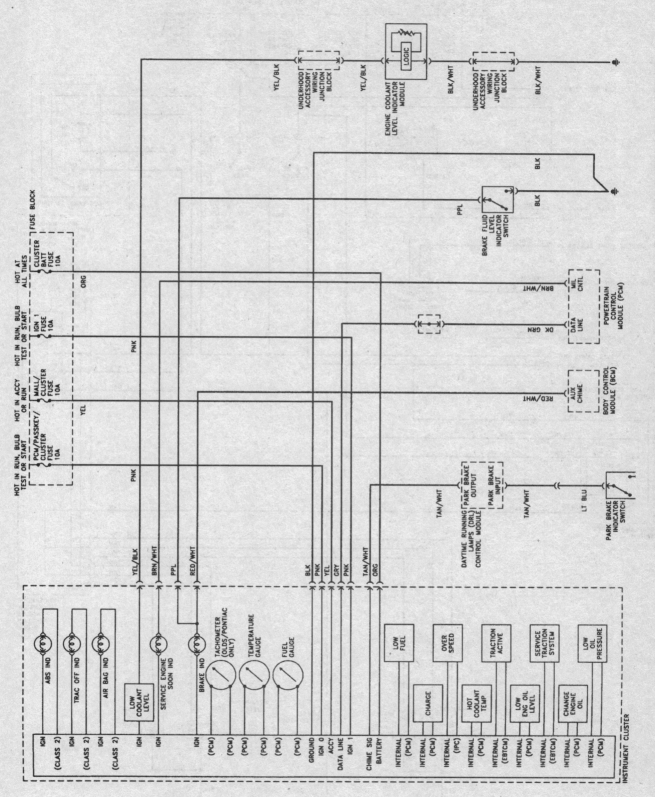

Instrument panel gauges and warning lights system

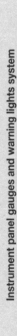

12

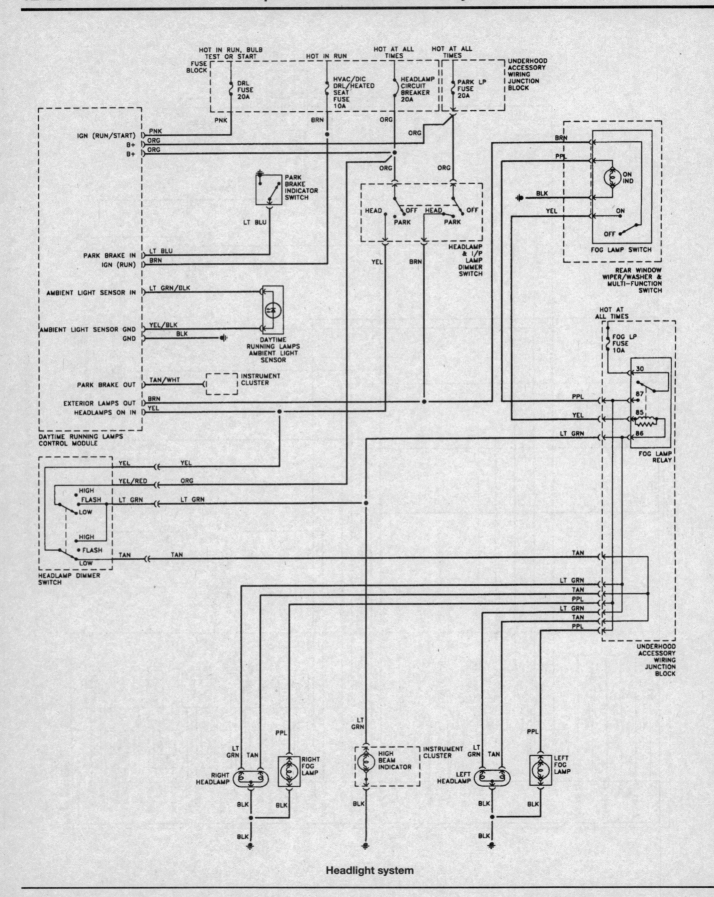

Headlight system

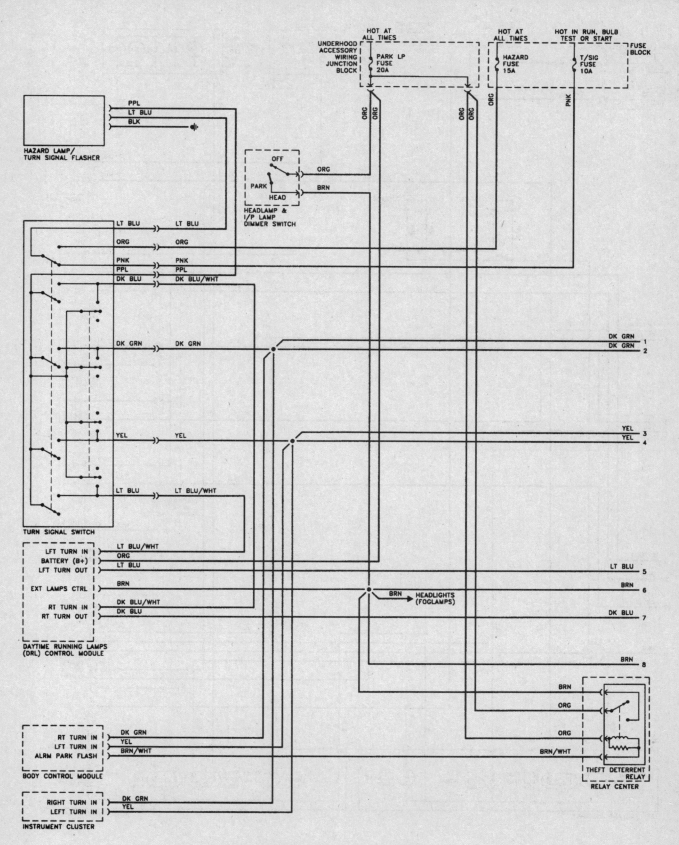

Exterior lighting system (1 of 2)

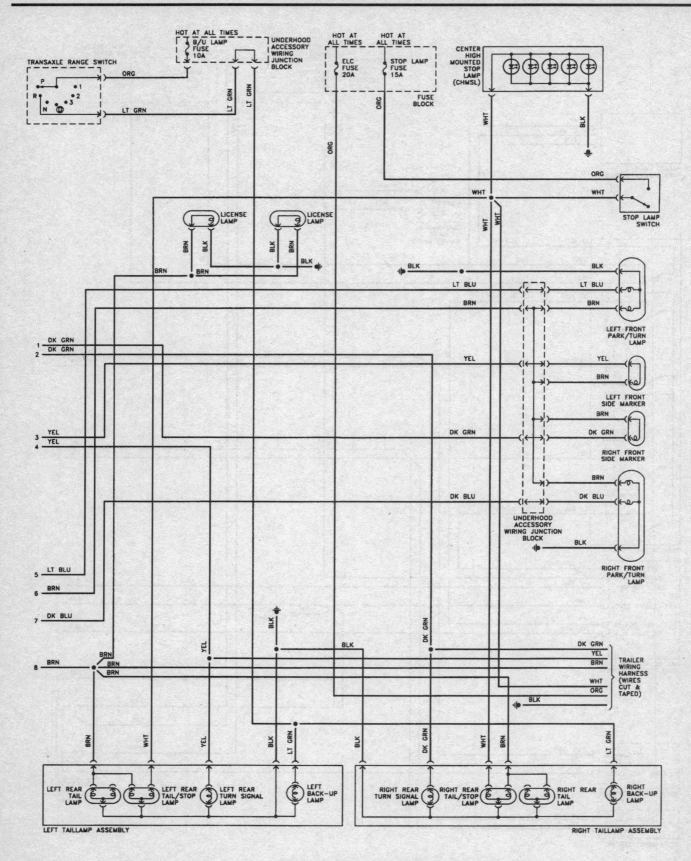

Exterior lighting system (2 of 2)

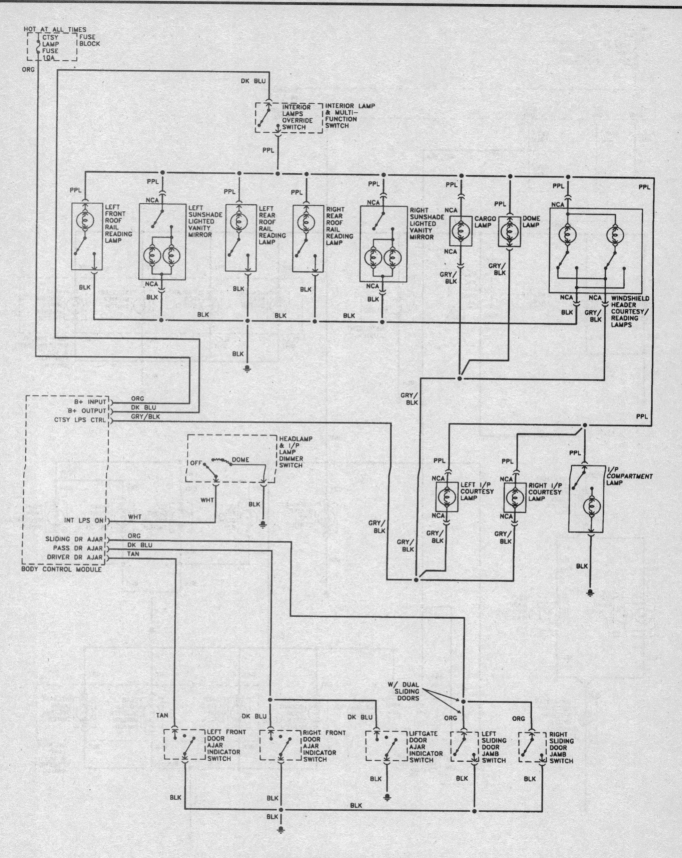

Interior lighting system (1 of 2)

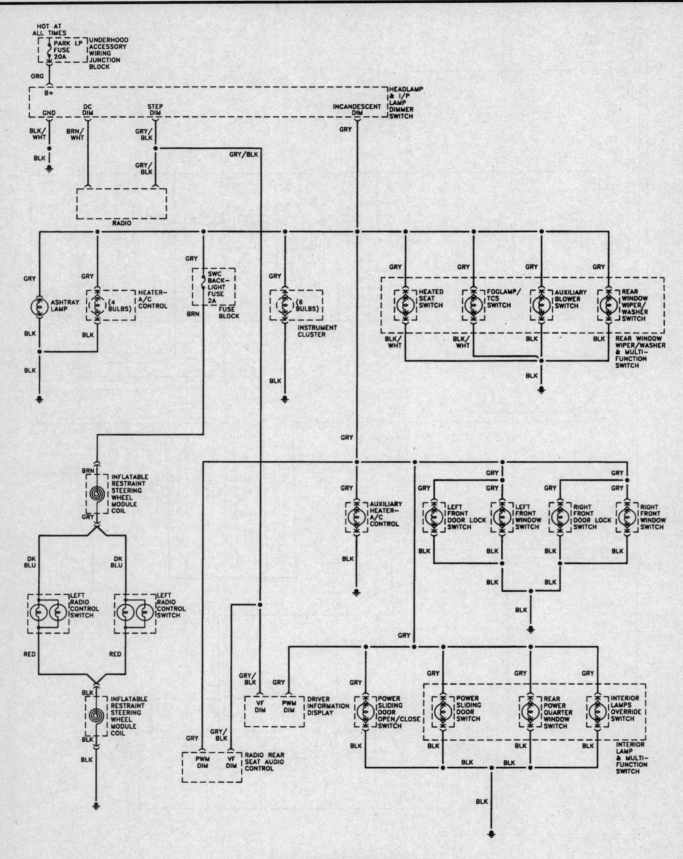

Interior lighting system (2 of 2)

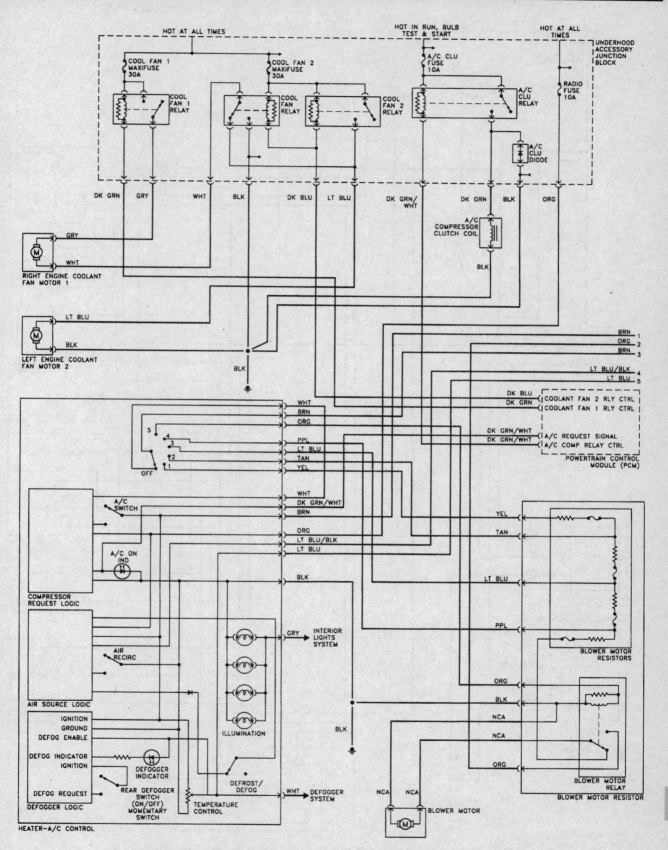

Heating, air conditioning and engine cooling fan system (1 of 2)

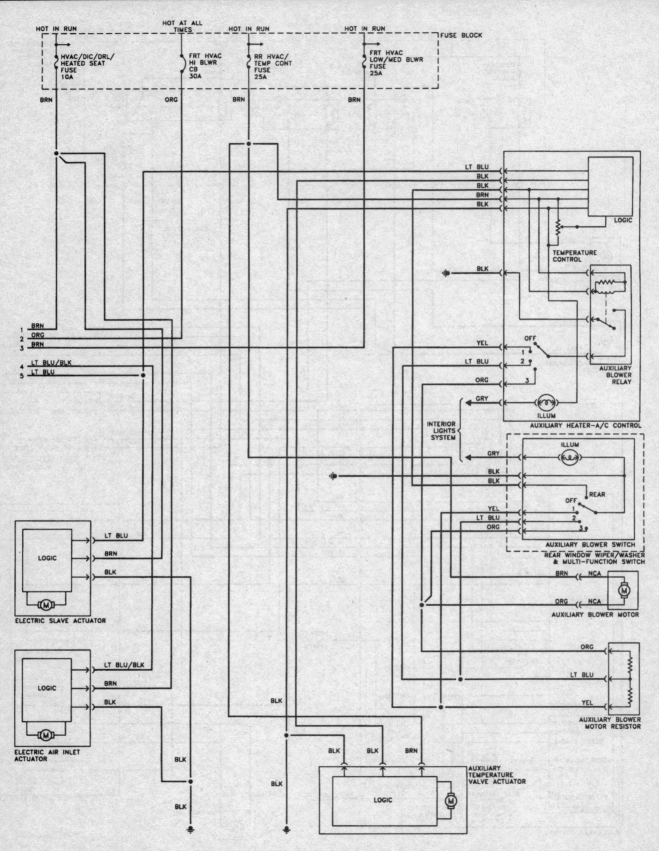

Heating, air conditioning and engine cooling fan system (2 of 2)

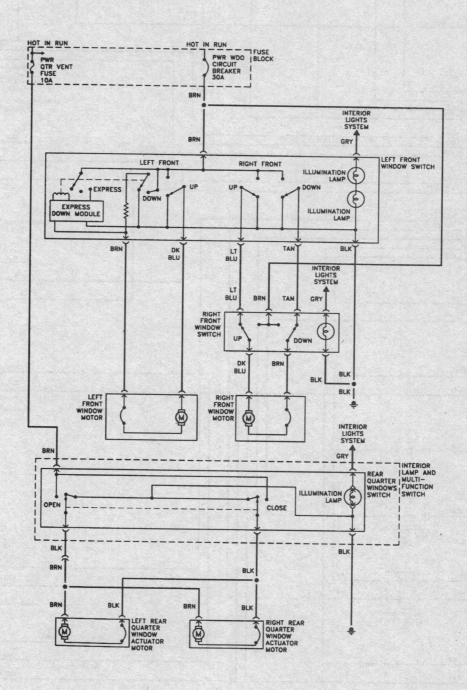

Power window system

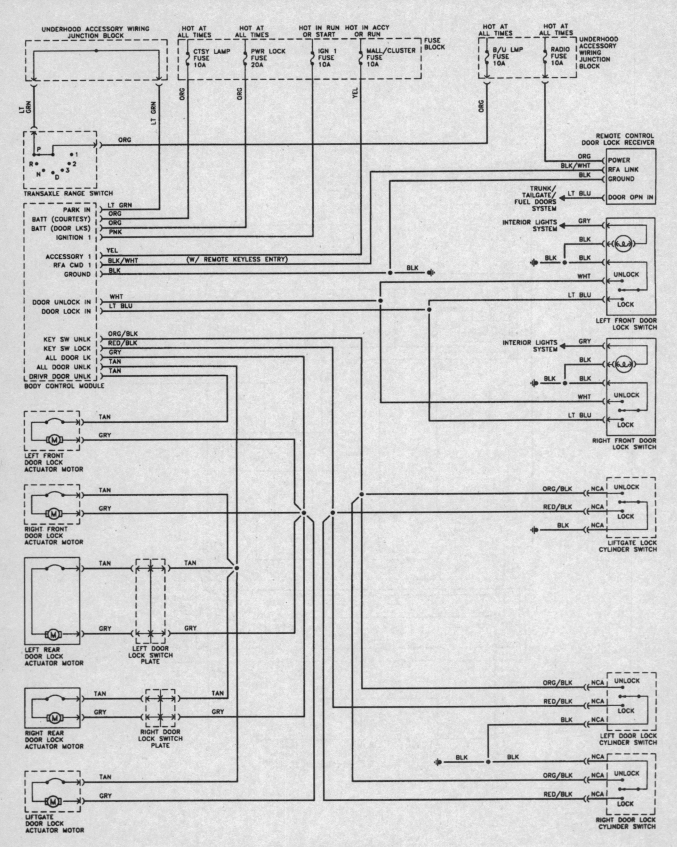

Power door lock system

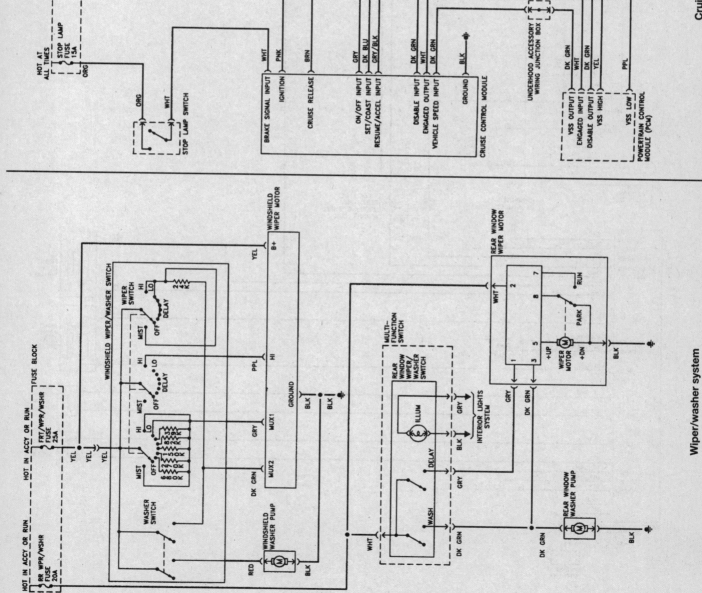

Cruise control system

Wiper/washer system

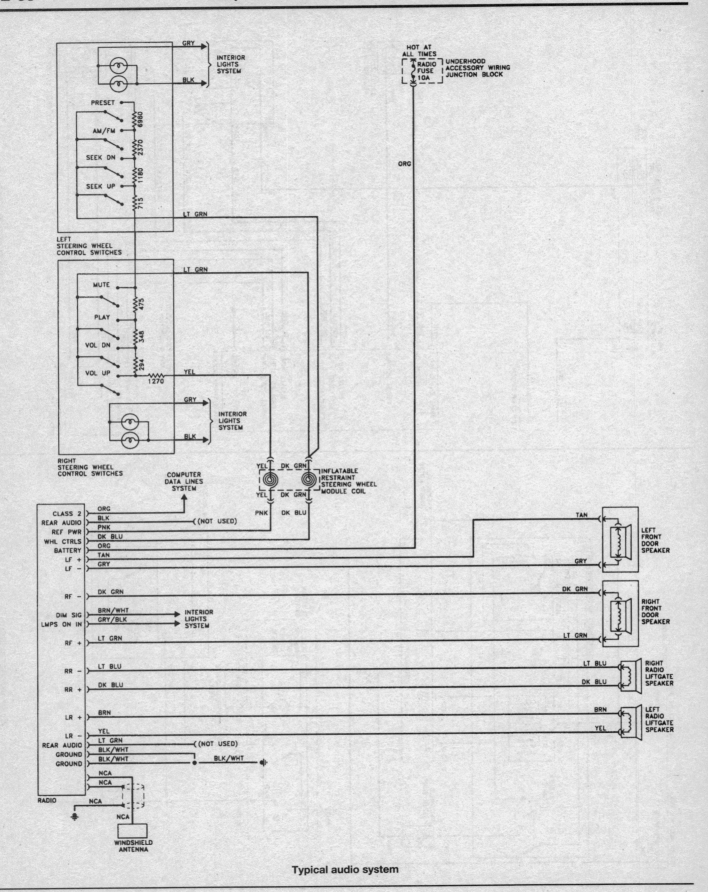

Typical audio system

Index

Haynes Automotive Manuals

NOTE: New manuals are added to this list on a periodic basis. If you do not see a listing for your vehicle, consult your local Haynes dealer for the latest product information.

ACURA
12020 Integra '86 thru '89 & Legend '86 thru '90
12021 Integra '90 thru '93 & Legend '91 thru '95

AMC
Jeep CJ - see JEEP (50020)
14020 Concord/Hornet/Gremlin/Spirit '70 thru '83
14025 (Renault) Alliance & Encore '83 thru '87

AUDI
15020 4000 all models '80 thru '87
15025 5000 all models '77 thru '83
15026 5000 all models '84 thru '88

AUSTIN
Healey Sprite - see MG Midget (66015)

BMW
*18020 3/5 Series '82 thru '92
18021 3 Series including Z3 models '92 thru '98
18025 320i all 4 cyl models '75 thru '83
18050 1500 thru 2002 except Turbo '59 thru '77

BUICK
*19010 Buick Century '97 thru '02
Century (FWD) - see GM (38005)
*19020 Buick, Oldsmobile & Pontiac Full-size (Front wheel drive) '85 thru '02
19025 Buick Oldsmobile & Pontiac Full-size (Rear wheel drive) '70 thru '90
19030 Mid-size Regal & Century '74 thru '87
Regal - see GENERAL MOTORS (38010)
Skyhawk - see GM (38030)
Skylark - see GM (38020, 38025)
Somerset - see GENERAL MOTORS (38025)

CADILLAC
21030 Cadillac Rear Wheel Drive '70 thru '93
Cimarron, Eldorado & Seville - see GM (38015, 38030, 38031)

CHEVROLET
10305 Chevrolet Engine Overhaul Manual
*24010 Astro & GMC Safari Mini-vans '85 thru '02
24015 Camaro V8 all models '70 thru '81
24016 Camaro all models '82 thru '92
Cavalier - see GM (38015)
Celebrity - see GM (38005)
24017 Camaro & Firebird '93 thru '00
24020 Chevelle, Malibu, El Camino '69 thru '87
24024 Chevette & Pontiac T1000 '76 thru '87
Citation - see GENERAL MOTORS (38020)
24032 Corsica/Beretta all models '87 thru '96
24040 Corvette all V8 models '68 thru '82
24041 Corvette all models '84 thru '96
24045 Full-size Sedans Caprice, Impala, Biscayne, Bel Air & Wagons '69 thru '90
24046 Impala SS & Caprice and Buick Roadmaster '91 thru '96
Lumina '90 thru '94 - see GM (38010)
*24048 Lumina & Monte Carlo '95 thru '01
Lumina APV - see GM (38035)
24050 Luv Pick-up all 2WD & 4WD '72 thru '82
Malibu - see GM (38026)
24055 Monte Carlo all models '70 thru '88
Monte Carlo '95 thru '01 - see LUMINA
24059 Nova all V8 models '69 thru '79
24060 Nova/Geo Prizm '85 thru '92
24064 Pick-ups '67 thru '87 - Chevrolet & GMC, all V8 & in-line 6 cyl, 2WD & 4WD '67 thru '87; Suburbans, Blazers & Jimmys '67 thru '91
24065 Pick-ups '88 thru '98 - Chevrolet & GMC, all full-size models '88 thru '98; C/K Classic '99 & '00; Blazer & Jimmy '92 thru '94; Suburban '92 thru '99; Tahoe & Yukon '95 thru '99
*24066 Pick-ups '99 thru '02 - Chevrolet Silverado & GMC Sierra '99 thru '02; Suburban/Tahoe/Yukon/Yukon XL '00 thru '02
24070 S-10 & GMC S-15 Pick-ups '82 thru '93
*24071 S-10, Gmc S-15 & Jimmy '94 thru '01
*24072 Chevrolet TrailBlazer & TrailBlazer EXT, GMC Envoy & Envoy XL, Oldsmobile Bravada '02 and '03
24075 Sprint '85 thru '88, Geo Metro '89 thru '01
24080 Vans - Chevrolet & GMC '68 thru '96

CHRYSLER
10310 Chrysler Engine Overhaul Manual
25015 Chrysler Cirrus, Dodge Stratus, Plymouth Breeze, '95 thru '98
25020 Full-size Front-Wheel Drive '88 thru '93
K-Cars - see DODGE Aries (30008)
Laser - see DODGE Daytona (30030)
25025 Chrysler LHS, Concorde & New Yorker, Dodge Intrepid, Eagle Vision, '93 thru '97
*25026 Chrysler LHS, Concorde, 300M, Dodge Intrepid '98 thru '03
25030 Chrysler/Plym. Mid-size '82 thru '95
Rear-wheel Drive - see DODGE (30050)
*25035 PT Cruiser all models '01 thru '03
*25040 Chrysler Sebring/Dodge Avenger '95 thru '02

DATSUN
28005 200SX all models '80 thru '83
28007 B-210 all models '73 thru '78
28009 210 all models '78 thru '82
28012 240Z, 260Z & 280Z Coupe '70 thru '78
28014 280ZX Coupe & 2+2 '79 thru '83
300ZX - see NISSAN (72010)
28016 310 all models '78 thru '82
28018 510 & PL521 Pick-up '68 thru '73
28020 510 all models '78 thru '81
28022 620 Series Pick-up all models '73 thru '79
720 Series Pick-up - NISSAN (72030)
28025 810/Maxima all models, '77 thru '84

DODGE
400 & 600 - see CHRYSLER (25030)
30008 Aries & Plymouth Reliant '81 thru '89
30010 Caravan & Ply. Voyager '84 thru '95
30011 Caravan & Ply. Voyager '96 thru '02
*30012 Challenger/Plymouth Saporro '78 thru '83
Challenger '67-'76 - see DART (30025)
30016 Colt/Plymouth Champ '78 thru '87
30020 Dakota Pick-ups all models '87 thru '96
*30021 Durango '98 & '99, Dakota '97 thru '99
30025 Dart, Challenger/Plymouth Barracuda & Valiant 6 cyl models '67 thru '76
30030 Daytona & Chrysler Laser '84 thru '89
Intrepid - see Chrysler (25025, 25026)
*30034 Dodge & Plymouth Neon '95 thru '99
*30035 Omni & Plymouth Horizon '78 thru '90
30040 Pick-ups all full-size models '74 thru '93
30041 Pick-ups all full-size models '94 thru '01
*30045 Ram 50/D50 Pick-ups & Raider and Plymouth Arrow Pick-ups '79 thru '93
30050 Dodge/Ply./Chrysler RWD '71 thru '89
30055 Shadow/Plymouth Sundance '87 thru '94
30060 Spirit & Plymouth Acclaim '89 thru '95
*30065 Vans - Dodge & Plymouth '71 thru '03

EAGLE
Talon - see MITSUBISHI (68030, 68031)
Vision - see CHRYSLER (25025)

FIAT
34010 124 Sport Coupe & Spider '68 thru '78
34025 X1/9 all models '74 thru '80

FORD
10355 Ford Automatic Transmission Overhaul
10320 Ford Engine Overhaul Manual
36004 Aerostar Mini-vans '86 thru '97
Aspire - see FORD Festiva (36030)
36006 Contour/Mercury Mystique '95 thru '00
36008 Courier Pick-up all models '72 thru '82
*36012 Crown Victoria & Mercury Grand Marquis '88 thru '00
36016 Escort/Mercury Lynx '81 thru '90
36020 Escort/Mercury Tracer '91 thru '00
Expedition - see FORD Pick-up (36059)
36022 Ford Escape & Mazda Tribute '01 thru '03
*36024 Explorer & Mazda Navajo '91 thru '01
36025 Ford Explorer & Mercury Mountaineer '02 and '03
36028 Fairmont & Mercury Zephyr '78 thru '83
36030 Festiva & Aspire '88 thru '97
36032 Fiesta all models '77 thru '80
*36034 Focus all models '00 and '01
36036 Ford & Mercury Full-size '75 thru '87
36044 Ford & Mercury Mid-size '75 thru '86
36048 Mustang V8 all models '64-1/2 thru '73
36049 Mustang II 4 cyl, V6 & V8 '74 thru '78
36050 Mustang & Mercury Capri '79 thru '86
*36051 Mustang all models '94 thru '03
36054 Pick-ups and Bronco '73 thru '79
36058 Pick-ups and Bronco '80 thru '96
*36059 Pick-ups, Expedition & Lincoln Navigator '97 thru '02
*36060 Super Duty Pick-ups, Excursion '99 thru '02
36062 Pinto & Mercury Bobcat '75 thru '80
36066 Probe all models '89 thru '92
36070 Ranger/Bronco II gas models '83 thru '92
*36071 Ford Ranger '93 thru '00 & Mazda Pick-ups '94 thru '00
36074 Taurus & Mercury Sable '86 thru '95
36075 Taurus & Mercury Sable '96 thru '01
36078 Tempo & Mercury Topaz '84 thru '94
36082 Thunderbird/Mercury Cougar '83 thru '88
36086 Thunderbird/Mercury Cougar '89 thru '97
36090 Vans all V8 Econoline models '69 thru '91
*36094 Vans full size '92 thru '01
*36097 Windstar Mini-van '95 thru '03

GENERAL MOTORS
10360 GM Automatic Transmission Overhaul
38005 Buick Century, Chevrolet Celebrity, Olds Cutlass Ciera & Pontiac 6000 '82 thru '96
*38010 Buick Regal, Chevrolet Lumina, Oldsmobile Cutlass Supreme & Pontiac Grand Prix front wheel drive '88 thru '02
38015 Buick Skyhawk, Cadillac Cimarron, Chevrolet Cavalier, Oldsmobile Firenza Pontiac J-2000 & Sunbird '82 thru '94
*38016 Chevrolet Cavalier/Pontiac Sunfire '95 thru '01
38020 Buick Skylark, Chevrolet Citation, Olds Omega, Pontiac Phoenix '80 thru '85
38025 Buick Skylark & Somerset, Olds Achieva, Calais & Pontiac Grand Am '85 thru '98
*38026 Chevrolet Malibu, Olds Alero & Cutlass, Pontiac Grand Am '97 thru '00
38030 Cadillac Eldorado & Oldsmobile Toronado '71 thru '85, Seville '80 thru '85, Buick Riviera '79 thru '85
*38031 Cadillac Eldorado & Seville '86 thru '91, DeVille & Buick Riviera '86 thru '93, Fleetwood & Olds Toronado '86 thru '92
38032 DeVille '94 thru '02, Seville '92 thru '02
38035 Chevrolet Lumina APV, Oldsmobile Silhouette & Pontiac Trans Sport '90 thru '96
*38036 Chevrolet Venture, Olds Silhouette, Pontiac Trans Sport & Montana '97 thru '01
General Motors Full-size Rear-wheel Drive - see BUICK (19025)

GEO
Metro - see CHEVROLET Sprint (24075)
Prizm - see CHEVROLET (24060) or TOYOTA (92036)
40030 Storm all models '90 thru '93
Tracker - see SUZUKI Samurai (90010)

GMC
Vans & Pick-ups - see CHEVROLET

HONDA
42010 Accord CVCC all models '76 thru '83
42011 Accord all models '84 thru '89
42012 Accord all models '90 thru '93
42013 Accord all models '94 thru '97
*42014 Accord all models '98 and '99
42020 Civic 1200 all models '73 thru '79
42021 Civic 1300 & 1500 CVCC '80 thru '83
42022 Civic 1500 CVCC all models '75 thru '79
42023 Civic all models '84 thru '91
42024 Civic & del Sol '92 thru '95
*42025 Civic '96 thru '00, CR-V '97 thru '00, Acura Integra '94 thru '00
Passport - see ISUZU Rodeo (47017)
*42040 Prelude CVCC all models '79 thru '89

HYUNDAI
*43010 Elantra all models '96 thru '01
43015 Excel & Accent all models '86 thru '98

ISUZU
Hombre - see CHEVROLET S-10 (24071)
*47017 Rodeo '91 thru '02, Amigo '89 thru '02, Honda Passport '95 thru '02
47020 Trooper '84 thru '91, Pick-up '81 thru '93

JAGUAR
49010 XJ6 all 6 cyl models '68 thru '86
49011 XJ6 all models '88 thru '94
49015 XJ12 & XJS all 12 cyl models '72 thru '85

JEEP
50010 Cherokee, Comanche & Wagoneer Limited all models '84 thru '00
50020 CJ all models '49 thru '86
*50025 Grand Cherokee all models '93 thru '00
50029 Grand Wagoneer & Pick-up '72 thru '91
*50030 Wrangler all models '87 thru '00

LEXUS
ES 300 - see TOYOTA Camry (92007)

LINCOLN
Navigator - see FORD Pick-up (36059)
*59010 Rear Wheel Drive all models '70 thru '01

MAZDA
61010 GLC (rear wheel drive) '77 thru '83
61011 GLC (front wheel drive) '81 thru '85
61015 323 & Protegé '90 thru '00
*61016 MX-5 Miata '90 thru '97
61020 MPV all models '89 thru '94
Navajo - see FORD Explorer (36024)
61030 Pick-ups '72 thru '93
Pick-ups '94 on - see Ford (36071)
61035 RX-7 all models '79 thru '85
61036 RX-7 all models '86 thru '91
61040 626 (rear wheel drive) '79 thru '82
61041 626 & MX-6 (front wheel drive) '83 thru '91
61042 626 '93 thru '01, & MX-6/Ford Probe '93 thru '97

MERCEDES-BENZ
63012 123 Series Diesel '76 thru '85
63015 190 Series 4-cyl gas models, '84 thru '88
63020 230, 250 & 280 6 cyl sohc '68 thru '72
63025 280 123 Series gas models '77 thru '81
63030 350 & 450 all models '71 thru '80

MERCURY
64200 Villager & Nissan Quest '93 thru '01
All other titles, see FORD listing.

MG
66010 MGB Roadster & GT Coupe '62 thru '80
66015 MG Midget & Austin Healey Sprite Roadster '58 thru '80

MITSUBISHI
68020 Cordia, Tredia, Galant, Precis & Mirage '83 thru '93
68030 Eclipse, Eagle Talon & Plymouth Laser '90 thru '94
*68031 Eclipse '95 thru '01, Eagle Talon '95 thru '98
68035 Mitsubishi Galant '94 thru '03
68040 Pick-up '83 thru '96, Montero '83 thru '93

NISSAN
72010 300ZX all models incl. Turbo '84 thru '89
72015 Altima all models '93 thru '01
72020 Maxima all models '85 thru '92
*72021 Maxima all models '93 thru '01
72030 Pick-ups '80 thru '97, Pathfinder '87 thru '95
*72031 Frontier Pick-up '98 thru '01, Xterra '00 & '01, Pathfinder '96 thru '01
72040 Pulsar all models '83 thru '86
72050 Sentra all models '82 thru '94
72051 Sentra & 200SX all models '95 thru '99
72060 Stanza all models '82 thru '90

OLDSMOBILE
*73015 Cutlass '74 thru '88
For other OLDSMOBILE titles, see BUICK, CHEVROLET or GM listings.

PLYMOUTH
For PLYMOUTH titles, see DODGE.

PONTIAC
79008 Fiero all models '84 thru '88
79018 Firebird V8 models except Turbo '70 thru '81
79019 Firebird all models '82 thru '92
79040 Mid-size Rear-wheel Drive '70 thru '87
For other PONTIAC titles, see BUICK, CHEVROLET or GM listings.

PORSCHE
80020 911 Coupe & Targa models '65 thru '89
80025 914 all 4 cyl models '69 thru '76

80030 924 all models incl. Turbo '76 thru '82
80035 944 all models incl. Turbo '83 thru '89

RENAULT
Alliance, Encore - see AMC (14020)

SAAB
*84010 900 including Turbo '79 thru '88

SATURN
*87010 Saturn all models '91 thru '02
87020 Saturn all L-series models '00 thru '04

SUBARU
89002 1100, 1300, 1400 & 1600 '71 thru '79
89003 1600 & 1800 2WD & 4WD '80 thru '94

SUZUKI
90010 Samurai/Sidekick/Geo Tracker '86 thru '01

TOYOTA
92005 Camry all models '83 thru '91
92006 Camry all models '92 thru '96
*92007 Camry/Avalon/Solara/Lexus ES 300 '97 thru '01
92015 Celica Rear Wheel Drive '71 thru '85
92020 Celica Front Wheel Drive '86 thru '99
92025 Celica Supra all models '79 thru '92
92030 Corolla all models '75 thru '79
92032 Corolla rear wheel drive models '80 thru '87
92035 Corolla front wheel drive models '84 thru '92
92036 Corolla & Geo Prizm '93 thru '02
92040 Corolla Tercel all models '80 thru '82
92045 Corona all models '74 thru '82
92050 Cressida all models '78 thru '82
92055 Land Cruiser FJ40/43/45/55 '68 thru '82
92056 Land Cruiser FJ60/62/80/FZJ80 '80 thru '96
92065 MR2 all models '85 thru '87
92070 Pick-up all models '69 thru '78
92075 Pick-up all models '79 thru '95
*92076 Tacoma '95 thru '00, 4Runner '96 thru '00, T100 '93 thru '98
*92078 Tundra '00 thru '02, Sequoia '01 thru '02
92080 Previa all models '91 thru '95
*92082 RAV4 all models '96 thru '02
92085 Tercel all models '87 thru '94

TRIUMPH
94007 Spitfire all models '62 thru '81
94010 TR7 all models '75 thru '81

VW
96008 Beetle & Karmann Ghia '54 thru '79
*96009 New Beetle '98 thru '00
96016 Rabbit, Jetta, Scirocco, & Pick-up gas models '74 thru '91 & Convertible '80 thru '92
96017 Golf, GTI & Jetta '93 thru '98, Cabrio '95 thru '98
*96018 Golf, GTI, Jetta & Cabrio '99 thru '02
96020 Rabbit, Jetta, Pick-up diesel '77 thru '84
96023 Passat '98 thru '01, Audi A4 '96 thru '01
96030 Transporter 1600 all models '68 thru '79
96035 Transporter 1700, 1800, 2000 '72 thru '79
96040 Type 3 1500 & 1600 '63 thru '73
96045 Vanagon air-cooled models '80 thru '83

VOLVO
97010 120, 130 Series & 1800 Sports '61 thru '73
97015 140 Series all models '66 thru '74
97020 240 Series all models '76 thru '93
97025 260 Series all models '75 thru '82
97040 740 & 760 Series all models '82 thru '88

TECHBOOK MANUALS
10205 Automotive Computer Codes
10210 Automotive Emissions Control Manual
10215 Fuel Injection Manual, 1978 thru 1985
10220 Fuel Injection Manual, 1986 thru 1999
10225 Holley Carburetor Manual
10230 Rochester Carburetor Manual
10240 Weber/Zenith/Stromberg/SU Carburetor
10305 Chevrolet Engine Overhaul Manual
10310 Chrysler Engine Overhaul Manual
10320 Ford Engine Overhaul Manual
10330 GM and Ford Diesel Engine Repair
10340 Small Engine Repair Manual
10345 Suspension, Steering & Driveline
10355 Ford Automatic Transmission Overhaul
10360 GM Automatic Transmission Overhaul
10405 Automotive Body Repair & Painting
10410 Automotive Brake Manual
10415 Automotive Detailing Manual
10420 Automotive Eelectrical Manual
10425 Automotive Heating & Air Conditioning
10430 Automotive Reference Dictionary
10435 Automotive Tools Manual
10440 Used Car Buying Guide
10445 Welding Manual
10450 ATV Basics

SPANISH MANUALS
98903 Reparación de Carrocería & Pintura
98905 Códigos Automotrices de la Computadora
98910 Frenos Automotriz
98915 Inyección de Combustible 1986 al 1999
99040 Chevrolet & GMC Camionetas '67 al '87
99041 Chevrolet & GMC Camionetas '88 al '98
99042 Chevrolet Camionetas Cerradas '68 al '95
99055 Dodge Caravan/Ply. Voyager '84 al '95
99075 Ford Camionetas y Bronco '80 al '94
99077 Ford Camionetas Cerradas '69 al '91
99088 Ford Modelos de Tamaño Mediano '75 al '86
99091 Ford Taurus & Mercury Sable '86 al '95
99095 GM Modelos de Tamaño Grande '70 al '90
99100 GM Modelos de Tamaño Mediano '70 al '88
99118 Nissan Camionetas '80 al '96, Pathfinder '87 al '95
99125 Toyota Camionetas y 4-Runner '79 al '95

---

* Listings shown with an asterisk (*) indicate model coverage as of this printing. These titles will be periodically updated to include later model years - consult your Haynes dealer for more information.

Nearly 100 Haynes motorcycle manuals also available

9-04

Haynes North America, Inc., 861 Lawrence Drive, Newbury Park, CA 91320 • (805) 498-6703